A Neurolinguistic Theory of Bilingualism

Studies in Bilingualism (SiBil)

Editors

Kees de Bot
University of Groningen

Thom Huebner
San José State University

Editorial Board

Michael Clyne, *University of Melbourne*
Kathryn Davis, *University of Hawaii at Manoa*
Joshua Fishman, *Yeshiva University*
François Grosjean, *Université de Neuchâtel*
Wolfgang Klein, *Max Planck Institut für Psycholinguistik*
Georges Lüdi, *University of Basel*
Christina Bratt Paulston, *University of Pittsburgh*
Suzanne Romaine, *Merton College, Oxford*
Merrill Swain, *Ontario Institute for Studies in Education*
Richard Tucker, *Carnegie Mellon University*

Volume 18

A Neurolinguistic Theory of Bilingualism
by Michel Paradis

A Neurolinguistic Theory of Bilingualism

Michel Paradis

McGill University, and Cognitive Neuroscience Center, UQAM

John Benjamins Publishing Company

Amsterdam / Philadelphia

™ The paper used in this publication meets the minimum requirements of American National Standard for Information Sciences – Permanence of Paper for Printed Library Materials, ANSI z39.48-1984.

Library of Congress Cataloging-in-Publication Data

Paradis, Michel
    A Neurolinguistic Theory of Bilingualism / Michel Paradis.
        p. cm. (Studies in Bilingualism, ISSN 0928–1533 ; v. 18)
    Includes bibliographical references and index.
        1. Bilingualism--Psychological aspects. 2. Bilingualism--Physiological
    aspects. 3. Neurolinguistics.

    P115.4 P37 2004
404'.2/019 -dc22   2004049728
  ISBN 90 272 4126 0 (Eur.) / 1 55619 738 1 (US) (Hb; alk. paper)
  ISBN 90 272 4127 9 (Eur.) / 1 55619 739 X (US) (Pb; alk. paper)

John Benjamins Publishing Co. · P.O. Box 36224 · 1020 ME Amsterdam · The Netherlands
John Benjamins North America · P.O. Box 27519 · Philadelphia PA 19118-0519 · USA

Contents

Preface

This book is the outcome of over 25 years of research into neurolinguistic aspects of bilingualism. It will therefore draw extensively on scattered previously published material, with an attempt at integrating many issues that have hitherto been dealt with in isolation. It represents an effort to infer from our current knowledge some general principles that may be considered passably established or on the way to being widely accepted. Some relevant but less central issues will not be dealt with in detail. Rather, the reader will be referred to works specifically devoted to these issues, particularly when these aspects have been thoroughly treated elsewhere.

It will be assumed that the reader is familiar with the most rudimentary concepts of neurolinguistics (see Stemmer & Whitaker, 1997) and neuropsychology (see Beaumont, Kenealy, & Rogers, 1996), the basic notions of neuroanatomy and neurophysiology of the processes involved in language representation and use (see Fabbro, 1999), and fundamental notions of aphasiology (Taylor Sarno, 1998). For the sake of clarity, a glossary provides the specific meanings of certain words, as they are used in the present volume. Paying careful attention to the meaning of the words we use is far from a display of pedantry. In scientific discourse, the words we use can have serious consequences. Too many controversies over the past quarter century have been caused by a failure to stipulate what researchers meant by a word, and sometimes this was a word that referred to the very object of their research; the term "language" is not the least of such cases. Using the same word for two different entities leads one to believe that the two entities are one and the same; eventually entities that are distinct and should be treated as such are lumped together. Using different words to refer to the same thing may suggest that we are dealing with two distinct entities, differing at least in some intrinsic property or context of use. In order to avoid possible confusion, ambiguity will be shunned, at the risk of having the text appear redundant or repetitious at times.

In the chapters that follow, our best current working hypotheses, whose interrelationships are at the basis of an integrated neurolinguistic perspective on bilingualism, are discussed. Because the various components of the proposed theory are so intricately interrelated that the presentation of each presupposes at least partial knowledge of others, it is difficult to describe any one hypothesis exhaustively before introducing another. As a result, it may become necessary, in the discussion of a construct, to refer briefly to a hypothesis that will be expounded more fully only in a subsequent section. Therefore, instead of presenting the various notions exhaustively, one at a time in a logical sequence, only those aspects necessary in the context of the ongoing discussion will be mentioned and other aspects will be addressed more completely later.

I apologize for the large number of references to my own publications, but after 30 years of focusing on the subject, it turned out to be difficult to do otherwise. The list kept growing with every new topic that was introduced.

Introduction

Henry Hécaen, one of the founders of the International Neuropsychological Symposium and co-founder of *Neuropsychologia*, which together established neuropsychology as an independent discipline, was the first researcher to use the term *neurolinguistique* in a publication (Hécaen, 1968). He defined it as a subdiscipline of neuropsychology concerned with the study of verbal deficits resulting from cortical lesions. According to him, it was to serve as a bridge between the neurosciences (neurology, neuroanatomy, neurophysiology, and neurochemistry) and human communication (experimental psychology, psycholinguistics and linguistics). Neurolinguistics integrates the models, methods and techniques of linguistics and psycholinguistics and adapts them to its own needs (Hécaen, 1972). Hécaen described the neurolinguistic enterprise as a four-step program: (1) description and classification of deficits on the basis of hypotheses about the underlying causes, (2) identification of correlations between such types of deficits and lesion sites, (3) interpretation of the role of cerebral mechanisms in language processing on the basis of the above, and (4) verification of these hypotheses (Hécaen & Dubois, 1971).

Hécaen defined aphasias as deficits in the use of specific rules at any of the various levels of language structure. However, he was quick to point out that these rules are determined by the linguistic model one selects. The grammatical description of a type of aphasia is therefore inherently limited by the capacity of one's linguistic theory. Yet, the fundamental problems of language pathology, namely the classification and explanation of language deficits, crucially depend on the theory of language which, in the final analysis, is at the basis of any neurolinguistic study (Hécaen & Dubois, 1971).

In North America, at about the same time, Harry Whitaker established neurolinguistics as an area of research within linguistics by teaching a course called "An introduction to neurolinguistics" at the 1971 Linguistic Society of America Summer Institute, publishing a book called *On the representation of language in the human brain* (Whitaker, 1971) in which he suggested that linguistic and neurological theories should be compatible, and founding the journal *Brain and Language* in 1974.

Four years later appeared Albert and Obler's seminal book, *The bilingual brain* (1978). It asked many of the questions that would inspire the research into neurolinguistic aspects of bilingualism for the next quarter century. Psychologists, neuropsychologists and aphasiologists focused on the issues raised about the nature of the bilingual lexicon, polyglot aphasia, language switching and mixing, cerebral organization and differential lateralization of a bilingual's languages. The fact that many of the authors' speculations either remain controversial or have not materialized as predicted does not diminish the value of the book, which remains an important landmark in the study of bilingualism. It is in this environment that an integrated view of bilingualism plants its roots.

Many aspects of bilingualism have been studied within different disciplines. These include psychological aspects, such as the effects of bilingualism on perception, cognition, memory and intelligence; sociolinguistic aspects, such as the study of languages in contact, and the influence of social context on choice of language, switching and mixing; sociopsychological aspects, such as bilinguals' attitude towards their languages, problems of allegiance (the desire to assert group membership), the evaluative perception of speakers of each of their languages or speaking with an accent associated with each language; anthropological aspects, such as biculturalism associated with speaking two languages and issues related to acculturation; political aspects, such as language planning, legislation affecting official languages and their domains of authorized or forbidden use; pedagogical aspects, such as the investigation of the best method of becoming bilingual; pedolinguistic aspects, such as the study of language development in children raised bilingually; psycholinguistic aspects, such as the mental representation of two languages; and linguistic aspects, such as what the grammars of a bilingual individual are like, and grammatical constraints on language mixing. In this book, it is the neurolinguistic aspects, namely the cerebral mechanisms and structures involved in the representation and processing of two or more languages in one brain, that will be investigated.

In any study of bilingualism, one needs to be keenly aware that bilinguals do not form a homogeneous group. In fact, a consensus does not even exist as to what constitutes a bilingual. The dictionary definition of a bilingual is usually "a person who knows or uses two languages." This leaves open for interpretation what it means "to know" a language, and to what extent each must be used before a person qualifies as bilingual. As a result, some authors consider their subjects to be bilingual as long as they have some reading knowledge of a language other than their native language (Macnamara, 1969), while others insist that a bilingual must understand and speak each language like a native in all modalities of use, all domains of discourse, and all sociolinguistic registers, that is, all levels of formality and informality (Thiery, 1976). Between these minimalist and maximalist criteria for bilingualism lie a whole range of possible definitions, and various authors have situated their requirements at intervals along a proficiency continuum, from ambilingualism, equilingualism, and diglossia to semilingualism (see below). Some authors stipulate that the use of both languages must be habitual, fluent, and accent-free.

There is in fact no such thing as *complete* knowledge of any language in all its varieties and in its full lexical range (Martinet, 1960). This is what Chomsky (1965) referred to as *idealized* competence, the theoretical linguist's field of investigation. *A fortiori*, no speaker has complete knowledge of *two* languages. However, as long as individuals speak each of their languages the way unilingual speakers do, with the same automaticity and accuracy with respect to the norm, they are considered to be "perfect" bilinguals or *ambilinguals* (Baetens Beardsmore, 1982). If they speak both languages with equal proficiency (irrespective of degree of mastery or accuracy) they are considered to be balanced (or *equilingual*). If neither of their languages is native-like and both languages together are necessary to express their thoughts, they are considered *semilingual*. A dominant bilingual is a person who speaks one language better (more fluently or accurately) than the other, and hence is not an equilingual. An equilingual (von Raffler-Engel, 1961), on the other hand, is either ambilingual if both languages are equally native-like or semilingual (Skutnabb-Kangas, 1980) if both are mastered equally poorly.

There are many other dimensions along which bilingual speakers differ from each other besides degree of proficiency or dominance—context of acquisition (age and manner); context of use (relative frequency, purpose, modalities, sociolinguistic status); structural distance between the languages; amount and type of interference; fluency; lexical, morphosyntactic, and phonological accuracy; auditory and reading comprehension; speaking, writing, and translating abilities each with the possibility of influencing the organization of the grammar. It is therefore extremely important to describe in detail the particular bilingual population used in experimental group studies, or the patient's bilingual background in clinical case studies.

The inquiry that led ultimately to the formulation of a neurolinguistic theory of bilingualism began with a review of the world literature on aphasia in bilinguals and polyglots (Paradis, 1977, 1983). It became apparent that the study of the various patterns of dissociation between the languages of bilingual aphasic patients should provide us with a window on the organization of two languages in the same brain (Paradis, 1985, 1987a). A number of hypotheses discussed in the literature at the time led to the investigation of various topics: (1) Code-mixing (Kolers, 1966; Jakobovits, 1970; Macnamara & Kushnir, 1971), together with other hypothetical constructs such as the bilingual monitor (Obler & Albert, 1978) and the language tag (Liepman & Saegert, 1974), led to the Direct Access Hypothesis (Paradis, 1980b, 1990c). (2) the organization of the bilingual lexicon (Kolers, 1968; McCormack, 1977, for a review) prompted the

Three-Store Hypothesis (Paradis, 1978, 1980b, 1997b). (3) The organization of two languages in the left hemisphere (Ojemann & Whitaker, 1978; Rapport, Tan & Whitaker, 1983; Berthier, Starkstein, Lylyk & Leiguarda, 1990; Gomez-Tortosa et al., 1995) inspired a number of hypotheses about the representation of two languages in the same brain (Paradis, 1981) and the Activation Threshold Hypothesis (Paradis, 1993a). (4) The participation of the right cerebral hemisphere in the language functions of bilinguals (see Vaid & Genesee, 1980; Vaid, 1983, for reviews) induced research into the actual role of the right cerebral hemisphere in language processing in general (Paradis, 1987b), which eventually caused (a) the rejection of the notion of qualitatively differential representation of the language system in the brains of bilingual individuals (Paradis, 1990b, 1992a, 1995a, 2003), and (b) the investigation of the use of pragmatics as a compensatory mechanism in healthy and brain-damaged bilingual individuals (Paradis, 1998a).

It soon became manifest that an instrument that would be linguistically and culturally equivalent in all of a patient's languages was needed in order to objectively and validly assess the relative degree of recovery of, and the nature of the deficits in, the various languages; hence the *Bilingual Aphasia Test* (for a description, see Paradis & Libben, 1987; 1993, 1999, 2003) was developed. At the time this book goes to press, the test is available in over 65 languages and 150 specific language pairs. It has allowed worldwide data collection from bilinguals who speak two closely related (Vilariño et al., 1997; Fabbro, DeLuca, & Vorano, 1996; Huitbregtse & De Bot, 2002) or totally unrelated languages (Nilipour, 1988; Erriondo Korostola, 1995; Mimouni et al., 1995; Nilipour & Paradis, 1995), and from speakers of languages for which there is currently no standard test available (Mimouni & Jarema, 1997; Semenza et al., 1999).

A number of issues (differential asymmetry, lexical representation, code-mixing, language acquisition and loss) discussed over the past 25 years have been muddled because of a lack of specification of what researchers mean by "language" and insufficient attention paid to fundamental distinctions between levels of representation (Paradis, 1995b); between implicit linguistic competence and metalinguistic knowledge (Paradis, 1994); between linguistic and pragmatic competence (Paradis, 1998c); between lexical and conceptual representations (Paradis, 1997a, b); between qualitative and quantitative differences (Paradis, 1995b); and between contents and process, that is, between *what* is represented and *how* it is represented.

These topics are explored in the succeeding chapters. Chapter 1 introduces the different cerebral mechanisms that subserve various components of verbal communication, namely implicit linguistic competence, explicit metalinguistic knowledge, pragmatics, and motivation. Chapter 2 discusses the relevance of procedural-memory-based linguistic competence and declarative-memory-based metalinguistic knowledge to issues in language teaching and language pathology. Chapter 3 investigates bilingual aphasia, data from which serve as the basis for the formulation of a number of hypotheses about the representation and processing of more than one language in the brain. Chapter 4 considers the issues of cerebral lateralization and localization of two languages in one brain that have arisen as researchers attempt to account for the observed bilingual aphasia recovery patterns. Chapter 5 presents the notion of neurofunctional modularity derived from the properties of the components of verbal communication introduced in Chapter 1 and the bilingual aphasia data described in Chapter 3. Chapter 6 examines the contribution of functional neuroimaging to the neurolinguistic study of bilingualism. Chapter 7 integrates into a coherent whole what we know of the cerebral mechanisms presented in Chapter 1 and the different hypotheses developed over the past 25 years to account for the observed normal and clinical bilingual phenomena.

CHAPTER 1

Components of verbal communication

For the past 150 years or so, when linguists, psycholinguists, neurolinguists and aphasiologists spoke of "language," they were referring to the language system, the code, the grammar, which has come to be known as *linguistic competence* and consists of phonology, morphology, syntax and semantics. But it has become apparent that whereas the grammar is indeed necessary, it is far from sufficient for normal verbal communication. At least three other functions, each of which relies on a different cerebral system, are directly involved in the production and comprehension of utterances, namely metalinguistic knowledge, pragmatics, and motivation. When one studies bilingualism, it becomes crucial to take these systems into consideration because different degrees of reliance on each system are a source of variability in communicative behavior and cerebral processing among bilingual speakers that is not seen among unilinguals. Each contributing system will be examined in turn below. The pervasive role of the cerebral systems' activation thresholds will also be discussed.

Implicit and explicit memory

The study of any neurolinguistic aspect of bilingualism can no longer ignore the procedural/declarative memory dimension. It is a crucial element that determines performance in the appropriation, use, and loss of languages.

In the following discussion, *implicit linguistic competence* refers to the knowledge inferred from individuals' systematic verbal performance, even though the individuals themselves are not aware of the nature of this assumed knowledge (Lewandowsky, Dunn & Kirsner, 1989; Graf & Masson, 1993). It is implicit in the sense that it is not overt but inferred. Through their methodical verbal behavior, speakers demonstrate the existence of an internalized implicit system that allows them, for example, to use the plural or the past tense marker in the appropriate contexts, or appropriately place the object before or after the verb, and the adjective before or after the noun. Such behavior can be described in terms of the application of a grammatical rule, but there is no guarantee that it is indeed the result of the application of that particular rule—or in fact of any rule. It might be the outcome, for example, of parallel distributed processing (PDP), consisting of frequency-of-occurrence-induced, statistical-probability-matrix-governed weighted connections (i.e., connections whose weight—or strength—is governed by a statistical probability matrix which itself is induced by the frequency of co-occurrence of any set of items (Ellis, 2002)). We can only say that the speaker's systematic behavior is *compatible* with the application of a particular rule. This is what linguists infer to be linguistic competence. But since a given behavior can be explained as the result of the application of different rules—or even of no algorithmic rule (e.g., PDP)—the form in which linguistic competence is actually represented remains unknown.

This competence is acquired incidentally (i.e., by focusing attention on something other than what is being internalized, as in focusing on the acoustic properties of the word while acquiring the proprioceptive programs that will allow one to articulate that word, or focusing on the meaning of an utterance while internalizing its underlying syntactic structure—which is not there to be observed); it is stored implicitly (i.e., not available to conscious awareness); and it is used automatically (i.e., without conscious control).

Explicit knowledge refers to knowledge of which individuals are aware and that they are capable of representing to themselves and verbalizing on demand; hence, it is characterized as being represented in declarative memory (Cohen, 1984). It can be consciously (even effortfully) learned, by focusing on that which is to be retained in memory. Its contents can later be recalled into conscious awareness and verbalized. On the other hand, one does not know—is not aware of—the contents of implicit competence. Whereas explicit knowledge entails conscious recollection of a fact or an event, implicit competence refers to the change in the subject's behavior attributable to such an event, without conscious recollection of the event (Cork, Kihlstrom & Hameroff, 1992). Implicit knowledge has been described as *knowing how* whereas explicit knowledge is depicted as *knowing that* (Cohen & Squire, 1980).

Implicit and explicit memory have been dissociated experimentally in numerous tasks (e.g., Reber, 1976; Reber et al., 1980; Graf & Schacter, 1987; Turner & Fischler, 1993; Winocur, Moscovitch, & Stuss, 1996; Paller et al., 2003; Pilotti, Meade, & Gallo, 2003; Zeithamova, 2003; Zizzo, 2003; to cite only a few of the early and the most recent studies). Implicit learning is invariant of IQ, whereas explicit learning covaries with it (Mayberry, Taylor, & Obrien-Malone, 1995).

Implicit memory is much more fundamental and more pervasive than explicit memory, which it precedes both phylogenetically and ontogenetically (Lockhart, 1984; Sherry & Schacter, 1987). Implicit memory may in fact be considered the norm, and explicit memory as the specialized capacity of only the most evolved species (Tulving, 1983; Schacter & Moscovitch, 1984; Nelson, 1988; Lockhart & Parkin, 1989; Parkin, 1989). During the first 12 months of life, the child possesses only implicit memory, while explicit memory emerges only later (Schacter & Moscovitch, 1984). Three-year-old children exhibit an implicit memory that is still considerably superior to their explicit memory (Parkin & Streete, 1988). This explicit memory continues to develop with age (Parkin, 1989).

The implicit competence which underlies the performance of motor and cognitive skills is said to be *procedural* (Cohen, 1984), because it relates to internalized procedures, genuine behavior programs, which eventually contribute to the automatic performance of the task. Procedural memory contrasts with *declarative* memory, which subserves everything that can be represented at the conscious level and subsumes both what Tulving (1983) called *episodic* memory, and Penfield termed *experiential* memory (Penfield & Roberts, 1959), i.e., memory of specific, consciously experienced events (e.g., the recollection of what happened on a particular occasion, and what psychologists call *semantic memory*, i.e., the individual's general encyclopedic knowledge (e.g., the knowledge that an event took place, whether or not one was present), including the knowledge of the meaning of words.

Typical examples of procedural competence are the ability to play a musical instrument *by ear*, or the set of computational procedures that permits the comprehension and production of utterances. Typical examples of declarative memory are one's knowledge of geography and chemistry, but also knowledge of what one had for breakfast in the morning, as well as the explicit knowledge of the pedagogical rules of grammar that results from deliberate learning by focalized attention. To sum up, declarative memory comprises one's encyclopedic knowledge (knowledge of the world) and one's episodic memory (recollection of one's past experiences).

Whereas declarative memory is very flexible in that it integrates information from various modalities, procedural memory is available only for very specific tasks; it is inflexible (each motor or cognitive skill is subserved by its specific procedural memory; deficits relating to procedural memory are clearly task-specific: aphasias and apraxias occur independently of each other, and may be broken down into still finer categories, such as constructional apraxia, dress apraxia, gait apraxia, or phonological, morphosyntactic, and lexical impairments in aphasia); its content remains opaque to introspection; and it improves only with practice (Cohen, 1991).

While attention is an essential factor in the memorization and recall of explicit information, it is not necessary for the acquisition of action programs or procedures. On the contrary, it would seem that focusing one's attention on the form to be acquired reduces the efficacy of the acquisition process, because the form is treated explicitly and hence is not internalized (Verdolini, 2002). One might object that gymnasts, for example, explicitly visualize the required movements of their routine in their mind's eye once some preliminary attempts have been made. But what they are conscious of is what they do or what is to be done, but not *how* it is actually done. Unless one is a phys-ed teacher or a physiotherapist, one does not know which muscles are involved, in what sequence, when one performs a certain movement. As long as there is no pain, you never notice which lower back muscle is involved in raising your right arm to pull down the blind. In fact, physiotherapists may have a declarative knowledge of what muscle does what, but they surely do not apply this conscious knowledge when they play tennis. They focus on which movements are to be performed, but what they internalize is the proprioception that underlies the schema for their smooth sequential production. This is the only sense in which focus on procedure can improve performance.

Segalowitz, Segalowitz and Wood (1998) measured the development of automaticity in over 100 English-speaking students learning French at Brock University. They report that words that were not the object of focused learning (that is, those never listed as vocabulary items to be studied), but that naturally recurred frequently throughout all learning activities, showed increased automaticity, thus further supporting the notion of incidental acquisition through practice.

The memory systems that most directly concern us here are those that underlie the acquisition and use of language. We will then consider whether the memory system that subserves the formal learning of a foreign language is the same as or different in nature from the one that subserves the acquisition of a first language or of a second language acquired in a conversational setting. Finally, we will examine implications this conclusion may have for differential types of recovery in bilingual aphasic patients, language rehabilitation and second language teaching.

Two systems: Two ways of speaking

There is no doubt that, to quote Nick Ellis (1994, p. 3), "children and adults can acquire and act upon rules and schemata; they can, for example, be taught grammatical rules for forming the plural." This is indeed what a number of second language learners do. This is also precisely what individuals with genetic dysphasia do in their native language (Paradis & Gopnik, 1997). These individuals demonstrate that learning explicit rules is not the same as acquiring the implicit competence that allows one to speak automatically in a way from which one may infer, as one does of most three-year-old children, that they have internalized a rule (or some computational procedure that can be described as a rule). Unlike three-year-olds who can automatically and unreflectively generate the plural of a nonword such as "wug → wugs," people with genetic dysphasia cannot do this by age 13, 43 or 63. They do, however, learn individual words in their plural forms and store them in their lexicon in the same way as non-impaired speakers store irregular, idiosyncratic plurals that cannot be generated by some form of generalization. They can also do it by the conscious application of an explicit rule. The same is true of the past tense of regular verbs in English, verb inflections in French, case assignment in Finnish and Turkish, *rendaku* (i.e., voicing in specific contexts) in Japanese, compounding in Greek, as described in the special issues of the *Journal of Neurolinguistics* (volume 10, issues 2/3, 1997) and *Folia Phoniatrica et Logopaedica* (volume 51, issues 1/2, 1999), respectively devoted to genetic dysphasia and cross-linguistic evidence thereof.

Such cases provide neurolinguistic evidence of how the use of meta-linguistic knowledge can compensate for gaps in implicit competence and strongly suggest that there are two systems: one that implicitly internalizes the competence that allows speakers to automatically and unreflectively engage in systematic behavior, and another that allows them to learn and apply a rule, with considerable interindividual and intra-individual variability in performance.

There are thus two ways of speaking: using implicit linguistic competence only, as illustrated by children and illiterates; using metalinguistic knowledge only, as illustrated by individuals with genetic dysphasia and incipient L2 learners. (Note that the distinction between metalinguistic knowledge and linguistic competence refers to the conscious versus unconscious nature of these representations, though the procedures involved in accessing them are unconscious for both types of representation.) In individuals who have acquired language normally, both systems are independently available. In normal circumstances, the implicit system, which is faster, tends to be used. One or the other may be selectively affected by pathology.

The idea that metalinguistic knowledge is separate from incidentally and unreflectively developed competence is not new (Krashen, 1981; Karmiloff-Smith, 1986); nevertheless, it has more recently received clinical support from studies of declarative and procedural memory (Cohen & Eichenbaum, 1993). Raichle et al. (1994) have shown that two distinct cerebral pathways are used, depending on the degree to which a verbal task is controlled or automatic. Developmental language impairment may be successfully overcome by metalinguistic training that provides a means to bypass impaired linguistic competence (Hirschman, 2000). In non-brain-damaged speakers of L1, metalinguistic knowledge is used to keep track of the output when sentences are long and complex, particularly in a formal context.

Neurolinguistic evidence

Pathology has shown that implicit and explicit memory are doubly dissociated. We have ample clinical, neuropsychological and neuroimaging evidence that implicit linguistic competence and metalinguistic knowledge are each subserved by separate, neurofunctional mechanisms. Patients with aphasia have damaged implicit memory for language (or impaired automatic use thereof) but spared declarative memory, resulting from circumscribed lesions in the perisylvian area (the traditional Broca's and Wernicke's areas; Figure 1.1), parts of the left basal ganglia, in particular the neostriatum, and the right cerebellum; whereas patients with amnesia have impaired declarative memory with spared procedural memory (including linguistic competence) subsequent to lesions in the hippocampal system, including the parahippocampal gyri and mesial temporal lobes.

Individuals with Alzheimer's disease (Gabrieli et al. 1992), alcoholic Korsakoff's syndrome (Canavan, Hömberg & Stelmach, 1992; Parker, 1992), and anterograde amnesia (Corkin, 1992; Keane, Clarke & Corkin, 1992) have their *explicit* memory impaired. Individuals with Parkinson's Disease have their *implicit* competence impaired (Saint-Cyr, Taylor & Lang, 1987; Ullman et al., 1997; Zanini et al., 2003). Anesthesia with isoflurane/oxygen spares implicit memory (Kihlstrom et al., 1990) whereas anesthesia with sufentanil/nitrous oxide does not (Cork, Kihlstrom & Schacter, 1992). While the latter example is not a double dissociation, it does show that different substances have differential effects on implicit and explicit memory. Vocabulary is affected earlier than syntax in the attrition of the native language (Andersen, 1982; Köpke, 2002). Lebrun (2002) provides additional clinical evidence of the distinction between implicit linguistic competence and explicit metalinguistic knowledge and concludes that procedural routines for phonology and morphosyntax involve subcortical structures whereas metalinguistic knowledge, including vocabulary and literacy, has its representation exclusively in the neocortex.

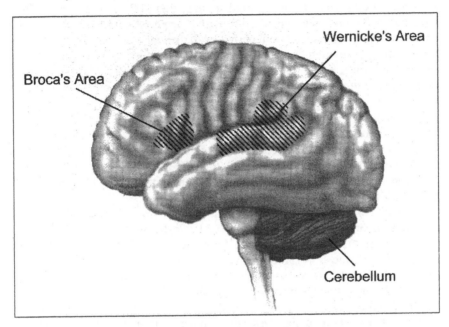

Figure 1.1. *The classical perisylvian language area*

Meguro et al. (2003) report that their Japanese-Portuguese bilingual patients with Alzheimer's disease had greater difficulty with kanji in Japanese and with irregularly spelled words in Portuguese whereas they were able to read Japanese kana normally and regularly spelled Portuguese words nearly normally. Unlike kana script and Portuguese regular spelling, kanji and irregular Portuguese words have no one-to-one correspondence between grapheme and sound. In other words, for these patients, the items that rely on declarative memory were selectively or considerably more impaired than the items that are derivable by internalized rules.

Reduced implicit linguistic competence in the context of available metalinguistic knowledge may explain the paradoxical recovery of a previously weaker second language to a greater extent than the native language in bilingual aphasia (Agliotti & Fabbro, 1993; Fabbro & Paradis, 1995). On the one hand, we have cases of aphasia where patients recover their second language better than their first, presumably because, while their linguistic competence in both languages is affected, they compensate by relying on their more extensive explicit knowledge of L2 (Paradis, 1994). On the other hand, amnesic patients have been reported to lose their L2, learned and stored explicitely, while retaining the use of their L1, acquired implicitly (Jamkarian, 2001). Loss of L2 has also been reported in Alzheimer's disease, a condition in which declarative memory is affected first (Hyltenstam & Strout, 1993; Hyltenstam, 1995; Obler 1999). Elderly bilingual individuals with dementia have a greater preference for their native language and converse less in an L2 learned after age 13; there is also a tendency for words and phrases from their native language to intrude into conversational speech in L2 (Mendez et al., 1999). They revert to their first language when interacting with speakers of their L2, but do not go in the other direction, which suggests that this is not a problem with switching per se, but a problem with a late-learned L2 (Hyltenstam, 1995). The same is true of healthy immigrants when they stop using the local language (de Bot & Clyne, 1989).

Recently, a number of neuroimaging studies have reported differential activation in certain cortical areas when L1 and L2 were used. Perani et al. (1996) report that the set of active language areas in a PET study was considerably reduced for the second language in their Italian-dominant speakers of English. There was also bilateral activation of the parahippocampal gyri for L2, suggesting an increased participation of memory-related structures. The following year, in an fMRI study, Dehaene et al. (1997) report considerable dispersion in the classical language area for L2, with concomitant activation of the anterior portion of the cingulate gyrus, thus suggesting increased use of controlled processing in the second, much less proficient language. The anterior cingulate cortex is known to be involved in conscious controlled tasks (Raichle et al., 1994; Casey et al., 1997). For one thing, it has been shown to be active during the ongoing evaluation of performance (Carter et al., 2001).

From the exhaustive assessment of Patient H.M.'s cognitive capacities (Milner, 1966; Milner, Corkin, & Teuber, 1968), we have learned that declarative memory, which is impaired in anterograde amnesia, is independent of procedural memory, which is spared. Not only H.M., but amnesic patients in general, perform as well as normal controls on implicit tasks (Cermak, 1993). H.M.'s inability to learn new words over the past 40 years (Cohen, 1991) attests to the declarative component of vocabulary: we are aware of the sounds and meanings of words, but not of the underlying grammatical structure of sentences. The dichotomy between the ability to learn words and to acquire syntax is well documented in studies of chimpanzees and gorillas. Most experimental primates have been able to learn an impressive number of words, but the best of them have been able to master only a very rudimentary syntax. Similarly, in children who are exposed to language after the age of seven (see Nanga (Lebrun, 1978) and Genie (Curtis, 1977), for example), the acquisition of grammar is arduous, whereas vocabulary expansion is relatively easy. In addition, Nanga is reported to have been hardly able "to derive grammatical rules intuitively from the numerous utterances she hears ... Syntactical relationships and constraints have to be made explicit before they can be grasped" (Lebrun, 1978, p. 190). A patient with semantic dementia showed progressive and profound loss of semantic memory, affecting both factual knowledge and vocabulary (i.e., the association of the phonological representations of words with their corresponding familiar objects), with preservation of basic syntactic processes (Hodges, Patterson, & Tyler, 1994). These converging data suggest that vocabulary is at least in part subserved by declarative memory (to the extent that we are aware of some properties such as the referential meanings and sounds of words), whereas the morphosyntactic and phonological aspects of language (those aspects that are implicit and can be described as rule-governed) are subserved by procedural memory.

Because the implicit/explicit memory dimension is a key concept of the proposed neurolinguistic theory of bilingualism, the next chapter will be devoted to discussing a number of its implications for L2 appropriation and bilingual aphasia.

Pragmatics

As mentioned above, the cerebral representation of the language system, comprising phonology, morphology, syntax and semantics, has been extensively studied for over 150 years. These efforts have resulted in the identification, in the left hemisphere, of the perisylvian cortex and some subcortical structures as being involved in the representation and processing of what linguists call a generative or sentence grammar (Caplan, 1987; Paradis, 1998c).

Not until the last couple of decades has it become apparent that individuals with right-hemisphere lesions exhibit verbal communication deficits of a qualitatively different nature, but equally—if not more—disabling. The right-hemisphere deficits described so far are of a pragmatic nature, comprising difficulty with comprehension and/or production of affective prosody, indirect speech acts, metaphors, and connotative meanings, that is, with the interpretation of the appropriate intended meaning of an utterance, i.e., whether it is said in anger, in jest, in earnest or as a metaphor. There are also deficits at the level of discourse, such as deriving the gist of a story or the moral of a tale, and in general, problems of cohesion.

More specifically, patients with right-hemisphere damage have been reported as exhibiting problems with discourse organization, cohesion, and logical coherence (Delis et al., 1983; Hough, 1990; Molloy, Brownell, & Gardner1990; Schneiderman, Murasugi, & Saddy, 1992; Hough & Pierce, 1993; Frederiksen & Stemmer, 1993; Tompkins et al., 1995, 1997; Albyn Davis, O'Neil-Pirozzi, & Coon, 1997; Brownell & Martino, 1998; Brownell, & Stringfellow, 1999); story or narrative processing (Joanette et al., 1986; Rehak et al., 1992; Nicholas & Brookshire, 1995); and script knowledge (Roman et al., 1987); and as showing insensivity to violations of Gricean maxims (Rehak, Kaplan, & Gardner, 1992). Overall, these patients seem to have difficulty using contextual information to interpret discourse (Dwyer & Rinn, 1981; Brownell, 1988). Patients are also reported to have difficulty with indirect requests, indirect commands, and indirect speech acts in general (Hirst, LeDoux, & Stein, 1984; Foldi, 1987; Weylman et al., 1989): with inferring the gist or main ideas and getting the point (Delis et al., 1983; Gardner et al., 1983; Brookshire & Nicholas, 1984; Wegner, Brookshire, & Nicholas, 1984; Brownell et al., 1986; Bryan, 1988; Hough, 1990; Rehak, Kaplan, & Gardner, 1992; Rehak et al., 1992; Schneiderman et al., 1992); with understanding jokes, cartoons, and humor in general (Gardner et al., 1975; Brownell et al., 1983; Dagge & Hartje, 1985; Bihrle, Brownell, & Gardner, 1986; 1988; Winner et al., 1998; Shammi & Stuss, 1999); in other words, with various pragmatic aspects of communication (Foldi, Cicone, & Gardner, 1983; Kaplan et al., 1990), including theory of mind (Siegal, Carrington, & Radel, 1996) and the ability to interpret the speaker's mood (Brownell et al., 1992). In addition, they seem to have difficulty dealing with any meaning other than the default, canonical, literal meaning (Pearce, McDonald, & Coltheart, 1998), such as figurative meaning (Bottini et al., 1994), metaphoric meaning (Brownell, 1988; Brownell et al., 1990; Tompkins, 1990; Gagnon et al., 2003), figures of speech (Brownell et al., 1990; Dravins & Bradvik, 1996), idiomatic expressions (Myers & Linebaugh, 1981; Tompkins, Boada, & McGarry, 1992), and connotative meaning (Chapman et al., 1980; Brownell et al., 1984; Brownell, 1988). Many have also been reported not to be able to use prosody to interpret (or convey) the emotional content of discourse (e.g., Weintraub, Mesulam, & Kramer, 1981; Heilman et al., 1984; Shapiro & Danly, 1985; Tompkins & Flowers, 1985; Tompkins & Mateer, 1985; Schlanger, Schlanger, & Gerstman, 1986; Bowers et al., 1987; Ross et al., 1988; Alexander, Benson, & Stuss, 1989; Behrens, 1989; Bryan, 1989; Cancelliere & Kertesz, 1990; Cohen et al., 1990; Blonder, Bowers, & Heilman, 1991; Lalande, Braun, Charlebois, &

Whitaker, 1992; Gandour et al., 1995; Borod et al., 1998). Similar patterns of communicative dysfunction are observed in nonretarded people with good literal language presenting with autism (Rumsey & Hanahan, 1990; Ozonoff & Miller, 1996) and schizophrenia (Langdon et al., 2002; Tenyi et al., 2002), suggesting that the right hemisphere contributes to these conditions. Right temporal cortex participation has also been reported during tasks requiring pragmatic cohesion in a recent fMRI study on healthy right-handed volunteers (Kircher et al., 2001). For a recent discussion of pragmatic language disorders, see Martin and McDonald (2003).

Whereas deficits in implicit linguistic competence have long been commonly referred to as dysphasia, there was no label to refer to impairments in the ability to infer what is meant from the context in which something is said. This is why the use of the term *dyshyponoia* was proposed (Paradis, 1998c). It is derived from the Greek ὑπονοώ, meaning to imply without actually saying what one means. It is used to refer to a difficulty in drawing appropriate inferences from extrasentential information, leading to problems in interpreting the unspoken component of an utterance (its illocutionary force or pragmatic meaning), with preserved comprehension of the literal meaning of a sentence, i.e., its semantics, derivable solely from the lexical meaning of words and morphosyntactic structure of a sentence.

The importance of pragmatics in deriving the meaning of an utterance should not be underestimated. In much of everyday speech, we do not say what we mean, not because we are devious, but because that is the way verbal communication normally works. We often say (1) less than what we mean, or (2) something other than what we mean, or even (3) something opposite to what we mean, and yet expect our interlocutors to understand exactly what we mean, which they most often do.

We seldom say everything we mean. This would be an extremely boring endeavor. Only with babies do we run a commentary on ongoing actions (e.g., "now we put your little hand through this sleeve, now this one through that sleeve; now we button this little white button. . ."). With adults, we avoid stating the obvious, whatever is there for the interlocutor to see. Nor do we explicitly mention obvious implications (e.g., if we are told "John drove Bill to the hospital; he had a broken leg," we do not need to be told which one had a broken leg).

Very often, we say something other than what we mean and use figurative speech so that our utterances are not to be interpreted literally but, taking various contexts into consideration, as an idiomatic expression (e.g., "she has a green thumb"), as a metaphor (e.g., "the President's nose lengthens with each new explanation"), or as an indirect speech act (e.g., "do you know what time it is?").

An ironic or sarcastic remark will be interpreted as meaning the opposite of what is said when the circumstances call for it (e.g., "that was smart" when somebody just did something plainly stupid; or "you are very generous" when a little boy puts a candy in his mouth and gives you the wrapper).

In addition, the same sentence can have many different meanings depending on the circumstances of its utterance. For example, the sentence "the dog is sleeping on the mat" can be understood as a reproach (i.e., "I told you 100 times not to let the dog shed its hair on the mat"), a congratulatory remark (i.e., "you finally managed to train the dog to sleep on the mat rather than on the couch"), a warning (i.e., "watch for the dog as you open the door"), an excuse (i.e., "I can't vacuum my room because the dog is sleeping on the mat in front of the door"), or information (i.e., as an answer to the question, "where is the dog?"). In some other cultures its translation equivalent might even have an idiomatic meaning, as in the proverbs "let sleeping dogs lie, or "every dog has his day."

Some aspects of pragmatic capacity, the ability to infer meaning from nonlinguistic clues (i.e., clues other than grammatical) in the context of verbal communication, are just as implicit as linguistic competence and also remain so forever unless they are specifically studied as part of education. Some clues, such as pupil size (Hess, 1965), for instance, are known to exist only by specialists, and yet they have an impact on our interpretation of an interlocutor's state of mind and communicative intentions (although the speaker may be just as unaware of producing those clues as the listener is in making use of them). Speakers constantly emit signals of which they are not aware, though this does much to determine their behavior (Watzlawick, 1976).

Such implicit pragmatic competence is phylogenetically and ontogenetically prior to implicit linguistic competence (your dog might run under the couch the moment he hears you mention the vet; children catch pragmatic cues long before they utter their first word). It is part of what Lamendella (1977a, b) called the general communicative system. Just as concepts are shaped and refined by language-specific constraints, pragmatic capacity is shaped and refined by cultural-specific implicit pragmatic conventions. Thus, a native speaker of Italian will implicitly infer some particular meaning from some specific nonverbal behavior accompanying an utterance which is different from the meaning inferred by a speaker of Swedish or Dutch on the same occasion.

Semantics and pragmatics in the interpretation of an utterance

For purposes of interpreting an utterance, both grammar and pragmatics are necessary and neither is sufficient. Both have a constitutive role in the interpretation of the meaning of every utterance. But this is not to say that they cannot be dissociated for purposes of analysis. Verbal communication makes simultaneous use of both implicit linguistic competence and implicit pragmatic competence, each subserved by its own neural substrate and selectively isolable by pathology. Some left-hemisphere-damaged patients understand the (unspoken) pragmatic component of the meaning of an utterance, though not the meaning of the actual sentence, and some right-hemisphere-damaged patients are able to derive the meaning of the sentence (independent of its context of use, its "semantic" component) but are unable to interpret the (unspoken) meaning of the utterance (its pragmatic component). Hirst, LeDoux and Stein's (1984) results suggest that the pragmatic and grammatical aspects of language are differentially affected by damage to different brain structures. When processing indirect speech acts, the right-hemisphere-damaged patients had difficulty with the pragmatic component while the left-hemisphere damaged patients had difficulty with the linguistic component.

Both right- and left-hemisphere damage causes deficits in the normal use of language, but these deficits are qualitatively different and in complementary distribution over the hemispheres. And, just as aphasic patients demonstrate the capacity to utilize extralinguistic cues to discern the contextually conveyed intended meaning of implicit speech acts (Wilcox, Albyn Davis & Leonard, 1978), speakers of a second, weaker language are able to compensate for their lack of linguistic competence by relying on pragmatic cues.

Like agrammatic patients (Hirst, Le Doux & Stein, 1984), children, genetic dysphasics and second language learners are able to derive the speaker's intentions without going through the syntactic decoding process. To do this, they use right-hemisphere-based skills, in particular, inference from context and general knowledge. In a PET study with non-brain-damaged participants, Bottini et al. (1994) observed greater activation in areas of the right hemisphere roughly homologous to Broca's and Wernicke's areas during tasks requiring metaphorical comprehension as compared to literal comprehension of sentences. In another PET study, Nichelli et al. (1995) also reported that activation increased in right frontal and temporal regions when their participants made judgments about the moral of a fable as compared to judgments about the literal meaning of a story.

Dissociations between grammar and pragmatics have been described in a number of different populations. Nass and Gutman (1997), for example, present the case of an ASL signer who suffered a right parietal-occipital lesion. In the performance of a particular narrative device known as role play, this patient maintained full command of sentence-level grammatical elements but not of extragrammatical, pragmatic ones. This is in striking contrast with the way in which children learning ASL as a native language do it: The first identifiable role plays produced are marked only by pragmatic elements. In the beginning, children use all pragmatic features successfully, rendering the role play unambiguously recognizable as such, even though it lacks the grammatical elements. The right-hemisphere-damaged patient had access to the necessary abstract, complex syntactic capacities but could not use the pragmatic capacities acquired by children before these grammatical markers (Loew, Kegl, & Poizner, 1997). Corina et al. (1992) also demonstrated dissociations between linguistic and non-linguistic gestural systems. And Papagno (2001) reported a double dissociation between the comprehension of propositional (i.e., literal) language and figurative language (metaphors and idioms) in a group of patients with Alzheimer's disease.

It is, of course, not the case that all right-brain-damaged patients necessarily exhibit all of the symptoms that have been reported, but when they do have communication impairments, they are of a particular kind. They are not only qualitatively different from aphasic symptoms, but complementary. This situation is no different from that experienced by left-brain-damaged patients: Not every left-brain-damaged patient has aphasia—only those with lesions in specific areas do. But when they do, their deficits have certain characteristics which differ qualitatively from those subsequent to right-hemisphere damage.

While it is true that the derivation of the meaning of an utterance depends equally on grammatical and pragmatic clues, it is also true that implicit linguistic competence functions independently of pragmatic competence, and that the two, dealing with the said and the unsaid respectively, in parallel or rapid succession, work together to arrive at the intended meaning (or what is perceived as the intended meaning). Semantics and pragmatics are independent in the way that phonology and syntax are independent. Each has its own underlying rules (or implicit modus operandi), which differ in their objects and, to a great extent, in their internal structure—and yet both are necessarily used in concert, for every utterance.

Foreign language speakers are more likely to understand the semantic than the pragmatic meaning of utterances. Apart from literary metaphors, taught in literature classes, L2 learners usually get acquainted mostly with literal meanings. The pragmatic components are acquired from practice in natural cultural settings.

Culture-specific pragmatic features: Diversities within similarity

The use of pragmatic and paralinguistic clues is as much a part of the implicit microgenesis of an utterance as its linguistic material. As with linguistic processes, cues tend to be underlyingly universal, with different surface manifestations in different cultures. Some of them may be genetically programmed, such as paying attention to particular features, which in turn may have slightly (or not so slightly) different manifestations and/or meanings (e.g., hand gestures, gaze direction, etc.). The shape and movement of the hand may differ from culture to culture within certain limits to indicate "come here" or "go away", or dozens of other meanings. The gesture for "crazy" often involves a finger (or fingers) pointed toward the head, from tapping the head with one crooked finger to drawing circles around the temple without touching the head (English), to applying the index on the temple and rotating it ninety degrees to the right and to the left in rapid succession (French). The same gesture (pointing to the head) may mean "crazy" in one language, but "smart" in another, just as *burro* means "butter" in Italian and "donkey" in Spanish. The gesture for "yes" in French (nodding head up and down) is very similar to the gesture for "no" in Arabic (jerking the head up), while the French gesture for "no" (repeated movements of the head from right to left and left to right) is the gesture for "what?" in Arabic. (The fact that the Arabic "what?" gesture is faster than the French "no" gesture or that the Arabic "no" gesture is only part of the French "yes" gesture goes unnoticed by speakers of the other language.)

A question representing a proposal in English (e.g., "would you like a beer?") can only be a genuine question in Polish, Russian or Spanish, and not an invitation to have a beer. The equivalent of "why don't you" questions would be interpreted in most languages as a combination of a question and a criticism, and would be downright impolite in Korean, for instance. "Why don't you sit down?" would be interpreted as a reproach and a request for a justification for not sitting down. Some linguistic devices associated with respect in English are associated with hostility and alienation in Polish (Wierzbicka, 1985). Eye contact, required in American culture, is interpreted in other cultures as threatening, aggressive, or a sign of insubordination. Because of differences in prosodic conventions between British English and Indian English, what sounds to British ears like a statement where a question would be appropriate, and hence is perceived as unfriendly if not rude, is meant as an offer in Indian English (Gumperz, 1982).

Wolfson (1981) shows that Americans pay compliments in situations where complimenting would be quite inappropriate in another culture. Not only do some American compliments become the object of ridicule to Athapaskan

Indians, as reported by Basso (1979), but the reaction of the French, an apparently much closer culture, would in some cases be also very different from the standard American response. Told, for instance, "I like your tie", a Frenchman, instead of the traditional "thank you", would likely declare that he bought it on sale at the cheapest department store (or make some other equally deprecatory statement about his tie). A Moroccan, in the same circumstances, would feel obliged to offer his tie to the complimentor.

All cultures use compliments, express gratitude and apologies, and have politeness markers, but these differ from culture to culture. Universal (or natural) principles (involving gesture, posture, prosody, gaze, eye contact, loudness, as well as indirect speech acts, metaphors, and jokes), are modulated by language/culture-specific conventions. Different forms of indirectness (implicit performatives), for example, are used in different languages for the performance of a particular speech act (Blum-Kulka, House, & Kasper, 1989). Spatial deixis, relative location, what is considered in front of, next to, or behind something is not invariant from language to language (Weissenborn & Klein, 1982). These differences do not exist just between Papuan, African, Amerindian or East Asian languages and European languages, but between languages as close as German and English and cultures as geographically contiguous as Mexico and the United States.

The unconscious, uncontrolled pragmatic features (pupil size, pulse rate, skin coloration) are more likely to be universal (though again, natural skin pigmentation may differ and thus flushed or pale complexions would look different). Other clues are within the awareness of the speaker and their surface manifestations are consciously perceived by the listener (just as the spoken form of the utterance is)—even though their production may be just as automatic as the production of the phonological component of the utterance. Facial expressions, gestures, voice quality, and loudness, are variations on a universal theme. However, the baseline may be different across cultures. For example, one "raises one's voice" in anger from a "normal" level which may be higher or lower in another culture, so that the baseline in one language/culture may be perceived as "raised" by a speaker from another culture.

While right-hemisphere-damaged bilingual patients have not yet been systematically tested for dissociations between the ability to interpret, or appropriately produce, conventional gestures and other language-specific pragmatic features in each language, it is not unreasonable to expect that such dissociations will be observed when such patients are tested. Because systems of conventional inference and cues for signaling speech acts differ from one language/culture to another, cross-cultural differences in the realization of various pragmatic functions might be expected to exhibit (1) unidirectional interference, i.e., simply translating utterances into L2 without adopting the pragmatic features of the second language (conventional speech acts, politeness markers, conventional metaphors, etc.) and interpreting body language and other pragmatic features in accordance with L1 conventions; (2) bidirectional interference, whereby pragmatic conventions of each language have permeated the other and clues from one are interpreted as clues in the other, reciprocally; and (3) no interference, using the culturally appropriate pragmatic features in each language. To the extent that conventional pragmatic practices differ between two languages/cultures, there is an opportunity for misinterpreting the L2 speaker's intentions.

Coulmas (1978) discusses such pragmatic interference. If the various pragmatic phenomena are subserved by neural structures in a way that parallels linguistic phenomena, one may expect pragmatic interference and selective impairment subsequent to (right) brain damage to mirror the dissociations observed in bilingual aphasia. The study of bilingual pragmatic deficits subsequent to right-hemisphere damage should eventually help us determine whether pragmatic inferences rely on "central systems of mind" (Kasher, 1991, p. 575) or on language-specific pragmatic neurofunctional modules.

Pragmatic competence includes the implicit knowledge of social conventions, such as, in the case of bilingual speakers, the necessary conditions for language switching to be appropriate. Two types of language-switching deficit may be observed: the loss of grammatical (or probabilistic) constraints on code-switching (as is sometimes reported in aphasia) and the loss of sociolinguistic constraints on language switching, as may be expected to occur subsequent to some right-hemisphere or prefrontal lesions (Abutalebi, Miozzo, & Cappa, 2000; Fabbro, Skrap & Aglioti, 2000). This is still speculative since no systematic study has investigated the latter type of impairment. In retrospect, one may recall one or two cases compatible with this hypothesis, but a focused study has yet to be undertaken.

All individuals with dyshyponoia seem to have difficulty in inferring the speaker's intention from a variety of clues (including tone of voice, facial expressions, situational context, and discourse features), that indicate when a message contradicts the literal meaning of an utterance. This strongly suggests that, in addition to implicit linguistic competence and metalinguistic knowledge (which allow one to understand and produce grammatical sentences with appropriate semantic meanings), pragmatics (irrespective of the specific sites of its neural substates) is another necessary component of verbal communication. It is most likely that those aspects of pragmatic capacity that are implicit (i.e., pragmatic competence) are subserved by circumscribed areas of the right hemisphere whereas those that are explicit (metapragmatic knowledge) are bilaterally distributed over extensive areas and involve various mechanisms of conscious reasoning.

Motivation and affect

The human brain contains not only the most recently evolved structure, the neocortex, of which certain areas subserve the higher cognitive functions, including language, but also, as in all other less evolved animals, a central nervous system, responsible for vital functions, arousal and tonus, and a limbic system (Lamendella, 1977b), located between the two, responsible for drives, desires, emotions and motivation. A neural mechanism consisting of the amygdala, the ventromedial prefrontal cortex, the nucleus accumbens, the dopamine system and the peripheral nervous system assesses the motivational relevance and emotional significance of stimuli such as the desirability of an L2 (Schumann, 1990, 1998). Inputs to the orbitofrontal cortex and the amygdala allow these brain structures to evaluate the reward value of incoming stimuli; outputs of the evaluative cerebral structures project directly to the basal ganglia to allow implicit responses to be made on the basis of the hedonic evaluation of these stimuli (Rolls, 1999). These assessments are made on the basis of whether or not the stimulus is pleasant, enhances an individual's goals and needs, and is compatible with his or her coping ability, self-image and social image (Schumann, 1998).

Motivation in acquisition and learning

Lamendella (1977a) suggested that, during acquisition, the native language is integrated into the phylogenetically and ontogenetically earlier communication system, and thus possesses a solid limbic base. Formal foreign language learning, according to Lamendella, leads to exclusive use of neocortical areas, without integration into the communicative system, and hence without limbic participation. The knowledge of a foreign language would then be represented in the same way as any other abstract knowledge, such as geography or chemistry. Just as there is a dissociation between the availability of abundant factual knowledge and the absence of any emotional response to it in patients with frontal damage (Damasio, 1994), formal second language learning, because of the lack of emotional involvement during development, never seems to connect to the relevant limbic structures that underlie native language acquisition (Lamendella, 1977a): Remove the drive, and you will not acquire mastery of a skill (Damasio, 1994). Additional evidence for the impact of affect on verbal behavior may be found in dynamic aphasia, a condition in which there is no damage to the cortical areas that subserve language *per se*; rather, a disconnection between the limbic system and those areas leaves patients unmotivated to speak, and they must continually be prompted. The reverse effect is observed in cases of global aphasia, in which patients are unable to put two words together but loudly produce whole phrases or short sentences when their emotions are aroused by some sudden discomfort.

Under normal circumstances, every utterance produced by a speaker starts with an intention to communicate a message. At the root of every utterance there is therefore some limbic participation. This is true in the course of language acquisition: Young children are highly motivated to say what they want to say and to understand what is said to them. This is the dimension that, to the present day, has been lacking in foreign language teaching methods. It is obvious that this dimension was absent in traditional grammar-translation methods (still in use in many post-secondary institutions). For instance, there is no urgency in a statement like "the pen of my aunt is on the desk of my uncle" nor any great motivation to produce it other than the possible desire to learn a particular language structure. The audiolingual methods that were popular in the late 1950s and 1960s, focused on structural pattern drills without much concern about the meaning of consecutive sentences or the context of their use, since there was no context for the repetition, substitution and transformation exercises (Pattern example: I lost my hat; stimulus: cat—response: I lost my cat; hair—I lost my hair; mind—I lost my mind; father—I lost my father; temper—I lost my temper; reputation—I lost my reputation... .) Nevertheless, soldiers in WWII who received intensive training in audiolingual drills before they were sent behind enemy lines are said to have quickly mastered enough language to pass for natives (presumably, provided they did not engage in long conversations) and to understand what was being said around them. This is a good example of the impact of motivation. These soldiers were eager and enthusiastic, unlike high school students who were reported to find the exercise boring, tedious, and pointless.

The audiovisual and structuroglobal methods added the semantic and pragmatic dimensions, insisting that every utterance should be used in a situational context, provided by microfilm projection. Learners were thus supposed to be always conscious of the meaning of their utterances and of their appropriate context of use. For example, it was necessary to look at the map on the screen in order to correctly answer the question: "Where is the pharmacy?" However, both the question and the answer were motivated solely by the fact that it was Student A's turn to ask the question, and Student B's turn to answer it. The question was not asked because Student A had a headache and wanted to get a pain killer. In order to ask the question, Student A had to use phonology, morphology, syntax and lexical items, and in order to answer, Student B had to understand the question and in addition had to take the pragmatic situation into account and check the proper location on the map. However, the first phase (the intention to communicate a message—limbically driven) of the microgenesis of the student's utterance was missing, as it usually is in most L2 formal learning contexts.

In the communicative approaches to second-language learning that were introduced later, the learner is placed in a game-like situation in which success at communicating the relevant information is the key to winning; it may be assumed that the initial phase of the microgenesis of utterances in this context may somewhat approximate that in the infant, thus providing, at least to some extent, the beneficial surge of dopamine from the amygdala (Schumann, 1998).

Additional anecdotal evidence of the role of motivation comes from English-speaking students of French in Montreal in the late 1950s and during the 1960s. It was a concern to the school board that, in spite of having been taught French from Grade 1 (age 6), the vast majority of students matriculating in Grade 11 (age 16) could hardly understand a word of spoken French and certainly not a sentence in a normal conversation, nor could they produce an unrehearsed coherent statement. The situation was blamed in turn on the inadequacy of the method used and on the teachers (many of whom, admittedly, could not speak French and hated having to teach it). But note that the situation changed little when French-speaking teachers were recruited from Europe and North Africa, nor when new audiovisual methods were introduced.

What was surprising was that often students who arrived from Poland or Pakistan in Grade 7 without any knowledge of French were doing much better by the end of the year than their classmates who had been taught French since Grade 1. How was this possible? A close look at the sociopolitical situation of the city at the time may provide an answer. Most English-speaking residents of Montreal had little respect for the French-speaking majority, who were considered less educated and definitely positioned lower on the socio-economic scale, and with whom they did not wish to interact. For the immigrants, however, French represented a prestigious language, a language of culture, one that one would be proud to be able to speak. Outside the classroom, they availed themselves of the multiple opportunities offered by French television and contacts with French-speaking people. The difference is thus one of sociolinguistic status. There was no motivation for the English Montrealers to learn a language associated with people they considered inferior, and because of the political circumstances, there was even a counter-motivation. In spite of their parents' paying lip service to the importance of speaking French, the children sensed their resentment for a culture they did not wish to associate with (for one thing, the parents never invited a French-Canadian to their homes, and always referred in unflattering terms to the provincial government as "they").

The situation rapidly changed in the late 1970s after the not-so-Quiet Revolution, when French was made the only official language of the province and it became mandatory to speak French in any job involving contact with the public. Most English-speaking Montrealers under the age of 40 who did not leave the city for Toronto or the rest of Canada in the late 1970s now speak French.

In addition to the differences between native and later learned languages, the extreme variability in success among second-language learners themselves has also drawn attention to the important role of motivation. Second-language teachers will often assert that degree of motivation is one of the best predictors of success in L2 appropriation (Savignon, 1976; Olshtain, 1990; Kraemer, 1993). In fact, motivation is as good a predictor of success as aptitude (Gardner & Smythe, 1974a), in particular integrative motivation (Gardner & Smythe, 1974b).

Different kinds of general motivation behind the appropriation of a second language have been identified, from *instrumental*, such as wanting to learn a language to improve one's professional status, to *integrative*, namely the desire to become part of another linguistic community (Lambert, 1968; Gardner & Lambert, 1972). Anecdotal evidence abounds in support of the strong facilitating effect of learning the language of a significant other (especially during courtship). This situation is probably facilitative for a number of reasons, including the motivation to be accepted as a valid partner, which not only stimulates the dopaminergic system, but also encourages the learner to multiply practice sessions, thus facilitating incidental acquisition. Schumann (1990) further postulates that the attitude towards the L2 and the L2-speaking community has an influence on the acquisition of the L2: Efficiency of L2 appropriation is a function of the emotional appraisal of the linguistic input and the learning situation. Such observations find a neurofunctional explanation in Schumann's proposal that one of the functions of the amygdala is to appraise the subjective emotional significance of incoming sensory stimuli. Hence, in a positively evaluated environment, the learner would be much more receptive to intake, given that the amygdala would project more opiates to the specific sensory processing cortical systems involved and thereby facilitate retention of the material in long-term memory.

The Activation Threshold Hypothesis

A pervasive component of the model, not associated with any particular anatomical area or functional system but physiological in nature and operative in all higher cognitive representations, whatever their domain, is the Activation Threshold Hypothesis (Paradis, 1987b; 1993a). This hypothesis proposes that an item is activated when a sufficient amount of positive neural impulses have reached its neural substrate. The amount of impulses necessary to activate the item constitutes its activation threshold. Every time an item is activated, its threshold is lowered and fewer impulses are required to reactivate it. Thus, after each activation, the threshold is lowered—but it gradually rises again. If the item is not stimulated, it becomes more and more difficult to activate over time. Attrition is the result of long-term lack of stimulation. Intensive use/exposure to one of the languages in a bilingual environment leads to a lower activation threshold for that language (i.e., it requires fewer resources), even in early, fluent, behaviorally balanced bilinguals (cf. Perani et al., 2003).

The selection of a particular item requires that its activation exceed that of any possible alternatives (Luria, 1973; Green, 1986). In order to ensure this, its competitors must be inhibited, i.e., their activation thresholds must be raised. Thus, as an item is targeted for activation, its competitors are simultaneously inhibited, i.e., their activation thresholds are raised and consequently more impulses are required to activate them (though the threshold is not usually raised high enough to prevent comprehension of incoming signals). In other words, the appropriate item comes to be activated by raising the activation thresholds of competing items (i.e., all other possible candidates) as much as by actually activating the targeted item. Since the availability of an item is a function of the frequency and recency of its activation (Luria, 1974), expressions may be more available (because they have been activated more often and/or more recently) in one language than in another.

When bilingual speakers use one of their two languages, the activation threshold of the other is assumed to be automatically raised so as to avoid interference. The activation of a word in unilinguals involves not only the activation of the cerebral substrate that subserves it but also the concomitant inhibition of the underlying substrate of all other semantic fields, then of all other words within the same field, until all words except the one that is selected are inhibited. It is not unreasonable to assume that the same principle applies to the use of two languages: Dutch is inhibited (i.e., its activation threshold is raised) while French is in use, and particularly the Dutch translation equivalents of the items selected in French.

A word (or any other linguistic item such as a syntactic construction or a phonotactic schema) must reach a certain activation threshold in order to become available (evocation, self-activation, retrieval) during the microgenesis of an utterance. The activation of a word or any other item (i.e., the amount of impulses needed to activate its neural substrate) will fluctuate as a consequence of its recency and frequency of use (and to some extent of the recency and frequency of use of its immediate network and its entire subsystem).

Production of an item (i.e., recall, self-activation) is more difficult than comprehension of the same item because, among other things, the underlying neural substrate must generate the excitatory impulse from within, as opposed to being excited by stimulation from the incoming auditory or visual signal that impinges on the sensory peripheral organs. This means that production requires a lower threshold than comprehension. In other words, at a certain threshold level one may not be able to produce a word or use a particular syntactic construction (i.e., self-activate their neural substrate) while nevertheless being able to comprehend these items. Consistent with the general principle that comprehension does not require an activation threshold as low as production does and that it is sensitive to frequency of use, Muñoz and Marquardt (2003) report that (1) bilingual individuals with aphasia who lived in a community where, on average, they had more opportunities to use English than Spanish, obtained higher scores on a naming task in English than in Spanish; (2) the cross-linguistic differences evident in language production were not evident in comprehension and recognition tasks; and (3) whereas identification scores were significantly higher than naming scores in both languages, this discrepancy was even more marked in the less used language.

Pathology (or age-related functional changes) may disrupt the normal threshold levels, causing, for example, word-finding difficulty. As will be examined in Chapter 4, aphasia would correspond to the blanket raising of the threshold for a system or subsystem or module, thus selectively or differentially affecting either the entire language system, or one language, or only the phonology, syntax, or lexical access in one language. The hypothesis may account for recency and frequency effects, priming phenomena, and language attrition.

The activation threshold hypothesis is based on a generalization from, or an analogy with, what is known about neuron action potentials. Individual neurons have a critical threshold, or level of activation that must be reached for the cell to generate an action potential (Kandel, Schwartz, & Jessell, 1991; 2000). Moreover, the magnitude of the receptor potential and the synaptic potential is *graded* (in both amplitude and duration) and a neuron does not generate an action potential until the sum of incoming signals has reached its threshold (Kandel et al., 1991; 2000). One may thus hypothesize that a linguistic item is activated when the action potentials of the neurons involved in its representation have reached the required threshold. The mechanisms of neuron activation and signal transmission which apply to cell assemblies (i.e., groups of neurons or systems of neurons that are concurrently activated or inhibited as a result of the flow of chemical/electrical signals) may be supposed to be involved in the activation of mental representations in general and linguistic representations in particular. The computations performed by a group of neurons are determined by the flow of information (activating/inhibitory impulses) through the interconnections of the network they constitute. In the case of linguistic representations, we may surmise that the operations performed by a group of neurons result in the activation of the corresponding item (word, syntactic construction, phonotactic schema, etc.).

Conclusion

In sum, verbal communicative competence comprises linguistic competence (phonology, morphology, syntax and the lexicon), metalinguistic knowledge (the conscious knowledge of language facts used to keep track of the output when sentences are long and complex, particularly in a formal context, and to compensate for lacunae in linguistic competence in later learned languages), pragmatic competence (the ability to infer meaning from discourse and situational contexts, paralinguistic phenomena and general knowledge, and to use language effectively in order to achieve a specific purpose), and motivation (the desire to acquire a language in order to communicate, modulated by a range of affective factors that result in great variability among second-language learners). Each of these systems is necessary but not sufficient for normal verbal communication and relies on its own specific neural substrate which is susceptible to selective impairment. Speakers who have learned a second language after the native language has been acquired will compensate for gaps in their implicit competence by relying more extensively on the other components of verbal communication, namely metalinguistic knowledge and pragmatics. The type and degree of motivation may influence the level of success in both the appropriation and use of a second language.

  To the extent that the teaching method is formal, it will involve declarative memory (and result in metalinguistic knowledge); to the extent that it provides motivation, it will engage the dopaminergic system (and improve performance in both learning and acquisition); to the extent that it is communicative, it may involve procedural memory (and result in some implicit linguistic competence). Practice will either speed up controlled processing or promote implicit competence.

A language needs to be used in order to keep its activation threshold sufficiently low to prevent accessibility problems. Within each language, the ease of access to its various items is proportionate to the recency and frequency of their use. Affective factors and pathology may modify this correlation.

CHAPTER 2

Implicit and explicit language processes

The distinction between implicit and explicit language phenomena is fundamental to the proposed neurolinguistic theory of bilingualism. It has a considerable impact on applied linguistic theory (linguistics applied to language teaching) and on the interpretation of some paradoxical recovery phenomena in bilingual aphasia. Some of its implications are examined below. The basis for the distinction was established in the 1950s with Brenda Milner's first description of Patient H.M. (Scoville & Milner, 1957) and subsequent studies (Milner, Corkin, & Teuber, 1968) that led to the discovery of two different types of memory: conscious declarative memory and implicit procedural memory.

The nature of implicit rules

The expression "implicit computational procedure" will be used to refer to what linguists often call an implicit rule, namely, a shortcut for "whatever it is that allows speakers to behave in such a way that their output can be described (by inference) as resulting from the application of a rule or rules, but without assuming that what has been internalized is (or is not) a rule or set of rules, and certainly not one of those that have been proposed over the years, from pedagogical grammars to various types of theoretical grammars, no matter how compatible they are with the systematic verbal behavior of speakers." There is at present no criterion for selecting among competing proposals, since we have no basis for assuming that the brain processes implicit linguistic competence in the most "elegant" or "economical" way—the criteria generally appealed to in order to assess theoretical constructs. In fact, it is unlikely that these properties, which theoretical linguists value most in weighing the merits of grammars, are those in accordance with which the brain actually operates, since, in general, it has been shown that the brain favors redundancy rather than economy in its functioning. Speakers may behave "as though" they have internalized a particular explicit rule, but this only means that, through practice, they have internalized computational procedures that allow them to produce (and understand) sentences that *can* be described in terms of a particular explicit rule. Generally, more than one explicit rule can account for a particular form. There is no known way to ascertain which (if any) is the actual representation in implicit memory that is used automatically. Grammar rules are abstractions, not descriptions of actual cerebral computational procedures.

An implicit linguistic representation is not isomorphic with the corresponding element of explicit knowledge. The lack of conscious awareness of syntax is demonstrated by the repeated unsuccessful attempts of professional theoretical linguists over the past 40 years to characterize the simplest underlying syntactic algorithm, and the radical disagreement between their various attempts, from the transformational, government-binding, and minimalist approaches to generative grammar, to structural, stratificational, tagmemic, relational, cognitive, functional, or case grammars, not to mention the pedagogical grammars that are encountered in the course of learning a second language. If learners did not lack conscious awareness of the underlying syntax, surely linguists would have agreed by now on what it is. Native speakers' intuition only concerns whether a string is acceptable or not; and the way that string is generated remains unavailable to introspection. For the same reason, irrespective of how a learner may have consciously analyzed any particular grammatical pattern, it is unlikely that it corresponds to the actual form in which it has been internalized. This is why Chomsky (1965) called it *implicit* linguistic competence.

Only what is noticeable can be noticed

Conscious noticing of what becomes an internalized rule (an implicit computational procedure) is not possible because the rule is not there to be noticed. What can be noticed is the surface form of a sentence, not its covert underlying structure (which is a theoretical construct inferred from the observed systematic verbal behavior of speakers), nor the actual cerebral computational procedures that in fact generate the surface form. Yet it is such a covert set of computational procedures that is internalized and allows speakers to generate novel sentences of the same (invisible) underlying structure. Intake is an aspect of input of which the acquirer is not consciously aware (and never becomes aware).

Schmidt (1990) cogently points out that, in the context of language learning, "unconscious" is used with different meanings: (1) not aware of having learned something; (2) learning something that is not consciously noticed; (3) effortless and without focused attention; (4) unconscious induction of principles, rules and algorithms; (5) unintended; and (6) unable to report. In the context of this book, "conscious" and "unconscious" will be used with meanings relevant to (2), (3), (4), and (6). Sense (1) is ambiguous in that it could mean that a person may not remember where and how something was consciously learned (a frequent phenomenon but of no interest in the current discussion), or—what I wish to maintain about acquisition, though not about learning—that implicit linguistic competence is acquired incidentally and hence leaves no memory of having been acquired (since speakers are not even aware of what has been acquired, but only of the fact that they are able to perform). Sense (5) is an altogether different meaning, and often a misleading one because a distinction needs to be made between the (conscious) intention to communicate a message and the (unconscious and automatic) linguistic processing of the message. The intention is deliberate, the processing is not.

With respect to (2), unconscious acquisition does not mean "picking up" stretches of speech without even noticing them, but noticing stretches of speech while "picking up" something other than what is noticed, namely the covert implicit underlying structure. Whereas it may not be possible to *learn* aspects of a second language that are not consciously noticed, it is not only possible but always the case that the acquired computational procedures that constitute intake are not consciously noticed. With respect to sense (3), whereas in the process of incidental acquisition, noticing is indeed required, what is noticed is *not* what is internalized, as just mentioned. Regarding sense (4), the internalized computational procedures may be described as the induction of principles, rules, or algorithms only in a manner of speaking, for in reality, these algorithms are theoretical constructs inferred from the behaviors of speakers, and the actual form in which they are stored and processed in the mind/brain are not known. And, finally, with respect to sense (6), individuals must be able to demonstrate that they know what they claim to know by verbal description. Implicit competence, on the other hand, may indeed be demonstrated only by performing accurately, without being able to explain how or why one behaves the way one does.

A great deal of discussion is obscured by a failure to distinguish between acquisition and learning. Traditional models of learning generally do not bear on acquisition. Identification of short-term memory with consciousness and the claim that processing in short-term memory is necessary for permanent storage, for example, seem accurate when they refer to learning, but do not apply to acquisition. It is true that skilled use of a second language often begins as controlled processes that gradually appear to become automatic. In reality, controlled processing is gradually replaced by the use of automatic processing, which is not just the speeding-up of the controlled process, but the use of a different system which, through practice, develops in parallel. Practice engages entities other than those that are controlled, e.g., the controlled application of an explicit rule is replaced by the automatic use of implicit computational procedures (explicit rules and implicit procedures being of a different nature and having different contents).

Awareness of observable input and output—not implicit linguistic competence

Whereas we are aware of what we hear (input) and of what we say (output), we are not aware of the implicit computational procedures that allow us to generate the sentences that we produce or understand. We can only observe *what* has been produced, not *how* it was produced. We can only notice or pay attention to what is observable.

The actual computational procedures that generate sentences, though not undiscoverable in principle, are unlikely to correspond to any of the linguists' theoretical constructs, known as "underlying structures," or to the various pedagogical grammars available for L2 instruction, if only because the descriptions of underlying structure are varied and ever-changing—a testimony to the tenacious opacity of the actual form of implicit linguistic competence.

"Perception of and selective attending to linguistic form" that facilitate "paying attention to specific linguistic features of the input" and "comparing the noticed features with those the learner typically produces in output" (N. Ellis, 1994, p. 8, reporting on R. Ellis) is what the monitor does (Krashen, 1977); it is only indirectly relevant to acquisition, as will be examined below (pp. 50-53).

A complex process involves the use of *some* mechanisms that operate automatically while *others* are under conscious control (Jacoby, 1991). As a skill becomes more proficient, processing shifts from the use of one mechanism (controlled, declarative) to another (automatic, procedural). By eliminating or reducing reliance on higher-level supervisory processes, performance becomes less subject to monitoring by specialized attentional mechanisms (Shallice, 1982). In L2 appropriation, there is a shift from reliance on mechanisms that depend on general knowledge (declarative memory) to processing modules (that depend on procedural memory). Practice leads to the *replacement* of controlled processes by automatic processes, thus improving automaticity.

The development of metalinguistic awareness during the course of implicit early L1 acquisition is based, not on the underlying structure that has been internalized (which remains covert), but on the output of that implicit linguistic competence (one's own or interlocutors') and hence on the surface structure of phrases and sentences and the acoustic properties of sounds, in other words, those aspects that are available to conscious awareness.

The process of noticing is necessarily a conscious one (Schmidt, 1990). What is noticed, however, cannot be what is internalized as implicit linguistic competence. What can be noticed are the surface features of a sentence. What is internalized is an invisible implicit underlying structure (i.e., computational procedures that allow the processing of sentences of that type). The underlying structure is not available for verbal report.

According to Schmidt (1994), attention to input is necessary for implicit learning. Possibly, but it must be attention to some aspect of the input other than what is implicitly (incidentally) internalized. Explicit memory is indeed necessary for learning some features of natural language—those that end up consciously known, such as the phonological form and referential meaning of words.

Acquirers are totally unaware of the underlying structure of the sentences they hear, even though they are aware of the perceivable input (the surface form of utterances, including acoustic properties, from which they internalize an underlying structure (i.e., a set of implicit computational procedures) and covert proprioceptive feedback (both of which are totally unobservable in the input, and hence not available for noticing or attending to) that allows them to understand and generate well-formed sentences of a particular type and to articulate and produce the appropriate sounds. (In both cases, the person remains totally unaware of the cerebral computational procedures by which such structures are generated and produced.) As will be explored in more detail below, conscious strategies may be employed to infer the meaning of an utterance from the context, but over and above and independently of (or in replacement of) the implicit linguistic procedures.

Acquirers do not notice the relevant input as such (contra Schmidt, 1990) but only the observable aspects of the input, which may be of an altogether different nature from what is acquired, as in the case of phonatory-articulatory movements or the morphosyntactic computational procedures, which are nowhere to be noticed.

The only aspects that can attract a child's attention and be held in memory (Slobin, as cited by Schmidt, 1990) are the *observable* aspects, those of which the child may possibly be aware. One cannot hold in conscious memory anything of which one is not (consciously) aware. Only objects within the domain of declarative memory can be noticed, held in short-term memory and processed to pass on to long-term (declarative) memory. Schmidt's (1990) arguments may hold for items that depend on declarative memory, but they cannot apply to those items that are subserved by procedural memory. What is acquired incidentally piggybacks on something that is noticed, but is itself unnoticeable.

The conscious knowledge that is developed about the structure of language (e.g., most pedagogical rules) is based on a conscious analysis of actual productions (i.e., observable output). Metalinguistic knowledge develops on the basis of observations of the *outcome* of procedures that themselves remain implicit.

Knowledge is not automatic and competence is not controlled

In the context of the discussion of controlled and automatic processing, "controlled," unless otherwise specified, refers to "consciously controlled"; i.e., it does not refer to the cerebral control over autonomic functions such as heartbeat or kidney functions. "Automatic" does not refer to spontaneous, unsolicited, reflex-like behavior (in the Hughlings-Jacksonian sense, as observed in some patients), but to uncontrolled *processing*, once initiated. Likewise, "involuntary" refers to behaviors not consciously controlled, as opposed to the Hughlings-Jacksonian sense of "not deliberate, unsolicited, without intention". Nor does "automatic" in this context refer to what is sometimes called automatic speech, namely, overlearned material such as prayers, poems, and song lyrics.

Here is a good example of why it is important to define the words we use. In his theory of instructed L2 acquisition, Rod Ellis (1994) claims that (1) implicit knowledge can exist in a form that is available for use in controlled processing, and explicit knowledge is available for use in automatic processing, and (2) explicit metalinguistic knowledge can convert into implicit linguistic competence and vice versa.

The author asserts that equating controlled processing with explicit knowledge and automatic processing with implicit knowledge "is inexact to say the least, as Figure 1 makes clear" (p. 87). There is a sense in which this statement would be true, namely that controlled processing cannot be "equated with" explicit knowledge. Explicit knowledge is a representation in memory whose *use* is controlled when processed. But this is not what Ellis wishes to refute. What he means (as his Figure 1 makes clear) is that explicit knowledge can be used automatically and that implicit knowledge can be controlled—an oxymoron in both cases, for which a solution is not provided. Figure 1 (reproduced here as Figure 2.1) begs the question. It is not the representation of a fact but of a (controversial at best, plainly false at worst) hypothetical construct that can hardly be used as evidence to refute someone else's hypothesis. Ellis's assumptions need to be grounded in fact (at least to some minimal degree) before they can be used as evidence of the incorrectness of an account that is itself supported by abundant clinical, neuroanatomical and neuropsychological evidence.

R. Ellis (1994) proposes a model of two types of knowledge (explicit and implicit) and two types of processing (controlled and automatic), and states, on page 86: "It is assumed ... that both controlled and automatic processes can occur with or without awareness. ...both explicit and implicit knowledge can be represented in the mind of the learner as either controlled or automatic processes or both" (see Figure 2.1). How one can *assume* that implicit knowledge (i.e., competence) can be represented in the mind as a controlled process needs to be explained; that is, how one can consciously control something of which one has no conscious knowledge (the definition of "implicit"). Before it can be assumed, it should at least be shown not to be impossible. One must therefore show how an implicit rule can be used in a controlled manner but without awareness, i.e., how we consciously control something of which we are not aware (cell C); and how the conscious use of a rule can be automatic (cell B), an apparent contradiction in terms, unless one

Types of knowledge	Types of processing	
	Controlled	Automatic
Explicit	(A) A new explicit rule is used consciously and with deliberate effort	(B) An old explicit rule is used consciously but with relative speed.
Implicit	(C) A new implicit rule is used without awareness but is accessed slowly	(D) A thoroughly learnt implicit rule is used without awareness and without effort

R. Ellis (1994) proposes two types of knowledge (explicit and implicit), each allegedly compatible with two types of processing (controlled and automatic), leading to four possibilities (A, B, C, D). Yet, if an implicit rule is used without awareness (C), it cannot be controlled. An explicit rule used consciously (B) cannot be automatic, irrespective of speed.

Figure 2.1. *Types of knowledge, from R. Ellis (1994, Figure 1)*

redefines "automatic," "implicit," "used consciously" and "controlled." Learners may indeed exhibit behavior (A), "a new explicit rule is used consciously and with deliberate effort" (which corresponds to the explicit use of metalinguistic knowledge), and (D), "a thoroughly learnt implicit rule is used without awareness and without effort" (which corresponds to the implicit use of competence). However, (B), "an old explicit rule is used consciously but with relative speed," cannot be automatic and conscious at the same time (by definition, conscious use cannot be automatic), it is merely speeded-up. As for (C), "a new implicit rule is used without awareness but is accessed slowly," a rule cannot be used without awareness and consciously controlled at the same time. Implicit rules cannot be controlled and explicit rules cannot be used automatically. Of all the properties of automatic processes, namely, being fast, effortless, consistent, and unconscious, only the latter is a monotypic characteristic. Controlled processes may be fast, effortless and, to a great extent, consistent, but, by definition, cannot be unconscious.

In fact, fluency and accuracy are not necessarily indicators of implicit linguistic competence. The former may be the result of speedier processing and the latter the result of efficient monitoring of such speeded-up (albeit controlled) performance. Controlled processing is not only slower but also more variable than automatic processing. Segalowitz and Segalowitz (1993), Segalowitz, Poulsen and Segalowitz (1999) and Segalowitz (2000) have demonstrated that the coefficient of variation (standard deviation divided by reaction time) decreases when faster reaction times reflect an increase in automaticity (and a concomitant decrease in controlled processing), whereas the coefficient of variation does not decrease in speeded-up controlled processing. Speeding-up involves no structural change in the organization of underlying mechanisms. Speeded-up processing thus represents a quantitative change, under executive control; automatic processing represents a *qualitative* change from control. A shift from controlled to automatic processing implies a change in what is processed (i.e., a replacement).

When a skill is automatized, the performance is carried out rapidly, accurately, and stably. When it is performed through controlled processing, performance is more variable (a situation that is reflected in bilingual PET and fMRI studies, as we shall see in Chapter 6). Language use involves both automatic and non-automatic facets—but different ones. (For example, in L2, syntax may be automatic while phonology is processed via a speeded-up controlled mechanism—or the reverse may be true.) The implicit and explicit components of a task can be identified with qualitative differences in the nature of the underlying processes (Parkin & Russo, 1990).

The acquisition of a new rule is best viewed as characterized initially by controlled processing (an explicit rule) and subsequently by automatic processing, not of the same rule, but of an underlying computational procedure that results in the automatic comprehension and production of sentences that can be described as implementing a rule. But there are *two* "rules": An explicit rule initially processed in a controlled manner (a rule which remains forever explicit and available for explicit recall—unless it is eventually forgotten) and a *second* "rule" or computational procedure that is implicit, and that is *not* the ever-faster use of the explicit rule, from which it differs in its very nature, object of application, and underlying neural substrate. The on-line production in French of the agreement of the past participle of a verb conjugated with the auxiliary *avoir* with its preceding direct object (as in *la remarque qu'il a faite* 'the remark that he made') is not the speeded-up use of an explicitly known rule that eventually becomes automatic. "Automatic" does not just mean fast—it also means without conscious control. "Relative speed" (cell B in R. Ellis's model) certainly does not make it automatic.

Acquisition is not a process of automatizing rules of which the learner is aware, but of automatizing computational procedures (of which the acquirer is *not* aware) that underlie the automatic comprehension and production of sentences that, by inference, at a high level of abstraction, can be described by linguists as corresponding to (pedagogical or theoretical) linguistic rules.

Indeed, as Rod Ellis (1994) puts it, reporting Krashen's viewpoint, "Explicit knowledge does not help the acquisition of implicit knowledge of the same rule" (p. 87) because it is not knowledge of the *same* rule which is incidentally internalized and available for automatic use. What *is* internalized is a computational procedure *other than* the rule of which we have explicit knowledge, which allows the speaker to generate sentences of the type from which linguists infer the explicit rule. Declarative knowledge is not "proceduralized" through practice. What is proceduralized is an altogether different kind of entity. Declarative knowledge does not admit of implicit proceduralization. A computational procedure automatically generates an output that may then become the object of declarative knowledge. The computational procedure is not the same as the output it produces. Only outputs are available for conscious inspection; only outputs are available to metalinguistic awareness. It is a category mistake to confuse output (and the rules that are constructed by linguists in order to describe or characterize its structure) with the implicit computational procedures that led to that output—and which do not necessarily coincide with any of the theoretical constructs (i.e., "linguistic rules") proposed by linguists.

Automatic processes can be voluntarily started or stopped, but they cannot be controlled once they are initiated. They can only be stopped midway and replaced by controlled processes. However, conscious control does not act upon the automatic procedure (even if the outcome of the controlled performance should be identical to that of the automatic procedure, though possibly slower); instead, the automatic procedure is momentarily replaced by controlled processing, which is of a different nature and involves different neurofunctional mechanisms subserved by different cerebral structures. The neural structures that mediate controlled processing and those that subserve automatic processing each have their own evolutionary history and place in ontogeny. The commands to the same muscle effectors thus come from different sources. Controlled (conscious) processing is vulnerable to the effects of a concomitant memory load, whereas automatic processing is not affected by such cognitive demands (Rafal & Herik, 1994). Once started, automatic processes run on to completion, unless they are stopped and replaced by controlled processing. The triggering of the automatic processing can be voluntary, but the processing itself is not. But, as demonstrated in Favreau and Segalowitz's (1983) study, an automatic process can occur even when the subject does not intend for it to occur (as in a Stroop test). This, according to the authors, is another true sign of automaticity.

In other words, automatic processes are entirely involuntary (in their unfolding) and cannot be controlled by voluntary effort. However, they are not necessarily carried out without intention. Intention initiates the verbal encoding of a message, but the encoding itself is either (1) automatic, i.e., dependent on implicit linguistic competence (as in casual conversation in L1), and to that extent cannot be controlled by voluntary effort; or (2) controlled, i.e., dependent on metalinguistic knowledge and consciously constructing sentences (as in the careful production of sentences by beginners in a formally learned L2). Automatic processes can be deliberately initiated. *Access* to conscious knowledge is automatic, even when the intention to access is deliberate (e.g., we intend to search for a word and therefore initiate the search but we do not know how the search is carried out, e.g., alphabetically or by semantic field— or some other process). This automatic access may be impaired in aphasia and in normal aging, causing word-finding difficulty, though the representations of words remain intact, as demonstrated by success on multiple choice tests.

Some aspects of language processing are automatic and others are under voluntary control. The performance of a task, such as the production of an utterance, involves antagonistic processes, which include both facilitating and inhibitory components. In fact, as mentioned earlier, the selection of an item for production (e.g., a word or syntactic construction) requires the inhibition of competitors (e.g., words of the same semantic field, translation equivalents, other syntactic constructions) (Luria, 1974; Luria & Hutton, 1977; Simpson & Burgess, 1985). Models of word processing incorporate automatic-reflexive and voluntary-controlled mechanisms, involving facilitation and inhibition (Rafal & Henik, 1994). Automatic processes can be inhibited, either voluntarily, or automatically by the simultaneous activation of antagonistic processes, or by pathology.

Here is another good example of why it is important to define the meaning of the words we use. R. Ellis's view is shared by Bialystok (1994) who claims that explicit knowledge may be conscious or not, and that it may be accessed automatically or not. In the normal acceptation of the words *explicit* and *conscious*, the statement that explicit knowledge (i.e., that which is consciously known) is not conscious (i.e., not consciously known) is a contradiction in terms. If the author means that not all knowledge is conscious at all times, and that therefore, at any particular time, only a limited number of elements are in consciousness, i.e., we are aware of them at that time, then her claim would be true (Damasio, 1989). Nothing is in our consciousness all the time. (Not only do we spend some time asleep, but there is a limit to what an individual can be actively conscious of at any given time.). Thus, when we say that explicit knowledge is conscious knowledge, we do not mean that it is present in consciousness at all times, but that, unlike the contents and structure of implicit linguistic competence, it is capable of being brought into consciousness and verbalized.

On the other hand, both explicit and implicit knowledge are accessed automatically, that is, without our conscious awareness of how we access that knowledge; we are unaware of the cerebral search procedures, and hence cannot control the search. Knowledge is conscious, but its access is automatic—even when we deliberately seek to access a particular piece of knowledge.

Bialystok goes on to claim that, without explicit notions of topic and predicate, one cannot learn basic word order. When two-year-olds put their first two words together, and even when by the age of three, they put together longer strings of words in perfect order (even if some morphological markings are still missing), it is most doubtful that they have *explicit* notions of topic and predicate, or any other explicit grammatical notions. (If *learn* here truly meant *learn*, as opposed to *acquire*, and referred to second-language *learning*, the statement might not necessarily be true, but at least it would not be downright impossible.)

(Conscious) knowledge and (unconscious) know-how

I know what movement I want to perform, but I do not know which muscle does what. I do not know *how* I do it, I just know *how to* do it. Some muscles are contracted, some are relaxed, some maintain their tonus. When my arm moves in a certain direction, I don't know which back muscle is involved until my fifth lumbar vertebra is slightly dislocated. The same thing applies to the numerous muscles involved in speech, as well as to the computational procedures that generate the sentences that I intend to use. I know what I want to say, but I don't really know how I say it (i.e., I do not know how the utterance is automatically put together); I only become aware of the output of the computing system (and can monitor it so as to consciously correct possible inadequacies of meaning or form). Automatization eventually and indirectly results from the actual practice of possibly deliberate actions.

One knows, in gross general terms, which movements need to be performed, and, at the beginning of the learning period, one deliberately performs these movements (however imperfectly) one after the other until, through practice, the smooth succession of precise movements is internalized via proprioceptive feedback and is performed automatically. Thus, in the beginning, one may perform each one very consciously. Even then, however, one is more conscious of *what* one wants to do than exactly *how* one is doing it. The underlying structure, or schemata, of the smooth succession of movements is what is internalized and eventually performed automatically, without conscious knowledge of the schemata that are involved. The extent of the participation of each muscle is not within one's awareness (if it ever was: we are conscious of controlling the limb, but not of which specific muscles are active and which are not). With some complex actions, such as riding a bicycle (which could be described in terms of the physical laws of gravity and balance—the application of which the learner is surely totally unaware, just as we are unaware of the computational procedures underlying the generation of a sentence), one might never be conscious of the movements to be performed, other than pressing on the pedals. Even then, one is not necessarily aware of whether it is the toes (and which toes) or the sole of the foot that pushes, and at what angle, with what force and for how long, and combined with body motion to the right or left. Just try to write your signature slowly (i.e., consciously), and it will look so distorted that it would not be accepted by your bank manager!

Just as we are conscious of the output of our generative grammar but ignorant of the computational procedures that generated it, we are conscious of the movements we produce, but not aware of the program for action that is stored. Nor are we aware of which of the several muscles is/are involved, and to what extent. Thus, skilled motor actions, such as skiing, cycling or driving a car are very much like cognitive behavior (and vice versa). No wonder the cerebellum is involved in both motor and cognitive behaviors—including language (Leiner, Leiner & Dow, 1991; Gordon, 1996; Fabbro, 2000; Fabbro, Moretti & Bava, 2000; Silveri & Misciagna, 2000; Barrios & Guardia. 2001; Marien et al., 2001; Xiang et al., 2003). It is involved not only in the articulatory and phonatory movements that are outside our awareness, but also in the microgenesis of each utterance. Corina et al., (2003) provide evidence of the role of the right posterolateral cerebellum in actual linguistic-*cognitive* processing.

Metalinguistic knowledge does not become implicit linguistic competence

In acquiring linguistic competence of a second language, it is not the material which constitutes metalinguistic knowledge that is used, worked upon, and eventually transformed or automatized. The point that metalinguistic knowledge does not *evolve* or *change* into implicit linguistic competence is fundamental because of its many implications. There is no metamorphosis for a number of reasons: (1) Once a caterpillar has become a butterfly, there is no more caterpillar. Yet, metalinguistic knowledge remains available as metalinguistic knowledge after implicit linguistic competence has been acquired (and hence it has not been transformed into implicit linguistic competence). We now have two different sources of knowledge, as suggested by Bialystok (1981): One that remains explicit, another that independently develops in the form of implicit competence. (2) The very nature of what is represented in metalinguistic knowledge differs from what underlies implicit linguistic competence (an explicit rule vs. a set of implicit computational procedures). (3) Metalinguistic knowledge and linguistic competence rely on different memory systems that have separate, anatomically distinct, neural substrates. (4) One does not internalize what one focuses one's attention upon. One cannot "notice" (Schmidt, 1990) what becomes internalized because it is not there to be noticed.

Explicit knowledge cannot be "converted" or "transformed" into implicit competence; it does not evolve into, change into, or become competence the way raw potatoes are transformed into French fries or puree, ice into water, or an egg into a turtle. In each of these instances, a particular substance is subjected to some external condition that acts upon it and changes its shape or internal organization. No such transformation is imposed upon explicit knowledge that would turn it into implicit competence. Even the fertilizer metaphor does not apply, for the fertilizer becomes part of the plant's tissue after its nitrates have been chemically transformed. No such transformation takes place from known (consciously perceived, noticed, focused upon, observable) metalinguistic knowledge to the implicit competence that remains covert while it generates observable systematic behavior analyzable in terms of the corresponding metalinguistic knowledge.

A transformation implies starting with some raw material and changing it by putting it through a number of processes, so that the final product is a transformation of the original substance. In the case of implicit competence, however, it is not explicit knowledge that, by being subjected to some process or processes, becomes implicit competence. What becomes implicit competence is not something that was explicit before. What becomes internalized as implicit linguistic competence (i.e., available for automatic use) is something *other than* what the acquirer has consciously focused upon, something of which the acquirer is never conscious at any stage of acquisition, because in many cases it is not there to be noticed in the first place (e.g., the covert underlying structure of syntactic constructions, the phonological system, and the proprioception underlying the articulatory planning of speech sounds—these are nowhere to be seen or felt; only their outcomes are heard or seen). We are indeed aware of the outcomes of implicit underlying computational procedures, but not of the structure of the procedures themselves; we know what is said, not how it is generated.

For example, when people learn to produce a new sound, they focus upon the acoustic properties of the target sound. During the individuals' successive attempts to produce the new sound, they monitor whether the outcome produced approximates the target sound, and they practice until they are satisfied that the sounds they produce possess those acoustic characteristics that they focused upon. Learners are conscious of their output, not of how the output has been produced. They are unaware of the cooperative participation of the approximately 100 muscles involved in its production—they do not even know whether a consonant is voiced or unvoiced. What they have internalized, however, are the kinesthetic articulatory programs acquired through proprioceptive feedback. Thus what has been internalized is different in nature from what has been focused upon. While the learner's attention focused on acoustic properties (auditory sensory material), what has been acquired through practice (i.e., the underlying mechanisms that allow the production of the sound) was altogether different (namely, kinesthetic motor programs). When attempting to produce a new sound, one can deliberately change the configuration of one's vocal tract by trial and error (admittedly, without knowing exactly what the configuration actually is) and perceive how that affects the output; however, the targeted sound will become automatically available only after much practice.

Explicit knowledge is qualitatively different from implicit competence. Explicit knowledge is conscious awareness of some data (utterances) and/or of their explicit analysis (structure). Implicit competence, on the other hand, is a set of computational procedures (of which the speaker is unaware) that generates sentences (which serve as data from which linguists or reflective speakers may construct a grammar—a set of rules—that becomes part of one's explicit knowledge). To claim that the difference is only quantitative would be to claim that (part of) competence is identical with (part of) our explicit knowledge. Given that claims about the structure of implicit linguistic competence have continuously and radically changed over the past 50 years, whose metalinguistic knowledge actually reflects implicit linguistic competence? That described in transformational grammar (Chomsky, 1965), government-binding-type grammar (Chomsky, 1981), the minimalist program (Chomsky, 1995), structuralist grammar (de Saussure, 1915), stratificational grammar (Lamb, 1966), case grammar (Fillmore, 1968), Tagmemics (Pike, 1971), functional grammar (Martinet, 1975), construction grammar (Fillmore, 1988), cognitive grammar (Langacker, 1991), psychomechanic grammar (Valin, 1994), one of the various pedagogical grammars, or a connectionist, parallel distributed processing, artificial intelligence neural-network-type model? It is not very plausible that grammar is actually represented in the brain in the form proposed by any one of these frameworks.

Competence, whatever its form, develops alongside explicit knowledge, has a different nature, and is subserved by different neural structures. Implicit competence develops through practice—or else it never develops, and explicit knowledge continues to be used (in a controlled manner), albeit possibly faster and faster. With practice, more and more tasks (or task components) fall into the province of procedural competence (and hence automatic processing), replacing the use of controlled declarative processing by independently developed procedures. Automatic routines thus exist side by side with explicit knowledge of rules.

An interesting question one might ask is why implicit competence develops in L2 if explicit knowledge will do. First, it remains to be demonstrated that implicit linguistic competence actually does develop and that observed fluency in a late-learned L2 is not simply the result of speeded-up controlled processes. Secondly, explicit metalinguistic knowledge "will do" only up to a point, at the cost of fluency and attention. Thus, it is preferable, when the mechanisms are available, to automatize as much of the language as possible: It becomes less effortful to use and is less vulnerable under conditions of noise, fatigue or stress. Because automatic processes are faster and more efficient than controlled processes, whenever an automatic system is available, it will spontaneously be used by default.

The type of grammar applied linguists generally have in mind is a traditional pedagogical grammar. There appears to be an underlying belief on the part of those who claim that knowledge of such a grammar becomes linguistic competence with practice, by using it very fast. The claim can best be construed as a metaphor that should be interpreted as, "speakers who consciously construct sentences by applying pedagogical grammar rules eventually get to behave verbally as though they had internalized those explicit rules (i.e., they automatically and systematically produce sentences that correspond to the structure described by the rule)". This interpretation would not be incorrect. However, this does not mean that the grammar rule, as taught, is now used automatically. Automatic language production does not correspond to the actual use of pedagogical grammar rules. It is not by saying, however quickly, "make the past participle agree in gender and number with the preceding direct object because the auxiliary of this verb is *avoir*, and hence the past participle must be feminine, because the object, *que*, it refers to, is placed before the verb and stands for *pomme*, which is feminine" that a speaker automatically produces *la pomme que j'ai prise* (Paradis, 1994), i.e., [priz] and not [pri].

As pointed out above, some researchers (e.g., Schmidt, 1990; Robinson, 1995) have claimed that the learner has to (consciously) *notice* the stimulus that serves as the basis for the acquisition of competence. However, what is internalized, i.e., becomes part of implicit linguistic competence, is not there to be noticed. The acquirer can only notice some aspect of the complex stimulus *other than* the one that is internalized; For example, one may focus on the surface form of a sentence while internalizing its (covert, non-observable) underlying structure. What is internalized is of a different nature than what is available for noticing. A learner's awareness of a perceptual entity (speech sounds) leads to the procedural memory for the automatic production of these speech sounds (a proprioceptive kinesthetic entity that is not available to awareness, no matter how hard one tries to introspect). It is not unreasonable to believe that such introspection, which is not available to university students registered in phonetics courses, is also not available to two- or three-year-olds acquiring their native language sounds, or to a foreign language learner at any age. There is no conscious control over one's vocal flap vibrations, degree of rounding, fronting or palatalization, let alone relative durations of voice onset times that could eventually "become" automatic. The reader is probably just as unaware as this writer is of the exact status of the one hundred or so muscles involved in articulation and phonation of any particular sound of their first or second language, that is, whether each muscle is contracted, relaxed or maintains its tonus at any given instant of speech production. One is even less aware (if it were possible to be less than zero) when the speech sound is used in the context of normal verbal communication, at the rate of 14 phonemes per second, when the muscular activity associated with its production is influenced by the phonemes that precede and follow it. All the while, word retrieval and morphosyntactic selection must be computed so they will be available in the following milliseconds to construct the remainder of the utterance. It would simply not be possible to juggle all these processes simultaneously if they were under conscious control.

The aspects of language that are implicitly acquired are those that a six-year-old has internalized without conscious awareness (and of which adults never actually become conscious), and those that are explicitly learned are those of which we are conscious, such as the recognition of the phonological form of a word and its (however incomplete) meaning (i.e., the fact that the sound [dɔg] has {🐕} as a referent).

During L2 development, there is not a continuum from metalinguistic knowledge to implicit competence (in the sense that the first gradually becomes the second); rather, there is a gradual shift from *using* metalinguistic knowledge to *using* implicit competence. It is comparable to the situation of a French boy who, over his adolescence, goes from drinking water at supper to drinking wine, by gradually adding more wine to his water. The water does not *become* wine over time, it is gradually *replaced* by wine. There is no transaccidentation involved. Nor is there any transubstantiation from metalinguistic knowledge to implicit competence. Gradually, reliance on the latter *replaces* the use of the former.

A person who is progressively becoming blind may gradually shift from reliance on sight to greater, and eventually perhaps total, reliance on hearing, in which case his reliance on sight has been *replaced* by reliance on hearing (though sight has not become, or been transformed into, hearing). In the same way, a second-language learner may gradually shift from sole reliance on metalinguistic knowledge to increased reliance on linguistic competence, in which case *use* of metalinguistic knowledge has been replaced by *use* of implicit linguistic competence. At the very beginning, a learner may rely 90% on metalinguistic knowledge and 10% on linguistic competence; years later, the same person may use 10% metalinguistic knowledge and 90% linguistic competence. (However, in this case, metalinguistic knowledge remains available, but is simply not generally used). Metalinguistic knowledge and implicit linguistic competence are not poles on a continuum, any more than sight and hearing are. What is on a continuum is the degree of reliance on one or the other. No more than one would say that the blind person's sight has become hearing (they are subserved by different sensory systems), would one wish to say that metalinguistic knowledge has become implicit linguistic competence (they rely on different memory systems).

The direction of the development of each component of language use (metalinguistic or linguistic, i.e., controlled or automatic) depends on the context of appropriation. In a situation of acquisition, e.g., acquiring the native language(s) under normal circumstances, implicit knowledge develops first, then declarative knowledge about language (metalinguistic knowledge) kicks in. This process starts slowly around age 2, and then definitely develops at school or through reflection in inquisitive adults. For the second language, to the extent that there is implicit competence, it develops in parallel with explicit knowledge. Explicit knowledge develops first, possibly followed by some implicit competence, with great interindividual variability, related in part to differences in the appropriation context: teaching (depending on the methodology, instruction time available and opportunities for practice outside), individual cognitive style, and degree and direction of motivation. Both competence and knowledge are age-driven (implicit memory develops first ontogenetically) and cognition-driven (metalinguistic knowledge requires more cognitive capacity than implicit linguistic competence) in individuals, and teaching-method-driven within institutions.

The role of metalinguistic knowledge in L2 acquisition

The fact that metalinguistic knowledge never becomes implicit linguistic competence does not mean that it is useless for the acquisition of a second/foreign language. Metalinguistic awareness obviously helps one learn a language; in fact, it is a prerequisite. But it may also help one *acquire* it, albeit only indirectly.

While practice itself is what leads to the internalization of implicit computational procedures that will eventually allow the individual to automatically understand and produce well-formed sentences, metalinguistic knowledge of the surface forms (as heard and/or read before, or possibly as deduced from the application of a pedagogical rule) serves as a model for practice and as a monitor for checking the well-formedness of the automatic output of the implicit system (Krashen, 1977); this process leads to further practice of the correct form.

Thus, "practice under the guidance of explicit knowledge" (N. Ellis, 1994, p. 4) may indeed facilitate the acquisition of implicit competence, though not because explicit knowledge eventually becomes implicit competence. The acquirer focuses attention on the form to be practiced (for example, on the fact that the stress is on the second syllable of the English word *distributed*, or that in French, *problème* and *système* are masculine, and hence their modifiers must be in the masculine form); meanwhile, the underlying implicit processes/mechanisms establish themselves. However, it is not the *knowledge* that leads to competence, but the *practicing* of the relevant form—without conscious awareness of what is being internalized (i.e., what constitutes competence). Ellis (2002) would suggest that the frequency with which an item is encountered is what drives its internalization. Maybe so, but remember that the acquirer is not aware of the frequency of occurrence of the various items (syllables, words, and morphosyntactic features).

Conversely, implicit competence never becomes explicit. What the speaker is conscious of is the *outcome* of implicit linguistic competence, not its contents (i.e., not the processes by which the observed outcome has been obtained). The development of self-awareness allows "reflective examination, analysis and reorganization," not of competence (i.e. implicit knowledge), which is unknown, but of *inferences* on the basis of the observed phenomena (what is produced); This process does indeed result "in new independent explicit representations" (N. Ellis, 1994, p. 4). These representations do not, however, have their basis in implicit linguistic competence but in its observable output.

The consequence is that, as suggested by Long (1983), formal instruction may very well have an indirect positive effect on L2 acquisition. The first reason is that attention is focused on items that need to be practiced—even though what is focused upon is not what is eventually internalized. The second is that instruction allows learners to monitor, with the help of metalinguistic knowledge, the output of implicit linguistic competence (Krashen, 1982). The third reason is that some (however little) practice does take place in the classroom (in fact, this minimal practice as such may have a direct effect).

If it is the case, as Nick Ellis (2002) proposes, that frequency of occurrence is a crucial factor in the acquisition of any form, then the frequency of practice of a particular form will facilitate its incorporation into implicit linguistic competence. As mentioned in the preceding chapter, according to the activation threshold model (Paradis, 1987b, 1993a), the activation threshold of an item is lowered each time it is activated, only to slowly rise again when it is not used. Thus, increased practice of the appropriate form—preferably while focusing on the message, not the form itself—should increase the likelihood of acquiring, and hasten the acquisition of, the underlying computational procedures. By focusing on what is observable (the acoustic properties of a sound pattern, or the surface form of an utterance) during practice, the L2 learner unconsciously acquires the underlying computational procedures that constitute competence, that is, the ability to automatically understand and produce the relevant correct forms.

Implicit competence and explicit knowledge are structurally unrelated and explicit knowledge is relevant to implicit competence development only indirectly, by focusing attention on items to be practiced and monitoring and correcting the output of implicit linguistic competence. Explicit knowledge can thus contribute secondarily to the development of implicit linguistic competence, even though it never becomes, or is converted or transformed into implicit linguistic competence, and is certainly not automatized or proceduralized. The term "convert into" can only be applied at a highly abstract metaphorical level, where explicit knowledge eventually results in (i.e., leads to) the acquisition of competence, without itself being transformed or converted into competence. Knowledge may help trigger competence or facilitate the development of competence, by providing a suitable environment; in this way, and in this way only, it may indirectly contribute to the acquisition of implicit competence.

Since adult learners tend to use declarative memory (metalinguistic knowledge) anyway, it may be useful to provide them with explicit descriptions of particular grammatical phenomena. This may help them not only to construct correct sentences (in a controlled way), but also to monitor and self-correct their production (the output of their implicit competence); once they have practiced the correct form a number of times, they will eventually internalize it (in whatever form the implicit underlying computational procedures may take).

Norris and Ortega (2000: p. 502; 2001: p. 519) place Paradis (1994) among the theorists who adhere to a non-interface position. They state that proponents of the non-interface position hold that true linguistic competence remains unaffected by instruction, in the form of rule presentation or negative feedback. This statement is valid, provided that "true linguistic competence" refers to implicit linguistic competence, which is available automatically. However, as we have seen, this does not preclude an indirect effect whereby rule presentation and negative feedback contribute to the development of metalinguistic knowledge, which may in turn monitor the output of linguistic competence, thus allowing conscious self-correction, which results in further practice of the desired form. The repeated practicing of the target form may eventually lead to the internalization of the implicit computational procedures that result in the automatic comprehension and production of that form. It is not the instruction and resulting knowledge that affect competence, but the extra practice provided by the use of the corrected form. Let us not forget that there is not necessarily an identity relation between the rule as enunciated and the implicit computational procedures that are responsible for the generation of the corresponding observable form.

The role of implicit/explicit memory in bilingual aphasia and amnesia

Some bilingual aphasic patients have been reported to recover one of their languages sooner or better than the other, irrespective of their relative premorbid fluency. Paradoxically, some have gained access sooner, better, or only, to the language they spoke the least well before insult. It has been difficult to account for such a phenomenon.

However, once it has been firmly established that linguistic competence and metalinguistic knowledge are two independent systems, each subserved by a different cerebral mechanism, represented and processed in different cortical loci, it is not unreasonable to expect that some bilingual aphasic patients who have lost access to parts of their linguistic competence will still have access to their metalinguistic knowledge. Given that the extent of metalinguistic knowledge relative to linguistic competence may differ in the two languages spoken by a bilingual individual (depending on the different contexts of appropriation of the two languages), this knowledge may be more extensive in the language they spoke least fluently before insult.

The first language is acquired implicitly during infancy, but the speaker may later gain some metalinguistic knowledge in school. In fact Obler and Mahecha (1991) report that bilinguals with less than a high school education tend not to recover their native language as well as their second language. Presumably, speakers with minimal education have little, if any, metalinguistic knowledge about their L1. The amount of metalinguistic facts taught depends on the educational philosophy of the school system, and to some extent on the orthography of the language (e.g., when spelling takes into account morphosyntactic facts not realized orally, such as agreement phenomena in French). In some cases, quite a bit of parsing and clause structure analysis are a standard feature of the curriculum. Thus, the higher the level of education in one's first language, the more extensive one's metalinguistic knowledge of it is likely to be. Similarly, for a second language, the more formal the teaching method, the greater the extent of metalinguistic knowledge. Therefore, while in most cases the causes of non-parallel recovery patterns may be found in the mechanisms of inhibition/disinhibition affecting the neural substrate subserving linguistic competence (Paradis, 1989a, 2001a), in some cases, what appears to be paradoxical recovery, i.e., better performance in the language spoken the least well before insult, may be due to the use of a compensatory strategy relying on the patient's metalinguistic knowledge of the foreign language. In such cases, linguistic competence is affected in both languages, but more metalinguistic knowledge is available for the foreign language that was learned formally, and patients manage to express themselves in that language; the fact that they tend to speak slowly and laboriously does not seem particularly anomalous for aphasic patients.

To the extent that the lesion is circumscribed to the classical cortical language areas, we may expect language deficits without any impairment of declarative memory. In fact, patients remember events distinctly, including their performance on various tasks on the previous day, such as which objects they were able to name on confrontation and which they were not. This intact episodic memory, however, did not help the patient described by Paradis, Goldblum and Abidi (1982) to retrieve the phonological form of the words she (correctly) remembered having successfully named the day before.

The adult second-language speaker's two sources of language data (declarative and procedural) are selectively vulnerable to lesions causing aphasia (affecting implicit competence) or amnesia (affecting explicit meta-linguistic knowledge). We should therefore distinguish between spontaneous recovery of a language (disinhibition of procedural competence) and ability to control production through the use of metalinguistic knowledge, which corresponds to the use of a compensatory strategy based on preserved explicit memory. Given that what is affected in aphasia is linguistic competence (or the automatic use thereof), we may assume that, to the extent that explicit knowledge has been learned through formal instruction and has not yet been forgotten (due to a lack of rehearsal over the years), patients must have access to their metalinguistic knowledge to help them substitute controlled production for the lack of automatic processing, in the same way as a foreign-language learner during the initial phases of formal language instruction.

Typically, non-standard dialects, lacking a conventional written form, are acquired implicitly and used throughout life without much metalinguistic awareness on the part of the native speaker. In many cases, speakers of such language varieties learn a second language, often a related standard language, in school (e.g., Alemanic Swiss / Standard German; Québécois / Standard French; Friulian / Italian). Some metalinguistic knowledge of the standard language, the language of instruction, is explicitly taught in school as part of the regular curriculum. Since aphasia is caused by a disruption of procedural memory (linguistic competence) subsequent to a focal cortical lesion, metalinguistic knowledge, being subserved by an altogether different neural system, should remain available to the patient. Thus, in the case of a bidialectal speaker, the amount of metalinguistic knowledge about the standard dialect used in school as the medium of instruction is likely to be much greater than that of the native dialect. As we have seen, the same may be true in the case of a bilingual speaker who has learned a foreign language formally. While the linguistic competence for both languages or dialects may be affected to the same extent, metalinguistic knowledge obtained during the learning of the second language may still be available. To the extent that metalinguistic knowledge in the non-native standard or in the foreign language exceeds that in the native language, patients may give the impression of having recovered their non-native language better (when in fact they rely on metalinguistic knowledge of that language).

Because of the lack of systematic reporting in the literature of the manner of acquisition of the foreign language, it is not yet possible to verify the hypothesis that patients may compensate for their lack of access to linguistic competence by using their metalinguistic knowledge. In most cases of paradoxical non-parallel recovery reported in the literature (Paradis, 1983, 1989a, 2001a), it is not possible to determine the extent of formal instruction. Consider the case of Gaston, an 18-year-old Frenchman described by Hegler (1931). Subsequent to a cerebral vascular accident, he was able to speak only (somewhat broken) German, a language he had learned only over the previous six months, even when speaking to his brother who had come from France to visit him and who did not understand German at all. However, Hegler does not mention the manner in which the patient had learned German, in particular whether he had used grammar books or had attended evening school. The same is true of the soldier reported by Bychowski (1919) who, after cerebral trauma, could only speak Russian, a language he had known only marginally before insult. While the patient had never attended school in his native Poland, he had been taught to read and write Russian in an army commando school. One may suspect that a formal method of instruction was used, and the fact that the patient expressed himself in a slow, syllabified manner in Russian suggests such an explanation, but there is a lack of conclusive evidence.

Similarly, the patient examined by Byng et al. (1984) recovered English, which had been formally learned at school, better than his native Nepalese. Schwalbe's (1920) German-speaking patient could speak only Hebrew, which he had never used colloquially. Sträussler's (1912) German patient recovered French, a language learned in his youth but not much practiced since. Gelb (1937) observed that a foreign language, or better still, a classical language, may be recovered preferentially, precisely because it is less automatic. Gelb speculates that the greater mental effort required for the foreign language may stimulate the injured mechanism. It may also be the case that these patients rely on a mechanism other than the one injured, and subserved by different cerebral substrates, in this case, the intact metalinguistic knowledge. It is also of interest to note that the only language in which the trilingual patient reported by Paradis and Goldblum (1989) never exhibited aphasic symptoms in French, the language learned at school as the language of instruction and to the study of which, as in French schools in general, a significant portion of the curriculum was devoted. This is in contrast with his two native languages (Gujarati and Malagasy) which presentyed a pattern of antagonistic recovery over a period of 8 months.

Not only have numerous cases of better recovery of a previously less fluent second language been published but a case of loss of the L2 in an amnesic patient has recently been reported (Jamkarian, 2001). An Italian man emigrated to France at the age of 20; he learned French as a second language and continued to work there while living with his Italian wife. At age 60, he suffered a stroke. Seven years later, he still suffers from a chronic retrograde amnesia and has lost the ability to speak French. This case suggests that when a language is learned after the age of 20, even informally, it is learned with sufficient awareness of the form of the language input that it is subserved by declarative memory, and thus is vulnerable to amnesia.

There appears to be a paradox in that structural distance between languages seems to have no effect on recovery pattern, whereas it does seem to be a major predictor of the transfer of therapy benefits from the treated to the untreated language. Although maximum transfer has been reported to occur only in those areas where two languages are structurally closest (either phonologically, morphologically, syntactically, or lexically), patients spontaneously recover either both or only one of their languages, irrespective of whether the two languages are structurally very close or very distant. This paradox may be resolved if we assume that aphasia affects implicit linguistic competence whereas therapy impacts mainly on declarative metalinguistic knowledge (given that exercises are generally quite explicit).

If it is true that the benefits of language therapy transfer only to those aspects of the nontreated language that are structurally similar to the treated language, and if it is true that the reason for this is that declarative memory is involved (as suggested by the lack of generalization to aspects not explicitly practiced in therapy), then not only should such positive transfer occur in these circumstances, but there should also be erroneous transfer. For example, treated structure A in, say, Japanese may be transferred to structure A' in

English in instances where the structure of Japanese differs from that of English. In other words, one should not only look at what has been correctly transferred to languages with similar structures but also, when the patient's languages are dissimilar, see whether inappropriate transfer has taken place. In other words, after therapy, do the patients use the treated structures of Japanese in English and thereby make interference-type errors in English? Such a finding would support the notion of transfer of declaratively learned material (as opposed to the generalization of implicitly acquired underlying procedures).

The fundamental import of implicit/explicit memory for the study of bilingualism

The implicit/explicit distinction in language representation and processing is pervasive and crucial, with many implications for L1/L2 comparisons, and with numerous phenomena distinguishing between lexical and grammatical items. It applies to all aspects of language appropriation, use, and loss, and cannot be ignored by researchers in any of the language sciences. For example, given the very premises of the Chomskian claim that language is a function independent of and different from all other cognitive functions and therefore cannot be learned by general cognitive processes, researchers working within the Principles and Parameters framework who try to ascertain whether L2 speakers have access to UG (Universal Grammar, as postulated by the theory) can test access to UG only through tasks that cannot be performed by the use of declarative memory. Metalinguistic knowledge is a part of general cognition, similar to conscious knowledge of anything, and hence, within the generative grammar framework, not a part of the postulated innate language module. Any task that can be performed through the use of declarative memory (the conscious application of a pedagogical or idiosyncratically formulated rule, or the memorization of phrases) cannot serve as evidence that the speaker has access to UG. The task must demonstrably tap implicit linguistic competence.

Because they can be arrived at through metalinguistic knowledge, grammaticality judgments are not necessarily evidence of implicit competence; they are not evidence of explicit knowledge either, because they can also be arrived at without knowing why a sentence is right or wrong. Grammaticality judgments are evidence only of some level of metalinguistic awareness—i.e., that a sentence can or cannot be said this way. A sentence can be judged to "sound right" and yet the related structure can be produced incorrectly if it has not yet been internalized for automatic use; it can also be judged to sound right in the absence of the metalinguistic knowledge of *why* it is right. An individual can thus succeed on a grammaticality judgment task either without implicit competence or without metalinguistic knowledge of the structure of sentences correctly judged as acceptable or unacceptable.

The problem with grammaticality judgments by L1 speakers is that they may well respond in accordance with what they perceive as the "correct" form, namely the prescriptive form, and reject structures that they actually use frequently. Some speakers will also reject sentences on pragmatic grounds, in spite of careful instructions to the contrary. With L2 speakers who have a good knowledge of their L2, the concern is different. They are likely to correctly rate the stimulus sentences on the strength of their metalinguistic knowledge, even though they would make errors in spontaneous speech because the structures are not part of their automatic implicit competence.

Tomioka (2002a) has shown that some native speakers of Japanese, in a repetition task involving English sentences of about 17 words in length (i.e., too long to be repeated verbatim and thus necessitating the generation of the sentence on the basis of remembered facts), made errors on the very grammatical items for which they had obtained perfect scores on a grammaticality judgment task containing sentences identical in structure and length. In addition, some ungrammatical sentences were correctly rejected for the wrong reasons (participants were asked to underline the errors in sentences they considered ungrammatical).

Whenever one speaks of "learning a language late," one must be explicit as to whether one refers to implicit linguistic competence, acquired incidentally, stored implicitly, and used automatically, as is generally the case with L1 under normal circumstances, or whether, in addition to possibly impoverished implicit linguistic competence, greater reliance on the use of metalinguistic knowledge in a fluent, albeit controlled manner, are also considered.

Viewed from this perspective, Smith and Tsimpli's (1995) idiot-savant, who was reported to be able to speak several languages, albeit with a strong English accent and English syntax, cannot be said to have acquired implicit linguistic competence in these languages, but only an extensive vocabulary and morphological knowledge. Instead of linguistic competence, he has considerable knowledge about the languages. Given the quality of his performance in English, it is doubtful whether he can be said to rely on implicit competence even for his native language.

The description of a language deficit will vary depending on whether it is cast in terms of the observable surface features or of the (theory-dependent) inferred underlying structure, e.g., loss or impairment of a transformational rule (e.g., Naeser, 1975), of a trace (Grodzinsky, 1986, 1990, 1995), of a case filter and theta-role assignment (Schwartz, Saffran, & Marin, 1980), of binding chains or government chains (Hickok & Avrutin, 1995), of a number of hierarchical nodes (Haarmann & Kolk, 1991) or of connections in the network (Lamb, 1994). But in each case the account will go no further than a linguistic description, meaningful only within the theory in terms of which it is formulated. There is no guarantee (and in fact very little likelihood) that any of these descriptions corresponds to the way the language system is actually represented and/or processed (and hence damaged) in a patient's brain.

The critical period hypothesis

The critical period hypothesis applies to implicit linguistic competence. The decline of procedural memory for language forces late second-language learners to rely on explicit learning, which results in the use of a cognitive system different from that which supports the native language. It is the acquisition of implicit competence that is affected by age both biologically (gradual loss of plasticity of the procedural memory for language after about age 5) and cognitively (greater reliance on conscious declarative memory for learning in general and, consequently, for learning a language from about age 7). If we assume that normal language acquisition and use refer to the incidental internalization and automatic use of implicit linguistic competence, then a critical period affects the *acquisition* of language. (This period is admittedly longer than that observed for various skills in animals, but then humans take longer to mature.) It is a gradual process within a window between the ages of 2 and 5, give or take a few months in view of the considerable interindividual variability in the rate of maturation in general and of development of the language areas in particular. (Similarly, some individuals do not have to shave more than once a week until they are over 20 years of age whereas others must shave twice a day by age 15.) The critical period refers to the period during which individuals must be exposed to language interaction if they are to acquire linguistic competence. This period has an upper limit that varies with respect to which component of the implicit language system is acquired, namely, in chronological order, prosody, phonology, morphology, and syntax (including syntactic features of the lexicon). But the vocabulary, i.e., the sound-meaning pairing of words, is conscious and hence subserved by declarative memory; consequently, it is not susceptible to the critical periods that apply to the various components of implicit competence.

Speakers process their late-learned second language differently than their native language and the resulting performance is rarely (if ever) the same. It may in some cases appear to be the same. (Highly competent L2 speakers can fool most people much of the time, though a keen and persistent observer and experimental tasks (e.g., Favreau & Segalowitz, 1982, Segalowitz, 1986) will uncover differences.) Even if their-second language production and comprehension were observably identical to those of L1 speakers, the fact that they use speeded-up control rather than automatic processing would be evidence that, after a certain age, one has to resort to an altogether different processing mechanism because the acquisition of implicit competence is no longer possible (or extremely time-consuming and difficult). Various differences between the processing and/or representation of L1 and L2 have been reported even when the L2 is acquired at a very early age. Perani et al. (2003) for instance, found that bilingual speakers who had been exposed to the second language from the age of 3 (and who had used both languages in daily life ever since, with comparable levels of proficiency in the comprehension of both) showed less extensive cerebral activation during lexical search and retrieval in the language acquired first, suggesting that additional resources were recruited within a dedicated network when generating words in L2. See Mack (1984, 1986) for experimental evidence of differences in relatively early bilinguals.

In addition to (and irrespective of) the undeniable influence of social and educational variables and changing cognitive styles that occur with age, there is a fundamental biological reason for the difference between the appropriation of the native language(s) and later learned languages, namely the gradual (or not so gradual) inability to acquire language incidentally, using procedural memory, so that it becomes available for automatic use. This inability is compensated for by relying on conscious learning, using declarative memory.

The critical period that applies to implicit linguistic competence can thus be masked to some extent by reliance on compensatory mechanisms. To the extent that proficient L2 is subserved by declarative memory, like vocabulary, it is not susceptible to the critical period.

Some studies claim that with short, intensive training, it is possible to acquire a second language's phonological contrasts. But as Sebastian Gallés and Bosch (2001) point out, in spite of a 10 to 20 percent increase on identification or discrimination tasks, performance does not reach the native speakers' level. The improvement likely reflects speeded-up (but controlled) performance, in which case it would be considered as additional evidence in favor of a biologically based critical period.

Conclusion

The procedural/declarative dimension is a critical element in the appropriation, use and loss of languages. Implicit linguistic competence is acquired incidentally, stored implicitly, and used automatically. In the context of this neurolinguistic study of bilingualism, implicit linguistic competence refers to the cerebral representation of a set of computational procedures (the form of which is not overtly known). The implementation of these procedures is automatic. We cannot consciously control their use since we are not aware of their structure. Competence (know-how) is subserved by procedural memory, as opposed to knowledge ("knowing that") which is subserved by declarative memory.

Implicit linguistic competence and metalinguistic knowledge are distinct, as suggested by neurofunctional, neurophysiological, and neuroanatomical evidence, and recently confirmed by a number of neuroimaging studies on bilinguals. They have different memory sources (declarative vs. procedural), each subserved by neuroanatomical structures and neurophysiological mechanisms that differ from those subserving the other (hippocampal system and extensive areas of tertiary associative cortex vs. cerebellum, striatum, and focalized cortical areas), and bear on different entities (e.g., surface form vs. underlying structure; acoustic properties vs. proprioception). The former is consciously controlled, the latter is used automatically.

Implicit competence and explicit knowledge coexist. Neither one becomes the other. Second-language learners may gradually shift from the almost exclusive use of metalinguistic knowledge to more extensive use of implicit linguistic competence. Whatever appears in the output of L2 speakers is not evidence that a given structure has been incorporated in their implicit linguistic competence. It may be the result of controlled use of explicit knowledge (albeit relatively fast). When control processes are speeded-up, they may give the illusion of automaticity. But a task component cannot be more or less automatized. It is automatized or it is not. It can be more or less speeded-up, that is, more or less efficiently controlled. Control admits of degrees of velocity in the performance of a task. We cannot have more or less control over computational procedures that we are unaware of. Hence, automaticity does not admit of degrees. It is systematic whereas a speeded-up process is variable.

Speakers can only notice and pay attention to what they can perceive. What is internalized as implicit linguistic competence cannot be noticed. Speakers are aware of the output of the computational procedures that underlie implicit linguistic competence, not of the procedures themselves. One can only observe *what* has been produced, not *how* it was produced.

CHAPTER 3

Bilingual aphasia

The manifestations of aphasia in persons who spoke two or more languages before insult have served as a valuable source of data for the elaboration of hypotheses about the cerebral organization of cognitive functions. The study of bilingual aphasia has also allowed researchers to better understand how language per se is represented and processed in the normal brain of unilingual speakers. Some of the findings have helped clinicians devise approaches to rehabilitation.

Recovery patterns

When proficient bilingual individuals regain consciousness after a stroke or a traumatic accident, one would expect them to recover all of their languages at the same time and to the same extent. If they were more fluent in one of their languages premorbidly, one would expect this difference to be reflected in the extent of impairment in each language, with higher scores in the previously stronger language. This pattern is indeed exhibited by a number of patients. It has been called *parallel recovery* because the aphasic speech parallels the previous relative abilities in the two languages. However, a number of exceptions have been reported where patients recover their languages in one of several other, nonparallel, patterns. The term *differential recovery* has been used to refer to cases where one language would be recovered much better than the other relative to their premorbid fluency; either the language spoken the least well before insult is the best recovered, or it is simply not recovered to a lesser extent, as might have been expected. Minkowski (1963) referred to these first two patterns as "synergistic" because the recovery of one is accompanied by the recovery of the other, as opposed to *antagonistic recovery* when the two languages are not concurrently available. In cases of antagonistic recovery, only one language is available to the patient at first; then, as a second language gradually becomes available, the first recovered language proportionately regresses and eventually disappears. If this pattern repeats itself, that is, if the available and unavailable languages switch more than once over time, it is called *alternating antagonism*, as the languages alternate over periods of from 24 hours to a week or even months. Patients have also been reported to unwittingly mix their two languages and not to be able to speak only one language at a time. For lack of a better term, this pattern was reluctantly labeled *mixed* recovery. The term *blending* recovery is now preferred because it better describes what the patient is doing, namely blending two languages in the way that some unilingual patients blend words or syntactic constructions, and it avoids the possible confusion with mixed aphasia (i.e., combined symptoms of both Broca's and Wernicke's aphasia) or "mixed polyglot aphasia" (Albert & Obler, 1975, referring to what was later called "differential aphasia"—see below). *Selective aphasia* refers to the presence of aphasic symptoms in only one language without measurable deficits in the other(s).

There does not seem to be any single dimension along which all patterns could be classified, other, perhaps, than the underlying hypothesized cause, the control of inhibition, which we shall explore later. The terms that have been used to refer to these patterns are merely labels to describe what the patient does and have no theoretical foundation. Like the descriptions of the grammars of bilinguals, they apply to a given situation at a particular time. They are not mutually exclusive over time (an initial alternating antagonistic recovery may end up parallel after a few weeks or months—e.g., Paradis, Goldblum & Abidi, 1982); moreover, different pairs of languages in a multilingual patient may show different patterns (a patient may exhibit an antagonistic recovery of two languages and a successive recovery of a third—e.g., Nilipour & Ashayeri, 1989; or an antagonistic recovery between two languages over a period of eight months with no measurable deficits in a third—e.g., Paradis & Goldblum, 1989).

Patterns of selective aphasia and differential and selective recovery can be seen as points on a continuum of severity (Fig. 3.1). In selective aphasia, one language is not affected but the other is. In differential recovery, both languages are affected, though one more than the other. In selective recovery, both are affected, one so severely that it remains unavailable. In parallel recovery, both languages are equally affected. In antagonistic recovery, they are alternately affected over periods of time. In blending recovery, both languages are affected by a lack of selective inhibition.

Reviewers have reported five, six, seven or more patterns, depending on whether certain patterns are counted as different, or as subsets of a pattern (e.g., synergistic: parallel and differential; antagonistic and alternating antagonism). With time, new patterns may be encountered and when they are, they are generally given a descriptive label, in the absence of a theoretical classification scheme. Thus, *differential aphasia* was reported by Albert and Obler (1975) and Silverberg and Gordon (1979), when they thought they had identified patients with symptoms of one type of aphasia (e.g., Broca's) in one language and another type (e.g., Wernicke's) in another language. Three cases were described as fitting this pattern.

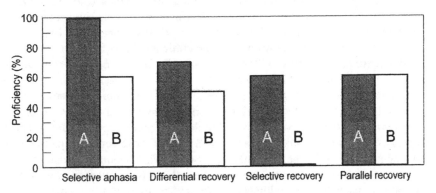

Languages A and B independently move along the proficiency axis (from 0 to 100), e.g., A 100 / B 60 (selective aphasia); A 70 / B 50 (differential recovery); A 60 / B 0 (selective recovery); A 60 / B 60 (parallel recovery). Percentages are merely illustrative of one random possibility and may vary from 99 to 0 for each language.

Figure 3.1. *Selective aphasia, differential recovery, and selective recovery on a continuum*

Albert and Obler (1975) reported symptoms of Broca's aphasia in English and Wernicke's aphasia in Hebrew in their polyglot patient on the basis of her better comprehension and lesser fluency in English than in Hebrew and the presence of more paraphasias in Hebrew than in English (Hungarian, her native language, and French, acquired in childhood, were intermediate). But as the authors themselves noted, it is rare to find equivalency of fluency or comprehension in the several languages of healthy polyglots (Albert & Obler, 1975, 1978). It should therefore not be too surprising that, post-onset, comprehension and/or accuracy and fluency should likewise be different, reflecting a premorbid state of affairs. Two factors may have conspired to give the appearance of Wernicke's aphasia in Hebrew: the premorbid quality of the patient's Hebrew, a language learned after the age of 19, and the interpretation of substitutions of inflectional morphemes as indicative of paragrammatism. The patient's initial gross impairment of auditory comprehension in all languages improved more rapidly in English than in Hebrew. Albert and Obler suspected that a possible different brain organization for each language may have been responsible for their patient's symptoms. In this case, however, it appears that the pattern was one of differential recovery rather than differential aphasia (i.e., a different degree rather than a different type of impairment) and that the patient exhibited symptoms of Broca's aphasia in both languages. Agrammatic symptoms in Hebrew (Grodzinsky, 1984; Goral, 2001) are manifested by the substitution of inflectional morphemes (the hallmark of paragrammatism in English, hence of Wernicke-type aphasia), rather than omissions (the hallmark of agrammatism in English, hence of Broca-type aphasia). This may also have influenced the clinicians' interpretation.

Silverberg and Gordon (1979) described two cases. Three days post-onset, the first patient seemed to present with nonfluent aphasia in Spanish, her native language, and fluent (i.e., Wernicke's) aphasia in Hebrew, a language she began to learn at age 23. One month later, she had recovered Hebrew faster and more completely than Spanish, with similar comprehension deficits in both languages. This again would appear to be a case of more severe impairment of one language (Spanish) than the other (Hebrew). The diagnosis of one form of aphasia over another is dependent in part on the classification criteria of each test battery, according to the kinds of tasks and rating scales. Patients may fall into one category or another depending on whether they are assessed on the basis of the *Aphasia Quotient*, the *Porch Index of Communicative Ability*, the *Boston Diagnostic Aphasia Examination*, or some other evaluation scheme. Here again, Hebrew is the language said to exhibit symptoms of Wernicke's aphasia.

The second case reported by Silverberg and Gordon is that of a 54-year-old Russian physician who had been exposed to Hebrew for only one year, and had only rudimentary knowledge of the language. His ability had been rated "very poor" as it was below average compared to others in his class. He still required the help of an interpreter in his conversations with patients at the hospital. During the first days after his stroke, he was reported to have global aphasia in Hebrew and word-finding difficulty in Russian. Two and a half months post-onset, his Hebrew had only slightly improved, his Russian, considerably. He had virtually no residual anomic deficit. Six months after the stroke, his Hebrew had still not improved to its premorbid state. Again, it should not be too surprising that this patient had globally lost his practically nonexistent Hebrew, while presenting milder symptoms of anomia in his native and considerably more fluent Russian. This hardly meets the criterion of differential aphasia and looks more like a selective recovery evolving into a differential recovery over time.

Bychowski's (1919) patient has sometimes been cited as a further case of differential aphasia, with transcortical motor aphasia in German (no spontaneous speech, good repetition, reduced comprehension), a milder form of the same in Polish (word-finding difficulty with limited spontaneous speech), and symptoms somewhat closer to amnestic aphasia in Russian. But, by Bychowski's own admission, the differences between transcortical motor aphasia and amnestic aphasia are not entirely clearly defined, with amnestic aphasia being characterized clinically and theoretically as a reduced form of transcortical motor aphasia. Bychowski further pointed out that even authors who wish to dissociate the two must admit to certain connections. More likely, as Bychowski himself suggests, the differences may reflect different stages of recovery over time, influenced by the kind of verbal stimulation provided by the environment. Here again, it appears to be a case of differential recovery, with Russian recovered better than Polish, and German being almost nonexistent.

Wald (1958, 1961) also described a polyglot patient as exhibiting conduction aphasia in Russian and motor aphasia in Yiddish, English, and German. He might as well have added global aphasia in French, Latin and Hebrew. In fact, the evidence he presents is consistent with the patient's Yiddish, English and German simply being more impaired than her Russian, a language in which she was able to produce some spontaneous speech, unlike the other languages, in which she could not produce any expressive speech. Her French, Latin and Hebrew were even more impaired in that they were totally unavailable.

Dronkers et al. (1995) also report two cases of differential aphasia. The authors are nevertheless aware that the data on the basis of which a diagnosis of differential aphasia was arrived at are very weak, both quantitatively and qualitatively.

For Patient MI (conduction aphasia in English, anomia in Japanese), the scores are very similar in both languages, except for the repetition task, where the score is lower in English. However, as mentioned by the authors, MI's pattern of errors "was rather different than that usually seen in conduction aphasia" (p. 62), namely, omission of articles and plural *s* marker (which turns out to be an artifact of the local English dialect). When the score was adjusted for dialect (based on controls), the patient's scores were compatible with anomia in both languages. In fact, the patient had complained of word-finding difficulty in both languages before testing.

For patient SM (Wernicke's in English, Broca's in Japanese), the authors considerably temper their claim when they stipulate that it is impossible to tell whether the patient chose not to speak more Japanese or was disabled by the aphasia. It is also likely that the patient's English was superior to his Japanese, for a number of reasons. On the authors' own account, he switched frequently to English when speaking Japanese. The alleged equal degree of premorbid fluency is based solely on the patient's claim to have spoken Japanese well, even though he had never been in the habit of speaking it. He had not spoken Japanese with his co-workers for the 28 years that he worked as a fisherman. He resided with his daughter, who spoke only English. It is not surprising that the patient's scores on comprehension were higher than on production in Japanese since, in a weaker language, comprehension is usually easier than production. Thus, given the few data that we have, it is more likely that the patient exhibited differential recovery (not differential aphasia).

The authors themselves concede that the evidence is weak. In fact the gist of the article is to emphasize the difficulty of assessing the bilingualism of the subjects whose languages are being compared. In one case, the discrepancy is explained by the English dialect of the patient—he is not exhibiting conduction aphasia after all; in the other, it is not unlikely that Japanese was weaker beforehand, which would explain the patient's avoidance of Japanese and his better scores in English.

The incidence of the various recovery patterns is not known. It can only be tentatively inferred from the few group studies reported so far. Most published cases are single case studies, generally because of their unusual symptoms. From 1843 to the present, about 300 cases have been published, including four series of 10 to 50 unselected patients each (see Paradis, 1983, for cases published from 1843 to 1975; Paradis, 1989a for cases from 1976 to 1985; and Paradis, 2001a, for cases from 1985 to 2000). Based on the 138 unselected patients from these series, it would appear that parallel recovery is the norm: 105 are reported to exhibit equal impairment in both languages (76%), 17 differential (12.3%), 9 blended (6.5%), 6 selective (4.3%), and one antagonistic (0.7.3%). Because they do not present striking phenomena, single cases of parallel recovery are not often reported, but the relative frequency of occurrence of all types of nonparallel recovery reported in the literature roughly corresponds to that found in the group studies.

Cases of selective aphasia may go unnoticed when patients are tested only in the language of the hospital staff. The one case reported so far was examined in Paris (Paradis & Golblum, 1989). Had the patient been assessed only in French, his selective aphasia in Gujarati would have remained undiagnosed.

Attempted explanations

Three basic questions may be asked in relation to recovery patterns (Paradis, 1993b). (1) What brain mechanism makes these various patterns possible? Assuming that we have an answer to this question, (2) what determines that a given patient undergoes one type of recovery, and another patient a different one? And, once the other two have been answered, (3) assuming a patient exhibits a selective recovery, why is one language (say, English) preserved rather than the other (say, Japanese)?

At first, clinicians searched for possible factors that could provide an answer to the third question. Ribot (1881) had casually noted that, in accordance with his primacy principle whereby the oldest memories are the most resistant to pathology, the native language was generally recovered first or better. Pitres (1895) pointed out that the native language was usually also the most familiar to the patient, and when this is not the case, patients recover the most familiar language before or better than their mother tongue. Minkowski (1928, 1949, 1965) proposed that the language best recovered was the one for which the patient had the strongest affective ties. Others suggested the language most useful to the patient (Goldstein, 1948; Bay, 1964), the language of the environment or the language heard or spoken last before insult was the best recovered. None of these factors seem to apply in more than half the cases (for further details, see Paradis, 1977, 1983).

Pitres (1895) had also attempted an explanation as to why differential and selective recovery were possible in the first place. He convincingly argued that selective recovery could not be due to differential localization of each language, because, given that there are several cortical sites devoted to language, there would have to be several lesions in exactly the areas that subserve one language and not the other. Instead, he proposed that selective recovery was not the result of the physical destruction of the neural substrate of one language, but the consequence of the physiological inhibition of one of the languages, either temporarily (successive recovery) or permanently (selective recovery).

In recent years, Green (1986, 2002) has proposed an explanation in terms of control over limited resources, which contributes to the inhibition of one language or the other. In the Activation Threshold Hypothesis, this inhibition is viewed as subject to degrees (commensurate with variable amounts of available resources) rather than as an absolute on/off phenomenon. This hypothesis is compatible with the various recovery patterns reflecting permanent inhibition (selective recovery), temporary inhibition (sequential recovery), alternating inhibition (antagonistic recovery), greater inhibition of one language (differential recovery), and loss of inhibition (blending).

Although, since Pitres, most researchers have rejected the notion of a different location for each language, it was revived, from the late 1970s onward, with Albert and Obler's (1978) suggestion that bilinguals might have their languages less asymmetrically represented over the cerebral hemispheres than unilinguals. It was thus assumed that selective or differential recovery might result from one language being less lateralized than the other and hence still available, at least in part, after unilateral damage to the brain, as seems to be the case with left-handers. Another modern version of differential localization comes from Ojemann and Whitaker's (1978) proposal that the representation of languages overlaps at the core of the language area but that, at the periphery, some areas subserve only one of the languages. These two proposals will be examined in Chapter 4. For current explorations of causal accounts of recovery patterns in bilingual aphasia, see Green and Price (2001).

The assessment of bilingual aphasia

A review of the world literature from the middle of the nineteenth to three-quarters of the way into the twentieth century (Paradis, 1977, 1983) revealed that most of the reported bilingual aphasic patients were not assessed with a comparable instrument in each of their languages. In fact, in many cases, the patients were examined thoroughly in the language of the hospital but only cursorily in their other language, sometimes by clinicians who had only a minimal knowledge of that language, as evidenced by the ungrammaticality of the questions that they sometimes report having asked (e.g., "*who are you born?*" Pitres, 1895). It must therefore have been easy to misjudge a patient's performance. At other times, clinicians relied solely on anecdotal reports from the patient's relatives.

Because no factor has been identified that can predict the status of one language relative to another, it is imperative that aphasic patients be assessed in all the languages that they spoke premorbidly. Indeed, some patients have been reported to have best recovered the language they spoke the least well before insult, even when they had no particular affective bias in its favor. Assessment in only one language is therefore inadequate for at least two major reasons. Not testing one of a patient's languages may have detrimental social and/or clinical consequences. On the one hand, patients may be unaware of which of their two languages is more affected or may erroneously believe that one of them is better recovered. In one such case observed in Montreal, this situation had led to the patient's husband's drastic decision to abandon his business and go back to the couple's country of origin, where he hoped he could start anew, a less than certain outcome when one is over 50. Testing revealed that the patient had not recovered her native Dutch any better than English, the language of her environment, thus rendering the move unnecessary. On the other hand, specific symptoms may be detectable in only one of a patient's languages, either because of the particular structural features of that language (Nilipour & Paradis, 1995; Paradis, 2001c) or because of a differential recovery in which the nontested language is the more severely affected. For example, a Hungarian-English patient, also tested in Montreal, showed no clear symptoms when tested in English, the language of the hospital, but definite signs of agrammatism when tested in his native Hungarian, which he used to speak daily with his wife and coworkers.

Too often a patient is assessed with a standardized battery only in the language of the hospital, and quite casually in the other(s), relying for the most part on the subjective impressions of either a professional who has only a rudimentary acquaintance with the language or a lay speaker of that language who knows little about aphasia. It is not uncommon for professionals to have the impression that the language other than the one they themselves speak is more fluent and hence much better recovered, without realizing that what the patient produces is actually pathological jargon. Thus, not only must all languages be tested, but they each must be assessed with an equivalent instrument so that the results obtained may be validly compared.

It was with a view to the above considerations that a battery, *The Bilingual Aphasia Test* (BAT), was developed as an instrument for the assessment of aphasia in speakers of more than one language. It was designed to be equivalent across the 65 languages for which it is currently available. Additional tests are constantly being produced in other languages. The various versions of the BAT are not mere translations of each other, but culturally and linguistically equivalent tests. The criteria of cross-language equivalence vary with each task, because the translation of standard aphasia batteries into languages other than the one in which they were constructed will not be adequate, for a number of reasons. The stimulus items may be culturally inappropriate. They may refer to objects that either are not part of the culture or look or work differently, and hence are not recognized or are misunderstood. The translations may test grammatical constructions that present very different levels of difficulty than the original. Moreover, any task that is based on phonological minimal pairs or rhyming words will simply not work at all in any other language. Some series, such as the days of the week or months of the year, are not available in some languages. Words may have a frequency of use that varies widely from that of their translation equivalent. Common syntactic constructions, such as the passive in English, are rarely if ever used in some languages. The point need not be further belabored. Suffice it to say that most translations will not yield interpretable results. Corresponding items in another language must be selected so as to tap the same information as the original, in accordance with the rationale that motivated the construction of the items in the first place. Such a transposition may yield a test in which the items have no obvious surface resemblance with the original—and yet are much more valid than a mere translation would have been (i.e., they test the same characteristics as the original, albeit through different means).

The BAT includes tests (Part C) that were designed to cater to the particular bilingual situation and are language-pair specific (e.g., translation of words and sentences, grammaticality judgments based on sentences containing contrastive features from another language spoken by the patient, etc.), as well as classic tests (e.g., naming, pointing, commands, verbal fluency, etc.) and some not-so-classic ones (e.g., syntactic comprehension, auditory verbal discrimination, etc.) that test proficiency in each language, irrespective of the other language(s) spoken by the patient (Part B). The latter contains 32 tasks. It examines language performance in all four modalities—hearing, speaking, reading and writing. In each modality, performance is investigated, yielding a score in terms of linguistic level (phonological, morphological, syntactic, lexical, and semantic) and linguistic task or skill (comprehension, repetition, judgment, lexical access, propositionizing), at the level of the word, the sentence and the paragraph, and at different levels of spontaneity, from extemporaneous speech to more formal tasks such as writing to dictation. Because many bilinguals are not truly literate in both of their languages, even if they speak both like a native and have been highly educated in one, the stress is on oral language with only few samples for each reading and writing task. The number of stimuli may be increased when a task is of particular interest.

Bilinguals do not form a homogeneous group. They differ along a number of dimensions, ranging from age and manner of acquisition to degree of mastery and pattern of use of each language. These differences are bound to have an impact on the relative availability of each language, if only due to activation threshold variations. There may even be resulting neuropsychological differences. In fact, it has recently been realized that maybe early and late bilinguals may not use the various cerebral mechanisms involved in verbal communication to the same extent (Weber-Fox & Neville, 1996; Perani et al., 1996). In order to compensate for gaps in their implicit linguistic competence in their second language, speakers of a language learned after infancy may rely to a greater extent than early bilinguals on metalinguistic knowledge and pragmatic competence. It is therefore important to obtain a detailed description of the patient's history of acquisition and pattern of use for each language. These data will help the clinician interpret possible differential scores in light of an informed estimation of the patient's premorbid relative fluency in the respective languages. To that end, the BAT starts with a 50-item branching questionnaire on the patient's history of bilingualism (Part A)—and any test for bilingual aphasia should start with at least as much. This questionnaire needs to be administered only once, in the language of the hospital or the language best spoken by the patient, and information may be gathered from relatives, friends or colleagues. The questions concern the patient's linguistic environment at home as a child and the language(s) of education. They are supplemented by the first 17 questions of the actual language test (Part B), which investigate the pattern of use of, and degree of literacy in, each language. The manner of acquisition—whether at home as an infant or at school as a teenager or adult—may have an impact on the extent to which different cerebral mechanisms have been drawn upon and hence on the differential vulnerability of each language to a left hemisphere stroke (depending on the extent of implicit linguistic competence developed) as well as on the differential availability of compensatory mechanisms such as metalinguistic knowledge and pragmatic competence (Paradis, 1993c, 1998b; Paradis & Gopnik, 1997).

It is important to remember that the scores on the BAT are only suggestive and must be interpreted in light of the respective premorbid proficiency in, and patterns of use of, each language, the patient's socioeconomic and education level and the grammatical structure of each language (Nilipour & Paradis, 1995; Paradis, 2001b). The BAT History of Bilingualism questionnaire plus the questions from the language background questionnaire at the beginning of each language test (Part B) may be supplemented with additional questions such as those found, for example, in the *Language Use Questionnaire* (Muñoz, Marquardt, & Copeland, 1999), easily adaptable to any pair of languages and any bilingual environment.

Because the native speakers who administer the BAT are not necessarily language pathology professionals, the scoring procedure has been made as objective as possible and the instructions given to the patient do not admit of any deviation from the text provided. For the same reason, scoring does not require an opinion or judgment on the part of the examiner. Most scoring consists in circling a symbol that corresponds to what the patient said or did (e.g., circling the digit 3 if the patient touched picture number 3 on the stimulus page).

Cross-linguistic equivalence of the various tasks

Because it is crucial for all languages to be assessed with comparable instruments if the data are to be useful for verifying hypotheses about language representation and processing, the equivalence criteria used in the construction of the BAT will be described in the pages that follow.

Each task requires a different criterion of equivalence, depending on the rationale behind the design of the task (i.e., what it is that we want to measure, and why) and on the structural distance between the languages and the cultural differences between the communities.

Pointing and naming. The items must be appropriate to the cultural and climatic conditions of the relevant community.

Verbal auditory discrimination. Minimal pairs differ from language to language. Hence, in each language, without any consideration of translation equivalence, different stimuli are constructed along the same principles, namely words of the language that differ only in their initial consonant, and by as few phonetic features as possible (e.g., *bear/pear* in English). In addition, the illustrations of the stimulus words must conform to the realities of the relevant community.

Syntactic comprehension. To the extent that languages differ structurally (e.g., with either relatively free or strict word order, or with various degrees of complexity of inflectional morphology—marking person, gender, tense, aspect, and/or mood), the complexity of a particular construction (say, the passive) will vary. Therefore, a sentence with structural complexity equivalent to an English passive (as measured by the number of changes from the canonical active form, the age at which it is usually acquired by children, whether it is notoriously vulnerable in agrammatism or not, etc.) may require an altogether different construction in another language (e.g., a cleft object construction). In other words, if the equivalence criterion is syntactic complexity, a structure of similar complexity (quite possibly not the passive) must be selected.

When a language does not have arbitrary gender, pronominal reference is tested using not masculine and feminine objects but reflexive and non-reflexive reference (*he washes him / himself; she dresses her / herself*). In languages with no gender, even for humans, the singular / plural distinction is used for subject and object pronominal reference (*it pushes them / they push it / they push them / it pushes it*).

Semantics. The stimuli for the semantic categories may be the closest translation equivalents in the various languages, provided that, as in the pointing task, they are culturally appropriate. The same is true of the synonym and antonym recognition tasks and the semantic opposite production task, depending on the availability of synonyms and antonyms in each language. When translation equivalents are not available, words from the same semantic category and their synonym/antonym are used.

Grammaticality judgment. The nature of the alterations depends on the structure of each language. In all languages, sentences are made ungrammatical by the deletion or insertion of a grammatical morpheme, the use of an inappropriate morpheme or, when applicable, the use of the wrong word order.

Repetition and lexical decision. The words for repetition are selected in accordance with the same criteria in each language, namely monosyllabic, disyllabic and trisyllabic words (again, without consideration of translation equivalence) and phonologically acceptable nonwords. In languages like Oriya in which no monosyllabic words exist, disyllabic words are selected instead. In the sentence repetition task for each language, the stimuli are selected from among the syntactic comprehension items corresponding to the same structural criteria: a standard canonical sentence, two sentences with pronominal reference, two nonstandard sentences of one type (e.g., cleft object in English), one negative nonstandard of another type (e.g., passive in English), and one standard negative sentence. The sentence type refers to the degree of complexity, not to the type of construction (whose complexity may vary from language to language—see syntactic comprehension above).

Series. The same series are used in all languages (days of the week, months of the year, counting to 25). In languages in which months do not have specific names (e.g., in Japanese, where they are called the first month, the second month, and so on up to the twelfth), some other similarly overlearned series is substituted (e.g., in Vietnamese, the year of the mouse, the year of the ox, the year of the tiger, etc.; in Chinese, the color spectrum, which is memorized from childhood). In territories formerly under foreign domination, native speakers of the local language know the names of days of the week or months of the year only in some more or less phonologically integrated form of the former colonial language.

Verbal fluency. Initial consonantal sounds that are productive in each language are selected; these are not necessarily the same sounds in every language.

Sentence construction. Translation equivalents are used to the extent that they are culturally appropriate in each language. The order of presentation of words is modified to avoid having successive nouns that form noun phrases in each particular language (e.g., to avoid the equivalent of *house/cat, dog/house*).

Derivational morphology. The type of derivation varies from language to language depending on its morphology (adjectives from nouns, adverbs from adjectives, nouns from verbs, etc.). Whenever there is no variety in derivational forms for morphological opposites (e.g., the prefix *nie-* occurs before every adjective in Russian, without exception), another type of derivation is selected, different from the other morphological task used in this version of the test.

Narrative description. The same story, illustrated by six consecutive drawings, is used in all languages. The pictures are ordered from left to right or from right to left depending on the reading direction associated with each language. The characters' clothes are adapted to the relevant customs. The ambulance depicted bears a red cross, a red crescent, or whatever symbol is characteristic of emergency services in the given environment.

Text comprehension. In both listening comprehension and written comprehension tasks, a different story is used in each language. The structure of the paragraph is the same, the sentences are of the same type and length, and the number of referential noun phrases and predicates is the same. Only the lexical items, and hence the story, differ across languages; the information load is identical in all.

Reading aloud. Words for reading aloud and reading for comprehension, as well as for the copying and dictation tasks, are selected from the foil pictures of the verbal auditory discrimination test. Their equivalence resides in the fact that, in each language, they form minimal pairs with the verbal auditory discrimination stimuli for that language. The complexity of the spelling-sound correspondence varies as a function of the type of writing system, which unavoidably limits the task's cross-linguistic equivalence. Sentences for reading aloud and reading for comprehension, as well as for the sentence dictation task, are selected from among the stimuli used in the syntactic comprehension section of that language's test. The same type of criteria are used as for the selection of sentence repetition items: a standard canonical sentence, two sentences with pronominal reference, two nonstandard sentences of the first type, two nonstandard sentences of the second type, two negative nonstandard sentences of the first type, and one standard negative sentence.

Extemporaneous speech and writing. The samples of spontaneous speech and spontaneous writing collected during the testing period are subsequently analyzed with respect to quantity and quality of production. A measure of syntactic complexity is obtained by computing the mean length of utterance and the length of the five longest utterances, the number of verbs per utterance, and the number of subordinate clauses. A measure of accuracy is obtained by computing the numbers of neologisms, phonemic, verbal and semantic paraphasias, perseverations, paragrammatisms, word-order errors, and omitted grammatical morphemes in obligatory contexts. A measure of the size and quality of the patient's lexicon is arrived at by counting the total number of words, the number of different words, the type/token ratio, and the numbers of circumlocutions, intraphrasal pauses, and stereotypic phrases.

When assessing the richness of a patient's lexicon, a cross-linguistically comparable measure must be used. That is, the measuring criteria should have similar consequences in all languages and should not yield a considerably larger or smaller count when applied to languages with certain structural characteristics. The type/token ratio is a good measure of the diversity of the lexicon at the patient's disposal. It is obtained by dividing the number of different words (types) by the total number of words (tokens) found in the corpus. The more varied the vocabulary in a corpus (i.e., the greater the number of different words used), the closer the ratio is to 1 (a score of 1 would correspond to a corpus in which not a single word was repeated). A high type/token ratio is thus indicative of a rich and diversified vocabulary, whereas a low ratio indicates a restricted vocabulary.

However, cross-language equivalence is threatened by the structural diversity of languages. A simple indiscriminate word count would not allow a valid comparison between languages. Languages without articles or copulas would yield higher type/token ratios than languages in which articles, accompanying every noun, account for many tokens of the same type. Languages in which noun phrases are commonly realized as compound words would have relatively fewer words in a corpus of equal length because what counts as three words in more analytic languages would count here as only one. Also, some languages mark case as inflections on the nouns (and hence a case-marked noun would count as only one item) while other languages use prepositions (and articles, which compound the problem by adding to the word count). Similarly, subject pronouns are used obligatorily in some languages and are either optional or obligatorily dropped in certain contexts in other languages. Therefore, only lexical items (that is, excluding grammatical words—articles, copulas, pronouns, auxiliaries, prepositions, and conjunctions) are counted for the purpose of the type/token measure. In languages in which noun phrases are realized as compound words, each constituent word of the compound is to be counted as one word. In this way, the Dutch word *gemeentereinigingsdienst* counts as three words, since *gemeente, reiniging*, and *dienst* each have an entry in a Dutch dictionary, and the rendition in English would also yield three lexical items: *municipal cleaning service*. In an even more analytic language, like French, the count would be the same because, even though there are four actual words, there are only three lexical items: *service municipal* de *nettoyage*. (For more detailed explanations, see Paradis & Libben, 1987, pp. 28-30.)

Some additional cultural concerns related to testing may have to be taken into account. The patients' responses are to be considered in light of their topolect and sociolect (Paradis, 1998b), with respect to both pronunciation and morphosyntax. As suggested in the test instructions, how patients are addressed will depend on local customs. In languages with different pronouns for different categories of addressees (*tu/vous* in French; *Du/Sie* in German; *jij/U* in Dutch, etc.), the BAT specifies that the pronouns used should be a function of age, sex, and perceived status relative to the interviewer, in order that the patient should be made to feel as comfortable as possible. In some cultures, men will feel uncomfortable being tested by women or by younger persons, *a fortiori* by young women. In other countries, women will feel uncomfortable being tested by men.

Reversible contrastive features

This section is intended to help researchers who wish to construct their own language-pair-specific test, by defining the reversibility of contrastive features, providing examples, and suggesting areas of the grammar where suitable contrasts are likely to be found.

   In Part C of the BAT, it is important to ensure that it is equally difficult to translate sentences in both directions between a specific pair of languages, e.g., from English to Spanish and from Spanish to English; the grammaticality judgment sections for each language (in which sentences in one language incorrectly contain features of the other) must also present equivalent difficulties. To achieve this end, sentences are constructed so as to include reversible morphosyntactic features. A morphosyntactic feature is reversible if its word-for-word translation from Language A into Language B is un-grammatical and the equivalent would be equally ungrammatical when translated word for word from Language B to Language A. In certain contexts, for example, the future is obligatory in French whereas the present is obligatory in English; in such cases, the present in French will be as ungrammatical as the future in English (e.g., I will call (future) you as soon as he arrives (present) → *Je te téléphonerai* (future) *dès qu'il arrivera* (future)).

   To be reversible, the contrastive feature must be obligatory in both languages. If it were optional in one of them (e.g., in Greek, either the present or the future is grammatical in the specified context), this feature could not be used in a comparison between Greek and English or Greek and French, because, whereas it would be possible for Greek speakers to use the wrong tense in English or French, it is not possible for English or French speakers to use the wrong tense in Greek because either present or future is acceptable. The same situation would occur if the feature existed in only one of the languages. For example, articles do not exist in Japanese. Thus, whereas it is possible for a Japanese speaker to omit an article in an obligatory context in an English sentence, it would not be possible for an English speaker to inappropriately use articles in Japanese because there are no articles available. Likewise, arbitrary gender can be a reversible contrastive feature only between languages both of which possess arbitrary gender, but in which the gender of the equivalent word differs, e.g., *voiture* ('car' feminine in French) and Wagen ('car' masculine in German). Speakers of French or German could not use the wrong gender in English because inanimate objects have no gender in that language.

Grammaticality judgments of sentences containing such reversible contrastive features have proven to be an excellent means of determining language dominance at the time of testing. Patients will accept sentences in their weak language that contain a feature from their strong language, but will reject sentences in their strong language that contain a feature from their weak language.

In the translation section of the test, sentences increase in difficulty with a corresponding increase in the number of contrastive features. The first two sentences contain one feature each, the next two, two each, and the last two, three each. The sentence structure in each language is identical to that in the other language, except for the contrastive feature. There is therefore no other element of structural complexity. Sentence complexity and information load are equal in both languages. Only the lexical items differ. In languages that differ fundamentally in obligatory word order (e.g., SVO and SOV), the basic canonical structure will necessarily be contrastive in every sentence and will therefore not count as one of the selected features.

Features that are contrastive from a prescriptive point of view but freely used in their noncontrastive form by native speakers are not to be used. Only reversible contrastive features which are evidenced in everyday speech should be used. For example, if prescriptive grammar stipulates that the future should be used but native speakers often use the present instead, the contrast is not reversible. To be reversible, contrastive features must be obligatory in both languages (i.e., not optional in one, and *a fortiori*, not optional in both), and the translation equivalent of a feature must exist in the other language, but be used in different contexts. The selected features must be productive (i.e., not idiomatic expressions—where a particular construction is restricted to one or two expressions in the entire language). The stimulus sentences should be short and plausible (i.e., sound natural).

Note that the nature of the contrasts will depend on the structural properties of the specific language pair involved. Part C of the test is therefore equivalent only for any given pair and not across pairs. The Farsi → Hebrew translation sentences are equivalent to the Hebrew → Farsi sentences, and the ungrammaticality of the Farsi sentences is equivalent to that of the Hebrew sentences in the grammaticality judgment task, but the Farsi-Hebrew contrasts are not equivalent to their Farsi-English or Basque-Spanish counterparts.

In Table 3.1, the reader will find a list of Italian-Slovenian reversible contrastive features, followed by an English rendition of the stimulus sentences for the translation and grammaticality judgment sections of the Italian-Slovenian

Table 3.1. *A list of reversible contrastive features followed by their incorporation into the translation and grammaticality judgment stimuli from the Italian-Slovenian BAT.*

Italian →   Slovenian
1. to   →   on   (go to / on the market, the seaside)
2. Ø →   on (to play a musical instrument, e.g., to play / play on the violin, piano)
3. intransitive V   →   reflexive V (to laugh, cry / laugh, cry oneself)
4. without + infinitive   →   without + gerundive (without to eat / without eating)
5. N + color Adj   →   color Adj + N (red dress, blue hat / dress red, hat blue)
6. Ø   →   in (on 'Saturday'; Saturday / in Saturday)
7. masc. N   →   fem. N (e.g., book, snake; masculine in Italian, feminine in Slovenian)
8. Ø   →   of (genitive) (the 15th December / the 15th of December)
9. by (*per*)   →   from (*iz*) (by principle, habit / from habit, principle)
10. prep + prep (*a*) + N   →   prep + Ø + N (near of, in front of the car / near, in front the car)
11. V + prep (of) + infinitive   →   V + Ø + infinitive (to try, decide of eat / to try, decide eat)
12. quantity + Ø + N   →   quantity + of + N (much, little money / much, little of money)
13. accusative   →   dative (to help, follow someone / to help, follow to someone)
14. to have Adj.   →   it is Adj. to me (I have cold, warm / it is cold, warm to me)
15. dative   →   accusative (to force to someone / to force someone [to do something])
16. negation + infinitive   →   negation + imperative (not to eat / do not eat)
17. plural   →   singular (there are 7 o'clock / it is 7 o'clock)
18. of   →   on (proud, jealous of someone / proud, jealous on someone)
19. twenty-five   →   five and twenty
20. singular   →   plural (on Sunday / on Sundays)

Translation

458. The President forced him to resign   (15)   470. The nurse taught her to swim
460. The mother is proud of her daughter   (18)   472. The farmer is jealous of his brother
462. The gardener planted 25 trees near the wall   (19,10)   474. The priest saw 32 soldiers in front of the church
464. The driver decided to follow the bus   (11,13)   476. The teacher tried to help the student
466. Tanja will go to a very sunny beach on Saturday   (1,6,5)   478. Giorgio will go to a very big market on Monday
468. On the 3rd of May Peter will play the piano   (2,8,4)   480. On the 5th of June Mary will play the violin
           without singing   without complaining

Grammaticality judgment

Bad Italian (except 486, 492 =correct)

482. Ivan cried *himself* when he read the news (3)
484. The beggar has little *of* money (12)
486. There are nine o'clock (17) (correct)
488. The customer broke *these vases* (feminine)(7)
490. Valeria goes to church on Sundays (20)
492. The boy is warm (14) (correct)
494. *From* habit he never wears a hat (9)
496. Luca, don't drink too much (16)

Bad Slovenian (except 500, 404 = correct)

498. Adam laughed (*not reflexive*) when I told the joke (3)
500. It is seven o'clock (17) (correct)
502. The traveler has much time (accus./not genitive) (12)
504. The girl is cold (14) (correct)
506. The student bought *these books* (masculine) (7)
508. On Fridayø Sonja goes to the cinema (20)
510. *Per* principio he never watches television (*not iz*) (9)
512. Ana, don't *to eat* too many sweets (16)

test (items 459 to 517). The numbers in parentheses in the translation and grammaticality judgment examples refer to the contrastive feature(s) listed in the first section of the table that are incorporated into the corresponding sentences. Table 3.1 represents only one of the 150 currently available language pairs, and is given as an example to help those who may wish to adapt the BAT to their own language and/or dialect pairs while making it compatible for comparison with any of the other BAT versions.

When selecting reversible morphosyntactic features in order to construct translation sentences and grammaticality judgment stimuli for a specific pair of languages, there are a number of areas where one can look for examples, that is, areas where languages often differ.

Local word order. The place of the adjective relative to the noun (N + Adj / Adj + N); sometimes, only specific types of adjectives, such as color adjectives, inalienable properties, possessive adjectives, etc., will contrast. The place of the adverb relative to the verb or auxiliary (V + Adv / Adv + V); again, sometimes only some types of adverbs, such as adverbs of quantity, time, or manner, will contrast. The place of the object pronoun relative to the verb or auxiliary (V + Pro / Pro + V). The place of the direct object pronoun relative to the indirect object pronoun (dir. obj. + ind. obj. / ind. obj + dir. obj.). Note that the previous two features may be combined in the same sentence, thus providing two features for a translation sentence that requires two or three, and helping to keep the sentence short (e.g., *He has given it to her / he has to her it given*). The place of the Wh word in questions (*Where is Peter? / Peter is where? / Peter where is?*).

Tense. The tense used in the following contexts may contrast systematically: after 'without' (+ gerund / infinitive / tensed verb); after 'when' or 'as soon as' in the subordinate clause, when the main clause is in the future (when + future / when + present / when + past); in conditional sentences, in the subordinate clause, after 'if', when the main clause is in the conditional (if + imperfect / conditional/ subjunctive); after 'if' when the main clause is in the future (if + future / present).

Prepositions and case. Different prepositions (or equivalent case-markers, including word order or postpositions) in the same context (e.g., *on / at the third floor, on / (Ø) King Street*). Preposition / no preposition in specific contexts (when the equivalent preposition does exist and is used in other contexts, e.g., *in the morning / the morning*). Double preposition / single preposition (e.g., *behind, under X / behind, under of—or from—X*). In some languages, case is not marked by a preposition but by a case-marking affix. In such cases, a particular case marker (e.g., instrumental case) may generally be marked by, say, the preposition 'with' in the other language. A reversible contrast will exist when, in some contexts, the instrumental case is translated, not by the usual 'with,' but by a preposition that usually indicates a different case, such as 'of' or 'from' (e.g., *covered with snow* → *covered of snow*, i.e., the structure uses the case (or preposition or postposition) that is usually translated as *of*). With containers, a preposition is or is not used, (e.g., *a glass (of) water, a box (of) chocolates, a bottle (of) milk, a bag (of) potatoes, a cup (of) tea*).

Articles. Use of definite / indefinite article in specific contexts, as well as article / no article, provided that articles exist in both languages and are used in other contexts (e.g., *$10 a / the pound, box, bag, kilo*). It does not matter whether the article is used before the noun or as a suffix. What counts is that a definite article, however it is marked, corresponds to a definite article in the other language, and in some contexts, must be omitted or replaced by what corresponds to an indefinite article in one whereas the definite article is obligatorily used in the other. (Note that, as with the order of pronouns relative to each other and their placement relative to the verb or auxiliary, the definite / indefinite article contrast may be combined with the presence / absence of a preposition (e.g., *a/the package (Ø) nuts, a/the box of cookies*), and thus provide two features —and at the same time help keep translation sentences short.) In reference to body parts, some languages require the definite article in place of the possessive adjective (e.g., *he raised his hand / he raised the hand*); a reflexive verb instead of a transitive verb may also have to be used when doing something to a part of the body (e.g., *she broke her leg / she broke the leg (to) herself*). Some languages require articles before proper nouns (*the Peter came, I saw the Mary*).

Verbs. Verbs requiring different types of object case (direct object / indirect object), e.g., *I phoned, answered, obeyed John* → *I phoned, answered, obeyed to John*. Some verbs are reflexive in one language and transitive or intransitive in another (e.g., in French, 'to faint,' 'to remember,' 'to complain'; in Russian, 'to laugh,' 'to cry' are reflexive). Modal verbs may be followed by the infinitive, the gerund, or a tensed verb when the subject of both verbs is the same (e.g., *I want to go, I want going, I want I (should) go*). The pattern may be different when the referent of the subject is not the same for each verb (e.g., *I want him to go, I want him/he going, I want (that) he goes*). Either or both subject and tense of the second verb may contrast. The subject of the second verb may or may not be expressed; a conjunction may or may not be used (in either case, obligatorily). Some languages, such as English, accept a beneficiary as the subject of a passive (*she was given a watch*); others, such as French, do not. In some languages, certain verbs require a preposition before a following infinitive (V + prep + infinitive); other languages do not permit such a preposition or must use a different one (e.g., *of* / *to*). Some languages require the use of a double negative (*nobody did not come*; *he did not eat nothing*); others forbid it (*nobody came*; *he ate nothing*). In certain languages, some verbs require a preposition before their object whereas their translation equivalent is marked by the accusative case or is in direct object position (e.g., to *ask for, to pay for* / *to ask, to pay* + *direct object: John paid (for) the tickets*; *Peter asked (Ø) a drink*); different prepositions may be used (e.g., *in* → *by*; *she lectured, spoke, wrote, taught in* / *by Spanish*).

Numbers. Cardinal vs. ordinal number in reference to time, year, month, season, or date, with an article and/or a preposition (*on the 23rd of October* / *(Ø) the 23 October*). The order relative to 'first' or 'last' (e.g., *the first three houses* / *the three first houses*; *the last/past three months* / *the three last/past months*). The order of constituents in numbers over 20 (*twenty-five* / *five and twenty*). The number after proper names (*King Peter the Second* / *Peter Two*).

Language (or language family) specific contrasts. Some languages or language families may have characteristics that are rarely encountered in other languages, and hence are likely to contrast with most languages, e.g., the redundant object pronoun in relative clauses of many Semitic languages (*the book that I read it*); prepositions after adverbs of quantity in French (*enough of cheese, too much of cheese, how much of cheese?*). In Friulian, the subject is replicated with a pronoun (whether the subject is a noun or a pronoun). In East Asian Languages (Chinese, Japanese, Korean), a person's title follows his or her name (*Lin Doctor, Kennedy President, Jones Mrs.*). German contrasts with many other languages with respect to the word order in subordinate clauses. Languages often also differ with regard to the comparative (*X is bigger than Y*) along several parameters, such as word order and the use of different prepositions. In sentences where the gender of the possessor and the possessed differ, possessive adjectives may agree with the possessor, the possessed or both ('his aunt' → *sa tante*, in which case the possessive adjective is feminine, even though it refers to a male possessor; 'her father' → *son père*, in which case the possessive adjective is masculine, even though it refers to a female possessor).

How to cope with what is available and be creative

The Assessment of Bilingual Aphasia (Paradis & Libben, 1987) places the BAT in the context of neurolinguistic perspectives on bilingualism and provides the clinician and researcher with the test's theoretical framework, a detailed description of each of its various tasks, implementation and scoring procedures, and suggestions for the interpretation of results. It also provides detailed instructions for producing new versions in languages currently not available. It serves as a BAT user's manual. It is also available in Spanish (Paradis & Libben, 1993), Italian (Paradis & Libben, 1999), and Chinese (Paradis & Libben, 2003). Each manual uses the relevant BAT version as reference, i.e., in the Chinese version, all references to the BAT are based on the tasks and illustrations of the Standard Modern Chinese BAT.

The Italian version of the BAT has been adapted for computer use and is commercially available from E.M.S., Bologna, under the name EasyLogo. EasyLogo comprises two parts: First, an assessment portion, namely the BAT, is presented task by task, with colored pictures and with instructions provided auditorily by the computer. The speech rate is adjustable. The patient answers orally or by using the mouse, depending on the task. At the end of the assessment, the computer program is able to suggest a plan for treatment, based on the patient's performance on the different skills at the various levels of linguistic structure. EasyLogo also offers different rehabilitation sessions based on the BAT. The patient can perform the rehabilitation exercises at home or at the clinic. All results are stored in the computer (including actual answers and response times). The program is also designed to detect whether significant progress has been achieved over time in one or more tasks (e.g., phoneme discrimination in the verbal auditory discrimination task).

Because the BAT was designed to selectively test the linguistic competence of bilingual speakers in each of their languages, additional tests are required to assess their actual communicative capacities. For this purpose, the patients' pragmatic abilities will also have to be evaluated. These too are to a great extent culture-specific. Paralinguistic phenomena such as facial expressions and gestures, especially conventional ones, as well as conventional indirect speech acts and possibly even certain conventional intonation patterns will have to be assessed. This serves the practical purpose of determining what remains available and can be integrated into the communicative ability rehabilitation program, giving the patient access to compensatory strategies (Paradis, 1993c, 1998a). As pointed out by Holland and Penn (1995), increased grammatical complexity does not necessarily guarantee better communication; cultural factors are at least as important as linguistic factors in cross-linguistic therapy, if not more so. Attitudes and beliefs about the aphasic condition, the value of testing, and therapy may differ. Indeed, in some cultures, therapy is a foreign and perplexing concept (Holland & Penn, 1995).

Language pathologists may of course choose to adapt any of the existing standardized aphasia tests, modify one of the existing versions of the BAT to suit their specific purposes, or produce a new version by following the instructions provided by Paradis and Libben (1987, 1993, 1999, 2003). But regardless of which aphasia battery one wishes to use in a language other than the one in which it was conceived, developed and normed, failure to apply the above principles will yield a translation the results of which are unlikely to be very meaningful; they will certainly not provide a valid comparison to those obtained in the original language.

In sum, two principles must be taken into account when designing cross-linguistic test materials: cultural adaptation and linguistic equivalence. Cultural adaptation requires careful selection of pictorial stimuli, propositional contents of stimulus sentences, and the appropriateness of objects used for pointing and naming. Linguistic equivalence does not correspond to the translation of an original test. The equivalence criteria vary with each task, in keeping with the rationale behind the task design.

The heterogeneity of bilingual speakers

Bilingual speakers differ along a number of dimensions, ranging from age and manner of acquisition to degree of mastery and pattern of use of each language. These differences may have an impact on the relative availability of each language. Early bilinguals may have developed equal implicit linguistic competence in each of their languages, while late bilinguals, in order to compensate for gaps in their implicit linguistic competence, may rely to a greater extent on metalinguistic knowledge and pragmatic ability. Since these involve different cerebral substrates, each language may be differentially vulnerable to a focal lesion within the left perisylvian classical language area (Paradis, 1994, 1997a). This is why it is so important to obtain a detailed description of the patient's context of acquisition and pattern of use for each language.

In some communities, switching languages in the course of conversation, even in mid-sentence, is the norm. Members of such a community are likely to continue to code-switch after a stroke and, as Grosjean (1985) pointed out, this should not be interpreted as a pathological symptom. There are, nevertheless, clear cases of pathological language-switching and they are of two kinds: sociolinguistic and grammatical. The first is reflected in apparent lack of awareness of the inappropriateness of using one of their languages with unilingual speakers of the other one. The second is manifested by a violation of grammatical and/or psycholinguistic constraints on code-switching (Sridhar & Sridhar, 1980), as in blending monomorphemic words (Zwörpö, a blend of German Zwerg and Hungarian Törpo, both meaning 'dwarf'—Gloning & Gloning, 1965); borrowing prepositions in isolation (je parle anglais to mes *enfants*, using an English preposition in a French sentence; using a French clitic subject pronoun with an English verb (*je* speak to them—Paradis & Lecours, 1979); using a German derivational suffix on an English noun in a repetition task ("conscious...*heit*", then, "conscious...*ung*" while attempting to repeat *consciousness*—Schulze, 1968).

In order to distinguish the normal from the pathological, a number of precautions must be taken. The first concern is the psychological set created by the environment. A unilingual environment will put the speaker in what Grosjean (1989, 1998, 2001) has called a monolingual mode; a bilingual environment, on the other hand, will put the speaker in a bilingual mode, and encourage switching, if that person was living in a free-switching community before insult. Therefore, each test should be administered by a (preferably unilingual) native speaker of the relevant language so as to put the patient in a unilingual mode. If the interviewer understands the patient's other language, it is likely that her body language will give her away; the patient will quickly realize that she can speak the other language and hence will not make the effort to search for a word in one language (e.g., English) when one is readily available in the other (e.g., Spanish). This could be indicative of Spanish dominance if the borrowings or switches are always in the same direction, but since the purpose of the test is to assess the patient's ability in English, the use of Spanish is not to be encouraged during the testing session.

For the same reasons, a unilingual speaker of English and a unilingual speaker of Spanish should be present when the patient is tested with the English/Spanish Part C of the BAT, so that the translation tasks feel more natural, in that the patient is translating Spanish words and sentences for the benefit of the English speaker, and vice versa. These are optimal conditions. In the real world, they cannot always be met. When they are not, one should be aware of the possible impact on patients' performance when one interprets their switching and borrowing.

Experience with the use of the BAT has shown that grammaticality judgments of sentences containing reversible contrastive morphosyntactic features are a good means of determining language dominance at the time of testing. It has also become obvious that a detailed history of the contexts of acquisition and use of each language is indispensable if we are to obtain a valid interpretation of the results in light of the premorbid situation.

In some languages, the BAT is used with nonbilinguals and sometimes even with nonaphasics. In Italy, for example, it is reported to be routinely used in the assessment of cognitive impairment in unilingual patients with multiple sclerosis (Zivadinov et al., 2001), Parkinson's disease (Moretti et al., 2001a, 2002e, 2003; Zanini et al., 2003), motor neuron disease (Moretti et al., 2001b,

2002d), cortical-basal ganglionic degeneration (Moretti et al., 2002b), olivopontocerebellar atrophy (Moretti et al., 2002c) and with cerebellar vermis lesions (Moretti et al., 2002a). It has also been used to assess the effects of normal aging (Juncos-Rabadán, 1994).

Implications of the implicit/explicit memory dissociation for bilingual aphasia

Right from the beginning (Paradis, 1977), it was apparent that recovery patterns could not be determined by a single factor, but by a combination of factors, including such biological factors as aging. To the extent that normal aging affects declarative memory more than procedural memory, one may expect older aphasic patients to have greater difficulty with their later-acquired language. This is in fact what was reported by Obler and Albert (1977); based on the case literature of the last century, they found that, unlike young and middle-aged patients, elderly aphasics did not recover their second, most familiar language, better. In other words, a larger percentage of elderly patients tend to have more difficulty with their second language. Rather than a consequence of Ribot's rule of regression, according to which the oldest acquisitions are the most stable and thus the most resistant to morbid dissolution, this may be a result of the impairment of the age-sensitive declarative memory that subserves the second language (in addition to whatever effects aphasia may have on implicit linguistic competence in both languages). Implicit memory is also reported to be more resistant to forgetting (Nilsson & Bäckman (1989).

Based on the declarative/procedural memory distinction, a number of predictions can be made: (1) Because of the differential reliance on declarative memory, one may expect that the older the patient is, the more likely it is that the later-learned language will be affected. (2) In younger and middle-aged patient populations (i.e., before the normal decline of declarative memory), some individuals with aphasia may appear to retain their second language better than their native language: Procedural-memory-based implicit linguistic competence is impaired subsequent to lesions circumscribed to the left cortical perisylvian areas, the basal ganglia, and/or the cerebellum, but the patients' metalinguistic knowledge of their second language, subserved by intact declarative memory, remains available. (3) Individuals with retrograde amnesia may selectively lose access to their second language (like other items subserved by declarative memory) whereas they retain access to their native language (not affected by amnesia).

The contribution of bilingual aphasia research

A single case does not tell us how the brain of a bilingual speaker works. But it does tell us what *can* happen. When several cases display the same symptoms, they allow us to infer how the system functions, by showing one of the ways in which it can break down. Eventually, cases exhibiting different symptoms will show the range of ways in which the system can break down and give us a first approximation of its structure. The model thus inferred can then be verified experimentally by designing tasks that specifically check one aspect of the hypothesized system. One can also see whether it is compatible with other observed behavioral phenomena.

A number of constructs developed to account for bilingual aphasia phenomena have been advantageously extended to increase our understanding of how the brain processes language in general. The various recovery patterns have led to the notion of neurofunctional modularity. Sociolinguistic registers in unilinguals have come to be viewed as neurofunctionally fractionable, in the same way as two languages in the brains of bilinguals. Bilingual aphasia research has also led to the notion of an activation threshold for the various representations in unilingual language subsystems. The search for an alleged greater right hemisphere participation in the representation of language in bilinguals has led to the study of the role of pragmatics in verbal communication, with special attention to its potential as a strategy to compensate for the lack of linguistic competence in second language speakers, unilingual aphasic patients, and 2-year-old first language acquirers. The dissociation between linguistic competence and metalinguistic knowledge in second-language learners has led to a better grasp of the roles of procedural and declarative memory in language acquisition and use. The differential use of the emotional system in first- and second-language appropriation has drawn attention to the role of the amygdala and the dopaminergic system in unilinguals (Paradis, 2000c). Findings in each of these areas have implications not only for our understanding of the way languages are represented and processed in the brain, but also for a better diagnosis and rehabilitation of neurogenic communication disorders. These will be discussed in the chapters that follow.

Implications for rehabilitation

Before research into bilingual aphasia therapy may proceed, we must identify the questions that need to be addressed. They are numerous and varied and many of them have not yet been formulated. One multifaceted question is whether therapy should be provided in both languages simultaneously (and if so, why? if not, why not?), or successively. If it is provided in only one of them, then which one (the native language, the one that was most fluent premorbidly, the best recovered, the language of the hospital or of the home environment)? Another type of question concerns whether there is a transfer of therapeutic benefits (if any) from the treated to the nontreated language, and if so, whether the transfer is a function of (1) structural distance between the languages, (2) order of acquisition, (3) dominance pre-onset, (4) dominance post-onset, (5) type of aphasia, (6) pattern of recovery, and/or (7) type of therapy. If there is an effect, is it directional (e.g., from the native language to the second language—or vice versa; from the most to the least fluently recovered—or vice versa; from the most fluent to the least fluent pre-onset—or vice versa). Should translation be used as a deblocking device, or should it be avoided for fear of increasing inhibition? Are various therapy techniques equally efficient in different languages, or is their efficiency a function of the structure of the language (e.g., morphology-rich vs. morphology-poor; configurational vs. nonconfigurational; with vs. without tones)? Does degree of transfer covary with the efficiency of a particular technique in the treated language, or is transfer greater with a technique that produces fewer gains in the treated language? As yet, most of these questions remain unanswered (Paradis, 1993d).

Premorbid proficiency influences the degree of habitual reliance on metalinguistic knowledge and/or pragmatic features. The actual extent of metalinguistic knowledge is also important: the greater the knowledge, the better the chance of using it as a crutch when recovering verbal communication. When implicit linguistic competence is lost, it is practically irrecoverable in older patients; only compensatory strategies seem to be efficient. Given that aphasia affects implicit linguistic competence, to the extent that such competence existed in L2 there will be deficits in that language (comparable to the L1). Nevertheless, differential, selective, successive, and alternating antagonism may affect the implicit linguistic competence of each language independently of premorbid fluency. There are several factors at work in the loss and recovery of languages in bilingual aphasia, and they interact to give a very confused picture.

Do therapy benefits transfer to nontreated languages?

Even though a number of papers on rehabilitation in bilingual aphasia have been published over the years, it is not known at present whether therapy in one language has beneficial effects on the nontreated language. If it has, we do not know in what proportion, in what manner (i.e., specific or general improvement), and in what circumstances it applies, that is, whether it is linked to the history or type of bilingualism, the structural distance between the languages, the type of aphasia (site and size of lesion) or the pattern of recovery (whether the degree and pattern of impairment is equal in both languages, or whether one language is recovered sooner or better than another; whether the two languages are uncontrollably mixed, or whether each language is accessible for alternating periods of time).

Most authors seem to agree that concurrent therapy in both languages exerts an inhibitory influence upon speech restitution in general (Chlenov, 1948) and can hinder the recovery of all the languages used premorbidly (Wald, 1958, 1961). Hence they insist that therapy should be provided in only one language, at least initially (Chlenov, 1948; Wald, 1961; Hemphill, 1976; Lebrun, 1988). Chlenov (1948) even goes so far as to suggest that it is essential to forbid patients to practice languages other than the one involved in therapy on their own. Of course, once the restoration of the basic language has progressed to a significant degree, even Chlenov agrees that therapy in a second language is acceptable.

There is less consensus when it comes to deciding *which* language should be treated first. Krapf (1961) suggests that it should be the mother tongue. Chlenov (1948) proposes that one must assist the restoration of the language which appears spontaneously: The tendency for preferential recovery displayed by the patient should not be overridden. Hilton (1980) agrees that, as a general rule, therapy should focus on the language currently exhibiting the strongest spontaneous recovery. Lebrun (1988) suggests that if the patient lives in a bilingual environment, it would be desirable for his interlocutors to use only the patient's best recovered language. Hilton (1980) recommends that, if it is determined that the patient's language preference is different from that of the clinical staff, every effort should be made to recruit a family member or friend to help with therapy in the patient's preferred language.

Little actual evidence has been published so far. Watamori and Sasanuma (1976, 1978, case 1) report only partial transfer from the treated to the nontreated language in a 69-year-old right-handed male English-Japanese bilingual patient with Broca's aphasia. The degree of improvement in the treated language (English) was clearly greater than that in the nontreated language (Japanese) across all modalities, and particularly in writing, which seems to have benefited most from therapy. Two factors may have interacted here: (1) The patient preferred English from the start, and (2) the writing systems of English and Japanese differ radically. There was some limited transfer of oral abilities from English to Japanese, but hardly any in writing. Hence it would appear that, in this case, the transfer of the benefits of language therapy was proportional to the degree of similarity between the various aspects of the two languages. Later, therapy was provided in Japanese as well as English. After 8 months, the patient's writing in Japanese had improved considerably, which suggests that the improvement was directly related to therapy for each specific task. To the extent that the nature of the task differed in the two languages, transfer did not occur. Sasanuma and Park (1995) also report findings that are largely consonant with the structural distance hypothesis. As a result of treatment in only one language (Korean, L1) in a Korean-Japanese bilingual aphasic patient, comprehension improved in both languages (whose syntactic structure is very similar) but there was no transfer of treatment for writing (the systems are very dissimilar). Similarly, Laganaro and Overton Venet (2001) report transfer of gains from treated to nontreated language for aspects that require the same strategy in both languages but not for tasks that involve language-specific processes.

Even when therapy is provided in both of the patient's languages, it may affect only one of them. The gap between English and Japanese in the oral production of Watamori and Sasanuma's (1976) patient did not narrow even after therapy in Japanese had been provided. The patient's oral ability in English improved after 12 months of therapy in that language, even though he had no occasion to speak English outside the clinic, but his Japanese did not improve in spite of 31 months of therapy in that language, and in spite of the fact that he was living in a unilingual Japanese environment. This case demonstrates that it is possible for a bilingual patient to be selectively responsive to therapy in only one of his languages.

Therapy in the second language (when it is also the language of the environment) has been reported to have a positive effect on the nontreated native language as well as on the treated language. Weisenburg and McBride (1935) rehabilitated aphasic polyglots mostly in one language and observed notable progress in their other languages as well. Voinescu et al. (1977) report that intensive therapy exclusively in Rumanian (after 11 months without spontaneous progress) had a significant, albeit lesser, effect on each of their patient's other three languages, including his mother tongue. Some report an even greater effect on the nontreated native language (Durieu, 1969; Linke, 1979). Therapy only in German resulted in substantial improvement in Italian, Linke's patient's native language, with only minimal improvement in the treated second language, even though for the previous 16 years the patient had spoken German exclusively. Durieu (1969) reports a patient's wife's observation that his native Spanish had improved more than French, subsequent to therapy in French only. The patient had lived and worked in France with his Spanish wife for over 20 years and had spoken French since adolescence. Differential impairment may remain severe, with poorer performance in the treated language (Muñoz & Marquardt, 2003). Fredman (1975) reports that speech therapy in the second language (Hebrew, the major language of the environment) of her 40 patients had a positive effect on their nontreated mother tongue as well as on their treated second language. Interestingly, Gelb (1937) considers a foreign language that is used only reflectively and deliberately, even a dead language like Latin, to be an excellent tool for the rehabilitation of the native language. Hinckley (2003) reports that, in a patient with aphasia of roughly equal severity and of the same type in both languages, picture-naming treatment yielded much greater improvement in L1, in spite of the alternating treatment design that gave equal time to each language.

Some authors predict that the benefits of therapy in one language will be transferred to the nontreated language on the grounds of the commonality of neurophysiological or linguistic structures. Peuser (1978) predicts concomitant improvement in the nontreated languages known premorbidly by the patient. Voinescu et al. (1977) postulate a level of "deep structures" which are involved in meaning (i.e., semantic structures) and "basic deepest structures" involving "cerebral psychophysiologic processes" where "the linguistic meets the psychologic and the physiologic, which are the basis of linguistic communication in any language whatsoever" (p. 175); they hypothesize that "the deep psycho-linguistic structures" are "more or less the same for all languages" (p. 174). Consequently, according to them, therapy in one language would transfer its effects to all other languages at these levels, though not at the level of "superficial structures". This can be interpreted to mean that therapy would transfer its effects for any aspects two languages have in common (any parameters they share) but not for those aspects for which parameters differ. It could also mean that languages are more similar at the semantic than at any other level, and that gains at the semantic level are therefore more likely to transfer than those at the syntactic, morphological or phonological levels.

Other authors report a lack of transfer in the nontreated language. Denès (1914) reports that his patient's French improved after therapy in that language but that his native Italian did not. Byng et al. (1984) attribute the discrepancy between their patient's poorer production in the mother tongue (Nepalese) than in the second language (English) to the fact that the patient had received intensive speech therapy exclusively in English.

On the other hand, Bond (1984) suggests that *bilingual* stimulation should be the most effective approach to language rehabilitation among bilingual aphasics. Several different kinds of language processing could be stimulated. In particular, translation may be an appropriate means of rehabilitating a patient's second language, especially when translation skills are less impaired than other language skills. Falk (1973) reports having successfully retrained an aphasic translator in two languages.

Thus, in the literature, we find reports of partial transfer of benefits from the treated to the nontreated language; of benefits only in or greater in the nontreated mother tongue subsequent to therapy in the second language; of lack of transfer to the nontreated language; as well as of treatment in both languages resulting in improvement in only one. We may therefore conclude, at the least, that it is *possible* for therapy to be effective in only one of a patient's languages and not in the other, even though at the onset of therapy both languages present the same qualitative and quantitative picture (i.e., the same symptoms to the same degree). Hence, if therapy shows no effect in one language, that does not mean that it should not be attempted in the other.

Compensatory strategies in rehabilitation

Based on observations and previous published data, at least three compensatory strategies that could be used in rehabilitation come to mind: The use of metalinguistic knowledge, to the extent that declarative memory is not affected; the substitution of pragmatics where syntax and/or lexical access are unavailable; and the use of translation, possibly via metalinguistic knowledge (Strategy 2, in Paradis (1984); see also Christoffels & de Groot, 2004), at any level of linguistic structure.

In fact, in the 1960s, 1970s and 1980s, in an effort to retrain lost or inhibited language functions, many language therapists used exercises that, if not always deliberately or even consciously, focused on metalinguistic knowledge. Patients were made to practice linguistic material by explicitly drawing attention to surface features of language. The structural approach to language therapy greatly resembled the grammatical exercises used in textbooks for second-language learning. In some cases, the patients' attention was oriented to the formal structure of words and sentences (e.g., Cubelli, Foresti, & Consolini, 1988). Whereas it is unlikely that these techniques helped the patients re-acquire the lost components of their implicit competence and their ability to use them automatically, they may have served as a means to circumvent the difficulties and improve the patients' communicative effectiveness, as is sometimes reported in the assessment of various methods.

Another compensatory approach is an attempt to circumvent the syntactic impairment by substituting pragmatic means of communication, since it has been shown that pragmatic skills are well preserved in aphasia and may provide an alternative resource. Methods such as Visual Action Therapy (Helm-Estabrooks, Fitzpatrick, & Barresi, 1982), Promoting Aphasics' Communicative Effectiveness (Davis & Wilcox, 1985), Functional Communication Treatment (Aten, 1986), and Communicative Strategies (Holland, 1991) aim at improving the patient's social interaction abilities without necessarily expecting a linguistic change per se. The tendency in the 1990s was to focus on patients improving their ability to communicate rather than on the need to produce grammatical sentences (Perkins & Lesser, 1993).

Because some bilingual aphasic patients are able to translate into a language that is not available to them at the time for spontaneous speech or even naming common objects (Paradis, Goldblum & Abidi, 1982), it has been suggested that translation might be used when words in one language are not available (Bond, 1984). Trudeau et al. (2003) report that their patient, who had considerable language impairments following a left functional hemispherectomy, was able to compensate for her severe lexical access deficit by accessing words in the other language. She was also able to use gestures when a word was not accessible in either language.

Conclusion

Bilingual individuals with aphasia do not necessarily recover their languages at the same time and to the same extent. There is no known correspondence between which language is better recovered and any single biological or ecological factor. Sometimes the second language may appear to be recovered better than the native language because patients rely on metalinguistic knowledge in their second language.

• All languages of a person with aphasia must be assessed with an equivalent instrument, not a simple translation of a standardized test from another language.

• The fact that therapy is ineffective in one language does not mean it will not work in another.

• When implicit linguistic competence is unavailable, compensatory strategies such as metalinguistic knowledge and pragmatic abilities may be used.

• Translation may be available when word retrieval is not.

• Motivation may improve performance.

• It can reasonably be argued that late bilinguals, to the extent that they possess an incomplete linguistic competence in L2, will compensate by relying to a greater extent on pragmatic aspects of verbal communication and hence on right-hemisphere-based cerebral mechanisms.

• To the extent that they use declarative-memory-based metalinguistic knowledge, they may also rely on bilaterally represented information.

CHAPTER 4

Cerebral lateralization and localization

Of all the attempted explanations for nonparallel recovery patterns in bilingual aphasia, lateralization and the localization of languages in the brain are the two most controversial and most widely discussed proposals of the past 25 years. Beyond trying to account for recovery patterns, these issues have been central to the concerns of recent neuroimaging studies, as will be examined in Chapter 6. The questions concern (1) whether two languages are equally lateralized or whether one or both has/have an increased right-hemisphere representation; and (2) if both are equally represented in the left hemisphere, whether their representations overlap or are subserved by separate areas.

Differential lateralization

The issue of language laterality in bilingual speakers, that is, whether the two languages are represented and processed in the left hemisphere to the same extent as in unilinguals is an interesting and legitimate one from a theoretical perspective.

Over the last three decades, numerous experimental studies have looked into the question of the lateralization of language in bilingual speakers. Although the researchers have not generally defined what they mean by "language," given the experimental paradigms and the stimuli that were used, one may safely infer that they had implicit linguistic competence, i.e. the language system, the code, the grammar, in mind. Hence, for the purpose of this exposition, "language" will refer to sentence grammar (phonology, morphology, syntax, and the lexicon). An utterance, on the other hand, is a sentence used in context, which requires inferences from the situational or discourse contexts and/or from general knowledge (i.e., pragmatic features) in addition to grammatical processing, in order to arrive at an interpretation of its meaning. It has been well established over the past one hundred years that language (as defined) is subserved by specific areas of the left hemisphere, and there is increasing evidence that pragmatic aspects are subserved by the right hemisphere in right-handed unilingual populations.

Experimental data

For a review of the literature on language lateralization in bilinguals, the reader is referred to comprehensive treatments in Vaid and Genesee (1980), Vaid (1983), and Vaid and Hall (1991). Suffice it to say that, after no laterality differences could be found in bilinguals in general, differences have been reported for very specific subgroups of bilinguals and/or under very specific conditions, such as greater involvement of the right hemisphere only for early (Orbach, 1967) or for late (Sussman, Franklin & Simon, 1982; Albanèse, 1985) bilinguals; for early or late bilingual women but only for late bilingual men (Vaid & Lambert, 1979); only when the subjects' eyes are closed (Moss, Davidson, & Saron, 1985), for talented second-language learners, as compared to untalented learners (Schneiderman & Desmarais, 1988); or for balánced bilinguals as opposed to speakers with a dominant language (Mägiste, 1992). Decreased asymmetry has been claimed to hold (exclusively) for just about every possible subgroup of bilinguals and its opposite: *Proficient* late bilinguals who have learned their second language *formally* (Bergh, 1986) versus only those late bilinguals who are at the *beginning* stages of acquiring their second language *informally* (Galloway & Krashen, 1980). In other words, one author claimed to have found differences only in proficient late bilinguals (as opposed to beginners) who learned their second language in a formal setting, whereas another found no difference in this group but only in people at the early stages of the informal acquisition of a second language. Bergh's results are in direct conflict with the predictions of the manner-of-acquisition hypothesis (that there is greater right-hemisphere participation only when L2 is appropriated *informally*) and the modified stage hypothesis (The right hemisphere is involved only when L2 is appropriated *late* and informally). Usually, proponents of differential language laterality try to explain away these multiple contradictions by invoking differences in methodology or procedures. This would be an acceptable argument only if it were shown *why* procedure X yields result A whereas procedure Y yields result B. Both procedures cannot tap the same entity, namely, language (or whichever component of language is claimed to be investigated) as they nevertheless claim to do. It is not sufficient to explain the discrepancies by attributing them to differences in methodology. One must specify the reason why each method obtains the results that it does, and explain which one is valid for investigating language (Paradis, 2003).

    Not only can we not generalize to bilinguals in general from any given subgroup, but in view of the contradictory nature of the results on the same bilingual subgroups, we cannot even generalize to any subcategory of bilinguals, no matter how they are subdivided according to sex, degree of proficiency, or age and manner of acquisition. Evidence contradicting the stage hypothesis (that there is greater right hemisphere participation at the beginning stages of L2 appropriation) abounds (see Vaid, 1983). There is also evidence inconsistent with both the manner of acquisition and the stage of acquisition hypotheses (Bergh, 1986). Furthermore, many studies have reported no difference between various subpopulations of bilinguals and unilinguals (e.g., Barton, Goodglass & Shai, 1965; Kershner & Jeng, 1972; Kotik, 1975; Schönle & Breuninger, 1977; Walters & Zatorre, 1978; Carroll, 1980; Gordon, 1980; Hynd, Teeter & Stewart, 1980; Piazza Gordon & Zatorre, 1981; Soares & Grosjean, 1981; Galloway & Scarcella, 1982; Soares, 1982; Rapport, Tan & Whitaker, 1983; McKeever & Hunt, 1984; Soares, 1984; Obrzut et al., 1988; Hoosain & Shiu, 1989) or even *greater* asymmetry in bilinguals (Starck et al., 1974; Shanon, 1982; Ben Amar & Gaillard, 1984; Workman et al., 2000). Bilingual men but neither unilingual or bilingual women nor unilingual men are reported to display less accuracy in the left ear but not right ear or both ears (Persinger, Chellew-Belanger & Tiller, 2002), suggesting more left-hemisphere representation only in bilingual men. Equal involvement for each language, and greater as well as lesser involvement of the right hemisphere have been claimed for L1 only, for L2 only, and only for early or late stages of informal acquisition or of formal learning. Vaid and Hall's (1991) meta-analytical study could find no evidence of greater participation by the right hemisphere in any subpopulation of bilinguals. As Berquier and Ashton (1992) would say, good reason to do more such studies. But surely, before doing more, one would have to show that the paradigm that is forever being refined is valid in the first place.

There was a time when it was legitimate to look for subgroups within the bilingual population, once it had been shown that the differential right hemisphere participation hypothesis did not hold for bilinguals at large. But why should we now wish to show at all costs (and what is even the rationale for suspecting) that there must be some small subset of bilinguals to which this hypothesis applies, such as proficient female late acquirers in informal settings, provided they keep their eyes closed (Moss et al., 1985) or block one nostril (Shannahoff-Khalsa, 1984)? In point of fact, it is conceded that "it is questionable whether, even if properly tested, the predicted differences in the extent of hemispheric involvement in the two languages of bilingual subgroups can be reliably detected by current procedures, especially since the size of ear or visual field asymmetries may be influenced by factors other than degree of cerebral lateralization" (Vaid, 1983, p. 328). On the basis of a statistical reanalysis of available data, Sussman (1989) concludes that previous findings and theoretical conclusions based on time-sharing laterality results may be meaningless, and he seriously questions the continued use of the time-sharing paradigm as a behavioral index of language lateralization. In addition, experiments with commissurotomized patients have shown that, following the section of the corpus callosum, under dichotic stimulation, the left ear score drops to near zero whereas with monaural stimulation it is normal (Milner, Taylor, & Sperry, 1968); this strongly suggests that the left ear score reflects the amount of information successfully transferred from the left ear to the left hemisphere (via ipsilateral connections)—not information processed by the right hemisphere.

And yet, studies continue to appear, with increasingly implausible interpretations. One troubling fact is that authors fully aware of the methodological, theoretical and statistical problems with their studies nevertheless go ahead and publish them in the full realization that their results, based on "an impoverished measure," with stimuli "hardly representative of 'language'," using a method "subject to many criticisms," and without a unilingual control group, cannot be readily generalized (Richardson & Wuillemin, 1995). Obler et al. (1982) and Zatorre (1983, 1989) are often cited for pointing out the methodological, theoretical and statistical problems with these studies, but the authors who cite them go ahead anyway. Likewise, authors may mention that the selected clinical cases published are of no statistical value, but then they cite percentages in favor of their standpoint anyhow.

Over a quarter of a century ago, Satz (1977) already pointed out that the probability of left-brain language, given a left-ear or left-visual-field advantage, is 90%; the probability of right-brain language, given a left-visual-field advantage, is only 10%; this means that *the probability of misclassifying* subjects into a right-brain language group, if they have a left-visual-field advantage, *is on the order of 90%*. Colbourn (1978) warned that the interpretation of visual-field advantage as indicating differences in lateralization between various subject populations is unfounded because it has not been shown that the degree of performance asymmetry reflects the degree of lateralization for the task or stimulus material used. No proof has been forthcoming since then. Degree of cerebral asymmetry of function has not been shown to correspond directly with the surface measures actually being recorded. Moreover, different derived indices of laterality can produce different interpretations of the same data. Since we have no knowledge of the relationship between our surface measures and the underlying variables, Colbourn concluded that an interpretation of different hemispheric laterality for two different languages cannot logically be upheld on the basis of visual-field advantage. The same can be said of ear advantage, rate of finger tapping interference, or direction of conjugate lateral eye movements.

Dichotic, dichhaptic and visual half-field tachistoscopic tests are considered doubtful tools with low or non-existent intertest reliability, and hence they are poor predictors of the possible degree of functional lateralization in individuals or subgroups of individuals. They are founded on neither logical nor empirical grounds (Morais, 1981; Teng, 1981; Sidtis, 1982; Bradshaw, Burden, & Nettleton, 1986; Jäncke, Steinmetz, & Volkmann, 1992). Results may often be explained as artifacts of the statistical procedures by which they are analyzed (Dennis, 1984). Asymmetries are not present for over half of the subjects tested. Lateralization effects can be manipulated by varying the frequency of trials relative to the number of stimuli used (Chiarello, Dronkers, & Hardyck, 1984). Unilingual laterality studies typically report that only 70% of right-handers show a right-visual-field advantage for recognizing words (Kim & Cohen Levine, 1991). In Wexler, Halwes, & Henniger's (1981) dichotic listening study, out of the total group of 31 subjects, only 15 were reported to have significant ear asymmetries. In Chiarello, Dronkers, and Hardyck's (1984) experiment, most subjects did not show statistically significant asymmetries, despite a robust right-visual-field group advantage. In addition, individual subjects display remarkable versatility in response to laterally presented stimuli, so that individual performance is difficult to predict. In fact, visual field asymmetries not only shift from one task to another (Geffen, Bradshaw, & Wallace, 1971) and from one subject to another (Kroll & Madden, 1978) but also from trial to trial in the same subject (Schwartz & Kirsner, 1982). This led Schwartz and Kirsner (1984) to consider that visual field and dichotic listening studies produce unreliable results, and that studies that compare measures with differential reliability produce spurious results. Chiarello et al. (1984) warn that the group effects found in the analyses of variance conceal a wide range of individual differences in lateral asymmetry. They report substantial intrasubject variation; 23% of their subjects shifted the direction of their asymmetry when they were retested. Twenty to thirty percent reversals seem in fact to be the norm (Pizzamiglio, De Pascalis, & Vignati, 1974; Blumstein, Goodglass, & Tatter, 1975; Bakker, van de Vugt, & Clausheuis, 1978; Geffen & Caudrey, 1981). As Chiarello et al. (1984) point out, since the percentage of asymmetry reversals remains constant across various studies, it cannot be attributed to differences in subject populations, stimulus modalities, experimental procedures or materials, or laterality statistics. In general, only low-to-moderate reliabilities are achieved (Segalowitz, 1986). If about one-third of right-handed subjects fail to show left-hemisphere language dominance, or worse, switch the direction of their ear (Colbourn, 1978) or visual-field (Chiarello et al., 1984) advantage upon retesting, the experimental procedure is grossly unreliable and can hardly be considered to be a valid measure of language laterality.

Voyer (1998), who admits that there are no validated tasks to assess lateralization of functions, surmises that once a high level of reliability has been attained, a likely side effect will be an improvement in the validity of these measures. Therefore, Voyer (2003) seeks to find which tasks would improve the reliability and magnitude of laterality effects obtained with the dichotic listening technique. He finds that the largest and most reliable laterality effects are produced with a target-detection task. Of course, finding an effect is no guarantee that it reflects what is purported to be measured. Ironically, the largest and most reliable laterality effects are obtained with tasks that are the least likely to be valid (e.g., Voyer's (2003) target-detection task, which requires that participants indicate to which ear a target word was presented). Of all the tasks using single words as stimuli (see Chapter 6), this must be one of the least likely to tap language laterality because it is maximally remote from a natural language function. The effect may be reliable, but it is unlikely that the degree of language laterality is what is measured. Incidentally, to assume that the validity of the target-detection task is illustrated by the large percentage of right-ear advantages (REAs) it produces in comparison with other tasks (Voyer, 2003) is to beg the question: It is necessary to first demonstrate that magnitude of REA correlates with degree of language laterality—a belief which to this day has not been validated. As pointed out by Schwartz and Kirsner (1984), no index of group differences, no matter how reliable, is a useful laterality measure unless it can be shown that the task is related to underlying brain asymmetry. One ought to take seriously Voyer's (1998) prescription that "the measures of laterality must be subjected to the same validation procedures as any other form of measurement before valid theories can be formulated and tested." (p. 210), even though, as he deplores, most theorists seem to neglect that fact.

In addition, laterality scores obtained from various experimental techniques have been shown to be independent of each other; there is considerable discordance between the different laterality scores with respect to direction as well as amplitude of differences (Eling, 1983). It is therefore difficult to see how these various paradigms could be testing the same function. Since they all purport to test language laterality, they cannot all be valid. There is no criterion for discriminating between them. Furthermore, none of them correlates with the clinical and neuropsychological evidence. Under the circumstances, we can hardly disagree with Colbourn's (1978) conclusion that "it would be better if researchers did not attempt to impose a *false quantitative respectability* on data which has no foundation for it". (p. 287; emphasis his). One may indeed wonder why, given the ubiquitous awareness of the overwhelming (90%) possibility of error, anyone would continue to attempt to determine laterality in a multilingual subpopulation on the basis of a visual half-field tachistoscopic, dichotic listening, or time-sharing tapping procedure.

One might object that all these experiments use stimuli that yield results that cannot be generalized to language (digits, syllables, single words). This objection is moot, given the lack of validity of the basic premise of correspondence between degree of laterality and reported degree of ear or visual-field advantage or tapping interference in the first place. They cannot be claimed to be valid even for the specific stimuli that are used. Schwartz and Kirsner (1984) concluded their review of behavioral laterality studies with the observation that "much of today's laterality research can be compared with the phrenology of the last century" (p. 66). The situation remains deplorably unchanged twenty years later. Unfortunately, their article, which was primarily aimed at helping avoid further work along unprofitable lines, like those of their predecessors (Satz, 1977; Colbourn, 1978) and successors (Paradis, 1990a, 1992a, 1995a), fell on deaf ears.

Some researchers are beginning to hint that the results might reflect differences in pragmatic content, in spite of the fact that, on the one hand, these procedures are explicitly designed to tap exclusively linguistic material (and purported to do so), and on the other hand, the very nature of the stimuli used precludes any involvement of the pragmatic aspects of verbal communication, inasmuch as the latter relate to the processing of utterances in context. Vaid (2002), for example, contemplates the possibility that language lateralization is the same in both bilinguals and unilinguals and that what differs is the relative reliance of the groups on those aspects of language thought to be under right-hemisphere control. This is very likely to be the case, but it cannot be inferred on the basis of measures obtained with instruments such as dichotic listening and visual half-field tachistoscopic presentation of digits, syllables or words, which are specifically designed to tap left-hemisphere-based language.

Nevertheless, with blatant disregard for the notion of validity (and relying on premises long shown to have no foundation in fact, such as Lenneberg's (1967) assumption that there is a correspondence between the fact that language lateralization is not established until puberty and the critical period for language acquisition), Evans et al. (2002), using a split visual field paradigm, still claim to provide evidence that, of two groups of English-Welsh bilingual individuals who learned Welsh after 5 or 6 years of age, those who are assumed to have been less exposed to Welsh sounds during infancy are less left-lateralized for Welsh than those who are assumed to have been more exposed to Welsh sounds (see Paradis (2003) for a detailed critique of that study).

Clinical evidence

As for the evidence from clinical reports, it is not just "equivocal" (Vaid, 1983, p. 317) with respect to the role of the right hemisphere in language mediation, it is simply *nonexistent*. There is not a shred of clinical evidence in support of the claim that language representation is less asymmetric in bilinguals, for either or both of their languages. There is *no* statistically significant higher incidence of crossed aphasia in bilinguals than in unilinguals (see April, 1979; April & Han, 1980; Chary, 1986; Mendelsohn, 1988; and Solin, 1989, for reviews). Karanth and Rangamani (1988) report that the incidence of crossed aphasia in their sample is actually lower in bilinguals than in unilinguals. That study was replicated by Rangamani (1989) on an unselected sample of patients with a cerebral vascular accident, reporting crossed aphasia in 2/12 unilinguals and 0/26 bilinguals. Wada testing results are equally clear: Both languages are affected only by left-hemisphere injection (e.g., Rapport et al., 1983; Berthier et al., 1990; Gomez-Tortosa et al., 1995), even when one of the languages is American Sign Language (Damasio et al., 1986). But old myths die hard. For example, Kotik-Friedgut (2001) makes the unsubstantiated (and invalid) claim that "the probability of crossed aphasia among bilinguals is higher than among monolinguals" (p.106). She goes on to make the related claim, also without providing statistics, references, or any other type of corroboration, that "the probability of aphasia with left hemispheric lesions is lower in polyglots than in monolinguals" (ibid.). Based on their survey of the neurolinguistic aspects of bilingualism studies, Goral, Levy, and Obler (2002) conclude that the sizable literature on polyglot aphasia, supported by evidence from crossed aphasia and lateral dominance in non-brain-damaged individuals, suggests that the left hemisphere is dominant for all languages of most polyglots, as is the case for the language of most unilinguals.

To the extent that right-hemisphere damage is known to cause speech, language, and communication deficits (Alexander, Benson & Stuss, 1989), bilinguals exhibit such symptoms, but only to the extent and in the same form that unilinguals do. Subsequent to right-hemisphere lesions, bilinguals, like unilinguals, may be expected to exhibit impairment of affective prosody and the ability to handle humor, sarcasm, irony, inference, analogy, non-explicit speech acts, and in general, any nonliteral meaning. But the linguistic aspects of prosody or grammatical usage will not be impaired to a greater extent than has been reported in unilinguals (e.g., by Joanette et al., 1983; Joanette, Goulet, & Hannequin, 1990).

Some authors' conjectures concerning the role of the right hemisphere in subserving the languages of bilinguals occasionally lead them into contradictions. For example, Marrero et al. (2002) propose that (1) the more auto-matized language is subserved by the left-hemisphere perisylvian areas (the other language is in part if not *in toto* represented in the right hemisphere); (2) the more automatized language is more susceptible to left-hemisphere injury; and, apparently contradictorily, (3) the more automatized language is quicker to recover. If, as the authors rightly assume, the most automatized language is subserved by specific areas of the left hemisphere, then it is reasonable to suppose that this language is more vulnerable to injury in this area than a less automatized language that is presumably subserved, at least in part, by a different area, such as the right hemisphere. The more automatized a language is, the less extensive its neural substrate and therefore the more vulnerable it is to a small circumscribed lesion. (The older the individual, the smaller the relevant area, for example, the smaller the lesion required to cause jargon-aphasia. There is also neuroimaging evidence that the more automatized a task is, the less cortical space is activated—see Chapter 6.) Hence, subsequent to a lesion in this area, one would expect greater impairment, not better recovery, of the more automatized language.

Misguided applications

A number of studies do not hesitate to make recommendations for the application of the alleged finding of increased right hemisphere participation to foreign-language teaching (Albert & Obler, 1978; Shannahoff-Khalsa, 1984), the treatment of mental illness (Werntz et al., 1983) or the rehabilitation of aphasics (Albert & Obler, 1978; Marrero, Golden, & Espe-Pfeifer, 2002). Students have been trained to write in their second language with their non-dominant hand (reported by Seliger, 1982), encouraged to breathe through their left nostril (Shannahoff-Khalsa, 1984), and advised to learn a second language through dancing or singing (Albert & Obler, 1978), all in the hopes of involving the right hemisphere in the acquisition of L2. More than 20 years ago, Scovel (1981) already warned against such attempts to apply neurolinguistics directly to second-language teaching. According to Seliger (1982), "often the guilt for the misapplication of such research findings must rest with the researchers who present findings as if they are absolute and conclusive and ready for direct application to the classroom." (p. 307).

In this context, four questions come to mind: (1) Is L2 laterality research sufficiently advanced that some application can be reasonably contemplated? (2) Is it beneficial to force the second language into the right hemisphere? (3) If it is, do we know how to bring this about? (4) Are we sure it would not actually be detrimental? Before tackling these questions, though, we must determine what it is that we wish to encourage the right hemisphere to do. Several points should be emphasized here. First, there is no evidence that the language system is less asymmetrically represented in the brains of bilinguals than in those of unilinguals. Second, we have no evidence that the right hemisphere is involved in the early stages of the acquisition of the language system in unilinguals. Third, even if it were the case that the right hemisphere was used at the beginning of first language acquisition, it might not be a good idea to repeat this process for L2. Fourth, even if it were beneficial to involve the right hemisphere, we would not know how to do so. Fifth and last, the forced activation of the right hemisphere during the initial stages of the acquisition of a second language might actually be detrimental.

No use tampering with nature

Even if it were the case that the right hemisphere played a major role in the acquisition and/or learning of a second or foreign language, it might very well do so regardless of how that language is presented. We do not know how to force a language to be represented in a particular brain area, or prevent it from being represented where it would naturally be localized (save by removing the left hemisphere early in life—which, fortunately, no one so far has advocated).

Song, dance, instrumental music, or blocking one's left nostril will not force the grammar to be processed and/or represented in the right hemisphere, if that is not where it is naturally processed and/or represented. The mode of presentation might at best encourage particular processing strategies, but (1) even these are not demonstrably beneficial, and (2) the concurrent activation of the right hemisphere by means of music or dance may have adverse effects, as demonstrated by task-sharing studies: Interference is greater when two functions that rely on the same hemisphere are activated concurrently than when each function relies on a different hemisphere. If it were a fact that second-language learning usually does involve the right hemisphere, this would provide no assurance that utilizing the right hemisphere is the most efficient way of learning a second language. Indeed it might be an important factor in failure to acquire native-like proficiency since, once higher proficiency has been attained, greater asymmetry (i.e., left dominance) is reported. Goodglass (1978) suggests that, while in the early stages of first-language acquisition neurons are recruited bilaterally, in the course of language development, the most compact, fast-acting systems of the left hemisphere survive, while the slower, less efficient components of the right hemisphere's neural network drop out of the processing of language. It might therefore be considered more efficient to try to get the left hemisphere to process the second language as soon as possible (if one knew how to do this).

There is in fact no evidence that the grammar is ever subserved by the right hemisphere in children. In early childhood, most verbal communication does not contain much grammar, relying more on pragmatic aspects of language use and an increasing number of lexical items. For this reason, children's grammar develops more slowly than their ability to understand utterances in context (Bloom, 1974). It is not surprising that, before the age of three or four, a child who suffers symptoms subsequent to either right- or left-brain damage will display undifferentiated mutism. In the absence of right-hemisphere pragmatic support, the left hemisphere's labile incipient grammar is insufficient to sustain verbal communication. According to Kinsbourne (1981), language is left-lateralized from the very first word, and "the idea that language lateralization is progressive from bisymmetry to left seems to be totally misconceived" (p. 88). Functional asymmetries are present from the earliest measurable point in time (Aram & Whitaker, 1988). The widely accepted theory in the 1960s that lateral specialization is progressive, increasing with age from infancy to adolescence, has long been abandoned in the face of accumulated evidence that indicates that cerebral lateral specialization is established from early infancy (Harris, 1988) or even during fetal development (Turkewitz, 1988) and does not change over time (Best, 1988).

Yet some authors continue to take progressive language lateralization for granted. For example, in spite of his own finding, based on dendritic growth patterns, that Broca's area overtakes its right-hemisphere homologous site before the onset of language, Scheibel (1991) still refers to "the progressive lateralization of function that occurs during the first 6 to 10 years" (Scheibel, 1991, p. 346, citing Krashen, 1973, and Lenneberg, 1967). Scheibel further suggests that "at least some degree of functional symmetry may exist for several years after a high order of speech facility is attained" (p. 346). Scheibel bases his suggestion on two facts: (1) the nondominant cortex leads the other in terms of dendrite length for 3 to 6 months, after which the dendrite systems on the soon-to-be-dominant side overtakes the other, and a second burst of dendrite building at 12 to 18 months corresponds to the demands of early language learning and use and (2) there is a marked increase in the number of higher order branches on the left side relative to the right, which suggests enhanced dendritic growth activity at a time when the beginnings of internalization and conceptualization mark the onset of language competence in the child. However, this does not mean that the right hemisphere subserves grammar during its early period of greater dendritic growth. It more likely indicates that some pragmatic abilities dominate communication at that time, long before grammar develops—in the left hemisphere.

But even if it were beneficial for the second language to be processed in the right hemisphere, one might argue, as mentioned earlier, that any competing right-hemisphere function activated at the same time might be a hindrance (as the time-sharing task experimental paradigm would indicate if it were valid: finger tapping is reported to be more disrupted when it is performed with the right hand by right-handers). The moral would therefore be: "Do not overload the right hemisphere with materials (melody, choreography, etc.) that might require its attention."

To the extent that the right hemisphere is normally engaged in (first) language processing, it will be engaged in second/foreign-language processing as well—but no more. If it is a question of the extent to which certain bilinguals tend to use right-hemisphere-based strategies in language processing (Gordon & Weide, 1983; Vaid, 1983), then we no longer are looking at a phenomenon characteristic of bilinguals (or groups of bilinguals) per se but of some unilinguals as well. The degree of reliance on right-hemisphere strategies is a function of individual cognitive style and, to some extent, a substitute for the use of grammar—a process not limited to bilinguals.

Now, it happens that language teachers and language pathologists are turning more and more to the neuropsychological literature for guidance. This is a commendable endeavor that may ultimately prove fruitful. However, one cannot be too cautious in applying to language rehabilitation or classroom methodology theoretical constructs that are at best hypothetical and often quite controversial. In the face of contradictory experimental results and the total absence of clinical evidence, the claim of less asymmetric language representation and/or processing in bilinguals is unfounded, and should therefore not serve as a basis for researchers in neuropsychology to make any recommendation in the fields of pedagogy, psychiatry or language therapy.

These words of caution are not mere rhetoric. For example, Werntz, et al. (1983) report having observed alternating periods of greater relative amplitudes of EEG activity in one hemisphere, and then in the other. At the same time, measures of airflow in the right and left nostril have shown a similar alternation between the use of each nostril. Rhythms of the nasal cycle and hemispheric cycle have been observed to be tightly coupled. The authors concede that they cannot tell whether the increased EEG amplitudes observed are a reflection of increased or diminished mental activity in the hemisphere contralateral to the active nostril. This does not prevent them from suggesting that "future research in this area may be of clinical relevance in producing a noninvasive approach to selective hemispheric stimulation as a treatment for mental diseases of unilateral cerebral function" (p. 42). Nor does it deter one of the authors (Shannahoff-Khalsa, 1984) from suggesting that, since the balance of hemispheric dominance can be shifted by forcibly altering the phase of the nasal cycle, we could exert control over cognitive functions by forced breathing through the right nostril for 10 to 15 minutes, thus augmenting our language or mathematical skills. It might still be premature to recommend that foreign language teachers require students to block their left nostril to activate their right hemisphere in the hope of forcing language processing in that hemisphere (or the reverse). Remember that by the authors' own admission, we do not know which hemisphere actually increases mental activity.

A few years earlier, in the concluding sentence of their seminal book, Albert and Obler (1978) suggested that a second language might be more easily learned if it were taught through nursery rhymes, music, dance, or techniques employing visuospatial skills. This might be the case, but it would have nothing to do with language (as defined) being acquired via the right hemisphere. It might, possibly, increase the child's positive attitude toward the second language (Schumann, 1998), which in itself would not be an unwelcome consequence. Note that some authors do not hesitate to prescribe banning music from the child's environment on the assumption that any nonlinguistic activity will disrupt the progress of cerebral dominance training (Delacato, 1966).

In sum, to answer the three questions posed at the beginning of this section, (1) It does not seem to be a good idea to force the second language into the right hemisphere; (2) even if it were, we would not know how to bring this about anyway; and (3) it could actually be detrimental, by promoting a process so ineffective that it is quickly abandoned in the acquisition of L1—if in fact it were ever attempted, which is doubtful. No experimental instrument has yet been validated for measuring *degrees* of lateralization of language (qua implicit linguistic competence). Given the absence of any form of clinical evidence of greater right-hemisphere participation in bilingual speakers, it seems most likely that whatever implicit linguistic competence speakers may have in their L2 is represented in the left hemisphere in the same proportion as linguistic competence in unilingual speakers.

Differential localization

While authors from Pitres (1895) to Penfield (1965) have argued against the notion that separate centers are specifically assigned to each language of a polyglot subject, a growing number of contemporary researchers are prepared to consider various kinds of differential representation, including distinct anatomical sites. Some authors feel that there are numerous reasons to believe that cerebral representation of language is not entirely the same in polyglots as in unilinguals (Lecours, Branchereau, & Joanette, 1984), and that it would be surprising if bilingualism had no effect on brain organization (Segalowitz, 1983). The two languages of a bilingual may not be subserved by exactly the same neuronal circuits; it may even be that they are differently lateralized (Lebrun, 1981). The hypothesis of a different location for each language was attributed by Pitres to Scoresby-Jackson (1867), who had merely suggested differential localization along the third frontal convolution as one of at least three possibilities. However, 120 years later, Kim et al. (1997) interpret their neuroimaging evidence exactly in the way hinted at by Scoresby-Jackson: Later-acquired languages might utilize cortical areas adjacent to the site in Broca's area devoted to the native and early-acquired second languages. Other authors propose that the two languages of a bilingual speaker are represented in partly different anatomical areas in the dominant hemisphere, with some overlap (Ojemann & Whitaker, 1978; Rapport et al., 1983). Another possibility is that languages are subserved by different circuits intricately interwoven in the same language areas, so that both are represented in the same area at the gross anatomical level, while still being independently subserved by different neural circuits at the microanatomical level (Paradis, 1977; Roux & Tremoulet, 2002).

A number of hypotheses concerning how representations of two (or more) languages are organized in one brain may be considered. Four of them were examined by Paradis (1981). According to the extended system hypothesis, languages are undifferentiated in their representation, and elements of the various languages are processed as allo-elements. The dual system hypothesis proposes that each language is represented independently in separate systems. In the tripartite system hypothesis, those items that are identical in both languages are represented in one single underlying neural substrate common to both languages, and those that are different each have their own separate representation. (Another form of tripartite system (Lambert & Fillenbaum, 1959) is the assumption that what has been acquired in the same context is stored in a common neurofunctional system and what has been acquired in different contexts is stored in separate neurofunctional systems.) Finally, there is the subsystems hypothesis, whereby bilinguals have two subsets of neural connections, one for each language, within the same cognitive system, namely, the language system. For a schematic representation of these types of organization of two languages in one brain, see Figure 4.1.

```
A B A B B A B A A B              A A A A A    B B B B B
B A B B A B A A B A              A A A A A    B B B B B
B B A B A A B A A B              A A A A A    B B B B B
B B A B A A B A A B              A A A A A    B B B B B
A B A B B A B A A B              A A A A A    B B B B B
A B A B A B A B A B              A A A A A    B B B B B
```

         Extended System   *Dual System*


```
A/B A/B A/B A/B                  A A A A A B B B B B
A/B A/B A/B A/B                  A A A A A B B B B B
A/B A/B A/B A/B                  A A A A A B B B B B
A A A A A    B B B B B           A A A A A B B B B B
A A A A A    B B B B B           A A A A A B B B B B
A A A A A    B B B B B           A A A A A B B B B B
```

         Tripartite System   *Subsystems*

Schematic representation of the various hypothetical organizations of two languages in the same brain. In the extended system, the number of elements is increased but they are stored undifferentiatedly. In the dual system, each language forms an independent system. In the tripartite system, elements identical in both languages (A/B) are stored once, used for languages A and B, and items that differ are stored independently, each in its own system. In the subsystems option, the larger language system contains two subsystems, one for language A, the other for language B. The symbol A represents elements (phonemes, phonological rules, morphosyntactic rules, lexical items) of language A, the symbol B represents elements of Language B, and A/B symbolizes the fact that these elements are equivalent and belong to the grammar of both language A and language B.

Fig. 4.1. *Schematic representation of various models of the organization of languages*

Only the fourth is compatible with all patterns of recovery as well as with the bilingual's ability to mix languages at each level of linguistic structure. Parallel impairment can be interpreted as the result of damage to, or interference with, the linguistic system as a whole, and differential impairment as the result of greater damage to, or interference with, one of the subsystems. Each language, as a subsystem, is susceptible to selective pathological inhibition. Yet, subjects with intact brains may choose to alternate the use of elements of one or the other linguistic subsystem or to quasi-simultaneously use elements of both. The frequency of code-switching and code-mixing may be an important factor in how the two languages are processed. Frequent mixing may lower interlanguage inhibition. It may also lead to the adoption of mixed or amalgamated strategies for sentence interpretation (i.e., using the same cues for both languages, regardless of their respective validity—see Wulfeck et al., 1986; MacWhinney, 1997).

Green and Newman (1985) rightly point out that, whichever of these hypotheses is adopted, we still need to characterize how items of each language are selected. However, the means of selection need not differ from that used by unilinguals to select a baby-talk word, for example, rather than a familiar-register or a formal-register word, given the appropriate circumstances. If choosing to speak one language rather than another requires the speaker to specify a language "tag" (Green, 1998), then a similar "tag" is necessary for unilinguals to select items from among their various registers and, within the selected one, from among possible synonyms, as well as between active, passive, or topicalized constructions (Paradis, 1980a). The selection mechanism between languages need not be different from that operating within each language. In other words, the selection mechanism used by a bilingual need not differ from that used by a unilingual. A direct-access hypothesis (i.e., access without the necessity of an additional language tag to first identify which language is spoken—see Chapter 7) is definitely consonant with the facts of comprehension (Grosjean & Soares, 1986). In production, the same selection process used by unilinguals suffices to account for bilinguals' choice of words, constructions, or pronunciation (accent), allowing them to choose to speak one language (unilingual mode), to freely mix (bilingual mode), or to use syntactic structures of one when speaking the other, with or without the pronunciation of the other (for special effects).

The language tag, as conceived in the 1960s, i.e., awareness of language membership, is a product of metalinguistic knowledge. In on-line processing, language awareness is of the same nature and as unconscious as the process that allows a unilingual speaker to understand (or select) the appropriate word in a given context. The process of selecting a Russian word by a Latvian-Russian bilingual person is the same as the process that allows a unilingual Russian speaker to select among the indefinite, almost unlimited, possibilities for encoding a given message. In order to name an object on confrontation, competing synonyms within the same language must be inhibited, just as translation equivalents (and their synonyms) must be. There is therefore no greater need to postulate a language tag specific to bilinguals than to postulate a bilingual switch or bilingual monitor, as will be examined in greater detail in Chapter 7. The mere fact that the various languages form subsystems is sufficient to account for their susceptibility to selective inhibition. Inhibition is neither necessarily global (i.e., affecting the whole system) nor total (i.e., not admitting of degree).

Of course, the processing of synonyms and of translation equivalents is not *exactly* the same. Language does play a role in their retrieval, given the raising of the threshold of the non-selected language. However, if the activation threshold of the translation equivalent happens to be lower for reasons of recency or greater frequency of use, then a translation equivalent may have the same chances of being activated as a synonym in the selected language. This is why the non-selected language must be inhibited (i.e., its threshold must be raised) during confrontation naming. Cross-linguistic Stroop test interference illustrates how difficult it is to totally inhibit the non-selected language.

Many researchers interpret selective or differential recovery of one or more languages as suggesting non-overlapping cortical representation (Gomez-Tortoza et al., 1995; Marian, Spivey, & Hirsch, 2003). Yet, the two cases cited in support by Marian et al. (namely, Nilipour & Ashayeri, 1989; Paradis & Goldblum, 1989), referring to the alternating temporary unavailability of one language, constitute prime data *against* the notion of differential localization. A more plausible explanation would be that the patients' languages were unavailable at different periods of time, not because one language, located at a different site, was selectively physically damaged, but because they were alternately physiologically inhibited (Paradis, 1996), a possibility granted by Gomez-Tortosa et al. (1996).

Goral, et al. (2002) report that cortical stimulation and imaging techniques suggest the existence of interspersed networks for multiple languages in the left hemisphere that largely overlap, and that these findings are confirmed by event-related potential (ERP) studies that report overlap in processing in proficient bilinguals, with greater differences for less proficient bilinguals. These findings no longer seem controversial. What is now required is a neurolinguistically informed interpretation of the findings. The proposed neurolinguistic theory of bilingualism predicts the overlap for proficient bilinguals and the differences for less proficient individuals. It also specifies the nature of the functions subserved by the areas of increased activation.

In a nutshell, the same cerebral areas are recruited by bilinguals to subserve the same functions as unilinguals, and the observed differences reflect the greater reliance on some components of verbal communication in order to compensate for lacunae in automatized implicit linguistic competence in their L2. Compensatory strategies rely on an increased use (relative to unilinguals) of certain cognitive functions (e.g., metalinguistic knowledge, pragmatics) and hence on the cerebral mechanisms that subserve these functions (parahippocampal gyri, right-hemisphere areas). Moreover, some of these functions are explicit and therefore rely on the use of cerebral mechanisms associated with attention and control (anterior cingulate gyrus, head of caudate nucleus).

The theory also predicts that studies that use single words should not find differences between unilinguals and bilinguals, irrespective of their degree of fluency in L2, whereas in language comprehension and production tasks, differences should increase as proficiency decreases; there should also be greater overall heterogeneity among bilingual speakers since different individuals use different compensatory mechanisms to different extents. In addition, because different bilingual individuals have internalized different components of implicit linguistic competence to different extents, the patterns of activation within the perisylvian classical language areas should also be heterogeneous, contrasting with the great homogeneity of implicit linguistic competence in languages acquired in infancy. These phenomena will be further discussed in Chapter 6.

In terms of a model based on control of resources (Green, 1986, 2002), in parallel recovery, degree of inhibition is about equal for each language (parallel distribution of resources); in differential recovery, one language is more strongly inhibited than the other (differential distribution); in antagonistic recovery, the inhibition switches from one language to the other, and if it does so repeatedly, the available language alternates (alternating distribution); in successive recovery, one language is inhibited until it is eventually disinhibited, while the other remains available (temporary selective distribution); in selective recovery, one language remains inhibited (permanent selective distribution); in blending recovery, neither language can be sufficiently inhibited to allow the use of one language at a time (uncontrolled distribution); in selective aphasia, inhibition is restricted to one of the languages (selective distribution).

In terms of activation threshold, in parallel recovery, the activation threshold is evenly raised in each language; in differential recovery, the activation threshold of one language is raised higher than that of the other; in antagonistic recovery, the activation threshold of one language is lowered while that of the other is concurrently raised, and if the pattern of higher and lower activation levels alternates repeatedly, the patient exhibits an alternating antagonistic recovery; in successive recovery, at first, the activation threshold of one language remains raised beyond access until such time as it is eventually lowered, while the threshold remains low enough for access in the other; in selective recovery, the activation threshold of one language remains too high for it to be activated, though possibly not high enough to prevent comprehension; in blending recovery, the activation threshold of neither language is sufficiently raised to allow the use of one language at a time; in selective aphasia, the activation threshold of one of the languages is normal (i.e., unaffected by pathology and remains a function of the usual factors of frequency, recency, etc.), while that of the other (or parts thereof) is somewhat raised, making it more difficult to access.

In the proposed neurofunctional model, each language is represented as a subsystem of the language system. When one language is selected for expression, the activation threshold of the other language is raised so as to avoid interference (i.e., the inappropriate activation of an item from the other language system). However, it is not raised so high that it could not be activated by an incoming verbal stimulus that impinges on the auditory sensory system and sends impulses to the corresponding representation. (This permits comprehension of one language even when the other is being spoken, and the Stroop effect.) Then, within the selected language, the activation threshold of the nonselected items is raised while the selected item is activated.

One controversial point is whether both languages can be active at the same time in the brain of a healthy bilingual speaker, or whether one is inhibited while the other is activated. Seemingly contradictory evidence emerges from experimental studies (e.g., Altenberg & Cairns, 1983; Scarborough, Gerard & Cortese, 1984). Green (1986) adopts the view that a language system (or any part thereof) can be in one of three states: dormant, activated, and selected, and that the unselected language may nevertheless be active. Likewise, in terms of the proposed model of activation threshold levels, the unselected language is not *totally* inhibited. Its activation threshold is simply raised high enough to prevent self-activation, but not so high as to preclude comprehension. Involuntary mixing is seen as a failure to exercise full control over a (relatively) intact system. A lack of control over the selection of appropriate items is at the origin of the production, in a sentence, of an unsuitable word that is either phonologically or semantically related to the target (a slip of the tongue). A similar situation prevails when a bilingual speaker inadvertently uses a word from one language while speaking the other.

Speech errors in the form of blends may occur occasionally in healthy unilingual speakers (e.g., the production of *assumably* or *presumedly* as a consequence of the co-activation of *presumably* and *assumedly*), or, to use a real and verifiable example, the production (ironically in the context of a discussion of inhibition and control of speech selection mechanisms) by Carr (1998, p. 84), of "I have misunderstand" (probably a blend between "I did not understand" and "I have misunderstood"). This also happens frequently in the form of paraphasias in the speech of patients with Wernicke's aphasia, where not only word forms are blended, but entire phrases, leading to paragrammatism. Similarly, bilingual persons with aphasia have been reported to mix their languages at the word level—for example, one patient produced *ochor*, a blend of German *Ahorn* and Czech *javor* ("maple") (Leischner, 1943)—and mixing words from the other language into their sentences.

As emphasized by François Grosjean, bilinguals move in and out of various speech modes when speaking to different interlocutors (Grosjean, 1989, 1995, 1997, 1998; Soares & Grosjean, 1984; Grosjean & Miller, 1994). Depending on whether they are conversing with unilinguals or with other bilinguals, the activation threshold of the language not currently in use will be raised to a different degree. For bilinguals who are used to constantly switching in their speech community, this threshold is likely to be lower than for bilingual individuals who are not used to switching back and forth.

Conclusion

There is no evidence to suggest that what is expected to be measured by experimental psycholinguistic methods (from dichotic listening to time sharing), namely the language system, is less lateralized in bilingual than in unilingual speakers. If these testing procedures were sensitive to anything other than the language system, such as pragmatics, they would be considered invalid since their purpose is to measure language. However, it is very unlikely, given the stimuli used in these experiments (i.e., digits, isolated syllables or single words without context), that pragmatics could be tapped (it is even questionable to what extent the results obtained with such techniques could be extended to the language system as a whole). There is no sound rationale for suspecting that bilingual speakers' language system should be less asymmetrically represented than that of unilinguals. In fact, there is no valid experimental evidence or clinical documentation of a difference in the asymmetrical representation of language functions between bilinguals and unilinguals.

Nor is there any evidence that the languages of bilinguals are each represented in a different locus in the brain. Both language systems seem to be represented as distinct microanatomical subsystems located in the same gross anatomical areas. To the extent that speakers of a second language have gaps in their implicit linguistic competence, they compensate by relying more heavily than unilinguals on metalinguistic knowledge and pragmatic elements. These differences are quantitative, not qualitative: the very same cerebral mechanisms are used, albeit to different extents. To the extent that they use compensatory strategies, late L2 speakers will rely more heavily on certain cerebral areas (hyppocampal gyri, frontal lobes, right hemisphere) but this does not mean that any implicit linguistic competence they have acquired is represented in areas other than the classical language areas. The cerebral representation of linguistic competence in the two languages may nevertheless be distinct at the microanatomical level and constitute neurofunctional subsystems subserved by dedicated neural circuits, as discussed in the next chapter.

CHAPTER 5

Neurofunctional modularity

The brain is not an undifferentiated mass. It is differentiated not only at the gross anatomical level but, more importantly, at the cytoarchitectural and biochemical levels. Different areas begin postnatal maturation at different times and develop at different rates. Neurology is moving in the direction of discovering more and more function-specific nuclei. For example, "rather than an amorphous collection of lacework, i.e., a 'reticulum,' the reticular formation turns out to be a collection of identifiable nuclei of neurons, each having specific functions to play" (Damasio, 1999, p. 246). Neville, Mills and Lawson (1992) suggest different neural subsystems with different sensitive periods.

It appears that language (*qua* implicit linguistic competence) is represented as a neurofunctional system divided into a number of neurofunctional modules, which respectively subserve phonology, morphosyntax and semantics; each module is subdivided into as many subsystems as there are languages spoken by the individual. This description of subsystems applies only to those portions of the languages that have been acquired incidentally and stored as implicit computational procedures. As discussed in Chapter 1, language itself is part of a larger system, the verbal communication system, which, in addition, comprises at least pragmatics (itself very likely constituted of modules, though this aspect has not yet been investigated as extensively as linguistic competence), metalinguistic knowledge and affect (which provides motivation).

Characteristics of neurofunctional modules

Neurofunctional modules are isolable (that is, selectively susceptible to impairment and/or inhibition) and computationally autonomous (i.e., the internal structure and computational processes of one module are independent of those of other modules), have a specific *purpose*, and function as a *component* of a larger unit. The output of one may serve as the input to another, or may be used in conjunction with the output of another, but the internal function of one module does not interact (or *a fortiori* interfere) with the internal function of another. Each module has access only to the *output* of another. The internal structure of one component has no impact on the internal structure of another (e.g., the structure of syntax has no influence on the structure of phonology; the algorithms of mathematics have no influence on specific language structures). For example, the phonological system of a language is independent of whether the language has a Subject-Verb-Object or Subject-Object-Verb word order. A language may have vowel harmony whether or not it has a rich inflectional morphology.

No external event of any kind can influence the underlying syntactic computational procedures—pragmatics, for instance, may influence the choice of one (say, a passive construction) over another (say, a topicalized object construction) but will not alter the procedures that lead to the generation of the passive. It is in this sense that the procedural memory for what linguists describe as syntax is computationally autonomous.

Neurofunctional modules are functionally independent, domain-specific, informationally encapsulated, and have a characteristic pattern of development. They may also be represented and/or processed in specific neuroanatomical locations, as evidenced by doubly dissociated selective impairment consistently correlated with specific lesion sites.

The neurofunctional modular system for language is susceptible to selective impairment (aphasia). The fact that other cognitive deficits (apraxia, agnosia) may occur (and often do occur) with aphasia is not theoretically relevant; so do toothaches. What *is* important is that aphasia can occur *without* memory deficits, agnosia or apraxia; that syntactic deficits *can* occur without concomitant phonological deficits; that kana or kanji *can* be selectively impaired in Japanese readers, etc. In other words, neurofunctional systems are *isolable* by pathology.

Some authors object to the use of the term "modularity" on the grounds that one or more characteristics depart from Fodor's (1983) original definition. To begin with, the set of criteria for modularity is not carved in stone (see Juszyk & Cohen, 1985), nor was it meant to be by Jerry Fodor, who presented it as a potboiler, a programmatic sketch (Fodor, 1985). There is no reason to be more Fodorian than Fodor himself, especially when one explores *neurofunctional* modularity, rather than the modularity of the mind, the discussion of which is at a different level of abstraction. If one is allergic to the term "module" on account of its historical baggage, it may be called something else, as long as it is characterized as a dedicated, structurally independent system, whose internal structure is impervious to the influence of other systems, from which it may nevertheless receive inputs, and to which it may provide outputs.

In order to avoid a barren terminological war, readers are welcome to substitute any label they prefer, such as "isolable subcomponent" or a combination of megasystem, system, subsystem and sub-subsystem, but they may find it heuristically convenient to use the phrase "neurofunctional module," with criteria slightly (and explicitly) modified from Fodor's characteristics, as they are typically understood in neuropsychology. (See Shallice (1988), who considers the Fodorian criteria too specific and the systems to which they apply, too limited.)

Neurofunctional modules do share the following properties with Fodor's (1983) modules: They are domain-specific (by virtue of being subserved by procedural memory—of which task-specificity is a characteristic property); they are mandatory (automatic computational procedures, such as those subserving syntax or phonology, are obligatorily applied: one cannot choose not to understand a sentence in a language for which one has implicit linguistic competence); their computational procedures are implicit (inaccessible to consciousness); they are fast (given that their processes are automatic, some of them lasting only a few milliseconds); they are informationally encapsulated and autonomous in their internal structure and functioning (e.g., music has no impact on face recognition) though, in the case of the language system, it is related to other cognitive, motor and sensory systems from which it receives inputs and to which it feeds outputs. Mature systems are associated with fixed neural architecture (albeit sometimes in multiple locations, but nevertheless all dedicated to a specific function), and they exhibit characteristic and specific breakdown patterns. Their ontogenetic development exhibits a characteristic pace and sequencing. (When two languages are acquired simultaneously, each is acquired in accordance with its own sequencing schedule: e.g., case suffixes may be acquired in one language before the equivalent prepositions in the other.)

Innateness

Innateness is one characteristic that is not considered a necessary attribute of neurofunctional modules. Sperber and Wilson (2002) agree that a cognitive ability may become modularized in the course of cognitive development (though they assume that many modular structures have a strong genetic component). Whether or not the structure that subserves implicit linguistic competence is innate, by the time it is operative, it has been established as an independent module.

According to Gerrans (2002), evolutionary psychology assumes that higher order cognitive processes exhibit a modular structure, with modules that have specific domains, exploit specialized algorithms or data stores and may rely on localized neural substrates. Gerrans then argues against an innate theory-of-mind module. However, the cerebral circuits specialized for processing certain types of computations need not be exhaustively innately specified ("pre-wired") but may develop in reaction to the appropriate stimuli in areas of the brain that are most suitable for the purpose by virtue of their genetically programmed general predispositions (e.g., their cytoarchitecture, motor and sensory connections, etc.).

The notion of neurofunctional modules presented here leaves open the extent and specificity of genetic determinism. (See Samuels (1998) and Gerrans (2002) concerning various types of modules.) Whether a system is hardwired (Chomsky, 1965; Fodor, 1983) or emerges through patterns of developmental experience (Geary & Huffman, 2002), once it has been acquired, it constitutes a module which attains neurofunctional independence. Neurofunctional modularity does not entail innateness. Innateness is compatible with it but not necessary. By the time a cognitive system is operative, it has been established as an independent module. Whether the communication system is genetically hardwired or an epigenetic outcome, it is neurofunctionally modular. It will be argued that modularity is in fact a general feature of neurofunctional organization. Note that the fact that some individuals process language in brain regions other than the classical language areas, as reported in neuroimaging studies, is not a priori evidence against the innateness (and hardwiring) of implicit competence or in favor of cerebral cognitive equipotentiality. One would need to demonstrate that areas active during verbal communication indeed support implicit competence rather than compensatory mechanisms such as the ones used by individuals with genetic dysphasia and incipient bilinguals who learn a second language in formal instructional settings.

Connectionism, distributed systems and neurofunctional modules

Distributed representations are often taken as a refutation of the modularity of a doubly dissociated function. There are two counterarguments to this proposal: (1) Connectionist models actually end up with modules; and (2) they lack biological plausibility—behavioral dissociations can often be shown to actually rely on different neural substrates (regardless of what computers can do).

In connectionist so-called neural networks, learning is said to result in the adjustment of the weight of connections between units, thereby in effect establishing dedicated pathways, the hallmark of neurofunctional modules. Dedicated weighted connections for a particular task constitute the connectionist equivalent of a module, a different metaphor for a modular system. Given that in the steady state, a specific set of connections is activated (and not others) for a particular stimulus, this particular set *is* the neurofunctional representation corresponding to the stimulus. Computer networks eventually build a discrete system of connections (defined in terms of weights) that correspond to a stimulus (or a range of stimuli). In other words, a number of specific connections are dedicated to subserving a particular representation (or set of representations). Once a system has established weighted connections, that is, dedicated pathways that perform a specific task, it has substantially developed a module, namely, a portion of the general network that is uniquely devoted to the performance of a specific task (even if it started off as a tabula rasa). The fact that it was arrived at on the basis of statistical probabilities is not relevant to the issue of modularity (though it does bear on innateness, or initial hardwiring). The notions of modularity and innateness should be separated. Computer "neural networks" may be used as arguments against nativism (i.e., hardwiring as the only possible explanation) but not against neurofunctional modularity resulting from neural development in response to experience.

Distributed representations or patterns of multiple activations are not random activations, but activation of the relevant neural nodes. Nodes and their connections are the item's representation. Thus a neurofunctional module may be represented as a number of connected cerebral areas which, *together*, are dedicated to subserving a particular function. Damage to any part of this dedicated network will result in impairment of the function, whereas damage to any other area will not. For instance, in a Japanese-English bilingual individual with aphasia, depending on the role of the affected neurofunctional module, either a component of the function (e.g., the syntax module, or the whole Japanese subsystem) or the entire cognitive function (language itself, i.e., both English and Japanese) will be affected. Such a distributed network is not incompatible with neurofunctional modularity in that each language is associated with fixed, dedicated neural architecture, although it may be represented in numerous interconnected locations.

Most artificial intelligence models have no biological plausibility condition built into them. The fact that a computer may reach a double dissociation through parallel distributed processing is no indication that this is how the brain does it, especially when it is known that the two cerebral functions of interest (e.g., declarative and procedural memory) are each subserved by a different set of anatomical structures.

Both overt and covert recognition may be elicited by a lesioned distributed computer neural network (Farah, O'Reilley & Vecera, 1993); in humans, however, they are impaired by lesions of different neuroanatomical structures and dissociated by biochemical agents that act upon different neural sites in proportion to their number of relevant receptors. It has now been sufficiently established that the hippocampal-amygdalar system is crucial for the obtainment of new declarative memories, though not for the acquisition of new motor or cognitive skills. Conversely, lesions in the perisyslvian area will cause aphasia (the impairment of procedural memory for language functions) without loss of declarative memory. Recall that the patient reported by Paradis, Goldblum and Abidi (1982) was able to correctly specify which objects she was able to name the day before, and which not, although her word-finding difficulty persisted.

Müller (1996) concedes that artificial networks are caricatures of biological brains and that, unlike most connectionist models, brains are not equipotential networks, but he cautions against equating regional specialization with modularity. Nevertheless, whereas regional specialization is not a necessary feature, it is often concomitent with other characteristics that together strongly suggest neurofunctional modularity.

Furthermore, producing double dissociation in distributed systems is not as straightforward as is often made out to be: A careful analysis of how these connectionist models operate reveals that there are in fact no reliable double dissociations in the models (Bullinaria & Chater, 1996). Even if it were possible for a fully distributed computer system to produce double dissociations by using a fully distributed system, we have ample evidence that this is not the way the brain actually does it.

The fact that a simple recurrent connectionist network, trained on 100,000 presentations of three-word SVO sentences of two artificial microlanguages of 12 words each, can reflect the overall separation of these two languages (French, 1998) does not necessarily mean that this is the way the brain actually separates two languages. In the real human brain, the proposed theory reasons that there are necessarily two lexicons because the lexical items are tied to specific language systems. The translation equivalent of a count noun in one language may be a mass noun in another. The translation equivalent of a verb that requires two arguments in one language may require three in another. The translation equivalent of a transitive verb in one language may be intransitive in another and take reflexive morphology in a third. Lexical items are therefore inseparable from the morphosyntax of the language subsystem to which they belong. The morphosyntactic features of lexical items are no less language-specific than their semantic features, and for the same reason must be represented within their respective language subsystems. The concept of transitivity may nevertheless be retained when the language-specific transitive feature attached to a particular verb is lost (through aphasia or attrition). French's experiment shows that a computer can (albeit in a very limited way:

the complexity of the human lexicon is qualitatively different from that of the vocabulary sample used in the experiment) obtain similar results by procedures other than those used by the brain. It does not, however, show that bilingual memory is organized in the brain as a single distributed lexicon rather than as two separately accessible lexicons corresponding to each language.

Noncontiguity

While acknowledging that Fodor does not have a monopoly on the use of "module," Müller (1996) objects to calling entities that are noncontiguous or distributed "modules." Neurofunctional modularity holds that a specific neural substrate subserves a particular representation, irrespective of its actual physical form, i.e., whether it is a specific set of neurons in a particular cortical location (Ojemann & Whitaker, 1978), a specific neural network (Lamb, 1998), or a specific set of neurons distributed over various specific cortical and subcortical areas (Pulvermüller, 1992). The representation could therefore be subserved in the form of either a circumscribed anatomical location or a dedicated set of connected neurons, which activates the representation when it reaches threshold.

The system of representations is considered to be neurofunctionally modular in that it is distinct from other neurofunctional modular systems, reacts only to certain specific types of stimuli, and works in accordance with its own set of computational procedures, which differ from, and are not permeable to, the computational procedures of other modules. Each neurofunctional module is independently susceptible to inhibition and selectively vulnerable to pathology. The output of one may serve as the input of another, or they may synergically function in parallel, but they do not interfere with each other's internal structure.

A neurofunctional module need not be *localized* in one specific anatomical area. It may be represented in a dedicated network involving corticocortical, limbic, basal ganglia and corticothalamic interconnected areas. There is no reason why neurofunctional modules could not have neurally noncontiguous or dedicated distributed systems as substrates. Information can be processed simultaneously and in parallel in various parts of the brain, and yet—or rather, thereby—constitute a neurofunctional module.

Even though everything is eventually connected to everything else, some well-defined portions of the overall network are responsible for specific functions. Parts of the global network constitute systems which may contain subsystems that possess their own unique set of procedures. Hence components of mental processes are hypothesized to be represented in specific (albeit possibly multiple) regions of the brain.

Micro/macro-anatomy

Two languages in the same brain are observably functionally independent. Both normal use and aphasias amply demonstrate this (Paradis, 1987c). However, there is no evidence of different gross anatomical localization (at least not between two languages acquired before the age of five). Yet languages, like any other mental phenomena, must be supported by some biophysical neural substrate. The two language subsystems are independent in their respective internal structure (their content), their selective activation, and their selective breakdown (or availability) in pathological states. They behave in every way as isolable modules. It is therefore not unreasonable to expect a bilingual's language subsystems to be represented in the same macro-anatomical cerebral area, but differentiated at the micro-anatomical level.

Gross anatomical localization is not a necessary property of neuro-functional modules. A module forms a subsystem, and relies on a specific network of neurons. Such a network may include cortical and subcortical components which may be distributed over many areas. One language subsystem may even intertwine with the other in the same anatomical area, as is likely to be the case with two acquired languages. The two languages of a bilingual speaker appear to be micro-anatomically independent within the same macro-anatomical areas.

In earlier reports of preoperative electrical stimulation of the brain, a few sites responding to only one language were identified at the periphery of the language area (Ojemann & Whitaker 1978; Rapport, Tan & Whitaker, 1983) It could be argued that, because of the characteristics of the technique (bipolar electrodes 5 mm. apart, with 5-mm. diffraction at each pole, thus interfering with a 50-mm^2 area), one could not be sure that successive applications stimulated identical areas. Moreover, because such language-specific areas were reported only at the periphery of the language zone, it might have been the case that the stimulation interfered with language only some of the time, with the electrode field falling just outside the language zone at others. However, an increasing number of cases of specific sites well within the classical language areas that respond to only one of the patients' languages have been recently published (Roux & Trémoulet, 2002). This might be a first step toward empirical evidence that two languages are represented as independent subsystems intertwined within the same area. In fact, given the capacity of bilinguals to speak one language fluently without interference from the other, and the fact that bilingual individuals with aphasia may recover one language and not the other, researchers are beginning to realize that, to the extent that phonological, morphosyntactic and lexical structures differ between languages, distinct neural circuits may independently subserve each language within the same cortical areas (Dehaene, 1999; Hernandez et al., 2001b; Halsband et al., 2002). To the extent that the meaning of a word differs from that of its translation equivalent, their lexical semantic representations will probably not activate entirely overlapping micro-anatomical substrates at the conceptual representational level. To the extent that phonemes and prosody differ between the two languages, phonotactic representations will probably overlap the least. The spatial resolution of current neuroimaging techniques is not sufficient to speak to the issue and it is unlikely that methods based on blood flow and metabolism ever will.

As pointed out by Marshall (1984), localization per se is not an issue, only the nature of the localization. As has long been recognized, cognitive skill modules may be characterized by mere distinctness of cells and fibers which, however, so far as position is concerned, may be interblended with others having different functions (Bastian, 1880). Such anatomically distributed modules are still distinct functional systems that rely on some specific material substrate, whether cells, synapses, groups of cells in particular assemblies, or even a specific pattern of firing of a dedicated distributed network of cells. The point is that cognitive skills are subserved by neurofunctional modules, i.e., isolable systems with their own internal structure and content. Mountcastle (1978) similarly conceives of distributed anatomical modules as participating in several functional systems. Brain damage may lead to modular dysfunction in a distributed neurofunctional module by inhibition rather than physical destruction of the neural substrate (Pitres, 1895).

Dedicated micro-anatomical circuits within the same general cortical area may be figuratively likened to the hands that each represent a subsystem of the "upper limb extremities" system. When the hands clasp each other with fingers intertwined, the fingers of each hand retain their individuality and can be wiggled independently. You may choose to wiggle either the fingers of the left hand or those of the right hand while they remain intertwined (with the hands clasping). Yet, if someone hits your fingers with a hammer, both sets of fingers will get smashed. If you paralyze only one hand by injecting it with a local anesthetic, you will inhibit one of the two subsystems: you may continue to wiggle only the fingers of the hand that has not been inhibited. In this analogy, each hand stands for a subsystem. Like the intertwined fingers, the circuits subserving the two cognitive subsystems may together be physically damaged by a large lesion or each may be independently inhibited by a physiological cause. Just as the fingers of both hands would be affected by epidural anesthesia, both subsystems (e.g., English and French) are inhibited when the system (language) as a whole is inhibited. And the English sub-system, like one of the hands, may be selectively inhibited.

Neurofunctional modularity does not entail localization in any specific gross anatomical region; it need not be a "single, bounded, and compact region of the brain" (Dick et al., 2001, p. 784). Distributiveness does not preclude dedicated neural networks. Once the cognitive system has been established, we have a dedicated neurofunctional module the internal structure of which can break down, not only as a result of physical destruction of a portion of the network (the hammer blow of the fingers analogy) but also as a result of physiological phenomena brought about by a depletion of resources or a raising of the activation threshold (the local anesthesia of the analogy). These phenomena result from a combination of effects involving neurotransmitter levels, electrochemical events, etc. In view of the corollary to Murphy's Law, it is not surprising that a system can break down in similar ways, whatever the etiology, in patients and in neurologically intact individuals under conditions of stress or fatigue. The same portions of the network are involved. The findings presented by Dick et al. (2001) do not provide evidence against a domain-specific organ localized in a dedicated network (i.e., a neurofunctional module) for grammar. Their argument is against a single gross anatomical location of the 19th-century "language center" type.

Neurofunctional modules are isolable but interactive

Obviously, the language system is not isolated. It is connected more or less indirectly to all the other cognitive functions, in one way or another, as well as to the sensory and motor functions. However, it is isolable by pathology and can be selectively inhibited, while all other functions remain unimpaired. Its internal structure and function are independent of those of other systems from which it receives input (e.g., the message to be transmitted from the nonlinguistic cognitive system) and to which it sends outputs (e.g., the articulatory and phonatory or digitomanual effectors that will render the verbal output in speech, sign or writing). The conceptual system generates a message to be encoded verbally. In keeping with the relevant pragmatic considerations, it selects the lexical and syntactic elements that best fit the intended message from among the possibilities offered by the grammar. The selection of items within the implicit linguistic competence system thus depends on input from other systems (e.g., the pragmatic system that chooses *tu* over *vous* in a particular context), but this does not alter the morphosyntax of *tu* or *vous* or their default definitions. The same is true of the choice of topicalized, pseudo-cleft, active or passive syntactic constructions, or the placement of phonological stress on a personal pronoun. The choices are limited by what is available in the grammar. For example, to place emphasis on the subject pronoun in English, one resorts to phonological prominence (stressing the pronoun). Since phonological prominence is not an option in French, a different means must be selected, such as morphosyntactic prominence (e.g., the use of a strong pronoun—*lui* instead of the clitic *il*). The same is true of modules *within* the language system. For example, a syntactic feature may be marked phonologically (e.g., in English, stress on the first syllable of a two-syllable noun, stress on the second syllable of (or in addition to) a two-syllable verb: súbject/subjéct), but the syntax can only select from among the available features in phonology. This option, not being available in French phonology, cannot be selected by French syntax. Hence, in French, morphological features will be selected instead, generally derivational or inflectional affixes, e.g., sujet / *as*sujet*tir*, transport/transport*er*. (These are among the kinds of cross-language equivalence alluded to in Chapter 3, section on assessment of bilingual aphasia.)

Whereas each module depends on other systems for its input and the implementation of its output, it nevertheless does not depend on other systems for the contents of its representations or the structure of its computational procedures. It is in this sense that the neurofunctional system for implicit linguistic competence may be called a module. It does not have to be innate, and does not need to be subserved by a single anatomical area; when it is represented in more than one area, the various loci and their dedicated connections together constitute the system, i.e., a neurofunctional module, independent of all other neurofunctional modules. Although other modules may interact with the language module, they do not affect the nature of its computational procedures. The internal functioning (i.e., the implementation of system-specific types of computational procedures) is not affected by the internal structure or even the output of another module (except for the selection for activation of a target item within the system, such as the choice of one particular form existing in the system over another).

Neurofunctional modularity and independence from other cognitive systems do not imply that language develops in isolation and has no effect on the development of other cognitive systems. In all probability, language influences the development of cognitive skills—albeit indirectly—as illustrated by the long-term effects of language delay, even when the language catches up later (Mogford-Bevan, 2000) and in deaf children without access to (sign) language during the period of cognitive development, i.e., before they enter school (Garfield, Peterson, & Perry, 2001).

Like all other neurofunctional systems, the implicit linguistic competence system requires glucose and oxygen in order to function. To this extent, the language system is dependent upon the operations of the heart (which, by the way, are controlled by other parts of the brain). But no one would wish to argue that the heart (or the brain mechanism that controls heartbeat) is part of the language system, any more than the reticular formation that regulates the degree of vigilance necessary to use language. The human organism is a whole, but you listen with your ears and you see with your eyes. The structure of the ear differs from that of the eye. The brain controls everything, but each separate function is controlled by a separate mechanism (or set of mechanisms, each making a specific contribution); the contents and structure of their representations/processes differ in each case, so that each is suited for its unique purpose. The general cerebral principles that govern all modules (including cognitive modules) may be the same, but each modular system is structured to suit its specific purpose.

Neurofunctional subsystems

Language is a system of systems. The language system (i.e., implicit linguistic competence) consists of independent subsystems or functional modules (e.g., phonology, morphosyntax, semantics). In bilingual speakers, each such modular language system contains two or more subsystems, one for each language. For example, the morphosyntax module contains as many subsystems as the person speaks languages. The surface realization of these systems (their output) may differ: A beneficiary may be marked by the dative case in one language, a preposition in another, and word order in a third. But the morphosyntax of each language performs computational procedures of the same nature (as opposed to the procedures performed by phonology, for instance). Correspondingly, the phonology of each language deals with the classification of articulatory and perceptual phonetics (i.e., characteristics of speech sounds) and not syntactic features. The quality and length of vowels and the voice onset time of consonants may differ between languages, but the phonology of both languages organizes language sounds. Phonology (subdivided into subsystems corresponding to the phonology of the various languages) constitutes a system that can be selectively inhibited. The same goes for morphosyntax. The phonological systems of the various languages spoken by an individual thus form a natural class: namely that person's phonology module. The different morphosyntactic systems form the morphosyntax, and so on. The phonological module of each language functions in accordance with parametric variations of general principles of phonology, the syntactic module functions in accordance with parametric variations of general principles of syntax, and so on.

But English—made up, among other things, of phonology, morphosyntax and lexical semantics—also forms a natural class, also susceptible to selective inhibition: a language. For these reasons, as illustrated in Figure 5.3, there are two sets of subsystems: One, represented vertically (Fig. 5.1), corresponding to each language (e.g., English, Japanese); the other, represented horizontally (Fig. 5.2), corresponding to the components of language as a cognitive function (phonology, morphosyntax, lexical semantics).

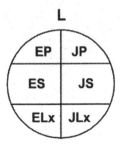

Figure 5.1. *Language subsystems*

The languages of a bilingual speaker, each of which forms a subsystem within the various language neurofunctional modules. Modules P, S, Lx; submodules: EP, JP, ES, JS, ELx, JLx.

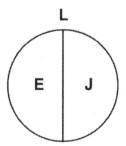

Figure 5.2. *Language modules*

Schematic representation of the language system (L) comprising 2 subsystems: English (E) and Japanese (J).

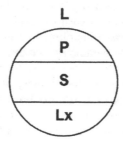

Figure 5.3. *Language modules*

Language as a collection of modules (neurofunctional subsystems): For the sake of simplicity, only three modules are represented: phonology (P), syntax (S) and lexical semantics (Lx).

A subsystem is neurofunctionally modular in that its internal structure differs from that of other subsystems (i.e., the computational procedures underlying English are not the same as those underlying Japanese in an English-Japanese bilingual speaker) and they are doubly dissociable—and indeed often *are* dissociated—by pathology (Fig. 5.4). It is also assumed that when one subsystem is active (say, English), the other (say, Japanese) is inhibited (i.e., its activation threshold is raised) in order to prevent interference. (In this section, the terms *system*, *subsystem*, and *module* may be used somewhat indiscriminately for the sake of a smoother exposition, in order to avoid ever-expanding phrases as a system is subdivided into subsystems, sub-subsystems, modules, and so on.)

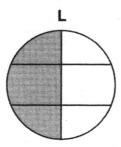

Figure 5.4. *Inhibition of a language subsystem*

One entire language is selectively inhibited.

The subsystems hypothesis is compatible with (and may in fact explain) instances of dynamic interference, nonce borrowings, and mixing. There can be no interference between the phonology module (or neurofunctional subsystem) and the syntax subsystem because each one deals with items and processes of a different nature and their underlying computational procedures are of a different kind, subject to different types of constraints. Rules that bear on nasalization or palatalization of certain consonants in particular phonological environments do not bear on theta-role assignment within or between languages. But both morphosyntactic modules (or subsystems) do have to assign theta-roles (mark the agent, patient, beneficiary, etc.), whether realized through word order, case inflection, or prepositions. The commonality of the nature of syntax across languages is captured by the notion of principles and parameters in Universal Grammar theory. (This does not imply that grammatical knowledge is necessarily innate, only that the general notion of principles instantiated in the form of parameters in each language subsystem is a useful heuristic device.) By virtue of the fact that the syntactic processes of both languages concern the same types of phenomena (e.g., assignment of theta-roles, marking of tense, aspect, plural, etc.), the morphosyntax of French has more in common with the morphosyntax of Farsi than with the phonology of either language. This is why the morphosyntax subsystems of any two languages are thought to be subsystems of the same module (the morphosyntax module of *language*).

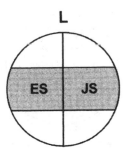

Figure 5.5. *Inhibition of a language module*

One module (syntax) is selectively inhibited, affecting both languages.

A glance at Figures 5.4 through 5.7 reveals why, within this framework, natural systems and subsystems, such as language as a whole (as opposed to other higher cognitive functions), and either each tongue, as subsystems of language (Fig. 5.4), or the syntax module, also a subsystem of language that encompasses English and Japanese syntax, can be selectively inhibited or impaired (5.5). Figure 5.6 shows how, in the case of selective recovery, one module may be selectively impaired in one language only, e.g., English phonology. Meanwhile, Figure 5.7 shows why it would be odd for the phonology of one language and the syntax of the other to be impaired at the same time: It would require the inhibition of two unconnected systems that do not form a natural class. They are neither part of the same language subsystem (English or Japanese), nor of the same language module (phonology or syntax).

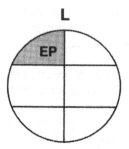

Figure 5.6. *Inhibition of one subsystem's module*
English phonology is selectively inhibited.

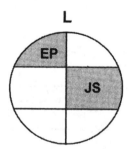

Figure 5.7. *Unlikely scenario*

English phonology and Japanese syntax do not form a natural subsystem. Even though the internal structure of ES is independent of the internal structure of JS, they both instantiate parameters of S (as opposed to parameters of P, for instance), which makes ES functionally more similar in nature to JS than to EP or JP. A co-occurrence of lesions affecting EP and JS simultaneously may not be altogether impossible in principle, but it is very improbable, given the different loci subserving the physiology of each neurofunctional submodule. It would take two different lesions (one affecting English phonology, the other Japanese syntax) to give rise to different aphasias in each language, namely qualitatively different symptoms.

Just as phonology can be considered to be a subsystem of the language system (phonology belongs to the language system—not any other cognitive system—and yet it has its own independent internal structure and is susceptible to selective impairment), a specific language (such as English or Japanese) is also a subsystem of the language system. Phonology is generally called a module (rather than a subsystem) because it must be integrated with other modules (e.g., syntax) in the course of normal functioning. While the phonology and syntax modules can be selectively impaired, they have no independent normal use. A language (e.g., Basque), on the other hand, is functionally self-sufficient and can be used independently of the other subsystem(s)—that is, other languages such as Spanish or French (even though it needs input from the conceptual system). If two languages happen to legitimately contain a similar feature, that feature is represented twice, i.e., once in each language subsystem, because features do not exist in a void but are part of a system, with reciprocal relationships with other features within that system.

From megasystems to embedded microsystems, there are different layers of modularity. Modularity applies, for example, (1) between declarative and procedural memory; (2) between different functions subserved by procedural memory (since procedural memory is task-specific) such as implicit linguistic competence and face recognition skills; and (3) between different components of a cognitive function, such as phonology and syntax within the language subsystem.

An imageable analogy would be to consider a large transparent plastic Easter egg in a candy store window (corresponding to cognition) containing several large chocolate eggs (each corresponding to a cognitive function, one being language). One of the large chocolate eggs (the one corresponding to the language system) contains three middle-sized chocolate eggs, one made of dark chocolate, one of milk chocolate and one of white chocolate, where each kind of chocolate corresponds to a language subsystem. Each of these eggs contains smaller eggs wrapped in different colored foil (corresponding to phonology, syntax, etc.) and different cream fillings (corresponding to each language subsystem): say, mint cream for the dark chocolate, raspberry cream for the milk chocolate, and lemon cream for the white chocolate. Note that each middle-sized chocolate (say, Arabic, French and English) contains eggs wrapped in the same colors as the other two (phonology, syntax, semantics), but whereas they all contain cream (i.e., "stuff" of the same kind), the cream flavors are unique to each kind of chocolate egg (*Arabic* syntax, *Arabic* phonology).

Van Orden, Pennington, and Stone (2001) deplore what they consider to be an unending fractionation into more modules. The fractionating systems into component modules will continue only so long as there is a component of a cognitive function that can be isolated because it is selectively vulnerable to pathology or susceptible to inhibition and has its own internal neurocomputational structure that is impervious to the influence of other modules. There is no reason to assume a priori that there is a given number of subsystems and component modules.

Whether we wish to consider memory as a system with two subsystems or modular components (procedural, declarative), or whether we wish to call declarative memory a system and procedural memory another system is a question of verbal convention. From a highly abstract point of view, both declarative and procedural memory share the property of storing representations (of facts in one, of schemata in the other). On the other hand, declarative and procedural memory constitute two independent systems that have only the term "memory" in common, reflecting the fact that both store and activate representations; still, these representations are of a different nature (facts vs. procedures) and involve different processes (explicit and controlled vs. implicit and automatic). They are distinct in that one deals with conscious material and the other with material that is not conscious. They rely on different anatomical substrates (hippocampal and mesial temporal lobe areas for declarative memory vs. right cerebellum, left basal ganglia and left perisylvian areas for language). It is also possible to consider each cognitive function (say, language) that uses procedural memory representations as a neurofunctional system, subdivided into, in this case, as many subsystems as there are languages, each with its own phonological and syntactic module. Everything will depend on the perspective, namely how much of the organism one wishes to consider at any given time.

As discussed in Chapter 4, the existence of distinct neural language (sub)systems (one subsystem per language) does not imply differential lateralization (as is too often assumed); in fact, it does not even imply gross anatomical differential localization within the left perisylvian area. Metalinguistic knowledge, subserved by declarative memory, is not part of the language subsystems, which are predicated only on implicit linguistic competence.

Cast in terms of connectionist theory, each language subsystem corresponds to a dedicated portion of the neural network. The connections between elements of L1 have greater weight than those between elements of L1 and elements of L2. The frequency of use of associated elements will determine the weight of the connections. Hence, individuals who frequently mix languages will have stronger connections between elements of L1 and L2 than individuals who do not mix (non-code-mixers). The subsystems are developed through repeated experience, and, even though they are not necessarily assumed to be innately preprogrammed, they end up as modular systems nevertheless.

There used to be a high school-level Canadian history book called *Unity in Diversity*. One way to characterize neurofunctional modularity would be as diversity within unity: Unity of the brain, where everything is eventually connected to everything else, but with specialized cerebral systems; unity of language structure, but with specific instantiations in each language; and finally, unity of the cerebral representation of the various languages of bilingual speakers at the macro-anatomical level, but with diversity at the micro-anatomical level.

Neurofunctional principles and parameters

In terms of Universal Grammar (UG theory), each set of parameters (L1 parameters, L2 parameters) constitutes a subsystem of implicit linguistic competence. In other words, UG principles are instantiated through L1 parameters and L2 parameters, respectively, and each such set of parameters is subserved by a neural substrate that constitutes a neurofunctional subsystem of the language system. Parameters (of UG principles) have in common that they are the same kinds of things (i.e., instantiations of UG principles) as opposed to the instantiation of other cognitive principles that may underlie music, arithmetic, or any other higher cognitive system. Language subsystems (the set of L1 parameters; the set of L2 parameters) are therefore more similar in nature to each other than to systems underlying other functions.

Two languages may happen to share some of the same parameters. Parameters that are the same in the two languages are hypothesized to be redundantly represented, that is, incorporated within the structure of each subsystem. Parameters that differ between L1 and L2 are represented only in their respective subsystem. However, to the extent that the speaker has not internalized an L2 parameter, its L1 analog may be redundantly represented instead in the L2 system (and may remain so for life). Such a speaker's L2 subsystem will then contain a feature deviant with respect to the L2 norm, namely that corresponding to the L1 parameter. This will constitute just one additional instance of redundancy of representation. The closer the two languages are structurally, the greater the number of features that are legitimately represented redundantly. The difference between (1) a hypothetical ideal speaker who possesses two languages, the representation of each of which conforms perfectly to its grammar and (2) a speaker who inappropriately incorporates some features from L1 (in addition to the legitimate ones) is merely a quantitative one that has no impact on the way the languages are represented (namely, as subsystems). In fact, a subsystem in which 10% of L2 syntactic structures are actually illegitimate L1 structures (say, a Basque subsystem illegitimately containing Spanish structures) may nevertheless contain fewer redundant representations than a system that contains subsystems for two structurally close languages (e.g., Catalan and Spanish) that may legitimately contain 30% or more of the same structures. In other words, there is no reason to expect a subsystem that contains illegitimate items from the other language (usually referred to as "interference") to be treated any differently from a system that contains only legitimate redundancies.

Evidence of modularity

One demonstration that implicit linguistic competence is subserved by a specific cerebral mechanism is that aphasia occurs in the absence of other cognitive, sensory or motor deficits. Of course paresis of the speech organs will prevent an individual from speaking, anopia will interfere with reading, and lack of vigilance will interfere with both speech and reading, but so will heart or lung failure. Impairments of other cognitive functions do not disrupt the language system per se.

Evidence from quadruple dissociation between reading and writing kana and kanji script in Japanese patients with dyslexia and dysgraphia, and double dissociation between the various languages of bilingual and polyglot patients with aphasia have been interpreted as supporting the hypothesis that cognitive processing is neurofunctionally fractionable into subcomponents, which themselves are further fractionable (Paradis, 1987c). Japanese patients were described who could read and/or write kana (syllabograms with a one-to-one correspondence between character and sound, and between sound and character) only or much better than kanji (morphograms with a many-to-one correspondence between character and sound, and between sound and character), whereas others could read and/or write kanji only or much better than kana characters. Some could read but not write, others could write but not read. It was therefore suggested that kanji reading and kana reading rely on different neurofunctional subsystems, and that kana writing and kanji writing were likewise subserved by separate subsystems. Kanji reading and kanji writing are further neurofunctionally differentiated, as are kana reading and kana writing, in patients with alexia without agraphia or with agraphia without alexia. The lesions responsible for these impairments clustered around sites in the left parietal-temporal-occipital area, somewhat more posterior and inferior for kana than for kanji (Paradis, Hagiwara, & Hildebrandt, 1985).

Nonparallel types of recovery in bilingual individuals with aphasia, in particular the selective, successive, and antagonistic patterns (which exhibit respectively permanent, temporary and alternating inhibition of the neural substrate underlying one particular language subsystem), provide evidence that two or more languages in the same brain are neurofunctionally isolable (cumulative evidence can be found in Paradis, 1977, 1989b, 2001a). Moreover, bilingual psychotic patients can present with either different or less severe psychotic symptoms, depending on the language they use (Bruce, 1895; De Zulueta, Gene-Cos & Grachev, 2001).

Hodges, Patterson, and Tyler's (1994) patient exhibited progressive and profound loss of declarative memory affecting factual knowledge and vocabulary in the context of preserved basic syntax. This led the authors to conclude that basic syntactic processes may operate independently of semantic (i.e., declarative) memory and are therefore independent cognitive modules. (This is, incidentally, one more indication that vocabulary (the relationship between word-sound and word-meaning) depends on declarative memory, whereas syntactic processes depend on procedural memory.) Kremin et al. (2000) describe a patient who presented a dissociation between L1 and L2 reading, with a pattern of letter-by-letter reading and surface dyslexia in her native language together with apparently normal reading in her second, learned language. (Not only is this evidence that one of a patient's two languages can be selectively impaired, but also that a later learned language may rely on declarative memory and not be affected by acquired dyslexia.)

Neuropsychology has revealed a cluster of functionally dissociable cognitive modules in the brain that are necessary to support various cognitive skills. There is indeed a great deal of evidence that cognitive subsystems are functionally and even, in some cases, anatomically distinct from those that support other skills as well as basic perceptual and motor functions (Donald, 1993).

Although sometimes the pattern evolves over periods ranging from 3 to 12 months, most of the time the nonparallel recovery patterns are observed in the first weeks post-onset and are probably due to the effects of edema (i.e., the swelling of brain tissue that interferes with normal processing until it subsides). The fact remains that, whatever the cause and duration of the inhibition, it is selective and affects each language differentially (even if for only short periods of time). "Natural" (sub)systems (phonology, syntax; Japanese, French;

language, pragmatics) are selectively vulnerable to impairment, suggesting that the activation threshold of specific portions of networks is raised, rather than random inhibition.

Even when the same muscle effectors are involved, in the absence of paralysis, they will selectively be operative or inoperative, depending on the module that sends the command; we therefore see a double dissociation, for example, between speech apraxia (when the command comes from the language system) and oral apraxia (when the command comes from the bucco-pharyngeal praxis system) (Johns & Lapointe, 1976).

Wilson, Scalaidhe, and Goldman-Rakic (1993) have shown that areas and pathways subserving object and spatial vision are segregated in the visual system: Neurons that code information related to stimulus identity are dissociable from those that code information related to stimulus location. In other words, the primate frontal cortex contains separate processing mechanisms for remembering *what* and *where* an object is. Ashby and Waldron (2000) and Waldron and Ashby (2001) present strong experimental evidence that normal category learning is mediated by at least two separate systems: an explicit, rule-based system, mediated by the frontal lobe cortex, involving the anterior cingulate and the head of the caudate nucleus, and an implicit, procedural-acquisitional-based system, involving the dorsal striatum and the tail of the caudate nucleus. (For a description of the biological nature of rule-based and implicit categorization, see Ashby & Waldron, 1999 and Ashby et al., 2002.) Maddox, Ashby and Waldron's (2002) analyses also bolster the functional independence hypothesis, suggesting that separate perceptual and decisional attention systems exist. Maddox, Ashby and Bohil (2003) provide further evidence in support of a multiple-systems approach to category learning and cast doubt on the validity of single-system approaches. Single-system models have difficulty with the reported dual-task category learning data and make incorrect predictions whereas a dual-system model naturally predicts these results (Ashby & Ell, 2002). Experiments by Zeithamová (2003) provide evidence in support of the existence of a declarative, verbal, rule-based system and an independent implicit, similarity-based system in category learning, corresponding to the distinction between explicit knowledge and actual performance.

It is not unlikely that neurofunctional modules map onto what Mountcastle (1978) describes as neuroanatomical modules (which are not necessarily—and in fact rarely are—gross anatomical areas) that vary in cell numbers, intrinsic connections, and processing modes, specific to each entity. Each neurofunctional module may thus depend on "a local neural circuit that processes information from its input to its output and in that processing imposes transforms determined by the general properties of the entity and its extrinsic connections" (p. 8). From this viewpoint, the neocortex is composed of local circuits that form modules with their intrinsic cytoarchitecture, structural organization and mode of neuronal processing, and these modules are grouped into entities (topographic macrosystems).

As suggested by Lieberman (1996), there is indeed no reason to suppose that the neurophysiology of the circuits that regulate human language is fundamentally different than those that regulate motor control, and in fact there are striking similarities between motor and cognitive skills. They are resistant to amnesia but vulnerable to damage to distributed neural circuits involving basal ganglionic structures. As Lieberman acknowledges, the individual circuits that subserve motor control, syntax and other cognitive processes may nevertheless be segregated; and this is the stamp of neurofunctional modularity.

Double dissociation

Whereas there is no need to postulate a module on the basis of simple dissociation, because if a dissociation is always in the same direction, then a hierarchy of difficulty (or vulnerability, or level of activation) can be assumed, the demonstration of a double dissociation between cognitive skills or between two components of a cognitive skill is traditionally taken as the criterion for neurofunctional modularity.

Not only are implicit and explicit memory deficits doubly dissociated behaviorally, but they occur subsequent to damage to clearly different neuroanatomical substrates. They clearly represent independent memory systems. This does not mean that there cannot be dissociations within each system, pointing to the existence of subsystems or domain-specific modules (within both declarative and procedural memory systems).

Within a neurofunctional modularity framework, dissociations both between and within declarative and procedural memory are not surprising, but only to be expected. Procedural memory is known to be task-specific, and therefore there is a different procedural memory module for each specific domain (language processing, bicycle riding, face recognition, etc.). The principles of procedural memory are the same for all domains (and different from those of declarative memory, which has different properties, such as being available to conscious introspection) and are instantiated by different parameters corresponding to each domain (subsystem) and each task (module).

Crowder (1989) questions the legitimacy of concluding that double dissociations in amnesics show the existence of different memory systems, one declarative, the other procedural, but suggests that amnesia appears to be "one element of normal memory—the knowledge *that* processing occurred in *that* context—is compromised" (p. 290). But it is not the case that retrograde amnesia affects only episodic memory. It also affects encyclopedic memories (generally referred to as "semantic memory" in psychology—Tulving, 1983). For example, a patient with a severe retrograde amnesia subsequent to traumatic head injury caused by a nail accidentally projected from a staple gun was followed by Isabelle Rouleau and colleagues for over 10 years; this man had lost a great deal of previously acquired information related to topics such as geography, history, literature, and music. He had to completely relearn the map of his hometown, could not name the continents, and thought Julius Caesar was a singer, for instance. He had to relearn most of the information pertaining to his work. In other words, the patient had not only lost episodic memory but also semantic memory, even though he retained premorbidly acquired skills, such as driving his car, skiing, swimming and skating, as well as highly complex skills such as repairing electronic circuits (Rouleau & Labrecque, 1991). Aphasia does not affect declarative memory. Amnesia occurs subsequent to lesions involving the hippocampal system (parahippocampal gyri and mesial temporal lobes), while aphasia occurs subsequent to lesions in the perisylvian area, basal ganglia and cerebellum. We thus have converging evidence, not only behavioral but also clinical and neuroanatomical, of a double dissociation between declarative and procedural memory. The same is true of other neurofunctional modules.

Ganis and Chater (1991) argue that inference from double dissociation to a particular modular structure of the underlying cognitive system is problematic because double dissociations can be observed in a fully distributed system—that is, a system that does not decompose into isolable subsystems. Their argument and that of many others relates to the modularity of cognitive processes, generally as modeled on artificial intelligence computer networks. Our inquiry concerns neurofunctional modularity, which imposes biological plausibility on the model. Unlike what happens in a fully distributed computer-simulated neural network, neurofunctional double dissociations occur when different systems are lesioned (i.e., inhibited or physically destroyed). The fact that dissociations can occur in a particular way in computers is not relevant to the way the brain actually functions. A robot's "vision" is based on systems very different from human vision even though its behavior may simulate vision as it avoids obstacles, picks up objects, etc.

Cognition: The Subsystems Hypothesis generalized

We are now in a position to generalize from conclusions derived from neurolinguistic aspects of bilingualism to cognition as a whole. It is tempting to propose, unlike Fodor (1983) in his *Modularity of Mind*, that neurofunctional modularity *is* the general fact about the cerebral organization of cognitive functions. Most of the properties he attributes to input systems can be retained and applied to any neurofunctional module. Modularity, as proposed by Shallice (1988), may well be "a general property of the systems underlying human cognition" (p. 20).

The application of general principles is parameterized in relation to the domain of application. The principles and parameters construct is hypothesized to apply not only to language, as seen earlier, but to all cognitive functions. General cognition refers to a constellation of numerous cognitive (sub)systems, each independent of the other with respect to its object, and while all may share basic principles (which makes them part of the system), each cognitive subsystem is developed in accordance with its domain-specific parameters. "Cognition" can thus be seen to be no more than an abstract entity that is the umbrella designation standing for the set of elements (dedicated domain-specific cognitive systems) that it contains.

As discussed earlier, whereas the establishment of a function may depend on distributed processes similar to simulations of computer neural networks, the end state is a dedicated set of neural connections, a domain-specific neurofunctional module. Language, pragmatics, musical ability, and face recognition, for instance, are hypothesized to be such neurofunctional systems, whether hardwired or not. Some of these systems (and subsystems) are, like individual languages, further divided into constituent modules. Each subsystem is associated with a fixed neural architecture, i.e., dedicated portions of the neural network established as a result of experience.

The internal structure of each subsystem is a specific parameterization of the general principles of its particular neurofunctional system. The general principles of one neurofunctional system (e.g., implicit linguistic competence) differ from those of other systems (e.g., pragmatics, music, arithmetic).

A neurofunctional cognitive subsystem is recognized as such when a double dissociation can be demonstrated between it and another subsystem. A double dissociation is taken as evidence of the subsystem's (or submodule's) susceptibility to selective inhibition (and selective impairment in pathology), pointing to its autonomy. This, in turn, is taken as evidence of dedicated neural circuits underlying the neurofunctional subsystem, module, or submodule.

Given the numerous reported cases of domain-specific selective impairments (specific apraxias, and agnosias), functions that rely on procedural memory are prime candidates for neurofunctional modularity. Functions that rely on declarative memory may be less obvious, though many deficits have been reported within specific fields constituting semantic memory (animals, furniture, tools, faces). More problematic are those functions usually considered as "general" or "central," and variously referred to as a central processor (Mandler, 1975); an executive system (Logan & Cowan, 1984); a supervisory system (Norman & Shallice, 1985; LaBerge, 2001; Schall, Stuphorn & Brown, 2002); a central cognitive system (Kasher, 1991); executive control (Roelofs, 2003b); or the central executive (Shallice, 1982; Baddeley, 1986). These functions have been assumed to centrally control all functions of a particular type (e.g., decision-making, general principles of intentional activity). The hypothesis proposed here is that even functions that have been considered all-purpose (i.e., "horizontal") may in fact fractionate into a number of vertical systems of the same type as those that have developed into domain-specific subsystems by virtue of the frequent co-activation of parts of the network (somewhat in the manner of a Hebbian cell assembly).

Cognition as a whole appears divided into a number of clusters of modules, each dissociable from the rest and possibly subserved by different cerebral mechanisms. For instance, some modules rely on procedural memory, while others rely on declarative memory). But even those modules that rely on the same type of memory are nevertheless dissociable from each other and form separate neurofunctional systems and subsystems. An increasing number of function-specific cerebral structures are being identified. As we have already seen, the reticular formation, for example, turns out not to be a reticulum after all (Damasio, 1999).

Verbal communication (as part of the general communicative system), for instance, comprises several components, each of a different nature and subserved by different cerebral mechanisms, including at least implicit linguistic competence, metalinguistic knowledge, pragmatic competence, metapragmatic knowledge, and motivation. It receives input from the conceptual and perceptual systems and provides outputs through the kinesthetic and kinesic systems (e.g., articulatory/phonatory, digitomanual), relying on different sensory modalities (auditory, visual, somesthetic, and proprioceptive).

More broadly, it may be hypothesized that, when a general function X is applied to a specific system Y, it forms a Y-specific subsystem of X; for example, English and French form two separate subsystems of the language system (*qua* implicit linguistic competence), each becoming isolable and doubly dissociable. As another example, language switching is not a property of language systems, but is of the same nature as other decisional systems—to do W rather than Z (Paradis, 1980a). However, whether a specific application of the decisional system might develop for language switching that would allow selective inhibition (in the way that two skills based on procedural memory are nevertheless isolable from each other) remains to be investigated. Is it the case, for instance, that whenever patients have difficulty with language switching, they also have difficulty switching between any other two tasks? (And vice versa, do bilingual frontal lobe patients who exhibit task-switching problems also exhibit language switching impairments?) Do people who have a linguistic pragmatic impairment also have a general pragmatic impairment (and vice versa)? Do pragmatic deficits segregate according to the nature of *what* is inferred or what something is inferred *from* (e.g., fact, state of mind, discursive context)? If the language subsystems analogy applies, then we should expect some—though not all—patients to have problems with X-specific subsystems (analogous to a selective recovery in a bilingual patient), while others, possibly the majority, have problems with the X-system as a whole, i.e., all X-specific subsystems (analogous to parallel recovery).

In other words, cognitive neurofunctional subsystems share the functional properties of the matrix system, but are dedicated to a specific instantiation of the general function of the system (e.g., English and Japanese are two subsystems of the implicit linguistic competence (matrix) language system; language switching and switching between two color schemes are two subsystems of the decisional system; linguistic pragmatics (inference from contexts to derive the meaning of an utterance) and non-linguistic pragmatics (inference from non-linguistic phenomena to derive a non-verbalized message, e.g., that it is likely to rain because dark clouds are observed to be quickly gathering) are two subsystems of the pragmatics system; within linguistic pragmatics, there as many subsystems as there are languages, that is, one for English, one for Navaho—remember that the system of English pragmatics differs from its Navaho counterpart; e.g., the Navaho translation of the polite invitation "have a cookie" is perceived as a bossy command).

Subsystems contain procedures of the same general type that differ with respect to their object, such as different phonological rules in L1 and L2 language subsystems. Although phonological rules of L1 are phonological rules (as opposed to syntactic rules), they are not the same as the phonological rules of the L2 subsystem. As we have seen, each set of rules constitutes parametric instantiations of the same general principles (those of phonology and the neural computational procedures that subserve them). By extension, different components of what is considered general cognition may function as subsystems of intelligence. Neurofunctionally, each cognitive subsystem is capable of specific inhibition as well as of different degrees of development. Some subsystems may in fact be hyperdeveloped while others are so reduced as to be nearly nonexistent (as in so-called idiot-savants).

This suggests a number of questions that deserve further investigation. For example, (1) Is there any central cognitive function that is not in fact made up of dedicated domain-specific subsystems? And (2) Is there an all-purpose central executive or general undivided function that participates in all (or several) cognitive functions (as opposed to parameterized, domain-specific executive subsystems)?

No central executive

Neurofunctional modularity (i.e., the organization of the cerebral substratum of cognitive functions into dedicated neural systems) is more pervasive than has generally been assumed and the hypothetical "central executive" may in reality be an abstraction referring to the summation of operations of local, domain-specific control systems.

The prevalent acceptance of a "central executive" goes back to the identification of mind with a unitary soul. The belief that our mind is one and that the self is doing the willing and making decisions is of course quite intuitive. But a multiple mind subserved by a modular brain would not be the first counterintuitive empirical discovery. Commissurotomized patients have shown that the mind is anatomically fractionable and that right and left hemispheres not only can act on their own, but may "want" to achieve incompatible goals, as demonstrated by a patient whose left hand tries to prevent the right hand from reaching its target. Each disconnected hemisphere appears to have a mind of its own (Sperry, 1974). When the cerebrum is divided surgically, it is as if the cranium contained two separate spheres of consciousness (Gazzaniga, 1967). Each hemisphere seems to have its own conscious sphere for mental activities (Sperry, Gazzaniga, & Bogen, 1969).

Just as "memory" is only an abstraction, so is the unitary central executive or self. We have to come to grips with the likelihood that there is no such faculty as intelligence, but rather several "intelligences" (Gardner, 1985), no will, but several wills, and no unitary central executive. The self is likewise an abstraction, the summation of a number of control systems. Just as there is no general-purpose perceptual analyzer (Marshall, 1984), no general-purpose memory (Pitres, 1895), and no general-purpose consciousness (Gazzaniga, 1967), there could well be no general-purpose central executive.

Goal-directed acts may be domain-specific, possibly contradictory, and a competition between different modular systems may result in carrying out the goal of the module that prevailed (i.e., that had the lowest activation threshold). There may in fact not exist any central processes (in the form of a unique general executive akin to free will). The illusion of free-willed decision-making may result from the integration of influences from several sources—a process that can be segregated, as evidenced by the independent, and sometimes contradictory, behavior resulting from right- vs. left-hemisphere control of actions in split-brain patients.

At some level of abstraction, one might speak of a central executive (subjectively perceived as self-consciousness and a feeling of free will), provided one realizes that, at the neurophysiological level, it simply refers to the summation of positive and negative impulses generated by the operations of local executives, *mutatis mutandis* analogous to the firing of neurons as a result of the computation of positive and inhibitory impulses from numerous sources.

When Green (1986), in an effort to account for alternating antagonism between the two languages of a bilingual aphasic patient, refers to a control system that regulates the attribution of resources to one or the other language systems, that control is specific to the language module (*qua* language faculty, as well as *qua* French and Arabic subsystems); it differs from the control mechanisms that distribute resources to other cognitive modules (since those modules operate normally and are unaffected by the aphasia). This allocation of resources does not seem to be centrally controlled, but locally controlled. Though clearly not within the domain of conscious, deliberate decision-making, these phenomena are suggestive of a general principle of modularized control systems.

A number of researchers consider that the currently available experimental evidence gives us some reason to take a massive modularity hypothesis very seriously; that is, they believe that the human mind is largely or perhaps even entirely composed of modules (Samuels, 2000). This perspective is congruent with Shallice's (1988) opinion that "it seems likely there is no simple higher-level system that directly controls the operation of the lower level modules" (p. 401). The processes of willed action, reflection, remembering, and speaking about something do not involve the same system. Many of what are generally called the central capacities are believed to be further fragmented into domain-specific modules (Jackendoff, 1987, 1992). Likewise, Service (1993), after concluding that different types of memories are modular, quotes J. Allman as saying that there is no memory manager putting everything together, i.e., no higher level of processing that reintegrates everything (though Allman does not recall having made such a statement (personal communication)).

In sum, as expressed by Michael Gardner two decades ago, one finds no need for a central system or executive process (Gardner, 1985). Indeed, as he assumed, modules can and do work together in any complex human activity. Such cooperation requires no higher-level supervision, nor does it need access to the inner workings of each module. Various modules work together cooperatively to carry out complex cognitive tasks, each using its own skill, without the need for a master executive. Thus, understanding the meaning of speech acts is not necessarily a central process. It is the result of the concurrent use of two sets of modules: the linguistic and the pragmatic modules.

As suspected by Marshall (1984), modularity may be far more pervasive than Fodor's account suggests. It may even be more pervasive than Marshall proposed: There may very well be no general-purpose mechanism, no central executive. In fact, neuropsychologists are beginning to envisage this possibility. For example, Shallice (2001) contemplates fractionating the supervisory system, suggesting that supervisory system processes should be considered to involve a range of different mechanisms. Dove et al. (2000) provide evidence that control is not exerted by brain areas exclusively involved in executive control, but within some of the areas involved in basic task processes. In other words, there is no evidence of a brain area devoted to executive control per se (not even for a specific task, such as switching).

The human organ analogy

Each organ in the human body is an independent structure with its own morphology, properties, and specific function. One could therefore say that the heart, the liver and the brain, for example, each constitutes an anatomico-physiological module, each of which necessary to the living organism (the human body) but none sufficient: None could survive in the absence of any of the others. These modules, stucturally independent as they are, interact with each other (the brain is nourished by the blood the heart pumps in, and in turn it controls the heartbeat). Other organs, such as lungs and kidneys could be brought into the picture, each with its own internal structure, morphology, properties, function, and modus operandi. Note that the heart is part of the blood circulation system which also comprises the veins and arteries—a complex system, yet isolable from the other systems with which it interacts. The heart can thus be considered a module within the circulatory system (as phonology is a module within the implicit linguistic competence system, which itself is a module of the verbal communication system).

The fact that all these organs—the heart, the liver, and the brain—evolved from undifferentiated stem cells, each cell originally capable of metamorphosing into a heart, or a brain, or any other organ, does not alter the fact that once a group of cells has become a heart, the heart has its own specific muscle structure and function; these are now quite separate from those of the liver and the brain, which each have their own structure and function, very different from those of the heart. Likewise, neurocognitive modules, such as language, need not be preformed any more than the kidneys which originate from stem cells which, placed in a different environment, would have developed into a liver. But once a kidney is a kidney, it cannot function as a liver, of which it has neither the internal structure nor the properties: It has become an anatomico-physiological module. Once implicit linguistic competence has developed, it has become a neurofunctional module, with its own dedicated circuits different from, and independent of, other cognitive neurofunctional modules. It might be argued that the heart and kidneys were genetically preprogrammed, and that therefore this analogy implies that *language* is genetically programmed. In fact, even this implication holds. The language function does have a genetic basis but, just as stem cells need a particular environment to differentiate into liver cells rather than heart cells, the gene or genes involved in the development of language (Lai et al., 2001) also need particular environments (of a biological and experiential nature) to express themselves as a normal procedural language system. The nature of prenatal levels, distribution and timing of exposure of the developing brain to sex hormones, primarily testosterone, has physiological, neuroanatomical and behavioral consequences (Lauter, 1998).

The heuristic value of this analogy is that even though these anatomico-physiological modules interact and they all originate from undifferentiated stem cells, they can be isolated and studied independently of each other and are independently vulnerable to specific types of dysfunction. Likewise, neurofunctional modules such as vision, hearing and motricity, but also cognitive modules, such as implicit linguistic competence, can be selectively inhibited or impaired. The liver is divided into several parts, each with its own endocrine or exocrine function (glycogen storage and glucose homeostasis, vitamin synthesis and storage, blood clotting factor synthesis, bile acid synthesis and excretion, drug detoxification and metabolism, bacterial destruction, etc). Similarly, each neurofunctional modular system (e.g., language) is fractionable into modules (e.g., phonology, syntax), and may be split into subsystems (English, Japanese). English and Japanese are part of the language neurofunctional system and as such comprise their own phonology and syntax modules.

Conclusion

Neurofunctional modules are isolable, autonomous, domain-specific and purposeful, and they constitute components of a larger unit. They are isolable but interactive. However, their interactions do not modify the nature of their computational procedures. They receive inputs and provide outputs but their internal structure is not influenced by that of other modules. When interacting, other modules merely select among items available within the system, without being able to modify them in any way (e.g., pragmatics may select among available syntactic structures to optimally conform to the message formulated by the conceptual system but it does not modify the syntax system).

Neurofunctional modularity is both representational modularity and process modularity. Representational modularity: There must be some neurally based trace (whatever its nature) that can be activated at successive times and is retained when we sleep so that we can still access it and speak the next morning without having to reacquire language (or rediscover where we parked the car the night before). Process modularity: Each neurofunctional module is processed in accordance with the parametric instantiation of the general cerebral processing principles of procedural or declarative memory depending on the type of cognitive information involved (implicit or explicit).

Whether or not implicit linguistic competence is innate is still controversial and very much depends on what one holds to be innate. However, innateness is not a necessary attribute of the language module. The properties of neurofunctional modules may be genetically programmed or develop through experience (and probably partake of both). The end result, which is what concerns us here, is the same.

The neural substrates that underlie neurofunctional modules need not be anatomically contiguous as long as the various components are connected and function as a unit. Modules are not even incompatible with computer-simulated connectionist distributed systems because the weighted connections established constitute *de facto* modules.

The neurofunctional system for language (i.e., the neural substrates of implicit computational procedures that constitute linguistic competence) contains modules (e.g., phonology, syntax), each of which has its own internal organization (in accordance with its general principles, i.e., the general principles of phonology and of syntax, respectively); for each subsystem of the language neurofunctional system (i.e., for each specific language, e.g., German, Italian) these principles are proceduralized in accordance with the parameters of that particular language subsystem.

The two (or more) language subsystems (i.e., their implicit linguistic competence) are not represented each in a separate gross anatomical location. Rather, they are distinguished at the micro-anatomical level within the same areas. Language subsystems are doubly dissociable by pathology and by antagonistic inhibition when interference is to be avoided (e.g., the activation threshold of one subsystem is raised when the other is in operation).

The notion of subsystems may be generalized to all cognitive functions. Cognition can be seen as the sum of independent cognitive systems. Cognitive functions that rely on procedural memory are prime candidates for neurofunctional modularity but specific deficits are also reported in domains subserved by declarative memory.

There may in fact be no central executive. The intuitive feeling of a unitary self that wills an action may simply be a subjective impression corresponding to the implicit summation of multiple decisions arrived at by various independent domain-specific computations.

CHAPTER 6

Neuroimaging studies of the bilingual brain

Neuroimaging is new, exciting, and colorful; it is also very expensive, and hence prestigious. As a result, it runs the risk of being overrated and used for purposes beyond its true scope. Some reasons for caution when using neuroimaging data as evidence for language representation and processing in general, and in bilingual individuals in particular, will be briefly outlined. At best, neuroimaging provides us with circumstantial evidence, and like all circumstantial evidence, its credibility rests on the amount of converging data from other sources. There may come a point when there are so many coincidences that they affect our belief—even if each piece of evidence is circumstantial. However, the problem with neuroimaging studies of bilingual speakers is that they provide evidence that conflicts considerably and is sometimes incongruent with evidence from other sources. For recent reviews of neuroimaging studies of language processing in bilingual speakers, see Abutalebi, Cappa, and Perani (2001) and Vaid and Hull (2002).

What do neuroimaging studies of language evidence? How do we know?

Neuroimaging techniques are supposed to determine which areas of the brain are activated during the performance of a particular task. When the task is a language task, two problems arise: either one uses a natural ("ecological") task such as the comprehension of a short story, in which case one must determine which component of the task is responsible for triggering which of the activated areas—and, supposedly, why. Alternatively, one attempts to target only one component of a complex task (e.g., single word comprehension, syllable detection, etc.), in which case one runs the not-so-unlikely risk of tapping into something other than what is used in a natural linguistic task. For example, syllables may be treated as meaningless sounds, rather than as *language* sounds, and thus may be processed by neural structures other than those that process syllables in a linguistic context; that is, they may fail to activate the procedural memory system that supports linguistic competence but instead activate structures involved in nonlinguistic acoustic pattern detection.

Consider one "language task" used to identify neural substrates of language: a word completion task (e.g., Chee, Tan, & Thiel, 1999b) in which the subject is asked to complete a word, given a morphologically and syllabically unmotivated string of letters either as the beginning of the word (e.g., COU___, where the subject is expected to say *couple*), or the end of a word (e.g., ___TER, where the subject is expected to say *water*). Under these circumstances, any task that has a language component would constitute a "language task." This kind of word completion task is at best extremely peripheral to language use. From this perspective, adding, subtracting or multiplying would also qualify as language tasks, although they would very likely activate neural substrates for arithmetic as well as those for word articulation. Symptoms of acalculia can be manifested in the absence of aphasia, and vice versa.

In neuroimaging, language tasks are commonly associated with activity in several cortical regions, in both the anterior and posterior parts of both hemispheres. The problem is therefore to determine which of the activated areas subserves which component of the task, and in what capacity. What the observed activation means is that something was detected by that particular technique. What that something *is* must be inferred (i.e., whether it is associated with the function in question or not, and if it is, with which component). Levels of activation depend on (1) the technique used, (2) what is selected as the baseline—running the danger of interaction between the baseline and task component(s), and (3) statistical threshold level settings. As a consequence, the fact that something is *not* detected is no indication that a particular area is not active—only that the technique employed does not pick it up (either because it is below the sensors' threshold or because it is masked by the baseline task). In Positron Emission Tomography (PET), for instance, the likelihood of observing a subtle and complex activation is influenced by both the study design and the image analysis technique employed (Price et al., 1996). Not only may some instances of activation not be detected (because of the limitations of a particular procedure), but individual differences, when observed, may reflect different strategies rather than topologically diverse representations. (In a word-reading task, for instance, it is difficult to know whether a stimulus word was read by the subject via grapheme-to-phoneme correspondence (without access to the semantic representation) or through direct pattern recognition of the entire word, with or without semantic lookup.)

With any type of cognitive/functional neuroimaging, the technique is likely to measure only one part or aspect of the complex process being investigated. The question then is, which one? The answer is only as good as the theoretical framework used to interpret the data, that is, to infer which component of what function is activated where—and why. Because of the inherent technical limitations, each procedure gives us at best a partial picture since each technique highlights one aspect of the function being explored, with varying degrees of temporal and/or topological resolution.

In addition, what is activated depends on the specific language task being used (comprehension of stories, comprehension of anomalous sentences, repetition of words or sentences, translation, production of synonyms or rhymes). Activation is further influenced by the study design and the image analysis technique employed: What is inferred to be significantly activated will depend on the task selected as a baseline (attentive silence, periods of rest during which subjects are asked to refrain from thinking of words or are instructed to empty the mind and avoid inner speech, random noise, word repetition or backward speech), on the rationale used (what is subtracted from what), on the statistical tools employed, and on the threshold settings. What is activated also depends on the context in which the stimulus appears and on the subject's "psychological set" (Hebb, 1972). The very same stimulus may be processed differently depending on whether it is perceived as speech or not, and depending on what type of linguistic task it is a component of. For example, Wang (1973) reported that, in an electroencephalographic (EEG) experiment, when a group of French speakers were asked to "listen to the following words" (all stimuli were CV words—the vast majority of CV syllables being real words in French), the subjects' left hemispheres showed increased activation. When subjects were asked to "listen to the following sounds" and the very same tape was played, they showed equal activation in both cerebral hemispheres. psychological set is thus a factor that cannot be ignored. Furthermore, the same stimuli (e.g., Chinese words in a tone discrimination task) will be processed differently depending on whether they are perceived as language (i.e., by a Chinese speaker) or not (i.e., by an English speaker). In an experiment by Klein et al. (2001), both Chinese and English speakers showed common regions of cerebral blood flow increase but only Chinese speakers showed additional activation in left-hemisphere areas; the English speakers, on the other hand, showed activity in the right inferior frontal cortex, an area associated with pitch perception.

I would like to present a couple of anecdotes to illustrate this point. The first involves visual perception. On January 26, 2001, Dr. Michela Gallagher gave a lecture at McGill University, as part of the Hebb Lecture Series, on "Neurobiology of the aging brain and cognition." Before her talk, she set up her PowerPoint computer and projected a picture on the screen. It remained there for several minutes while everyone was seated and she was introduced by the Chair of the Psychology Department. During all this time, I was looking at the picture on the screen, which looked like one of those fuzzy-shaped photographs of pieces of body tissue. Given the topic of the talk, I figured it must be a piece of hippocampus, though its shape was not at all obvious. As one tries to see something in a Rorschach blot or an unusually shaped cloud, after focusing on the picture for a while, I could make out something like a seal with its head pointing left, resting on one of its flippers, with the other in the air. I was quite conscious that this was pure invention, but I could not make anything else of this blotch. Then Dr. Gallagher started her talk by explaining that she was working on an animal model, namely with lab rats trained to swim to a platform below the surface of an opaque liquid. She then pointed to the picture on the screen and said, "This is a rat." At this instant, without trying, I clearly saw a rat. I did not have to search. There was a clear picture of a rat on that screen. Unlike the pictures where you see either a young or an old woman, depending on how you look at it, and you need someone to explain to you how to figure out how what you see as an old woman can actually be seen as a young woman, here the effect was instantaneous, without any explanation. The speaker simply said, "this is a rat," and I saw what most people in the audience had probably seen all along, namely a rat. I did not have to ask myself, where is the head, what position is it in, or anything of the sort.

The second anecdote involves auditory perception. Recently, on French television, a croupier explained that, at the roulette table, he once changed the words of the conventional call *les jeux sont faits, rien ne va plus* ('bets are placed, hold your bets') to *les oeufs sont frais, hier il a plu* ('the eggs are fresh, it rained yesterday,' keeping more or less the same vowels and number of syllables), and none of the gamblers seemed to notice. No one smiled or gave him a funny look. Both anecdotes illustrate the effect of state of mind. To a great extent, you see what you expect to see and hear what you expect to hear. There is a good top-down component to perception and comprehension. It is likely that many contexts have a non-negligible effect on what is activated in your brain while you are undergoing an experimental task.

Different neuroimaging techniques reveal different aspects of the overall picture. Some (e.g., Magnetic Encephalogram—MEG) are relatively insensitive to signals coming from any deeper than the side surface of the upper part of sulci, ignoring the vast cortical surface of the gyri and the subcortical structures involved. Others (e.g., PET) detect only what has modified the metabolism of areas activated for one minute or more (thus overlooking language processes that typically take milliseconds); furthermore, they can only give group results, thus missing any indication of individual variation.

It is true that neuroimaging studies often use different methods (functional magnetic resonance imaging (fMRI), MEG, or PET), different tasks (word generation, word translation, narrative generation, short story comprehension, or word completion), different baselines (word repetition, backward language, silence) and different subjects (of varying ages and experience in the use of L2). However, if the various techniques were equally valid *and* tapped into the same function, the activated areas should not differ and findings should not conflict. Therefore, it is likely that, at best, each study published so far has tapped into a different set of components of what authors broadly call *language*, or, at worst, that some have tapped into something other than language altogether. If different tasks correlate with different results, it is likely that each observed cerebral activation corresponds to each task, reflecting a different functional entity (hopefully, a component of language—though, because of numerous other problems with signal change, significance thresholds, baselines, statistical factors, etc., some may reveal something other than language, e.g., a sensory, motor, memory, attention, or executive component).

If one wishes to claim that very similar experiments designed to isolate the same language processes show activation in non-overlapping cortical areas because these studies use different methodologies, then one must be able to predict which variable will cause which observed activation, and why. To suggest that the discrepancy among neuroimaging study results "is likely due to differences in the experimental tasks, imaging procedures, and protocol" (Simos et al., 2001: 77) is to admit that none (or only one—though we have no means of knowing *which* one) can be valid, given that they all purport to identify the same entity, namely, the cerebral areas subserving L1 and L2.

If a given process is not a unitary function, then one ought to identify which component of the process is responsible for the observed results in each specific study. Until we can do this, we cannot know what causes the observed activation at any particular site (and one must eventually be able to show that *this* site's activation is the result of this variable, and *that* site's activation the result of another identified variable). We cannot simply invoke "methodological differences" without having a clear idea of the specific contribution of each methodological variable alleged to be responsible for the observed differences. We must also explain in what specific way(s) the method of presentation influences the activation sites. In other words, when factors are adduced to have an influence on the results, one must specify *how* (i.e., which factor has what influence on the results, and for what specific reason).

When one claims to identify areas that subserve a particular function, one ought therefore to be able to explain what the appropriate task that truly reveals the function is, what the appropriate presentation parameters and control conditions are, and why—since it is assumed that they will significantly influence the results (i.e., one must give a rationale for the method's validity). Unfortunately, not one study uses more than one method. Different studies purporting to measure the same entity arrive at contradictory findings, as revealed below.

The problems with neuroimaging studies

Howard Chertkow and Susan Murtha (1997) may have been a little over-enthusiastic when they stated that brain activation studies using PET have produced a breakthrough in our understanding of the neural basis of language. In fact, they themselves concede that cognitive neuroscientists have become acutely aware of the limitations inherent in the PET approach and they outline a number of pervasive problems: (1) the use of intersubject averaging (masking individual differences); (2) the subtraction paradigm (without empirical evidence of its validity); (3) the lack of knowledge of the physiological basis of cerebral blood flow (CBF) changes; (4) the influence of the rate of presentation of stimuli on CBF response (habituation phenomena); (5) the question of what to analyze in PET data (given the representations as networks of activity rather than simply increases and decreases at a particular point, and given the known predominance of inhibitory neural processing and inhibitory cognitive mechanisms, the increase/decrease CBF paradigm seems problematic); (6) the poor temporal resolution (averaging over one minute for phenomena that last milliseconds); (7) the distributed nature of cerebral processing (lack of circumscribed locus); (8) the multiple unintended secondary processes ("there is a high chance that you'll find something somewhere", p. 85).

Chertkow and Murtha even point out that "researchers are increasingly returning to brain-lesion data to help separate 'the wheat from the chaff' in activation studies" (p. 84) and they characterize the contribution of PET activation studies to our understanding of language and aphasia as "an intriguing and challenging pot pourri of results, some clear, some surprising, and others plain baffling" (p. 85). This does not prevent the authors from concluding that "Broca's initial finding of a left lateralized language area has been strongly supported." Maybe so, but not by PET studies: They consistently show concurrent and homologous right-hemisphere activation (Lassen, Ingvar, & Skinhøj, 1978; Müller et al., 1997; Perani et al., 1998).

Kent (1998) also considers that neuroimaging studies have greatly enhanced the potential to understand brain-behavior relationships in complex behaviors such as language, and that fMRI will contribute substantially to new knowledge about brain activation for language processing. Nevertheless, he too lists a number of pitfalls related to the reliability of imagery, control conditions, registration and normalization of data, and spatial and temporal resolution; he concludes that enthusiasm to use neuroimaging technologies should be tempered with caution and an understanding of their limitations.

Similarly, Démonet and Thierry (2001) concede that functional imaging techniques "suffer numerous deficits that might have been underestimated because of the rush for results that the scientific community keeps encouraging" (p. 49). The authors describe a number of methodological problems which they realize are not without theoretical consequences. Nonetheless, in their abstract they declare that "although brain mapping of language is still hampered by many methodological pitfalls, these methods now appear reliable" (p. 49).

There are in fact several additional problems inherent in neuroimaging techniques. To mention only a few, (1) many structures are smaller than PET's spatial resolution of 2 to 3 mm can detect. As a result, "the functional neuroanatomy of smaller structures such as the thalamus or particular areas of the hippocampus will be impossible to resolve using PET techniques". (Kertesz, 1994, p. 15). (2) "Depending on the proximity of different activation foci and the degree of smoothing used, activity from one focus may contribute significantly to the activation level of a neighboring focus" (Binder & Price, 2001, p. 193). (3) The ambient state (e.g., environmental conditions, diet, anxiety) will have a complex effect on the distribution and magnitude of the PET measured physiological variable (Hoffman & Phelps, 1992, p. 248). (4) It is virtually impossible to guarantee that subjects are doing nothing but the cognitive computation in question and hence systems other than (i.e., in addition to) those explicitly tapped in a given task are likely to be activated. "Therefore, it is rather difficult to interpret what the result of a subtraction represents in terms of cognitive processes" (Poeppel, 1996, p. 345). (5) Even the typical "resting state" is actually a condition characterized by rich cognitive activity (McKiernan et al., 2003). (6) "A cognitive module can be served by several brain areas and each brain area can be involved in multiple cognitive modules" (Friedman et al., 1998, p. 252). (7) It is not known whether all the active regions are essential for the performance of a specific task (Price & Friston, 1999; Brown & Hagoort, 2000). (8) Imaging studies converge only partially with lesion and stimulation findings (Illes et al., 1999). (9) The coupling of blood flow and neural metabolism is influenced by the size of the activated region, cell density, morphology of the vasculature and basal metabolism (Démonet & Thierry, 2001; (10) BOLD-related fMRI suffers from a shadowy theoretical relationship between neural activity and recorded data (Démonet & Thierry, 2001), i.e., the relationship between what is observed and reported (recorded data) and what this actually reflects (neural activity) is dubious. (11) An (arbitrary) change of the statistical threshold setting can result in an apparent increase of activated areas and even cause a shift in the asymmetry index (Chee et al., 1999a); (12) In language studies that directly compare PET and fMRI using the same tasks with the same subjects, there is no overlap between the activated regions (Vaid & Hull, 2002), suggesting that each technique measures something different related to the task, and not necessarily related to language processing. (13) Not only PET (as mentioned above) but also fMRI may simply not have the spatial resolution to detect the subtle differences that occur in language processing (Hernandez, Martinez, & Kohnert, 2000). Finally, probably most problematic of all, (14) fMRI measurements are quite variable within subjects who are tested for a second time both in terms of which brain regions are activated and in terms of the magnitude and extent of activation (Ramsey et al., 1996); variability in fMRI results have been observed both within and across sessions (Binder, 1995). All of this should give us serious cause for concern about the reliability and validity of PET and fMRI as well as neuroimaging in general. We are compelled to agree with Papanicolaou and Billingsley (2003) when they state that "without reliability, the images should not be considered as scientific data any more than ordinary behavioral data should under the same circumstances" (p. 253).

The reader will judge whether concern with unreliable results and contradictory findings constitute undue suspicion, on the grounds that for neuroimaging the rules of critical scientific appraisal should be considerably liberalized, or whether it is justified to expect that one should apply the criteria of functional specificity, reliability, validity, and spatial and temporal resolution proposed by Billingsley et al. (2003); in particular, as suggested by Papanicolaou and Billingsley (2003), the criterion that no image of cerebral mechanism should be considered to be accurate and realistic unless it has been externally validated, i.e., unless independently derived information corroborates the imaging data. It does not seem unreasonable to expect that tasks that purportedly tap the same linguistic function should, in principle, activate the same brain regions, and that the activation profile should be similar for the same individual in different sessions (Billingsley et al., 2003).

Before we can be confident of the validity even of MEG findings, a technique that is supposed to afford both the spatial resolution of fMRI and the temporal resolution of electroencephalographic evoked response potentials (ERPs), the following points remain to be demonstrated: (1) the extent to which the late components of the magnetic fields elicited by the stimuli actually reflect language-specific activation; (2) the extent to which the mathematical model for estimating the sources of these components is valid; and more specifically, (3) the extent to which the simple dipole source model, applied to the magnetic field distribution observed over each hemisphere separately, at 4-millisecond intervals following presentation of each stimulus, provides an accurate and complete picture of the brain activation associated with a particular language task (Simos et al., 2001). Note that a typical MEG paradigm requires at least 60 iterations of a given stimulus (usually single words) in order to ensure that reliable average event-related fields are obtained. Both single-word presentation and stimulus repetition are problematic.

A combined analysis of varied language tasks could improve the identification of regions involved in generic language functions rather than in functions specific to a single task (as proposed by Ramsey et al., 2001) only to the extent that the activation corresponding to each task actually correlates positively with a bona fide language component. Yet there is still a long way to go before this is ascertained.

One ought to be able to account for the considerable inter-individual variation reported among homogeneous groups of speakers. For example, in the Chee et al. (1999a) study, why do 2 of the 9 participants (23%) not activate their temporal lobe when processing text for comprehension, and of the 7 who do, why do only 6 show left posterior temporal gyrus *and/or* middle temporal gyrus *or* angular gyrus activation, while only 3 show activations in the anterior pole? Either (1) Brodmann's areas do not correspond to specific functional processes (i.e., temporal lobes need not be used to comprehend text, and when they are, different areas are used by different individuals to perform the same task); or (2) different cognitive processes may be engaged by different individuals performing the same task; or (3) the observed activation is a result of artifacts, such as, among others, the statistical threshold setting. In the Chee et al. (1999a) study, the interindividual differences cannot be attributed to incomplete implicit linguistic competence with concomitant use of different compensatory strategies (as could be the case, for example, in Dehaene et al., 1997), because all subjects were early fluent bilinguals who used both languages in daily life.

The results of neuroimaging studies with bilingual subjects are beginning to look as contradictory as those of bilingual lateralization studies using dichotic and tachistoscopic paradigms in the 1970s and 1980s (Paradis, 1990b, 1992a, 1995a, 2003): Some studies found a difference between early and late bilinguals, others did not; those that did find differences, found different ones. Similarly, some neuroimaging studies report less activation in the classical language areas for the weaker language (Perani et al., 1996; Dehaene et al., 1997; Halsband et al., 2001), while others report greater activation (Yetkin et al., 1996; Nakai et al., 1999; Chee et al., 2001; Hasegawa, Carpenter, & Just, 2002). Some report additional areas of activation for the weaker language (Perani et al., 1996;

Dehaene et al., 1997; Calabrese et al., 2001; Marian et al., 2003; Vingerhoets et al., 2003), while others report no difference (Chee et al., 1999a, b; Klein et al., 1995a, b, 1999). (As discussed further below, some differences may be explained by the type of task, i.e., text (procedural) vs. words (declarative), but here both single-word and text-comprehension tasks are represented in each set.) In various single-word tasks claiming to tap semantic processing, some studies report no right-hemisphere activation (Klein et al., 1995a, b), while others find greater right-hemisphere participation (Calabrese et al., 2001; Hernandez et al., 2001a) in the second language.

Demb et al. (1995) and Illes et al. (1999) interpret the fMRI finding of left inferior frontal region activation (Brodmann's areas 45, 46) as indicating that this region is involved in the retrieval of semantic information. Yet, the same area is reported by Sergent et al. (1992), Pugh et al. (1996) and Joubert (1999) to be activated during nonword reading, which is interpreted as indicating that this left frontal region is involved in specific forms of phonological processing and not semantic processing. Activation of Brodmann's areas 45 and 46 is thus interpreted by different authors as indicating the neural substrate for two opposing functional components of the task of reading single words (each to the exclusion of the other)—both using fMRI. Pillai et al. (2003) report conflicting results regarding activation topography in phonological versus semantic processing in bilinguals. Not only are the findings of Marian, Spivey, & Hirsch (2001) and Lee et al. (2002) which they cite not consistent with each other, but neither set of results is consistent with theirs. If these differences are related to differences in study design, then it would be important to stipulate which parameter causes which difference and why, and consequently to know which design actually reveals the areas involved in the processes of interest.

Hernandez et al. (2001b) present a pattern of findings exactly opposite to what Price, Green, and von Studnitz (1999) found. (1) The former found that the blocked condition shows activation not observed in the mixed condition, whereas the latter had found the reverse: increased activation in the mixed condition over the blocked condition. (2) Price et al. (1999) did not find any evidence of dorsolateral prefrontal activation in language switching, whereas Hernandez et al. (2001b) did. It is true that one study used PET and the other fMRI and that the two tasks were not identical. But then, neither study actually monitors natural processes of language switching. As indicated by Hernandez et al. (2001b), these studies do compare to any other task-switching study (e.g., Dove et al., 2000; Garavan et al., 2000), but not to normal language-switching. Not only is it difficult to establish that this particular task is representative of the entire range of bilingual language processing, as noted by Hernandez et al., but it is not even representative of normal language switching.

Whether they use words, sentences or text as stimuli, most studies find that early bilinguals activate common cortical areas when processing L1 and L2 (e.g., Kim et al., 1997; Chee et al., 1999b, 2000; Hernandez et al., 2000; Urbanik et al., 2001) even when L1 is not the dominant language (Hernandez et al., 2001b) and irrespective of the differences in orthography, phonology and syntax between the two languages (Chee et al., 1999a). Conversely, late bilinguals with moderate fluency in L2 are reported to use different areas (Perani et al., 1996; Dehaene et al., 1997; Kim et al., 1997; Urbanik et al., 2001; Nakai et al., 1999) or at least do not show complete overlap (Simos et al., 2001). However, some find that late fluent bilinguals activate the same cortical areas for L1 and L2 (Klein et al., 1994, 1995a, b, 1999; Perani et al., 1998; Illes et al., 1999; Pu et al., 2001; Tan et al., 2001b, 2003), even if they have only moderate fluency (Hasegawa et al., 2002). Even though, on a reading task, different L1s activate different areas specific to their orthography (i.e., English vs. Japanese), activation patterns associated with reading L2 are reported to be virtually identical to the patterns associated with L1 in late bilinguals (Nakada, Fujii, & Kwee, 2001).

Whether they activate the same or different areas, some studies report higher activation for L1 words or sentences (Perani et al., 1996; Dehaene et al., 1997; Chee et al., 2001), while other studies find higher activation for L2 words or sentences (Yetkin et al., 1996; Nakai et al., 1999; Hernandez et al., 2001a; Urbanik et al., 2001; Hasegawa et al., 2002; Luke et al., 2002). Some report that activated language areas increase with proficiency (Perani et al., 1998), others that they decrease with proficiency (Yetkin et al., 1996; Hasegawa et al., 2002). Languages not known by the subjects (and hence incomprehensible) are reported to activate Wernicke's area (Mazoyer et al., 1993; Perani et al., 1996; Nakai et al., 1999) or not to do so (Schlosser et al., 1998).

When tasks rely on declarative memory, the extent of the activated areas is likely to increase as a function of task difficulty; when tasks rely on procedural memory, the activated areas are likely to decrease as automatization increases. However, to the extent that the implicit morphosyntactic system is more extensive in the native language (or native languages in early bilinguals), the perisylvian classical language areas are likely to be larger and show less dispersion (see Dehaene et al.'s 1997 data) than for L2 processing.

Additional right-hemisphere activation during the processing of the second, weaker language is reported in some studies (Dehaene et al., 1997; Calabrese et al., 2001; Chee et al., 2001; Urbanik et al., 2001) whereas other studies report no right-hemisphere contribution to bilingual processing in late fluent bilinguals (Klein et al., 1994, 1995a, b).

ERP studies do not seem to fare much better. Whereas Weber-Fox and Neville (1996) found no difference in the processing of languages between unilinguals and early bilinguals (although late bilinguals did show differential processing), Proverbio, Cok and Zani (2002) find inter- and intrahemispheric activation asymmetries in early, highly fluent bilinguals.

In her contribution to the understanding of how different languages are represented in the human brain, Klein (2003) used a synonym generation task in a PET study of a bilingual patient about to undergo surgery for the removal of a posterior temporal cavernous angioma. In the abstract and the discussion, the author emphasizes that cerebral blood flow increases were observed for both languages in similar locations in the left inferior frontal gyrus and bilaterally in the cerebellum. This would indeed suggest that overlapping neural substrates are involved in L1 and L2. But even at this single-word level, there were also substantial differences in areas of activation (left middle frontal gyrus and right lingual gyrus for L2 only, and left superior parietal lobule and thalamus for L1 only). These differences remain unexplained. Yet they are consonant with greater involvement of implicit competence in L1 processing and greater effort in processing a weaker L2. The left middle frontal gyrus has been associated with inhibition of a cognitive set (Konishi et al., 2003), response inhibition (Brass, Zysset, & von Cramon, 2001), extensive control over working memory (Collette et al., 1999; Clark et al., 2000; Ranganath, Johnson, & D'Esposito, 2003) and attentional processes (Lepsien & Pollmann, 2002). The lingual gyrus has been associated with selective attention and monitoring in response inhibition and competition (Menon et al., 2001). All these processes are likely to be involved in a task like synonym generation where the stimulus must be inhibited in order to activate a response. The fact that these areas are more active in L2 is consonant with L2 being less fully mastered, as confirmed by the patient's lower scores in that language. The involvement of subcortical structures for L1 only (the thalamus) might confirm a more extensive competence for that language. The activation of the left superior parietal lobule is more difficult to account for (it is generally associated with visual motor and mental rotation tasks and visuospatial working memory), unless one is prepared to consider this an artifact of the selected threshold setting or of statistics. But then, why would the other findings not be artifacts as well?

Equally puzzling are the results reported by Klein et al. (2002) concerning another patient (with right cerebral language representation as determined by the sodium amytal test) who is also depicted as showing similar patterns of cerebral blood flow across all three of her languages (two native languages, L2 learned later). Here too several brain regions were active in relation to synonym generation, and these areas differed across languages. Activity in the right angular gyrus and bilaterally in the middle temporal gyrus was found for L1a and L2 but not L1b; bilateral activity in the inferior temporal gyrus for both L1s but not L2; and bilateral activity in the cerebellum for both L1s but unilateral in the left cerebellum for L2. The authors admit that these differences are difficult to interpret without a clear understanding of the functional significance of these regions in relation to language tasks. Results similar to those of Patient D.P. (Klein, 2003) were obtained: Perfect repetition score for all three languages, but 85% for L1a and 54% and 50% for L1b and L2 respectively on synonym generation, clearly showing that the patient was most proficient in her L1a. Admittedly, this patient differed from D.P. in that her speech was represented exclusively in the right cerebral hemisphere and she had a long-standing history of seizures, but neither set of activations is independently interpretable.

One might be concerned with the fact that, in neuroimaging studies, diverse individual brain shapes and gyral patterns (themselves not coextensive with cytoarchitecture—which is probably more relevant for functional localization) are averaged and further transformed to fit a pre-ordained common mold of standard representational maps (such as Talairach's (1988) standard templates), using a linear scaling method. But all the other, much more fundamental, problems make this one seem quite trivial by comparison, since, even if the measures were accurate, they might not be germane. Gross anatomy (in terms of gyri, as is usually reported) is likely not to be an appropriate measure of functional localization if, as proposed, languages are represented as subsystems that differ micro-anatomically in their dedicated neuronal circuitry, but are nevertheless located within the same macro-anatomical areas that subserve the various structural components of language (phonological, morphosyntactic and lexico-semantic). Hasegawa et al. (2002) pointed out that the analysis of cortical processing of languages is limited by the spatial resolution of the technology: When the location of the activation is similar in both languages, it is possible that the networks that are reflected in the activation are spatially adjacent within a 52 mm^3 voxel in which fMRI data are acquired.

Schwartz and Kirsner (1984) predicted that EEG and neuroimaging laterality measures were likely to be no more successful than dichotic and visual half field studies unless (1) the group studies are homogeneous, (2) the measures used are reliable and (3) the measures are valid indicators of cerebral functioning. (For an outline of the design characteristics of an ideal bilingual neuroimaging study, see Vaid, 2002.)

Let us conclude this section by remarking that another similarity with the experimental laterality studies of earlier decades is the threat that recommendations will be made prematurely concerning the direct application of neuropsychological speculations to second-language education. For example, Coggins, Kennedy, and Armstrong (2004) conjecture that the corpus callosum should be significantly larger in bilingual individuals compared to unilingual individuals. Based on "the preliminary findings" of "the first known study to address the relationship between the corpus callosum and bilingual capacity," and although the reported significance of the differences in the corpus callosum's midsagittal anterior midbody regional area "should be interpreted cautiously due to small sample size," the authors conclude that the results of their MRI study "could suggest that bilingual learning and use can have a profound effect on brain structure in general and the corpus callosum in particular." Coggins, Kennedy, and Armstrong are confident that, in spite of a lack of significant area differences between their two groups of subjects in the corpus callosum anterior third, the posterior midbody, isthmus and posterior callosum regions, these differences nevertheless "most likely exist but the sample size was too small to detect them." They go on to suggest that the role of the corpus callosum in bilingual processing should be further investigated for its potential application to second-language learning. Fortunately, the authors refrain from making any recommendation, however vague, but confine themselves to speculating that further studies will present "enormous educational implications with respect to second language education funding, instruction, and curriculum" and that, "considering the potential of important implications, funding for such studies would be a wise investment." The promise in the abstract that the paper discusses possible implications for second-language educators and students is not fulfilled. Not a single implication is hinted at; it is only repeatedly stated instead that they are enormous and important. Hopefully, funding agencies will be curious about the nature of these implications once we know whether the size differences between the corpus callosum of bilinguals and unilinguals that were reported not to be significant actually are, and whether the expected callosum adaptation to L2 is temporary or permanent (e.g., how can one grow a thicker corpus callosum in class, and for what specific purpose?).

The need for a neurolinguistically informed theory

Without a neurolinguistically informed theory, we can only observe that a particular parameter (task, procedure, baseline, etc.) has a particular effect, but we do not know why. As Carr (1998) warns, accurate task analysis is not easy, and it often turns out that even the simplest-seeming task requires considerable conceptual and empirical work to understand—yet it is essential for proper theoretical interpretation. A lack of sophisticated theoretical knowledge about the function being investigated (for example, the representation of languages in bilingual speakers) may lead to simplistic and naive interpretations. In the absence of any expectations of what one is likely to find on the basis of a sound neurolinguistic theory, one is liable to miss what, in light of an informed interpretational framework, would appear obvious. For example, in the late 1970s and early 1980s, David Ingvar (personal communication, 1981) was puzzled by the right-hemisphere co-activation that he and his co-workers were finding for language tasks, as measured by regional cerebral blood flow (rCBF), using inhaled xenon[133] (Lassen et al., 1978). It was surmised at the time that maybe this had to do with the hemodynamics of the neurovascular system, which might impose similar contralateral flow for the sake of symmetry. Another explanation, of course, is that right-hemisphere-based pragmatic competence is just as necessary to process verbal material as what was then considered "language." Similarly, Perani et al. (1996) and Dehaene et al. (1997) did not interpret the fact that L2 stimuli increased right hemisphere, parahippocampal gyri and anterior cingulate participation as possible evidence of an increased use of pragmatics and controlled metalinguistic knowledge.

Data by themselves do not tell us anything. They need to be interpreted. Their interpretation will only be as valid as the theory and background knowledge used to interpret them. Then again, the data themselves are a function of the hypothesis used to design the method for collecting them (even if this hypothesis is naive, commonsensical or covert). Data are not theory-free. They are only as good as the theory-driven selection of the task, stimuli, experimental procedure, and criteria for interpretation. Data are nevertheless important and cannot be ignored when they happen not to correspond to the researcher's expectations. They must then be reconciled with the theory by explaining them within its framework, or one must consider modifying the theory to accommodate them.

As mentioned earlier, a major problem with PET and fMRI data is that they tell us that some cerebral area is activated during the performance of a particular task, but they do not tell us what function is activated in this area. Since a language task is intrinsically complex, one must infer which component is responsible for the activation of each area on the basis of a hypothetical construct. This inference is also only as good as the theory on which the construct is based. Whether the interpretation of the function of an area activated in PET is valid depends on the task selected to isolate by subtraction the area involved in a given task or subtask (Warburton et al., 1996).

A good example of the lack of a neurolinguistically informed hypothesis, and corresponding lack of a sound rationale for the interpretation of findings, is the study by Nakada et al. (2001), confirmed by Nakada's (2002) refusal to address the problem (he sets off instead on a red herring attack on a straw man in his response to Tomioka and Paradis's (2002) comments). Readers are encouraged not to take my word for it, but to refer to the original, as it constitutes a paradigm case.

Nakada et al. (2001) reported that the cortical activation patterns associated with reading Japanese were significantly different from those associated with reading English in native speakers of these languages: Areas flanking the posterior aspect of the left inferior temporal sulcus were activated in all Japanese subjects and in none of the English subjects. The authors attribute this to the different cognitive processes required for reading two languages that differ substantially in their written coding architecture. They then hypothesize that literacy established in an individual's first language (L1) should have a significant effect on the acquisition of literacy in the second language (L2), and report that activation patterns associated with reading L2 were virtually identical to those associated with reading L1. They concluded that L2 represents a cognitive extension of L1.

Tomioka and Paradis (2002) pointed out that one faces an apparent (unresolved) contradiction. The type of writing system determines the cognitive operations used and hence different systems result in different cognitive operations, as manifested in the activation of different cortical structures in Japanese and English. This must now be reconciled with the fact that English readers of Japanese apparently process Japanese in the same way as English, and Japanese readers of English process English in the same way as Japanese. It therefore appears that reading strategies depend on something other than the structure of the writing system. One cannot both explain the differential activation by the difference in orthography and claim that people use the same cognitive processes to read the non-congruent system. What needs to be explained is how one can read English as if it were Japanese or Japanese as if it were English.

One major factor that may affect the results of the experiment is that kanji constituted less than 25% of the characters in the stimulus paragraphs used in the experiment. The activation pattern obtained with the Japanese subjects might therefore, to a great extent, represent the processing of kana rather than kanji. This would reduce the difference between the English and Japanese writing systems inasmuch as both would contain morphograms (kanji and irregular English words) and syllabically read words (kana and English words with a regular grapheme-to-phoneme correspondence).

Tomioka and Paradis concluded that Nakada et al.'s most unexpected results posed a challenge to the neuropsychology of bilingualism in particular, and possibly to the reliability and/or validity of neuroimaging findings in general. It is unfortunate that Nakada (2002), in what is purported to be a reply, chose not to address any of the points raised by Tomioka and Paradis (2002) in their comments on the earlier article. Instead, Nakada embarked on a critique of what he deems to be classical psychology's perspective of strong localizationist predetermined functionality, implying that this is Tomioka and Paradis's point of view. As a result, their questions remain unanswered, namely (1) how Nakada et al. (2001) can assume that the effect they observe is due to the specificity of kanji orthography, given the small proportion of such characters in the stimulus texts, and (2) how they can reconcile the claim that the architecture of the orthography determines which cerebral mechanism is involved (i.e., which brain area is activated) with the expectation (and finding) that the areas recruited on the basis of L1-specific orthography also subserve the reading of an L2 deemed to differ considerably in its orthographic architecture.

In fact, Tomioka and Paradis's (2002) arguments were based solely on Nakada et al.'s (2001) own localizationist statements, which Nakada (2002) judges to be "extreme" and assumes to be predetermined—an assumption neither held by Tomioka and Paradis nor hinted at in their comments. Tomioka and Paradis never mentioned, let alone adopted, the notion that there is an absolutely deterministic blueprint for cortical connectivity in associative cortices, as charged by Nakada. Their comments are perfectly compatible with functional localization's representing the result of cortical self-organization as a function of experience and task demands, as put forward by Nakada (2002). They refer only to Nakada et al.'s (2001) own localizationist claim that the posterior aspect of the left inferior temporal sulcus is uniquely recruited to subserve the specific architecture of the kanji writing system and no other writing system, such as that of English.

Nakada's suggestion that no deterministic blueprint exists is in fact, to a large extent, probably true, at birth. But, as implied by Nakada et al. (2001), once functions have established their neural substrate, they do rely on dedicated networks with specific connections. One cannot claim on the one hand that, because of specific functional requirements, a particular cerebral area develops in order to subserve a particular function, and at the same time that, once this area has self-organized to suit particular purposes, it can be used to subserve a different task with a very different set of stipulations—unless, as argued by Tomioka and Paradis (2002), one shows how the new task can adapt to the old processing characteristics. Once connections have been established, they serve a particular function and can be recruited to subserve another function only under duress, such as when a particular source of experiential information is absent or lost; in such cases, some of the cortical area previously dedicated to a lost function may be colonized by another. But it remains to be demonstrated that an area that is already committed *and still frequently used* can undertake to concurrently subserve a different function.

Cortical self-organization is presumably determined by the particular function a given brain area is meant to process. It will depend on demands of the architecture of the task (as in the physiological acquisition of kanji). The posterior aspect of the left inferior temporal sulcus is assumed to be recruited to subserve the particular computational procedures specifically required to read kanji. This means that, once this region has cortically self-organized to subserve reading kanji, this is what it does. (No other area does the same thing, nor does this area subserve any other reading strategy, as reported in Nakada et al.'s study.) The circuitry is established in such a way as to correspond to the processing of a particular set of computational procedures. (Note that Nakada et al. specifically assume that kanji and English, because of the specific characteristics of their writing architecture, require different computational procedures which cause kanji, but not English, to activate the posterior aspect of the left inferior temporal sulcus.)

One cannot at the same time claim (1) that a circumscribed cortical area organizes itself as a response to certain types of stimuli with specific computational demands and (2) that it continues to process these stimuli while, in addition, processing stimuli that require different procedures normally computed elsewhere. Either (1) kanji processing is not specifically attached to the posterior aspect of the left inferior temporal sulcus once kanji reading has been acquired (contra Nakada et al.'s claim), or (2) it is possible to use these kanji-specific procedures to process English text (in which case the procedures can no longer be considered specific to kanji, contra Nakada et al.'s claim), or (3) in Japanese native speakers, English-specific procedures are subserved by the posterior aspect of the left inferior temporal sulcus, in addition to the kanji-specific procedures that continue to rely on this cerebral substratum, while the reverse is true of English native speakers (in line with Nakada et al., 2001). Still, even though there may be no genetically determined maps, once a function has established itself in a region, that region is not known to be inclined to support an *additional* function that relies on different computational procedures.

Even if, as claimed by Nakada (2002), kanji were to be considered as "combination syllabograms" (and the only difference between kana and kanji were the complexity of the process of conversion from symbol to sound) and the differences in self-organization shown in Nakada et al. (2001) reflected differences in the process of decoding symbols, it nevertheless appears to be the case that this difference in processing is sufficient for kana and kanji to be subserved by different neural substrates (as Nakada et al. state themselves, citing studies in support). Each type of character is susceptible to selective impairment, as the numerous cases of double dissociation between acquired dyslexia for kana and for kanji (with different corresponding lesion sites) have demonstrated (Paradis, Hagiwara, & Hildebrandt, 1985). This occurs in spite of the fact that kana and kanji are learned consecutively with an interval much shorter than the period between the appropriation of one's native language and a second language learned in school. In other words, it appears that two processes, even processes as similar as kana and kanji, nevertheless do not result in the self-(re)organization of the same cortical area.

A more plausible explanation than the one proposed by Nakada et al. (2001) could be, for example, that implicit prosody, which accompanies silent reading (Fodor, 2002), is responsible for the observed activation: Japanese native speakers would read English with the (subvocal) prosody characteristic of Japanese (a mora-timed language), whereas native speakers of English (a stress-timed language, belonging to a rhythmic class very different from Japanese—Nazzi, Bertoncini, & Mehler, 1998; Rasmus, Nespor, & Mehler, 1999) would subvocalize Japanese using English prosody (C. Berckmoes[1]). The activation would have nothing to do with the particular writing architecture of kanji (which, given the small percentage of Kanji in the stimulus text, would not be surprising). Another possible explanation might be that L2 readers mentally translate the L2 text into their L1 (in line with Kroll & de Groot's (1997) model) and it is the L1 activation at the end of the process of translation that is reflected in the observed imaging results (D. Yeo[1]). I am not claiming that either of these explanations is necessarily the right one, only that each is more plausible than that proposed by Nakada et al. (2001), whereby the structure of the L1 orthography determines the cerebral structures involved in reading both L1 and L2.

Another example of lack of linguistic sophistication is a major confusion between phonology and orthography. For example, whereas Tan et al. (2001b) claim to localize the brain areas responsible for the phonological processing of

---

[1]Celine Berckmoes and Donald Yeo were participants in the International Neuropsychological Society 2002 Vivian Smith Advanced Summer Institute. They suggested the alternative interpretations reported above during a class discussion of Nakada et al.'s (2001) article.

Chinese (L1) and English (L2), they use a reading task with the rationale that "while English words map onto phonemes and abide by letter-sound conversion rules, Chinese uses characters with no parts in the character corresponding to phonological segments such as phonemes." (p. 612). First, letter-to-sound is only one of three possible routes for English reading, but this is not the issue here. The problem is that claims are made about the *phonological* processing of Chinese and English, on the basis of a rhyming decision task between written English words and Chinese characters said to rely on maximally differing grapheme-to-sound correspondences. Under these circumstances, it is difficult to decide whether the observed activations are due to (1) phonological processing (as claimed), (2) orthography-driven reading strategies, or (3) the metalinguistic awareness of the similarity or difference between the two sounds, once derived from the spelling. The authors' conclusion is illustrative of the oral/written confusion, as they interpret the observed common network of L1 and L2 as suggesting that the processing of L1 *phonology* at the syllabic level carries over to L2 processing, making Chinese readers less capable of processing English by recourse to an analytic *letter-sound conversion reading system*. Note that the reported common area of activation (BA 9 and 46) related to rhyme decision in both L1 and L2 is deemed crucial for Chinese *reading*.

Chee and Soon (2003) allege that fMRI can evaluate the lateralization of language functions and how two languages are processed in the brain. In order to do this, one would first need to be able to unambiguously interpret the observed data. Such an ability presupposes (1) that one has a means to ascertain the significance of the observed activations (e.g., whether they represent actual activation or inhibition of neural circuits in the region; what it is that is observed at given threshold levels), and (2) that one has a theoretical framework as to what function is being tapped (e.g., components of the language system or pragmatic aspects of language function). For instance, the fact that the right hemisphere is activated when a certain level of syntactic complexity is attained is not necessarily evidence that complex syntactic constructions are subserved by the right hemisphere; it more likely indicates that pragmatics takes over where syntax gives up and/or that the less frequent, more complex form is consciously constructed, hence involving declarative memory. Clinical investigations overwhelmingly point to an extremely limited linguistic potential for the right hemisphere—except when the left-hemisphere cortex is removed between one and five months after birth (Dennis & Whitaker, 1976). The right hemispheres of most split-brain patients do not show evidence of linguistic capacities of any kind; in the very few cases where they do, this is attributable to the presence of early left-brain damage (Gazzaniga,

2000). This is confirmed by the recent case reported by Trudeau et al. (2003) of a patient with Rasmussen syndrome who, subsequent to a left functional hemispherectomy, exhibited severely affected comprehension, even for single words, with production limited to only a few overlearned words. Even though the patient had suffered from epileptic seizures at age 5, suggesting early left-hemisphere damage, language had not relocated to the right hemisphere.

Another frequent problem is terminological ambiguity. For example, the term *semantics*, when used without specification, is multiply ambiguous. It may refer to the meaning of sentences, namely the computation of the meaning of words and the underlying syntactic structure. It may refer to the lexical meanings of words. In many neuroimaging studies, it is not clear whether it refers to the lexical meanings of words or to conceptual meanings. Semantic representations (meanings derived from verbal material) are not distinguished from conceptual representations (world knowledge and episodic knowledge). Nor is semantics distinguished from pragmatics, the meaning derived from utterances, taking into account the situational and textual contexts of their use and general knowledge. The reader can sometimes infer what the authors mean by the term, but this is not always possible. Hence most claims are uninterpretable and could be right or wrong depending on what the authors actually mean. This is a serious problem when claims are made about the increased participation of the right hemisphere in bilinguals: Is it a component of the language system or a pragmatic feature that is claimed to be less asymmetrically represented, or is it rather that late bilinguals rely to a greater extent on pragmatic cues? Similarly, when claims are made about bilinguals having either one or two semantic systems, are we talking about one common semantic system or one conceptual system (with possibly two corresponding language-specific semantic systems)?

Results cannot be generalized from single words to "language"

The majority of studies to date (28) have used single words as stimuli. Yet single words are the least likely candidates for investigating "language" representation, given that what makes language most specific as a cognitive function, i.e., the language system (phonology, morphology, syntax), is supported by procedural memory, whereas isolated words are supported by declarative memory and hence are less focalized in their cortical representation. Words stand apart from the rest of language structure in several ways: (1) Chimpanzees and gorillas are able to learn large numbers of words but acquire very little syntax—if any (Terrace, 1979; Bonvillian & Patterson, 1993). (2)

Children deprived of language input during infancy find the acquisition of grammar laborious, whereas vocabulary growth is relatively unconstrained (Lebrun, 1978). (3) The famous anterograde amnesic patient H.M. was incapable of learning new words even though he could still learn new motor and cognitive skills (Cohen, 1991). (4) Alzheimer patients usually retain functions supported by (implicit) procedural memory well after they have lost access to the functions supported by (explicit) declarative memory—including vocabulary (Chapman, 1996; Obler, 1999). (5) In L1 attrition, lexical items suffer by far the most from L2 interference (Köpke, 2002), presumably because words in both languages are supported by declarative memory whereas other aspects of the language system in L1 (and possibly, but not necessarily in L2) are supported by procedural memory. (6) Whereas late learners of a second language have difficulty acquiring its prosody, phonology, morphology and syntax, there seems to be no age limit for learning new words (Klein et al., 1999; Abutalebi et al., 2001). Most importantly, (7) early and late bilinguals, like unilinguals, treat single words in the same manner because they are of the same kind, namely, items in declarative memory, as opposed to the other components of language (phonology, morphology and syntax), which are part of domain-specific implicit computational systems (Paradis, 1994; Ullman et al., 1997), and likely of subsystems for each language. Reading isolated words is therefore unlikely to allow one to infer the cerebral localization of language areas.

Single-word recognition (Simos et al., 2001), word repetition (Klein et al., 1994, 2001), word reading (Chee et al., 2000; Price et al., 1999), cued word generation (Pu et al., 2001; Chee et al., 1999b; Klein et al., 1999), synonym generation (Klein et al., 2002; Klein, 2003), word translation (Klein et al., 1994, 1995a, b, Klein, 2003; Price et al., 1999), object picture naming (Pouratian et al., 2000; Vingerhoets et al., 2003), verbal fluency (Calabrese et al, 2001; Vingerhoets et al., 2003), judging whether a word refers to an animal (Ding et al., 2003), and deciding which of two verbs a noun is associated with (Pillai et al., 2001, 2003) can be considered, to some minimal extent, linguistic tasks. Some studies, however, use single words in non-linguistically-focused tasks, such as memorizing semantically unrelated word pairs (Halsband et al., 2002)—a memory task; deciding whether two written words rhyme or not (Tan et al., 2001b, 2003; Pillai et al., 2003)—a metalinguistic awareness task; recognizing the language of presentation (Rodriguez-Fornells et al., 2002)—another manifestly conscious metalinguistic task. Having to decide whether a word is concrete or abstract (Illes et al., 1999; Tan et al., 2001a) is a reflection on the properties of words, a task that is not part of any step in the processing of the meanings of lexical items. Counting the foreign words in a list of native words—or the reverse (Pihko et al., 2001a, b, 2002)—is a mathematical task (with a controlled metalinguistic element: as acknowledged by the authors, selecting words in a specific language from a list is a complicated process that involves several attention mechanisms). Discerning whether Chinese characters contain a certain radical or whether English words contain a certain letter (Ding et al., 2003) is so far from a linguistic task that it could be performed by someone who speaks neither Chinese nor English. Arguably, all these tasks may, in the course of their processing, access the meanings of the words involved, but it is still a far cry from the processing of words in normal language use. In the normal use of words, their lexical meanings are (1) modulated by their syntactic properties and how these relate to other words in the sentence, and (2) specified by the pragmatic contexts attached to the utterance.

Synonym generation is not "tapping the ability to find a word that conveys the meaning of a given thought or object" (Klein, 2003, p. 420), as it would be in the normal use of language or in confrontation naming, for example, but the ability to find a word whose meaning is close to that of the stimulus word provided. This task requires the inhibition of the stimulus word in order to access its synonym. As long as the phonological form of the stimulus remains in working memory, it will inhibit its semantically close competitors. This is a well-known cause of word-finding difficulty in ordinary speakers, even cross-linguistically: Finding a translation equivalent on demand is a difficult task for fluent bilinguals who are not professional interpreters. This difficulty is reflected in Klein's patient's scores, which are perfect on the repetition task but down to 85% and 63% accuracy on the production of a synonym in L1 and L2 respectively. In this context, the observed changes in cerebral blood flow have an even greater chance than usual of corresponding to inhibitory processes.

Alternating on cue the language used to name pictures (Hernandez, 2000, 2001b; Price et al., 1999), a task akin to any controlled switching task but not to normal, automatic, language switching and mixing in conversation, is particularly deceptive: Switching on demand is a task very different from natural switching in normal language use; it can only misleadingly be called "language switching" and can surely not be claimed to detect the language switch. In a bilingual environment, mixing and switching are guided by internal parameters such as the relative availability of a particular word (its activation threshold relative to that of its translation equivalent), the goodness of fit of a word in a particular language for a specific concept to be conveyed, etc. Once a word has been borrowed, it may trigger a language switch (Clyne, 1980). In such contexts, switching occurs implicitly, in the same way that words are selected on-line from among possible synonyms during a unilingual conversation.

In an fMRI study, Stephan et al. (2003) showed that the presentation of a word could activate either the right or the left hemisphere, depending on what the subjects were asked to do with the word. Yet, in each case, the stimulus was an identical four-letter word printed in black with one red letter. Language areas in the left hemisphere were not engaged automatically when a word was presented in a non-linguistic task (i.e., when subjects were asked to decide whether the red letter appeared to the right or left of the center of the word). This further underscores the fact that a word is not necessarily processed as a linguistic stimulus.

When words are used in any type of semantic task, such as judging the semantic relatedness of word pairs (Tan et al., 2001a), what is addressed is lexical semantics, namely one of the declarative aspects of words (sound being the other). Lexical meanings are known to be represented as a net of widely distributed connections to areas that were engaged in the acquisition of their conceptual representations (visual, olfactory, somesthetic, auditory, gustatory, and motor) and hence are the least localizable items at a gross anatomical level. It should not be surprising that single-word studies tend to find no differences between the representation of languages acquired early and those learned late in life, irrespective of proficiency level, given that the meaning-sound associations of words are supported by declarative memory in the native as well as the second languages. For example, Kiroy and Kotik (1985) required late bilingual speakers to differentiate names of animate and inanimate entities. Kotik-Friedgut (2001) interprets the similar latencies of evoked potentials in both languages reported in that study as indicating that, when stimuli in the two languages are used in a similar way, they are processed by the same cerebral mechanisms. She then aptly compares this ERP result with that of Illes et al.'s (1999) fMRI study: Both studies, in demanding semantic decisions about words, in fact used a task relying on declarative memory.

Words are not just "building blocks of sentences" (Chee et al., 1999b, p. 3050) that, presented in isolation, may contribute to the study of the structure of the language edifice. When they are presented out of context, they lose most of their language-specific properties. They are part of language, no doubt, but once they are isolated from the structure in which they are embedded and to which they contribute via their implicit morphosyntactic properties, results based on what remains (i.e., their explicit spoken and written form and default lexical meaning) cannot be generalized to the representation or processing of language in general. This is more than saying that it is dangerous to generalize from a part to the whole, for words do not just differ from syntax in the same way phonology differs from it, but they are also explicit pieces of knowledge, the representation and processing of which cannot be subserved by the same cerebral mechanisms as the rest of the language system. Experiments using single words can hardly speak to the issue of "a difference [or lack thereof] in brain organization between L1 and L2" (Chee et al., 1999b, p. 3053). At best, they may point to similarities or differences between the storage and off-line retrieval of vocabulary in L1 and L2.

Syntactic processing is not only more complex than single-word processing, as aptly suggested by Chee et al. (1999b), it is also supported by a different type of memory system (procedural as opposed to declarative) and consequently involves different cerebral structures in different anatomical locations. Indeed, because "the choice of probe and control tasks (Warburton et al., 1996) are important determinants of the pattern of language activation seen" (Chee et al., 1999b, p. 3053), one ought to be very careful not to generalize results from a particular single-word psycholinguistic or neuroimaging experimental task to language in general.

Intrahemispheric and interhemispheric differences in activation that occur between L1 and L2 in sentence-level studies are not observed in word studies. This may be partly due to the fact that lexical words, having a declarative component (probably the only component tapped in single word tasks), are the very language items that are likely to be similarly processed by L1 and both late and early L2 speakers, because they are of the same kind, namely, items in declarative memory (as illustrated by hippocampal activation: Halsband et al., 2002). However, grammatical words, which are processed as part of the syntax by L1 speakers, tend to be treated as lexical items by late L2 speakers (Weber-Fox & Neville, 1996), who also use declarative memory to process the morphosyntactic constructions they have not internalized.

The fact that Klein et al. (1999) failed to find support for the notion that languages acquired later in life are represented differently from languages acquired in infancy is therefore not surprising, given that they used a single-word generation task (a metalinguistic task). The authors are conscious that using single words may not reflect language in general but only vocabulary, which, among other things, appears to be relatively invulnerable to a critical period (precisely because it is declarative in nature). Activation of the left medial temporal region for both L1 and L2 further suggests the use of declarative memory in the task of deliberately generating a verb from a noun. Even though authors who used to claim to address the issue of the representation of *language* now add the caveat that their findings reflect the functional organization of the brain "at least at the single-word level" (e.g., Klein, 2003), it is not clear that researchers fully realize how much the special status of single words sets them apart from the rest of language, such that generalizations cannot be made from single-word data to language representation any more than from the processing of arithmetic. Although the *lexicon* is part of the language system, *vocabulary* is not. What happens at the single-word level is orthogonal to what happens at the phonological and morphosyntactic levels of organization. The lack of generalizability goes far beyond the usual caveats about generalizing from a sample. It is not just a matter of degree, loss of detail or influence of different contexts, but a complete incongruity because we are dealing with two qualitatively different sets of entities involving very different types of processing mechanisms.

Chee and Soon (2003) compare the study of cued generation by Chee et al. (1999b) with Kim et al.'s (1997) sentence-generation study and report that they did not replicate the finding of a different center of mass of activation for L1 and L2 in late language learners. Chee and Soon do not seem to realize the unsuitability of comparing a word-generation task with a sentence-generation task, nor to apprehend the reason why their results and Kim et al.'s should be expected to differ in exactly the way that they do (assuming, of course, that both techniques are valid).

A verbal memory task is a declarative memory task using either single words or semantically unrelated word pairs as stimuli. As such, it is a memory task, not a language task that speaks to the representation or processing of language. In Halsband et al.'s (2002) study, the control condition consisted in reading nonsense words without memorizing them, thus enhancing the memory component of the experimental task when compared to the control condition; in other words, memory becomes what is specific to the experimental task and in large part responsible for the extra activation over the reference task. It is not surprising that languages—even from structurally very distant linguistic groups—should show consistent activation of the same cerebral structures (precuneus and hippocampal areas) during memory retrieval of word pairs (Halsband et al., 2002).

Data from single-word experiments cannot support the overlap hypothesis (namely, that two languages are represented in the same cortical area) either: Overlapping activation patterns in single-word experiments reflect controlled metalinguistic processes that are not of the same kind as those that subserve linguistic competence. As discussed in Chapter 1, since declarative memory is not task-specific as procedural memory is, items from different domains are not expected to be separately represented in the way that items from two language subsystems would be, where each is subserved by its own independent set of procedures. These data, therefore, cannot be used to support the hypothesis that the closer the bilingual's level of proficiency is in the two languages, the closer the overlap in activation patterns will be. Although data from studies using story comprehension with less proficient bilinguals who show more L2 variability, are compatible with the hypothesis, they cannot be compared to studies using single words because the latter do not address implicit linguistic processes. Moreover, in story comprehension studies, only those areas that subserve the linguistic system per se (the left perisylvian area) are relevant to the overlap/separation issue. Additional areas (parahippocampal gyri, right hemisphere) reflect the use of non-linguistic compensatory mechanisms—in part those mechanisms that are involved in the processing of single words. This is a domain where task not only matters, but is crucial, because it either taps into the relevant function or it does not.

Considerable overlap in frontal activations is to be expected whenever a controlled process is involved, because it is controlled in both L1 and L2, as opposed to tasks that are automatized in L1 but can be controlled in L2 (in proportion to the lack of implicit competence in that language). Not surprisingly, in the Price et al. (1999) study, the main regions that were found to be most active during single-word translation fell outside of the classical language areas. Dehaene (1999) acknowledges that the bilingual brain seems to tackle the translation of single words and various word-generation tasks as it does any other non-automatized tasks, with the attention system of the anterior cingulate kicking in.

Reading single words is sometimes considered to be somewhat less controlled than other word tasks. However, whereas reading may be considered an automatized task to some extent, and reading single words is a task one performs occasionally when reading one-word signs (the total inventory of which is extremely limited), it remains an artificial task which differs from regular reading where words are syntactically related to each other and their meanings are modulated by the semantic and pragmatic contexts. In addition, in the second language, pragmatics is not required to compensate for any lack of automatized computational procedures, as would be the case in sentence reading (or listening).

In a similar vein, as was discussed in Chapter 2, grammaticality judgments present different concerns with respect to the interpretation of results for native speakers and speakers of L2, because they may use entirely different strategies, given that second language speakers are more likely to use metalinguistic knowledge to carry out the task. In a neuroimaging study (e.g., Wartenburger et al., 2003), a judgment of grammaticality, like the processing of words in isolation, is therefore not a natural linguistic task (i.e., is not normally involved in understanding or producing utterances) but a *judgment* task bearing on the form of sentences. We know from clinical studies, for instance, that some aphasic patients are able to correctly judge sentences that they do not comprehend (Linebarger, Schwartz, & Saffran, 1983). Researchers are beginning to recognize the importance of ecological validity (Owen, Borowsky, & Sarty, 2004), but there is still a long way to go.

Looking for converging evidence

The arguments presented in the previous sections do not mean that we should in principle disregard neuroimaging data stemming from studies of language in general, and bilingualism in particular, only that we should be fully aware of their limitations—which differ for each procedure—and realize that the validity of our interpretation of the results is directly proportional to the soundness of the theoretical framework used to infer what is happening. Consequently, our rationale has to be compatible with the data we get from many other sources, including clinical, anatomical and physiological data, and any discrepancies had better receive a reasonable explanation, again, necessarily based on a theory which itself should ideally have been constructed on the basis of many observations from different sources. Our interpretations will depend on what we know about the tasks and about the brain, in other words, on our current working hypothesis—which will be as valid as it is richly informed by many converging pieces of evidence from different origins (PET, fMRI, MEG, ERP, as well as clinical, histological, pharmacological, and experimental data, among others). At this time, the only neuroimaging studies we might take into consideration (albeit with a grain of salt) are those that are more ecological (i.e., that do not use single words as stimuli) if we wish to investigate bilingual *language* functions.

One may try to derive some pattern from these disparate and sometimes contradictory results. For example, in a true, natural linguistic task, such as the comprehension of short stories (Perani et al., 1996, 1998), the activation of the areas associated with procedural memory for language (left perisylvian area) increases with degree of proficiency (as measured behaviorally). On the other hand, in a word-generation task, that stipulates an initial letter—an eminently metalinguistic task (e.g., Yetkin et al., 1996)—activation of the left prefrontal cortex increases as fluency in the language *de*creases, suggesting an increased cognitive load and hence the use of controlled, metalinguistic processes. Dehaene et al. (1997) find an increased use of the anterior cingulate region in their participants' (weaker) second language. So it appears that the various results, as diverse as they are, are still compatible with the notion that, with increased implicit linguistic competence, speakers make greater use (i.e., increase activation) of the classical perisylvian area (whose surface diminishes with automatization), and that they compensate for gaps in their automatic competence by relying to a greater extent on right-hemisphere-based pragmatics and controlled metalinguistic knowledge (activating the mesial temporal areas, prefrontal cortex and anterior cingulate).

The findings of the Weber-Fox and Neville (1996), Perani et al. (1996), Dehaene et al. (1997) and Perani et al. (1998) studies provide converging evidence compatible with the hypothesis that late foreign-language speakers rely more on declarative-memory-based processes and less on implicit linguistic competence. The rationale is that these studies show less activation of those areas assumed to subserve implicit linguistic competence (the left perisylvian areas and right cerebellum) and greater activation of areas associated with declarative memory (i.e., parahippocampal gyri) and executive control (anterior cingulate gyri). Late second-language speakers process grammatical words in the same way as lexical items (Weber-Fox & Neville, 1996), another indication of the use of declarative memory in L2 when procedural memory is used in L1.

Interestingly, the following structures have been reported to be active only or to a greater extent when L2 is processed: the left precuneus, associated with the allocation of attention and hence indicative of conscious processing (Luke et al., 2002; Tan et al., 2001a); the anterior cingulate, associated with control (Dehaene et al., 1997; Wattendorf et al., 2001; Rodriguez-Fornells et al., 2002); and the parahippocampal gyri, associated with declarative memory (Perani et al., 1996, 1998; Luke et al., 2002). The anterior cingulate is known to monitor performance in order to regulate behavior (Devinsky, Morrell, & Vogt, 1995; Carter et al., 1998, 2001), and to mediate control of action (Casey et al., 1997; Price et al., 1999). Retrieval of lexical items in the least fluent language results in increased executive function in both early and late bilinguals (Hernandez et al.; 2001a). Calabrese et al. (2001) and Urbanik et al. (2001) impute the additional prefrontal activation registered during the use of L2 to a possible greater reliance on metalinguistic factors. The fact that a late-learned second language, even at the level of the perception of single words, relies to a greater extent on declarative memory is corroborated by the larger number of active voxels found during L2 than L1 processing (e.g., Marian et al., 2003, where the volume of activated voxels in the left inferior frontal lobe for L1 (84 mm^3) represents only 24% of that for L2 (350 mm^3) during the phonological processing of single words and 45% (317 mm^3 vs. 704 mm^3) during lexical processing). Cumulatively, these findings point to a greater use of conscious, controlled processes when using L2. To the extent that our assumptions about the role of the parahippocampal gyri and the anterior cingulate are valid, these studies support the hypothesis that late bilinguals compensate for their gaps in linguistic competence by using metalinguistic knowledge. To the extent that the right hemisphere is involved in subserving pragmatics, greater right-hemisphere activation in late bilinguals than in unilinguals and early bilinguals can be seen as indicating that they use their pragmatic ability as a compensatory mechanism as well.

Whether age of acquisition per se is responsible for the observed differences between high- and low-proficiency speakers is still controversial. Some authors argue that these differences are due to differences in proficiency per se, irrespective of age of acquisition (Ardal et al., 1990; Perani et al., 1998). In any event, it remains the case that, in individuals whose linguistic competence, for any reason, is not fully developed or has been impaired by pathology, cumulative evidence points to a decreased activation of the areas subserving procedural memory for language (i.e., the perisylvian area) with concomitant increased activation of areas subserving declarative memory and hence metalinguistic knowledge (i.e. the parahippocampal gyri, mesial temporal lobes, and anterior cingulate) as well as greater activation of areas subserving pragmatics (i.e., areas of the right hemisphere). It is noteworthy that Casey et al. (1997) have documented an increased *right* (but not left) anterior cingulate activation in controlled processes. This would contribute to an increased right-hemisphere participation during the controlled processing of metalinguistic knowledge. Thus, greater reliance not only on pragmatics but also on metalinguistic knowledge would contribute to an overall increase in right-hemisphere activation during the processing of a weaker language.

In their review of bilingual neuroimaging, Abutalebi et al. (2001) divide the studies into those that investigate language production and those that investigate language comprehension. They draw attention to the fact that, in the less proficient language, more extensive cerebral activations tend to be associated with production tasks and smaller activations with comprehension tasks. This is consonant with the proposed theory of bilingualism (Paradis, 2000a), which predicts that, for several reasons, comprehension is easier than production. Children understand long before they can speak, as discussed in Chapter 4, and comprehension tolerates a higher activation threshold, as discussed in Chapter 1. Whereas comprehension in L1 is automatically processed linguistically, in L2, because of the reduced competence, (1) there is less substratum to activate in the perisylvian area and what there is differs among individuals, and (2) other, more general and diffusely represented, higher cognitive processes are substituted. In production, because of incomplete linguistic competence, speakers of a weaker L2 must have recourse to (more effortful) conscious control and monitoring, thereby significantly activating regions outside the classical language areas.

Studies that use sentence comprehension or production report that both hemispheres are activated by the task. Presumably the left hemisphere is doing grammatical processing, while the right hemisphere is processing pragmatic features. Although there is right-hemisphere activation in both languages, processing in a less proficient L2 tends to elicit more activation than processing in L1 (Dehaene et al., 1997; Urbanik et al., 2001; Hasegawa et al., 2002; Luke et al., 2002). These data are consistent with the hypothesis that both languages rely on pragmatic features to process sentences, but that L2 relies on them to a greater extent.

Some cerebral areas that are purported to be the locus of the cerebral representation of a specific system or function, such as phonology in some studies (Sergent et al., 1992; Pugh et al., 1996; Joubert, 1999) and semantics in another (Demb et al., 1995), may in fact not be domain-specific but may instead process both phonology and lexical semantics when the tasks require control (Gold & Buckner, 2002).

Démonet and Thierry (2001) recognize that one of the main factors that make neuroimaging of language so complex is the unavoidable combination of automatic processes related to procedural memory and controlled processes related to explicit memory. They rightly predict that studying the interplay of procedural and explicit types of language functions will be of crucial importance for a future understanding of the neurophysiology and neuropathology of language. This is particularly true when investigating the processes involved in bilingual individuals.

Conclusions

Neuroimaging studies of language in general and of bilingual language functions in particular suffer from a lack of linguistic sophistication A number of consequences follow therefrom. (1) The tasks are often not linguistic tasks (i.e., not part of the natural use of language) and hence do not involve the implicit procedural computations that underlie the processing of a verbal message either in comprehension or production. (2) The selected stimuli often do not target components of language function and hence are not language-relevant. (3) Sometimes linguistic material is used, but in a non-linguistic context, and thus does not reveal any kind of language processing. (4) Researchers do not differentiate between implicit and explicit components of language and often generalize from words (whose form and meaning are supported by declarative memory) to language (whose implicit system—phonology, morphology and syntax—is supported by procedural memory). In addition, despite the ubiquitous attribution of contradictory results to methodological differences, there have been no attempts at replication (which should not be surprising, given that the techniques are known not to be reliable—see Ramsey et al., 1996 2001), and no two studies use the same task and the same technique with comparable subject populations. Until we have the means to decide which experimental task, used with which experimental procedure, according to which protocol, will reveal the relevant areas, any result is moot since it can be contradicted by another result and there is no way to determine which is right (i.e., valid).

Consequently, the literature on bilingual neuroimaging is fraught with inconsistent results and conflicting interpretations. To blame this confusion on methodological parameters is not sufficient. To be sure, data can only be compared to similar data. But, on the one hand, one should specify the effect of each parameter and hence explain why one gets result A with parameter α and result B with parameter β; on the other hand, one ought to replicate studies with the same type of subject, protocol, stimuli, and any other variable known to have an impact on the result, before one can consider a methodology to be reliable.

What neuroimaging studies of bilingual subjects set out to do is to determine which cerebral areas subserve language (or particular language functions, or language components). If different imaging methods (e.g., PET vs. fMRI, EEG vs. MEG) report contradictory findings, then these procedures cannot all be valid, i.e., they cannot all be doing what they set out to do; if they did, they would not activate different areas. At best, each may show activation of a different portion (or component, or aspect) of what it is they purport to identify. At worst, each activates something other than what they all purport to identify.

We cannot ascertain with any confidence what it is that is activated. It could be, at best, (1) only a portion of the language network (without knowing which one); (2) an antagonist function which is inhibited so as not to interfere with the actual task; (3) a functional area subserving a non-linguistic component of the task; or, at worst, (4) a random artifact of the technical and/or statistical parameters used.

Much external evidence from a variety of different sources is required to confirm the likelihood of an interpretation. In addition, each language task places different demands on cerebral processing. Given the great variety of tasks used in the various studies published to date (from listening to stories to mentally generating synonyms, etc.), caution is in order. Neuroimaging studies cannot yet claim to address issues of language representation in bilinguals more directly than clinical studies.

The promises of cognitive neuroimaging are enormous, albeit quite unrealistic. This does not mean that we should discard neuroimaging altogether. In fact, from a clinical point of view, neuroimaging techniques perform very well to identify hypermetabolism (e.g., malignant tumors) or hypometabolism (e.g., infarcts or degeneration); but they should not be applied to the localization of a cognitive domain until they have been shown to be valid for this purpose. Many reasons why they are inadequate and hence why their use is premature have been amply acknowledged (see above) but the very authors who denounce their shortcomings still go on to make statements about the role of a particular cerebral area in the processing of a particular language task based on these techniques. It is clear that results must be interpreted within the constraints of the neuroimaging technique that obtained them. One should refrain from generalizing to the language system when results are based on tasks that rely on declarative memory (such as any single-word task or metalinguistic task).

Nevertheless, many findings are consistent with an implicit/explicit account of language processing. Whenever differences are found in neuroimaging studies between L1 and L2 activations, they are compatible with the assumption that, insofar as speakers have an incomplete implicit linguistic competence in their L2, they compensate by relying more heavily on metalinguistic knowledge and pragmatics. The often-reported greater dispersion and weaker activation within the traditional perisylvian language areas during the processing of L2 may reflect a lesser reliance on implicit linguistic competence than when processing L1. Different individuals may compensate for their weaker implicit competence by relying, to different extents, on metalinguistic knowledge or pragmatic features, as suggested by the also often reported additional activation of mesial temporal, parahippocampal, and prefrontal areas (known to be involved respectively in declarative memory and conscious control) and areas of the right hemisphere (known to be involved in pragmatic inference). The greater intersubject variability in the processing of their L2 relative to the striking homogeneity across subjects in the processing of their L1 reflects the fact that linguistic processes are obligatory and automatic, and hence performed identically by all subjects; in L2, on the other hand, compensatory strategies are numerous and varied, and the implicit linguistic items actually internalized also vary from one speaker to another. They have not necessarily all incorporated the same parts of the grammar or even the same structures within each module into their linguistic competence (e.g., different individuals speak with a more or less pronounced foreign accent and the morphosyntactic features automatically available to them differ). In addition, implicit linguistic competence, being automatized, is faster and more efficient than any other means and is therefore selected whenever it is available (i.e., always in L1, less often in L2). One of the most robust findings in bilingual neuroimaging studies based on the processing of units longer than single words or phrases is the greater involvement, in later-learned languages, of regions subserving declarative memory and pragmatics.

In a nutshell, cognitive neuroimaging is still by and large at the "poking" stage (let's poke here and see what happens). And things do happen—in fact, lots of them. The problem is that in the absence of an existing theoretical framework, language research that is not linguistically informed is unable to interpret the varied, sometimes contradictory, findings that are reported.

Where something is represented depends on how it is processed, which in large part depends on whether it is supported by procedural or declarative memory. What is supported by procedural memory will be represented in circumscribed cortical areas and involve subcortical and cerebellar processing mechanisms; what is supported by declarative memory will be represented more diffusely (and hence will be more difficult to detect) and will involve frontal control mechanisms and parahippocampal mnemic processing mechanisms. The properties of what is represented (such as whether it is conscious or not) determine where and how it will be represented and processed.

As pointed out by Bub (2000), the conceptual validity of inferences underlying particular theoretical claims has yet to be established and the cognitive role of any activated brain region remains elusive. The host of methodological difficulties inherent in neuroimaging, as outlined above, must be resolved before neuroimaging techniques can be used to provide a testing ground for neuropsychological and neurophysiological theories of higher cognitive functions in general and of language in particular.

CHAPTER 7

An integrated neurolinguistic perspective on bilingualism

The preceding chapters have presented a number of hypotheses and have discussed evidence from various sources regarding the representation and processing of two or more languages in one brain. It is time to combine these hypothetical constructs with some additional ones into an integrated neurofunctional model of bilingualism. This model incorporates the Three-Store Hypothesis (Paradis, 1978), the Subsystems Hypothesis (Paradis, 1981), the Activation Threshold Hypothesis (Paradis, 1987a), the Direct Access Hypothesis (Paradis, 1990b) and the contributions of implicit linguistic competence, metalinguistic knowledge (Paradis, 1994), pragmatics (Paradis, 1998c), and motivation (Lamendella, 1977a; Paradis, 1992b; Schumann, 1998). Some of the constructs discussed in previous chapters will be briefly outlined to highlight their contributions to the overall model. In this model, there is no need to postulate any mechanism or hypothetical construct not already available in unilinguals. Interference and switching occur between languages as they occur between registers in a unilingual speaker. Translation between two languages corresponds to paraphrasing in a single language.

What is represented vs. how it is organized and processed

Each component of grammar of each of a bilingual's languages can independently contain various numbers of borrowed elements of different kinds (interference), in keeping with Weinreich's (1953) posited coordinate (i.e., no interference), compound (i.e., bidirectional interference) and subordinate (i.e., unidirectional interference) organization of languages.

There are in fact at least three aspects of each of the languages that are independently susceptible to unidirectional or bidirectional interference as well as selective impairment: (1) the grammar (phonology, morphology, syntax and lexical semantics), the only aspect traditionally considered; (2) cue strength in the interpretation of sentences (the relative strength of word order, subject-verb agreement and case-markers as a cue to who does what to whom), a dimension that has only recently been investigated (Wulfeck et al., 1986; Vaid & Chengappa, 1988); and, to the extent that they differ between languages, (3) pragmatic relations (rules that determine whether a figurative or literate meaning is to be selected, rules governing the use and interpretation of paralinguistic phenomena—facial expressions, gestures, prosody, voice quality) and indirect speech acts, aspects that have not yet been systematically investigated as a specific variable of bilingualism.

The *contents* of a representation (i.e., whether it contains illegitimate features from another language or not) are assumed to be orthogonal to the organization of two or more languages in one brain into one common system or as many (sub)systems as there are languages. The language system of a bilingual individual may present all three types of interference (i.e., unidirectional, bidirectional, or none) in various proportions at each level of linguistic structure (phonology, morphology, syntax and lexical semantics). The state of bilingualism is not constant: The various interlingual relationships will change over time, possibly differently at each structural level, as a result of experience.

Two types of interference must be clearly distinguished (Paradis, 1993a): (1) Static interference, which is due to deviant representations, in the sense that the individual's implicit grammar of one language (say, English) contains elements of another (say, French), and to the extent that the speaker systematically uses deviant elements when processing English—deviant, that is, with respect to the native English unilingual norm. This type of interference refers to the fact that the speaker's implicit linguistic competence contains elements that are different from those found in native speakers' competence. (2) Dynamic interference, which is due to performance errors, i.e., the inadvertent intrusion of a French element in the processing of an English sentence. In this case, even if the individual possesses two native-like internalized grammars, an element of French occasionally gets activated instead of an element of English, and the speaker produces a dynamic interference error (e.g., accidentally pronounces an English word with a French accent, uses an English word with the meaning of its French translation equivalent, or uses a French syntactic structure in an English phrase). Speakers often recognize such errors and repair them on the spot (or could repair them if their attention were drawn to them), in the same way as they would repair unilingual performance errors of the same type. For examples, see Poulisse, 1999.

Competence (i.e., static) interference is reflected in the systematic use of an element of one language when using another (in both production and comprehension of an utterance). It refers to the contents of the grammar of the language in question (i.e., to what is stored), not to the organization of the two grammars relative to each other (i.e., how they are stored in the brain). Both interference-free (or deviance-free) and interference-laden competence are compatible with any of the cerebral storage organization types considered in Chapter 4 (i.e., an extended system, a dual system, a tripartite system, or subsystems).

It is not necessary to assume that the extent to which the speaker masters both systems has any consequences for the *organization* of language within the brain (i.e., the organization into one system for both languages or two systems, one for each language) or *the way in which the system works*. Our best working hypothesis, which may be taken to be the null hypothesis, is that there is nothing in the bilingual brain that differs in nature from anything in the unilingual brain. Hence the mechanisms for comprehension and production in the bilingual brain do not need any additional component that is not already present in the unilingual speaker-hearer's brain. Nor is there any different component in the mechanism for a fluent as compared to a nonfluent bilingual. The only difference is the extent to which they make use of parts of the verbal communication system. Different types of bilinguals will make differential use of various parts of the system, depending on whether they switch a lot or not, or whether the only use they make of one of their languages is to listen to television broadcasts or whether they use both of them receptively and productively all day. At most, the activation thresholds of certain parts of the model may differ, but all parts must be available to all types of bilinguals and unilinguals alike.

Unilinguals can switch, suffer interference between registers, and paraphrase. Paraphrasing is a phenomenon which does not differ in kind from translation, i.e., saying more or less the same thing with different words and/or morphosyntax, even pronunciation. For example, baby or pet talk uses different intonation, pitch frequencies, etc., and even, on occasion, different phonemes from speech to adults. Here is an example of a different phoneme as one switches to a different register: I once published an insignificant paper on the comparison between baby talk (i.e., speech addressed to babies) in French and Québécois (Paradis, 1979) in which, among other things, I indicated that sometimes /s/ → /ʃ/ as in *c'est bon ça, hein*? /sɛbõsaːɛ̃/ → /ʃɛbõʃaːɛ̃/ ('that's good, isn't it?'). Two years later, I received a letter from a colleague at the University of Lyon, pointing out that in France the substituted sound is slightly different, i.e., /ç/ rather than /ʃ/. Though /ʃ/ is definitely used in the context, /ç/ can also be used, even as a substitute for /ʃ/ as in /ʃjẽʃjẽ/ → /çjẽçjẽ/ ('doggie'), in spite of the fact that the phoneme /ç/, a palatalized and somewhat rounded phoneme, does not exist in French adult speech outside of baby talk.

The neurofunctional system need not be organized differently for any language pair. Nor does it function differently for different language pairs. But *the extent* to which this or that aspect of the model is used depends on the languages' typology (e.g., whether a concept is lexicalized, grammaticized, or requires pragmatic inference), the extent of switching or of relative use (lowering the activation threshold), or any other aspect (e.g., extent of implicit linguistic competence and choice of compensatory mechanisms). The structural differences between the bilingual speaker's languages (and any other feature) are irrelevant to the organization of the neurofunctional system, but relevant to the degree to which any part of the system is put to use (or how high the activation threshold will be for a given item or function). A tone language is represented in a bilingual in the same way as in a unilingual. In other words, in different types of bilinguals, what changes is not the type of mechanism but the individual's grammar; not *the way* in which the two languages are represented, but *what* is represented; not the *organization* of the system but its *contents*.

Sociolinguistic considerations will not affect the organization of the system either—only the use of it. Just as sociolinguistic competence in unilinguals dictates whether to select *tu* or *vous* when addressing a particular person, given that both *tu* and *vous* are available in the speakers' linguistic competence (their language system), sociolinguistic factors will also determine which of two languages is used. Nevertheless, they will have no impact on the design of the model, only on its use.

The content of any type of representation in one of the languages (i.e., whether it contains foreign elements or not) is orthogonal to the way the representation is stored and processed. A representation is treated according to its type, irrespective of its specific parametric internal structure. Whether or not syllables of the second language of some bilinguals are bona fide syllables of L2, namely, in all respects identical to those of native speakers of that language, they are part of their L2 system. There is no a priori reason to believe that those aspects which are deviant with respect to native grammar (in that they resemble L1 more than they should) are treated by the brain any differently from those items that are legitimately similar.

In fact, the degree of semantic or any other kind of overlap between two languages is merely a historical accident. As long as a parameter is a genuine instantiation of a principle of human language, the brain has no reason to treat it differently just because it does not actually belong to a particular language in this decade. Natural languages continuously change over time. A particular feature of L2 may have belonged to L1 (or vice versa) as recently as 50 years ago or may be part of it 50 years from now. There is no reason to believe that, as a consequence, the brain will reorganize the way in which the two languages are arranged. Even though the *form* of certain items in the L2 subsystem may include more features from L1 than the actual L2 native speakers' language system does, these items are no different *in kind* from those of unilingual speakers.

The way the system operates may be compared to a city's transportation system. Different individuals may take various *available* routes to reach their destination. They may choose to walk, drive a car, take the bus or the subway. All these means are available. The subway may be cheaper and faster than the bus, while walking is cheaper and slower, but there is a limited number of ways of getting to one's destination, determined by the system of streets and tunnels and means of transportation. Some individuals will travel more quickly than others, some will use one particular route rather than another most of the time, but the system of roads and the transportation system are the same for all: There are no special paths for bilinguals. Speakers may not necessarily deliberately choose one path over another—the brain often does it for them. But the choices are there—and they are limited.

When bilinguals speak to other bilinguals, their choice of language may be conditioned by either (1) the greater availability of an item (easier verbalizability of the concept in one language, temporary word-finding difficulty, lower threshold of activation for the item in that language because of its frequency or recency of use) or (2) a deliberate choice. In the latter case, the choice is of the same kind as the choice of an implicit over an explicit request to turn on the lights. The choice of which language to use in a given utterance is governed by the same mechanism that, in unilinguals, is involved in choosing the register to be used, or in deciding whether to use a direct or indirect speech act to get someone to close the door or pass the salt. And the information on which this choice is based is also the same: the appropriateness of the situation, given the interlocutors. In other words, the decision is not part of the language system but is arrived at by a device (an operation) informed by the pragmatics system.

Neurofunctional modularity

While the brain is one, and everything is directly or indirectly connected to everything else, some portions of the network are dedicated to specific functions and, as such, constitute different neurofunctional modules. Each module can be selectively impaired by pathology. In the normal use of verbal communication, some modules process information in parallel, while the output of some serves as input to others. Episodic and semantic memory, encyclopedic knowledge, and information from various sensory sources serve as the basis for formulating messages which are optionally verbalized, involving at least four independent but collaborating neurofunctional systems: implicit linguistic competence, metalinguistic knowledge, pragmatics and motivation. The extent of reliance on each of these four systems will vary between bilingual speakers' two languages as a function of their proficiency in each.

Whereas all speakers will primarily rely on implicit linguistic competence to communicate automatically in their native language, they will differ with respect to their degree of proficiency in L2 and consequently will compensate for the gaps in their linguistic competence by greater (but variable) involvement of pragmatics and metalinguistic knowledge. Some will rely more on pragmatics, others on metalinguistic knowledge; the proportion may vary in the same individual depending on the circumstances.

The linguistic and pragmatic processes may operate sequentially (albeit in rapid succession, in milliseconds) or in parallel. Likewise, during decoding (the interpretation of language input), the pragmatic elements may be processed before or after linguistic processing, or in parallel, inferencing from each linguistic component (prosody, word selection, syntactic construction). Encoding may start with pragmatic considerations that guide the selection of linguistic elements, or proceed in parallel, influencing the selection of elements from each level in turn. In speaking, activation of concepts must precede that of the items selected to encode the conceptual message verbally.

The proposed neurofunctional model of bilingualism is thus a complex set of independent systems which collaborate at every step of the microgenesis of an utterance. One system (e.g., pragmatics) may influence the choices of elements in another (e.g., linguistic competence) but it will never interfere with the internal structure of that other system. Every component of the verbal communication system available to bilingual speakers exists in unilingual speakers as well. The only difference is the speaker's degree of reliance on each.

Language and thought in bilinguals

Macnamara (1970) argued that if Whorf's hypothesis were true, that is, if it were the case that differences among languages caused substantial differences in cognitive functioning, bilingual persons would find themselves in a curious predicament. They would have to conform to one of three patterns: (1) Function cognitively in the manner appropriate to L1 when using their L1 or L2 and then have great difficulty in understanding or in being understood by speakers of L2; (2) function cognitively in a manner appropriate to neither L1 or L2 and run the risk of understanding or being understood by nobody; or (3) function cognitively differentially, in accordance with each language. In the third case, bilinguals would be able to communicate with speakers of either language but (a) would have great difficulty communicating with themselves, and (b) would have difficulty in explaining in L2 what they had heard or said in L1.

Rather than improbable conjectures, all three situations and their consequences, including (3b), do in fact occur, but consequence (3a) does not. The first situation described by Macnamara corresponds to what Weinreich (1953) called *subordinative* bilingualism, namely when speakers use L1 meanings for L2 words, with the consequence that, to the extent that the lexical meaning of the L2 word differs from that of the L1 translation equivalent, there will be misunderstandings. The second situation corresponds to what Weinreich termed *compound* bilingualism, with the consequence that speakers will not refer to the appropriate concepts in either language and will consequently misunderstand and be misunderstood. The third situation corresponds to what Weinreich referred to as *coordinative* bilingualism, when speakers apply the appropriate concepts in each language, in which case they will indeed understand and be understood by speakers of both languages. But speakers who organize their concepts as native speakers do in each language may indeed have difficulty translating what they have just heard or said (consequence 3b), for a number of reasons.

Some concepts can be verbalized more easily in one language than in the other because a single word corresponds to the concept in one language whereas a cumbersome and awkward circumlocution may be necessary in the other. Words and their translation equivalents rarely if ever refer to the same set of conceptual features (Paradis, 1997b, 2000b). Therefore, a bilingual person may notice the salient features of a given experience without being able to verbalize them with equal ease in both languages (native speakers of each language would likewise find it more or less difficult depending on the codability of the relevant features in each). in fact, unilinguals often *do* have problems expressing a concept for which they do not find a satisfactory lexical item, and they keep paraphrasing and reparaphrasing. They also experience temporary word-finding difficulty—and the word is then often replaced by *thing* (or some other word used to denote indeterminate objects). This occurs no less often than with bilinguals (who have the possibility of having recourse to a translation equivalent instead of *thing*). Lexical retrieval problems are far from rare in non-aphasic unilingual speakers, and they become more frequent with age.

Bilingual speakers may perfectly understand a pun in one language without being able to translate it into the other, not because of a lack of mastery of the other language, but because the pun, by its very nature, cannot be translated. Comic strips translated from English into other languages sometimes make this point very clear: The translation makes no sense. For example, a Yogi Bear comic strip was published in a Saturday edition of a French Montreal newspaper relating the story of a shell collecting contest on a beach, in which Booboo brings back a shell from a neighboring army depot, and Yogi Bear tells him, "No, not that kind of shell." In French, a (sea)shell is *un coquillage*, an (artillery) shell, *un obus*. It turns out that the word *shell* was translated as *coquille* throughout (which means an eggshell). Unilingual French readers must have been perplexed. Why were the cartoon characters looking for *coquilles* on the beach, and what is the meaning of Booboo bringing back an *obus* (not considered the right kind of *coquille*)? Another strip, published in the national French newspaper *France-Soir*, depicted a woman paying a visit to Louis's mother. The mother asks Louis to keep the woman company while she makes tea. She is surprised to see the woman, obviously peeved, suddenly leave the house. Asked what happened, the young boy tells his mother that the woman asked him what his father did (i.e., what was his occupation) and he answered that "he minds his own business." The boy's words, however, (*Je lui ai dit que papa avait son propre travail et qu'il passait tout son temps à s'en occuper*) mean that he told her that his father is self-employed (runs his own business) and spends all his time attending to his work—no cause for getting into a huff.

However, contrary to Macnamara's assumption, bilingual individuals do not need to translate to themselves in L2 what they have heard or said in L1 (or vice versa) in order to communicate with themselves (3a). Each language is understood directly, just as it is by unilingual native speakers (see the Direct Access Hypothesis below). What this means is that bilinguals are able to organize their mental representations in accordance with the meaning of each language. This ability to adopt two perspectives might account for the results obtained by young bilinguals on intelligence tests. Far from being a handicap, as Macnamara (1970) would suggest, bilingual persons are reported to possess greater cognitive plasticity (Balkan, 1970; Bain, 1974) or greater cognitive flexibility (Albert & Obler, 1978; Bain & Yu, 1978; Rohde, 2001), which would explain their superior performance not only on metalinguistic tasks (Cummins, 1978) and verbal intelligence tests (Lambert & Tucker, 1972), but also on divergent thinking tasks (Landry, 1974; Torrance et al., 1970; Pricewilliams & Ramirez, 1977; Okoh, 1980), on concept formation and general reasoning tests (Cummins & Gulutsan, 1974), and in the discovery of underlying rules in problem-solving (Bain, 1974). Bilingual children are reported to perform better on tests of creativity and flexibility (Peal & Lambert, 1962; Jacobs & Pierce, 1966; MacNab, 1979; Ricciardelli, 1992). In Okoh's (1980) study, the Welsh bilingual group is reported to have obtained significantly higher scores than the unilingual group (by almost 10 points) for total nonverbal creativity, presumably thanks to a greater repertoire of cognitive cues, signs, meanings, and relationships to draw upon. The Nigerian bilingual group scored significantly higher on the verbal creativity tests. Hakuta and Diaz (1980) also report degree of bilingualism to be positively related to performance on a variety of cognitive tasks. The common finding in the disparate cognitive domains investigated by Bialystok (2004) is that bilingual children are more advanced than unilinguals in solving problems that require the inhibition of misleading information.

Bilingual persons who speak both languages like natives need not find themselves in any predicament: They may function cognitively differentially without any ill consequences. On the contrary, it is likely to enrich their general mental capacity. To the extent that they have native competence in both languages, they are able to organize their representations in accordance with the patterns of L1 when appropriate, and in accordance with those of L2 when that is desirable. They therefore have more ways of sorting out the same data of experience.

The Three-Store Hypothesis

The Three-Store Hypothesis proposes to separate the nonlinguistic cognitive store from the two language stores of bilingual speakers. It was meant to reconcile the contradictory findings of experimental psycholinguists of the 1960s and 1970s who found evidence supporting either one store or two stores. Kolers (1968) reported that his subjects' responses were fully compatible with neither the one-store nor with the two-store account, but rather were similar to responses to synonyms in the same language (Fig. 7.1). This led to the proposal of the Three-Store Hypothesis (Fig. 7.2).

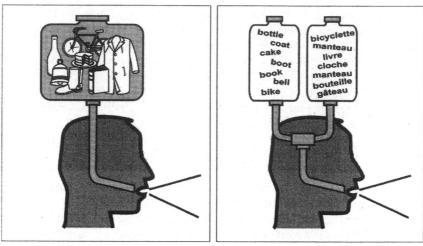

Figure 7.1. *The One-Store and Two-Store Hypotheses*

Two hypotheses about the way a bilingual person handles information are represented by two arrangements of tanks. One hypothesis (left) is that all his information is stored centrally, or in one tank, and that he has access to it equally with both languages. The other (right) is that information is stored in linguistically associated ways, or in separate tanks. Experiments by the author indicated that the actual situation of a bilingual person combines parts of both hypotheses (Kolers, 1968).

Because the question of the storage and retrieval of the lexicon in bilinguals has been cast for decades in terms of two stores or one, the proposed model was called the Three-Store Hypothesis (Paradis, 1978, 1980b). It postulates that a bilingual speaker possesses two language systems (one grammar for Lx and one for Lz, including a set of lexical meanings for words in each language) and one non-linguistic cognitive system which interacts with the two grammars in every act of comprehension or expression. The clearest evidence of a separation between conceptual representations and the linguistic system(s) comes from cases of paroxysmal aphasia (Lecours & Joanette, 1980). These patients show normal, intelligent behavior during bouts of total aphasia, that is, in the absence of any oral or written comprehension and production. Patients with severe aphasias are found with well-preserved nonverbal intelligence, visuospatial skills, and nonverbal learning and memory functions (Alajouanine & Lhermitte, 1964; Marshall, 1984; Gurd & Marshall, 1993).

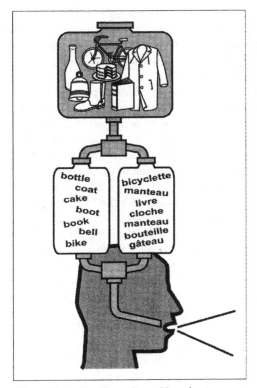

Figure 7.2. *The Three-Store Hypothesis*

The actual situation of a bilingual person may be illustrated by a third hypothesis: Both languages are differentially connected to the same conceptual-experiential information store (Paradis, 1978). Nonlinguistic conceptual features are grouped together so as to correspond to the lexical semantic constraints imposed by each language.

Research carried out over a period of more than ten years has shown that there is no correlation between aphasia (even severe jargonaphasia) and performance IQ or results on tests of general intellectual capacity (Alajouanine & Lhermitte, 1964).

Varley and Siegal (2000) describe a patient with severe agrammatism, unable to formulate propositions in speech or writing, make grammaticality judgments, match sentences with pictures, or identify the meanings of verbs (nor did verbs occur in his spontaneous spoken and written output), who nevertheless achieved a perfect score on causal reasoning, displayed theory-of-mind understanding of true and false beliefs, and successfully completed the picture arrangement test. The authors concluded that their patient's pattern of responses attests to a dissociation between grammar and cognition and to the modular nature of brain functioning.

Most psycholinguists today have adopted some form of the Three-Store Hypothesis in that lexical representations are considered to be connected through a common conceptual system (Paivio & Desrochers, 1980; Grosjean, 1982, 1998; Perecman, 1984; Klosty Beaujour, 1989; Malmkjær & Anderson, 1991; Grainger, 1993; Brauer, 1998; Hermans et al., 1998; van Hell & de Groot, 1998; Francis, 1999; Laganaro & Overton Venet, 2001; Larsen et al., 2002; Pavlenko, 1999, 2002; Abel, 2003). However, the Three-Store Hypothesis is not to be confused with the interdependence model (a one-store model) in which a single conceptual or semantic representation subserves the two lexical entries, nor with the independence model (a two-store model) in which there is a separate conceptual/semantic store for each language. Many authors who make a distinction between lexical item and conceptual representation actually seem to distinguish between meaning (organized in the conceptual store as described in the Three-Store Hypothesis) and lexical representations that appear to refer only to the lexical form that maps directly onto the conceptual features (e.g., Costa, Colomé, & Caramazza, 2000). The Three-Store Hypothesis, on the other hand, postulates that lexical semantic meanings are part of each language's lexical representations, and not merely their phonological and written form, as often seems to be assumed. Note that, in either case, "a common conceptual system" does not imply that the same concept corresponds to a lexical item in Lx and its lexical equivalent in Lz, but that they share some of the same conceptual features, though each may also (and most often does) contain features not included in the other (Paradis, 1978, 1997b; Kroll & de Groot, 1997; Costa et al., 2000).

The Three-Store Hypothesis posits two separate neurofunctional entities: The lexicon, which is part of the language system, and the conceptual system, which is ontogenetically prior and builds concepts through experience and, later, groups together conceptual features so as to match the semantic constraints of lexical items. The result is that the cognitive system eventually builds linguistically and culturally defined concepts and classification procedures in addition to the experientially derived ones. But the eventual one-to-one correspondence between word meaning and (language-induced) concept does not result in a single "semantic" system. Lexical semantics and concepts remain neurofunctionally separate, susceptible to selective impairment or access failure. Lexical semantics is part of the language subsystem; conceptual representations are not.

An individual's cognitive store contains several higher cognitive systems that represent the sum of that person's intellectual capabilities. The conceptual system is one of them, the language system another. The conceptual system stores *concepts*. "Concept," as used here, refers to the mental representation of a thing (object, quality or event) formed by combining all of its characteristics or particulars. A concept can be acquired through experience, by organizing features of perception into coherent wholes. With the acquisition of language, however, its boundaries (i.e., what it encompasses) may be reshaped, and new concepts may be formed. Features of mental representation are then combined in accordance with (language-specific) lexical semantic constraints to form a (language-induced) concept. The concepts evoked by a word and by its translation equivalent will differ to the extent that their lexical semantic organization differs in the two languages. In fact, some concepts may have a label in only one of the languages, and hence are not easily accessible through the other language. A concept expressed by a single word is said to be "easily verbalizable" (Clark & Clark, 1977). If one of the person's languages does not have a word for a particular concept—that is, if no word in that language will activate this concept or something equivalent (i.e., a slight variant, as for most language-specific concepts)—it is more difficult for unilingual speakers of that language to encode it verbally, and bilinguals will tend to use the label in the language that has one, and use a nonce borrowing in the other language, when in a bilingual mode. Just because bilingual speakers are unable to verbalize a given concept in one of their languages because an adequate expression does not exist in that language, it does not mean that the speakers do not have the concept in their mind. They could easily verbalize it in the other language. The distinction between nonlinguistic concept (or mental image) and linguistic concept (or lexically determined unit of meaning), which exists in unilinguals, is thus even more obvious in bilinguals.

The mental representations at the (nonlinguistic) cognitive level (i.e., concepts) are organized slightly differently by each language. The greater the typological and/or cultural distance between the two languages, the greater the difference in the organization of mental representations corresponding to a word or utterance and its translation equivalent. Note that, assuming that a concept comprises all the knowledge that an individual possesses about a thing or event, it is never activated in its entirety at any given time. Only those aspects that are relevant to the particular situation in which it is evoked are activated (Damasio, 1989). Thus, the exact same portion of the relevant neural network is not activated every time that a given word is heard or uttered. English and French words may activate exactly the same mental representation when the context focuses on features that overlap but will activate different representations when the context includes in its focus one or more features that are not part of the meaning of both the word and its translation equivalent.

According to the Three-Store Hypothesis, the conceptual component of verbal communication is not language-specific and there is a single nonlinguistic cognitive system, even though speakers group together conceptual features differently in accordance with the lexical semantic constraints of each language. The lexical items are part of the language system, but the concepts are not (Paradis, 1978, 1980b, 2000b). This is another instance of redundancy of representation, though here conceptual grouping is the mental representation that corresponds to the meaning of the relevant lexical item. In the case of a feature that is identical in two language subsystems, the redundantly stored features are of the same nature—both are within the language system (albeit in separate subsystems). In this case, though, the lexical meaning belongs to the language system whereas the mental representation belongs to the conceptual system (i.e., they are in different *systems*).

From a neurofunctional viewpoint, there is a case to be made for an anatomical-physiological distinction between lexical and conceptual representations. For instance, patients with Wernicke-type and global aphasia have lost access to lexical meanings, not to concepts. In brain-intact individuals, when lexical representations are activated, they trigger access to the corresponding conceptual features throughout the cortex, bilaterally. In split-brain patients (Sperry et al., 1969), the connection between the left hemi-visual field and the right hemisphere is severed, and consequently objects held in the left hand or seen in the left visual field, though conceptually recognized, cannot be named, because the corresponding lexical semantic features cannot be reached and the oral or written word cannot be accessed. In intact brains, language-specific lexical semantic constraints determine which conceptual features are activated, and which are not. The representations of lexical meaning are assumed to be connected to the appropriate conceptual features with links to the relevant sensorimotor associative cortical areas. Whereas conceptual features are thus represented bilaterally in multiple sites, the lexical semantic features specific to each language are represented, with the rest of the language system, in the left hemisphere.

Neuroimaging studies do not distinguish lexical from conceptual representations because whenever a word is accessed, both its lexical and its conceptual representations are activated. In bilingual speakers, the conceptual representation of an L1 lexical item varies in terms of micro-circuitry from the conceptual representation of its L2 equivalent, as a function of the similarity between their lexical meanings. Depending on how close the meanings of a word and of its translation equivalent are, the conceptual representation of the respective lexical items will overlap either more or less. But again, available neuroimaging techniques are not suited to address the issue.

The meaning of a word is language-specific. Each language specifies what is included in the meaning of each word and what is not. The meanings of translation equivalents generally overlap partly, but seldom, if ever, completely (Paradis, 1997a, 2000b). The conceptual store is language-independent. It contains the individual's knowledge of the world. Mental representations in the conceptual store are organized in accordance with the demands of the lexical constraints of the language to be encoded or decoded. Thus, to the extent that lexical constraints differ from one language to the other, the corresponding mental representation will also differ. (*chaise* evokes a different mental representation from 'chair': It cannot have any armrests; *balle* corresponds to a different mental representation from that for 'ball': it cannot be a basketball—it has to be small enough to be held in the palm of the hand.)

Not only nuances in meaning but critical attributes differ between words and their translation equivalents. Concepts that exist before language arises are vague and general, and verbal labels parcel them into different, more precise (language-delineated) concepts. Each language combines features of mental representation in different ways. The features themselves may be nonlinguistic, but their organization into meaningful *verbalizable* units is language-specific. The semantic field of a lexical label imposes its own structure on the conceptual field by grouping together only those attributes that are (semantically) relevant, and which are henceforth (i.e., from the time the label has been associated with just the right set of conceptual features) perceived as a meaningful entity. To each language corresponds a particular organization of experiential data, and to learn a new language is not to put new labels on known objects, but to get used to analyzing the object of verbal communication in a different way (Martinet, 1960).

In the same way that, within a single language, French children for instance have to learn to distinguish between *poil* and *cheveu*, as corresponding to two slightly different conceptual feature groupings, bilinguals must organize their conceptual features differently to fit the different lexical semantic constraints of words in one language and their translation equivalents. (*Un cheveu* is a hair that grows on human scalps; *un poil* is a hair that grows anywhere else on the human body, including the beard and moustache as well as the legs; and anywhere, including the head, on animals.) Note that *poil* and *cheveu* are not synonyms: They cannot be used interchangeably. *Le chat perd ses cheveux* ('the cat is losing its *cheveux*') could only be said as a joke; the expression *il n'a plus un poil sur le caillou* is slang (and slightly derisive) for *il n'a plus un cheveu sur la tête* ('he has not a single hair left on his head'). Yet, in English, both objects are referred to as *hair*, with no hint of a difference. Thus the concept evoked by *hair* will encompass the features of both *poil* and *cheveu*. New concepts may be formed through acculturation, as a result of living in an L2 environment for some time (Pavlenko, 1999).

In the course of development, first, experiential knowledge and innate tendencies to pay attention to certain features (objects, events, properties) of the environment give rise to conceptual meanings (non-linguistic mental representations). Subsequently, words draw attention to specific details of the environment (objects, events, properties) and specify (by lexical semantic constraints) what counts as a unit of meaning that corresponds to the word, and thereby creates a corresponding unit of conceptual meaning, i.e., a particular mental representation. In this way, language organizes conceptual material and creates new concepts by associating conceptual features (i.e., features of mental representations) into conceptual meaning units that correspond to language meaning units (i.e., words or expressions). Mental representations in the conceptual store, which are phylogenetically and ontogenetically prior to the appearance of language (even though language eventually imposes constraints on some concepts), are also microgenetically activated before the selection of the particular language takes place in the encoding process.

Mental representations are activated by a verbal, auditory, olfactory, somesthetic, gustatory or verbal stimulus or set of stimuli. The extent of the activated portion of the mental representation network is influenced by the context surrounding the perception of the stimulus. The individual's mind-set, partially influenced by desires, interests, previous discourse and concurrent or previous events that trigger expectations, also affects which neural substrates get activated, i.e., which portion of the concept is brought into consciousness. These neural substrates are self-activated when a mental representation is evoked in the absence of external stimuli (as a recollection) and may serve as the first phase in transmitting a message (verbal or otherwise).

The production of an utterance starts with the intention to communicate a message. The mental representation of that message is organized in accordance with the lexical semantic constraints of the language in which it is encoded, and is realized through selection of the relevant syntactic, morphological and phonological features from the grammar. This selection is guided by pragmatic concerns. Conversely, the comprehension of an utterance starts with phonological decoding and the final stage, modulated by pragmatic cues, is a mental representation of the meaning.

Comprehension is achieved when a nonlinguistic mental representation has been obtained (at the end of the decoding process). The bounds (i.e., the specific contents) of this mental representation are determined by the (language-specific) semantic constraints of the word or utterance that has been decoded. Expression starts with the activation of a mental representation that is cast into the most closely fitting mold provided by the structure of the selected language. The same principle holds for both unilingual and bilingual speakers. (The closest fit must be selected from among the available structures, e.g., an active vs. passive construction, choice of the most appropriate lexical items, qualifiers, etc., in keeping with pragmatic constraints.)

The Direct Access Hypothesis

Comprehension is effected through direct access: A word in either language is perceived as a word, that is, a sound with a corresponding meaning, irrespective of which language it belongs to. And just as a word and its synonym within the same language differ in sound, meaning (if only minimally), and/or context of use, so does a word from one language and its translation equivalent. There is therefore no a priori reason to believe that the mechanism for accessing a word and its translation equivalent should differ from that for accessing a word and its synonym within the same language. Thus, a word need not be tagged for language identity any more than a synonym is tagged so as to differentiate it from other words with very similar meanings but different forms within the same language (and yet, the appropriate synonym is generally selected on-line). Lexical meaning is what drives the selection of the appropriate conceptual features, whether the word heard be *dog, canine, hound, mutt, chien* or *perro*. An English-language context may facilitate the immediate recognition of an English word, but no more than any context will help the recognition of a word in unilinguals (e.g., the disambiguation of homophones or the perception of a word in a noisy background); This is simply another instance of the pragmatic role of the situational and discourse contexts.

It may therefore be assumed that each word, whether from within a single language (in unilinguals) or possibly from two (in bilinguals), is directly perceived as a word with its meaning, without the listener's having to first identify the language affiliation of that word *any more than* a unilingual must first identify the semantic category when, for example, the word *lemon* is heard (or, if one wishes to metaphorically state that the word is tagged for its semantic category, then *to the same extent that* the semantic category must be identified). Language may be identified after the word has been understood, not the other way around. The knowledge that *apple* is an English word, and not a French word, is metalinguistic knowledge, and is not used in on-line decoding. According to the Direct Access Hypothesis, a word is processed as follows: To the sound [æpəl] corresponds the meaning {ᗡ}, hence, this is an English word. The hearer does not reason that [æpəl] is an English word; hence it means {ᗡ}. (An alternate formulation is: the spelling *apple* corresponds to the meaning {ᗡ}; hence, this is an English word; and not: The spelling *apple* corresponds to an English word; therefore it means {ᗡ}.)

To the sound [dɔg] corresponds the meaning {🐕}, to the sound [tri:] corresponds the meaning {🌳}, and to the sound [klɔʃ] corresponds the meaning {🔔}. The fact that the first two are English words and the third a French word is not relevant to their comprehension by an English-French bilingual. Just as [dɔg] is immediately perceived as meaning {🐕} (and not {🌳}), and [tri:] is perceived as meaning {🌳} (and not {🐕} or anything else), [klɔʃ] is perceived as meaning {🔔 *cloche*} and not {ᗡ *pomme*}, {🐕 *dog*}, or anything else. Language-specific phonological characteristics are what distinguish the French *casserole* [kæsrɔl] from the English 'casserole' [kæsərol] in the same way that 'tránsport' is differentiated from 'transpórt' within the same phonological system. Just as *dog* and *tree* are distinguished by different sounds, so are [dɔg] and [klɔʃ]. The French word *dogue* and the English word *dog* are distinguished by subtle phonetic features (*dogue* = 'bulldog'), but each corresponds to a different lexical representation, in the same way as two similar-sounding words in the same language (such as *five* and *fife*). The more phonologically distinct the two languages are, the fewer the possible ambiguities.

When ambiguities do occur, they are resolved in the way all phonological or orthographic ambiguities are, namely by the context. In a psycholinguistic experiment, the written word *dent* could be interpreted as an English or a French word, just as *wind* could be interpreted as an English noun or verb (with their corresponding pronunciation and meaning). In a bilingual situation, relative frequency in each language, language dominance, language of last occurrence of the item, language of the experiment, etc., will serve to disambiguate the word. The same fundamental principles apply in the unilingual and bilingual conditions.

Schulpen et al. (2003) present experimental evidence consistent with the Direct Access Hypothesis by showing that lexical access is language nonselective but sensitive to language-specific characteristics of the input. Words, including interlingual quasi-homophones are distinguished by phonemic and subphonemic cues in the same way as minimal pairs within the same language are distinguished (e.g., pear/bear, dime/time, seal/zeal in English). As suggested by the authors, in the proposed neurolinguistic theory, interlingual homophones have two different representations, one in each language subsystem. The auditory input signal activates the representation that constitutes the best match. To the extent that two words in the same language differ (however minimally), they activate different representations within the same system. Likewise, and in the same way, as long as a word in Lx minimally differs (by a phonemic or subphonemic feature) from a quasi-homophone in Lz, it will be perceived as a word of Lx because it is in the Lx subsystem that it will find its representation. In English, /bæt/ will reach *bat* and /pæt/ will reach *pat*; in English-French bilingualism, [E]/pæt/ will reach *pat* and [F]/pæt/ will reach *patte* (in some English dialect and some French dialect (e.g., mine), respectively, though the vowel quality will change with each dialect). Subphonemic features become distinctive features that separate interlingual homophones just as they separate minimal pairs in languages in which such features (e.g., aspiration, vowel length or voice onset time) happen to be distinctive. Thus, they effectively create interlingual minimal pairs. Auditory input signals activate the representation in the language subsystem that is the best match with respect to sublexical and lexical characteristics. The ability to distinguish interlingual (quasi-) homophones will of course depend on the bilingual speaker's having internalized the relevant phonological and prosodic features of L2. If listeners have difficulty perceiving an L2 phonemic contrast, they will represent minimal pairs in L2 that differ by that contrast as homophones, as suggested by Pallier, Colomé, and Sebastián-Gallés (2001). Some such words will be perceived as cross-linguistic homophones and, according to the Subsystems Hypothesis, will be represented redundantly in each language subsystem.

In an experimental study exploring the recognition of guest words (nonce borrowings) in bilingual speech, Grosjean (1988) found that, when a word is borrowed from the language not currently in use, the phonotactics of the borrowed word, the presence or absence of a base-language homophone, the language-specific phonetics of the word, and the language that precedes that word all play a role in the recognition process. This finding illustrates how the recognition of a word is facilitated by a variety of contexts—language identity being one of them. Semantic expectations would be another, as attested by garden-path sentences and the use made of them by stand-up comedians. Grosjean (1995), in fact, remarks that the syntactic, semantic and pragmatic contexts of the sentence in which a word occurs affect its recognition. Grosjean's (1988) results are thus entirely compatible with direct lexical access. The word is recognized by its form, which corresponds to a meaning, and the knowledge that it belongs to one language or the other is not a precondition to its recognition. The recognition (on request) of a word's language identity is a conscious metalinguistic task.

Speakers have also direct, automatic access to one or the other of their languages for purposes of encoding a message. Once a language has been selected for expression, the neurofunctional subsystem subserving the other language is inhibited in order to prevent interference (i.e., unwanted competition) by raising its activation threshold to a point that makes self-activation difficult or impossible, but not high enough to prevent activation through perception of external verbal stimuli. Thus it is possible to understand utterances in one language while in the process of speaking another, as has been experienced by every bilingual person. The message is *directly* encoded and decoded in one or the other language, in a process not involving translation. This direct apprehension is what is usually (inappropriately) referred to as "thinking in a language."

Bilinguals cannot decide not to understand one of their languages. Bilingual Stroop tests cause interference. In other words, the input switch (as postulated in the 1960s and 1970s) cannot be turned off. Since it is an essential characteristic of a switch that it should have both on and off positions, there cannot be a bilingual input switch. Nor is there any necessity for an output switch (e.g., as proposed by Jakobovits, 1970) other than whatever mechanism allows the individual to switch any mind-set. The bilingual's decision to speak Spanish is no different in nature from the decision to gesture instead of speaking. Obler and Albert (1978) proposed to replace the input switch by a bilingual monitor that would continuously scan the incoming acoustic signal for clues to the language of the utterance in order to shunt the signal to the appropriate grammar. There is no basis on which this could be done. The linguistic cues on the basis of which such a monitor would operate could not be phonemes specific to one of the languages, since words of one language pronounced with phonemes from the other are still understood. It could not operate on the basis of specific consonant clusters because these are not present in every word, and probably not even in most words. Nor could the monitor identify the language on the basis of a syntactic structure peculiar to only one of them because the processing would have begun long before the syntactic structure was encountered (Paradis, 1980a). Because their experiments indicate that spoken language automatically activates both mental lexicons, Spivey and Marian (1999) conclude that there is no need to postulate a switching mechanism that is somehow voluntarily triggered.

The language tag, as awareness of language identity, is a product of metalinguistic knowledge. It may be considered as a convenient abstraction to refer to the fact that some words belong to the Lx subsystem, others to the Lz subsystem, in the same way that some words behave as (are tagged as) count nouns, others as mass nouns. In on-line processing, language awareness is as unconscious as the process that allows a unilingual speaker to understand (or select) the appropriate word in a given context; in fact the two processes are of the same kind. The process for selecting a Russian word by a bilingual person speaking Russian is the same as the process that allows a Russian unilingual to select among the indefinite, almost unlimited, possibilities for encoding a given message. In order to name an object on confrontation, competing synonyms within the same language must be inhibited just as translation equivalents (and their synonyms) must be in bilinguals. There is therefore no need to postulate a language tag specific to bilinguals any more than a bilingual switch or a bilingual monitor.

All these proposals (i.e., bilingual input/output switch, bilingual monitor, language tags) rest on the assumption that it is necessary to identify the language of a word (or utterance) before its meaning can be accessed; consequently, words (and presumably morphosyntactic rules) are "tagged" for language. The Direct Access Hypothesis proposes that words (and utterances) are understood directly, that is, without first having to identify the language, in the same way that unilinguals access the meaning of different words (and syntactic constructions) within the same language. Knowledge of the language identity of a word is of the same order of facilitation (and disambiguation), but not greater, nor of a different nature, than the knowledge of the semantic field or grammatical class of a word in a unilingual context (as wind/wind, bow/bow, *attention*/attention, *dialogue*/dialogue).

Access to the meaning of the lexical item is automatic, and the same in bilinguals as in unilinguals. Why should there be a special device to shunt *potato* to the English system and *échafaud* to the French system, when no such device is postulated to shunt *potato* to the meaning {potato} and not to the meaning {tornado}. When [poteːto] is perceived, the signal is automatically transmitted so as to activate the meaning {potato}, [tornedo] automatically activates {tornado} and, likewise, [eʃæfo], activates {*échafaud*} (Paradis, 1980a).

Just as *potato* is directed to its portion of the semantic network—i.e., vegetables—not vehicles or animals—*échafaud* is directed to its lexical representation in the French neurofunctional subsystem, because this is the connection that was established during acquisition. Eventually all lexical representations, English and French, activate the corresponding conceptual features in the single conceptual store, to give rise to a nonlinguistic mental representation.

The evidence usually invoked in support of the language identification hypothesis is the recognition of interlinguistically ambiguous items (i.e., forms that could be a word in either language, e.g., *son, dent, on*, in English and French). In such cases of interlingually ambiguous terms, as mentioned earlier, disambiguation surely follows the same procedures as disambiguation within the same language, generally through context. Interlingually ambiguous items have intralingual counterparts. They abound in French at the phonological level (e.g., *le livre est tout vert / le livre est ouvert* ('the book is totally green' / 'the book is open'); *le poteau rose / le pot aux roses* (the pink post / the pot of roses). They are also common orthographically in English (e.g., *read*: [ri:d]/[rɛd] (tense: present/past); *wind*: [wɪnd]/[wæ'nd] (grammatical category: N/V); or *read/red*, both [rɛd]. Such items allow for plays on words, puns, etc. English-language newspaper headlines abound in ambiguous readings of single lexical items or of whole captions. (For example, "Head cutter wanted" is not the caption for an article on a sheriff's appeal to bounty hunters to capture a psychotic killer, but an ad from a garment manufacturer who seeks a supervisor for the pattern cutting department.) The fact that a verbal stimulus is a French word as opposed to an English word is no more (or less) important than the fact that a word is a noun or a verb (e.g., *wind*) or in the present or past tense (e.g., *read*); the principle is the same in all such cases.

The fact that words that do not have a language-specific feature such as an initial consonant cluster to indicate the appropriate lexicon are recognized as fast as words that do possess such a feature, even when the word is a nonce borrowing phonologically adapted to the host language (Grosjean, 1988), argues in favor of direct access (i.e., there is no need to identify the language of a word before its representation can be accessed). The awareness of the language identity of a word is a metalinguistic phenomenon that occurs *after* the meaning has been accessed. The *word*-specific acoustic-phonetic characteristics of the word are more important than its language identity in determining the speed of recognition (the moment at which the word is recognized in a gating paradigm).

Whether it is a borrowed word or its base language homophone that is more frequent is a variable affecting the speed of the word's retrieval, showing that frequency of a given item is more important than its language identity. Frequency of the stimulus word plays a role independent of language identity: The recognition of a word is speeded up by its own intrinsic frequency. In a bilingual recognition task such as Grosjean's, a word will be perceived as its host language quasi-homophone as long as the quasi-homophone is more frequent, but as the guest language word if *it* is more frequent. In other words, the frequency of occurrence of a given item is more important than its language identity in guiding its interpretation. A bilingual recognizes known *words* (not French words or English words, just words, which upon analysis are identified as English or French). Words need not be "flagged as being English" (Grosjean, 1988. p. 255) before their lexical representation can be accessed. They are immediately recognized as meaningful words or not, and the fact that a particular word is English is determined by a post facto awareness.

This does not mean that the two lexicons are necessarily stored as one common store. It only means that each store is directly accessed in comprehension. The fact that each language subsystem is capable of selective inhibition demonstrates that, at some level, they are subserved by different neural substrata. In other words, direct access does not entail one extended language system common to both languages. The only claim is that words are perceived as meaningful, irrespective of their language identity. As long as the word is part of the bilingual's knowledge, its representation is activated automatically (i.e., immediately; that is, without the mediation of a language switch, monitor or language tag detector) when the word is heard or seen, on the basis of its intrinsic characteristics.

A word is automatically processed on the basis of its acoustic-phonetic and phonemic characteristics. Notwithstanding the fact that the two languages are represented as two separate subsystems within the language system, the claim is that a stimulus word automatically activates its own corresponding lexical representation in the appropriate subsystem simply because that is where it is stored.

Ambiguity resolution is no different in unilingual and bilingual situations. Items that are ambiguous across subsystems, or two homophonous items within the same subsystem, are activated simultaneously (unless the ambiguity has not been perceived because of a constraining context, and only one of the alternative interpretations is activated). When a homophone (or a cross-language homograph) is encountered, the activation threshold of both meanings is lowered, but only the selected item reaches the threshold. Cross-language pseudohomophones are disambiguated by their (minimal) differences in sound as are near-homophones within one language.

In a nutshell, bilinguals use the lexical-item-specific phonological or orthographic information available in the stimulus to access the appropriate *lexical item*; they do not use language-specific information to access the appropriate *system* (within which to access the item). Words are not necessarily cued "for one or the other lexicon" but for certain characteristics; when such characteristics happen to be limited to words in one language, then, in searching for words with those characteristics, the search will, as a logical consequence, involve only words in that language (because all words with these characteristics are in that language—a metalinguistic fact irrelevant to the on-line search). Words could just as well be stored in one common lexical system or in two separate systems. Direct access is independent of the type of organization of the two languages in the same brain (i.e., whether as an extended, dual or tripartite system or as subsystems).

The Subsystems Hypothesis

The Subsystems Hypothesis is a *neurofunctional* proposal, compatible with all the various known recovery patterns of bilingual aphasic patients, including alternating antagonism and selective aphasia. It acknowledges a separate neurofunctional cognitive system independent of the language system, and hence of the language systems of bilinguals (i.e., the conceptual system, as proposed in the Three-Store Hypothesis). In addition, it recognizes that language is an independent neurofunctional system, a neurofunctional module, receiving inputs from the conceptual system and providing outputs to the articulatory or digitomanual kinetic systems. Each language is a subset of the larger language neurofunctional system.

The Subsystems Hypothesis is by now shared by various psycholinguistic models (e.g., de Bot & Schreuder, 1993; Poulisse & Bongaerts, 1994; Dijkstra & van Heuven, 1998; Green, 1998; Schulpen et al., 2003). de Bot (2002) agrees that the Subsystems Hypothesis can explain how languages in bilinguals may be kept apart, but claims that it does not explain how the choice for a given language is made. In one sense, he is right. The choice of a given language is not determined by the subsystems but by the conceptualizer (i.e., within the nonlinguistic cognitive system). Nonce borrowing and mixing are made possible by differing activation threshold values. The conceptualizer determines which language is appropriate to the situation and activates elements of that subsystem in the same way that it determines the appropriateness, in a given context, of the register, the directness of the speech act, the literal or figurative form, the syntactic constructions used (in accordance with the desired focus), all of which will eventually determine the selection of the appropriate words and prosody.

Although the Subsystems Hypothesis by itself does not determine the choice of a given language, it makes it possible by offering the conceptualizer a choice of two networks. The raising of the activation threshold of the unselected language permits access to the desired language. A bilingual individual may decide to speak one language or the other, but this conscious intention merely initiates the implicit physiological function (an autonomous phenomenon); it does not consciously control the inhibition of the unselected subsystem. The inhibition of the unselected language occurs automatically, just as antagonist muscles are inhibited when one raises one's arm. The brain does it without the speaker's conscious control. It is a property of all cerebral systems (and subsystems), irrespective of their nature, that the antagonist function is inhibited (i.e., its threshold raised) when a given function is activated. Thus there is no need to postulate any mechanism specific to bilinguals in order to inhibit the unselected system.

Language choice (before verbal encoding) is not an all-or-nothing process that invariably runs straight from top to bottom (conceptualizer to articulator). Even unilinguals are able to change the structure of an utterance halfway through, for example when adjusting the structure of the sentence to fit the syntactic constraints of a particular late-selected lexical item; sometimes this results in the production of a blend, but it may be successful if the substitution occurs early enough in the process. The style (i.e., the selection of structures) may also change in mid-course upon the arrival of another interlocutor, requiring a different register (which may result in a different choice of lexical items, the avoidance of double negatives, and/or the adjustment of articulation and loudness). Similarly, because each language (subsystem) is part of the larger language (macro)system, when bilingual speakers encounter word-finding difficulties, or switch to use a conceptually better fitting word in the other language, they may activate a word or phrase from that other language (subsystem) and even decide to switch to the other language altogether from that point on, if it happens to be an acceptable grammatical juncture. This may be done automatically without any deliberate choice on the part of the speaker. The temporary word-finding difficulty may be caused by a significantly higher activation threshold for the word in the language currently in use than for its translation equivalent (possibly due to frequency or recency effects).

By virtue of being subsystems of the language system, two specific subsystems (say, English and Japanese) do share the properties of language whose principles they instantiate in the form of parameters (i.e., different rules of the same type, different forms of the same kind). There is therefore a fundamental structural similarity between the two subsystems. The specific parameters may differ between languages, but the nature of the parameters (i.e., instantiations of specific principles) is the same across language subsystems. The structural distance between two languages can be measured in terms of the number of shared parameters. Languages normally do share some parameters; not all of them will be different, especially in languages that are genetically close. This is why the number of identical forms that are either legitimately or deviantly present in two languages has no effect on the way languages are organized into neural subsystems. In other words, no matter how much static interference there may be in a language's representations (i.e., how many elements of L1 are illegitimately present in L2), L2 will be treated by the brain as a language subsystem. This intrinsic similarity between languages is what allows for borrowing and code-mixing. A parameter may be substituted for another parameter *of the same principle*. (As a heuristic analogy, blue, red, yellow, green, and orange are all different from each other, but they are all items of the same type, namely colors, as opposed to sounds or smells. As different as red is from green, they are both exemplars of color. You can change the color of your scarf from green to blue or red, but not from green to heavy, minty, liquid or putrid.)

Subsystems, switching and interference

Within a subsystems framework, it would appear that the implicit grammar of code-mixing requires no extra rule in addition to those of each of the two languages involved. The only constraint seems to be that each speech segment of a mixed utterance should not violate the grammar of the language of that segment. Decisions to switch within a sentence may occur, not necessarily only at the initial planning stage, but at every juncture where the switch will not violate the language of the segment preceding or following that switch. These junctures will differ for different pairs of languages, depending on how much parallelism there is between the two grammars. If, for example, both languages place the adjective before the noun, an adjective may be freely borrowed in isolation (as between Dutch and English, but not usually between English and French).

The activation of a specific language subsystem enhances the likelihood of elements of that subsystem being selected, but, indeed, as suggested by de Bot (2002), it is no guarantee of the selection of elements from that language only. This would be true only in a dual system model which, mainly for this very reason, was discarded in favor of a subsystems model (Paradis, 1981). The basic difference is that two subsystems constitute one language (macro)system, thereby allowing mixing by inserting into an utterance in one language elements of the same kind from the other.

When bilingual speakers are in a bilingual mode, i.e., when speaking with other bilinguals in a context where nonce borrowing and mixing are permissible, the conceptualizer selects a subsystem as the base language at the beginning of the conversational exchange but the subsystems construct allows the borrowing of a word or phrase from the other language (when the word in the base language is less easily accessible for any number of reasons— temporary word-finding difficulty, diglossic lexicon, lower activation threshold for the item in the other language, language-specific connotations, verbatim reported speech, etc.).

Code-switching that results from lack of knowledge (or temporary word-finding difficulty) reflects a property of subsystems (as opposed to a dual system) in that elements within the language system as a whole are accessed automatically as a result of differential activation threshold levels. If a word in a currently used language has a high activation threshold, its translation equivalent with a lower threshold will reach activation before it. It will be suppressed before reaching vocalization when in a unilingual mode, whereupon the speaker will take the trouble to retrieve the right word and possibly, as unilinguals invariably have to do, spend a few extra hundredths of a second in the process, or find a circumlocution. If code-switching is the result of an intentional strategy, it is deliberate, but still occurs by virtue of the same principles that make inadvertent code-switching possible. The bilingual speaker may willfully elect to use an item from one language over another for a number of reasons (e.g., for calculated emphasis, to mock somebody's speech habits, in a conscious attempt to be formal, etc.).

In the process of fitting the conceptual message into words, even though one subsystem has been selected (for whatever reason, for example, it is the language of the conversation so far or the interlocutor's perceived preference), a word from the other subsystem may nevertheless be chosen when it uniquely corresponds to the concept the speaker wishes to verbalize. The fact that the subsystems constitute one language system allows this to happen.

In his adaptation to bilingual processing of Levelt's (1989) language production model, de Bot (1992) adopts a subsystems framework for the lexicon and the formulator (i.e., the grammatical level of language encoding) but assumes what amounts to an extended system for the articulator in order to account for the presence of a foreign accent in the second language of bilingual speakers. Tomioka (2002b) argued that a foreign accent does not necessarily imply that bilingual speakers possess only one articulator for both languages. It can be accounted for within a subsystems framework if one assumes that the accent is caused not by dynamic interference (i.e., in the course of performance), but by static interference (i.e., as part of the representation of the kinesthetic programs themselves). Her argument is supported by the systematicity of foreign accents which reflects the form of the representations rather than a dynamic interference during performance.

This proposal is further supported by cases of differential speech apraxia such as the one described by Alajouanine, Pichot, and Durand (1949). Subsequent to a cerebral vascular accident sustained the previous year, their patient, a 63-year-old fluent English-French bilingual, presented with symptoms of what the authors call *anarthrie pure* (i.e., speech apraxia) that were much more severe in French than in English, even for phonemes and consonant clusters that are virtually identical in the two languages. It appears that when the kinesthetic commands came from the English subsystem, the patient's articulation was "perfectly realized" whereas it was "extremely deficient" (p. 265) when they came from the French subsystem.

The hypothesis is also supported by the case described by González-Álvarez et al. (2003) of a 51-year-old female patient who, subsequent to a small lesion in the right basal ganglia (affecting the head of the caudate nucleus, putamen and internal capsule), exhibited a selective foreign accent syndrome in her native language (Spanish) but not in her later-learned languages (French, Valencian, and English), which were not affected by the lesion. This case provides evidence in favor of either (1) pronunciation for each language being implemented by a different subsystem or, as discussed by the authors, (2) a distinction between the circuits that subserve the automatisms of the first language and the controlled ones that subserve later-learned languages. In either case, the articulator receives input from different sources and its output is language-specific.

On the basis of experimental evidence showing that Italian immigrants to the United States failed to establish a new phonetic category, namely, for English /e^l/, leading to a merger of the phonetic properties of English /e^l/ and Italian /e/, Flege, Schirru, and MacKay (2003) argue that the two phonetic subsystems of a bilingual person interact. But the nature of the interaction is one of static interference. Whether these immigrants have established a new phonetic category, continue to use the Italian category when speaking English, or have merged the properties of English /e^1/ and Italian /e/, they have a phonetic category for (their idiosyncratic) English. The kinesthetic engrams (the schemata or motor programs) for the production of phonemes, like any other component of language and speech, may exhibit representational interference in that their schemata may illegitimately incorporate any proportion of properties of the other language. The mergers are not caused by dynamic interference during the production process. Irrespective of the linguistic purity of its contents (i.e., whether the stored phonetic properties of English are actually those of English or not in the Italian's English subsystem), each language is stored as an independent subsystem.

The extent to which the phonetic output corresponding to a particular phoneme in one of a bilingual's languages resembles that of the other is irrelevant to the issue of whether there is one merged or shared representational system vs. two independent, separate systems (articulators). Even if the identical muscles are involved in the same configuration for the production of phonemes in either language, the fact that production can be impaired in the context of speaking one language and not the other shows that two different sets of commands (one for each language) rather than one common schema, are at work. This is similar to the demonstration that speech apraxia differs from oral apraxia. Just because a bilingual speaker has a foreign accent determined by prosody, it is not necessarily the case that, as postulated by de Bot (1992), there is only one articulator for bilingual speakers. It could equally be true that each articulator processes a larger number of similar intonation contours than is legitimate. Still, how is the brain to know whether these similarities are legitimate or not? For other pairs of languages, some of them would actually *be* legitimate. This reasoning applies to any aspect of the language system, including morphosyntactic rules and lexical meanings.

Roelofs (2003a) interprets accidental errors of using segments or applying phonological rules of one's L1 when speaking L2 (e.g., producing the English word *stuck* [stʌk] with the pronunciation of the Dutch word *stuk* [stük]) as suggesting that the phonological systems of the first and the foreign language are not entirely separate. This type of interference might be difficult to account for in a dual system representation (i.e., one system for each language) but is compatible within a subsystems framework. Depending on the relatively higher activation threshold of one item over its quasihomophone in the other language (induced by frequency and/or recency of use or properties of the context), the phonological form of the quasihomophone of the intended item may be selected from the other subsystem.

According to the subsystems hypothesis, neither encoding processes nor representations are shared between languages. When the phonological output is identical in the two languages, this does not entail that their representations are shared (i.e., that there is only one representation for both languages, as hypothesized in a tripartite system). Identical representations (including those of schemata) are redundantly stored in each language subsystem. For instance, in her study of gender interference in L2, Bordag (2003) hypothesizes that during the production of L2, when the gender of a noun differs from that of its L1 translation equivalent, their gender nodes compete for selection and the wrong gender may be selected. This account assumes dynamic interference during processing. In such a model, it appears that gender is not a feature attached to each individual noun, but a node common to all nouns, to which nouns must connect for gender selection during production. If this were the case, it is unclear how nouns would "know" which gender node to select. The subsystems hypothesis, on the other hand, assumes that gender is a feature attached to each noun, together with its other morphosyntactic properties, and that once a lexical item is selected, its semantic, syntactic, morphological and phonological features are activated. However, as suggested by Bordag (2003), during appropriation, lexical units of L2 tend to inherit the grammatical features of L1 until the differences are explicitly taught (or learned on the basis of contrastive phonological forms, e.g., o/a suffix alternation for masculine-feminine gender in Czech). The wrong gender thus appears to be part of the lexical item's representation, causing static interference until such time as it has been rectified through conscious exposure to negative evidence and, possibly, has been eventually internalized.

A corollary to Murphy's Law

Structural differences between the bilingual's languages should be irrelevant for the way the neurofunctional system works. The cerebral mechanism is the same for all bilinguals (and unilinguals). To the extent that X obtains for a given speaker-hearer, Y will result. This means that the more X is present, the more Y obtains. The less X is present, the less Y is used. If X is altogether absent, then there is no Y. But as long as there is one X, there will be some amount of Y. The mechanism is thus the same for all users, and there is only a difference in degree of use (not a difference in nature or in kind). This reasoning applies to any aspect of the proposed neurofunctional verbal communication system.

For example, in answering the question as to whether the same symptoms of surface, phonological, and deep dyslexia can be elicited in all readers, regardless of the structure of the writing system (e.g., Japanese and Chinese as well as English and Croatian), the reasoning is as follows: (1) All orthographies without exception allow deep dyslexia—a reader may recognize a word, whatever its form, and produce a semantic paraphasia. (2) To the extent that there are some regular graph-sound correspondences, and to the extent that there are exceptions to these correspondences, it will be possible to distinguish between surface and phonological dyslexia. (In Japanese, one can select and compare performance on *jukujikun* and *ateji* kanji (i.e., characters whose meanings do or do not match their default pronunciation in a given word), and on kana, by including among the stimuli the five exceptions to the otherwise regular grapheme-syllable correspondence (Paradis, Hagiwara & Hildebrandt (1985). In Chinese, characters containing phonic elements that do not contribute to the pronunciation of the character, and nonsense characters including common phonic elements can be used (Paradis, 1987c). This reasoning has been dubbed a corollary to Murphy's Law: Only that which is susceptible to break down will break down. In other words, possible errors are constrained by, and hence indicative of, the structure of the system (Paradis, 1987c, 2001c). This notion is reflected in Alexiadou and Stavrakaki's (2003) conclusion that grammatical disorders in bilingual aphasia depend to some extent on the specific properties of each language.

As another example, if we assume that the benefits of language therapy transfer to the untreated language only to the extent that both languages contain similar features, then one would expect the benefits of treatment in Spanish to transfer to Basque only in phonology, and not in syntax or the lexicon, while they would transfer to Catalan only in syntax and the lexicon, and not in phonology. The model that predicts this is a general model that works for both the Spanish-Basque and Spanish-Catalan pairs, and makes predictions about all combinations of languages. (In fact, it applies to unilinguals as well: Transfer from a treated feature will occur only for similar features in the language, e.g., training WH-movement structures is reported to improve the production of untrained WH-movement constructions but to have no effect on NP-movement structures— Thompson & Shapiro, 1995).

Cognates

Cognate recognition or priming is not evidence of an extended system (one common system for both languages) or of a tripartite system (with a common store for cognates only). Cognates have the same effect as synonyms within the same language, not because they are represented within a common system across subsystems, but because the form of the cognate serves as a cue to the recognition of the word in the other language (in the same way as completion does). It does this even when the cognate is in a language that the speaker has never heard or read before. When word forms sufficiently resemble their translation equivalent in a language known to the reader, they are immediately understood (in accordance with the Direct Access Hypothesis).

When French tourists arrive at Bucharest Airport for the first time, not only are they able to understand the meaning of the signs that read *Aeroportul Bucharesti* and, until recently, on a large building, *Partidul Communisti*, but they would also be able to understand the long notices that accompany pharmaceutical products. Romanian words can be recognized through the speakers' French lexicon. What is true of an unknown language is even more true of a known one. When a word in a known language is a cognate of a word in another known language, it is recognized by both language subsystems: directly in one, and by immediate "completion" in the other. This should be expected, given that words are generally recognized fairly globally, even when the order of some of the letters inside the word is reversed. Cognates from known or unknown languages should likewise be recognized immediately.

Words that sound or look alike in both languages but have a different meaning in each (i.e., "false friends"—e.g., resume ('to start again') → *résumer* ('to summarize'); deceive ('deliberately misguide') → *décevoir* ('to disappoint'), have their unilingual counterpart in homophones and homographs with different meanings, e.g., bank ('riverside') and bank ('financial institution'). In the absence of a compelling context, they could trigger either meaning (or both). Given a context, such words may trigger only one meaning. (Even if, in the process, the activation threshold of the other meaning has been lowered, it is not sufficiently low for it to reach activation.)

Words that have a similar meaning in both languages (translation equivalents) have their unilingual counterparts in synonyms. Cross-linguistic priming and other experiments with such words should therefore be expected to elicit the same effects as when synonyms in the same language are presented. It is well known that when [kæt] is produced, [ræt] also receives some activation (i.e., its threshold is lowered somewhat); it is therefore not surprising that when a word is activated, its synonym, homophone or translation equivalent should also receive some activation.

Marian et al. (2003) examined the neurological and cognitive aspects of bilingual language processing in late Russian-English bilinguals, using a head-mounted eyetracking device. They interpret the fact that subjects would look briefly at a stamp (*marka*) when the target was *marker* as evidence of a single lexical store for both languages of a bilingual speaker. However, the *marka*/marker effect may be indicative, not necessarily of a common store for both lexicons but, more plausibly, of an ambiguity of the same nature as that between two words with similar form and different meanings within the same language (e.g., potion/portion; paper/piper). This effect would be predicted by the Direct Access Hypothesis and does not contradict the notion of a separate (sub)system for items of each language.

The simultaneous activation of the two languages (i.e., no extra processing time in cross-linguistic priming) in various experiments discussed by Marian et al. (2003) does not obligatorily imply that the two lexicons are part of one single store, but may reflect either (1) the similarity of lexical meaning between a word and its translation equivalent at the conceptual level, or (2) the fact that any extra processing time for the recognition of a cognate in the other subsystem is insignificant. Priming effects should increase with degree of semantic and/or form overlap (culminating in written cognates in which both overlap maximally, e.g., French *direction* and English 'direction'). Marian and Spivey (2003) conclude from their experiments that, during spoken language processing, bilinguals encounter competition for items between their two languages in the same way as within their two languages. Bilingual listeners simultaneously accumulate phonetic input into both their lexicons (Marian & Spivey, 2003). This represents a challenge to the dual system but not to the Subsystems Hypothesis and is predicted by the Direct Access Hypothesis.

The integration of pragmatics

As mentioned in Chapter 4, in the 1970s and 1980s, experimental psycholinguists were exploring the possibility that one or both languages of bilingual speakers might be less asymmetrically represented in the brain than the language of unilingual speakers. Experimental findings remained contradictory in spite of the ever-shrinking target population, while there was no clinical evidence whatsoever in favor of any difference of language lateralization in any bilingual subpopulation (Paradis, 1990a, 1992a, 1995a,

2003). This led to a search for what the right hemisphere might be contributing in such cases, since it obviously was not subserving grammar. After a number of possibilities were considered (Paradis, 1987b), it appeared that the right hemisphere specializes in processing the pragmatic aspects of language use, which turn out to be at least as important for successful verbal communication as sentence grammar (i.e., the language system). The evidence comes from right-hemisphere-damaged patients with dyshyponoia (Paradis, 1998c).

This adds a new component to the model, given that some pragmatic features are language-specific. It brings another dimension to the possibility of unidirectional or bidirectional interference, namely the interpretation of L2 pragmatic clues with their L1 value, resulting in misunderstandings and faux pas. Not only do idiomatic expressions and proverbial phrases have different interpretations in various languages (e.g., 'to come off one's hinges' means 'to be insane' in Latvian and 'to be angry' in French), but plain indirect speech acts do too, not to mention differences in body language, facial expressions and prosody. What counts as a possible indirect speech act, what context determines the use of this or that form of address, conventional metaphors, conventional gestures and facial expressions all vary in accordance with each language and culture. Thus, in a neurofunctional model of bilingualism, pragmatics too needs to be integrated.

Each level of linguistic structure (prosodic, phonological, morphological, syntactic and lexical-semantic) is affected by pragmatics during the encoding and decoding of utterances. The listener derives meaning from prosody, the selection of specific words (e.g., *san/chan*, formal/informal way of address in Japanese), and syntactic constructions (e.g., passive vs. active; topicalized subject or object). A passive construction places emphasis on the patient rather than the agent of the verb and may be reinforced or contradicted by stress at the phonological level, in addition to prosody, facial expression, conventional gestures and the like. The use of *tu*, which will, in one context, be interpreted as a sign of friendliness or intimacy, will, by the same hearer in another context, be interpreted as a sign of contempt. There is no available empirical evidence as to whether a bilingual individual can lose access to the linguistic pragmatics of only one language. Nor is there any evidence that would help us decide whether linguistic pragmatics is stored as one extended system or whether, similar to the linguistic systems, the pragmatic features associated with each language constitute a subsystem of linguistic pragmatics. Our hypothesis is that the second possibility is probably correct, but this will have to be empirically verified. Because linguistic pragmatic inference/implicature procedures are specific to each language, we may assume that they form a natural class and that, as such, each is likely to form a subsystem connected to its respective language subsystem. The schematic representation in Figure 7.3 is an attempt to visually represent the theoretical construct referred to above.

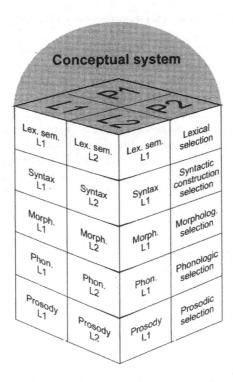

Figure 7.3. *The integration of linguistic pragmatics*

Schematic representation of the integration of linguistic pragmatics and the conceptual system into the verbal communication system.

Pragmatics is an important dimension of bilingualism, although until recently it has tended to be neglected in clinical and neurolinguistic research. Lack of pragmatic competence in L2 leads to communication breakdowns at least as important as those resulting from lack of grammatical proficiency. Individuals with dyshyponoia are known to encounter social problems, and ignorance of L2 pragmatics (especially for speakers with good linguistic skills) can be similarly disruptive. Speakers of a second language may understand what native L2 speakers *say*, but not necessarily what they *mean*. In turn, they may use inappropriate speech acts or other pragmatic devices and thus be misunderstood—possibly disastrously so.

The integration of conscious and unconscious processing

As discussed in Chapter 1, implicit linguistic competence and metalinguistic knowledge constitute two independent systems, both necessary but neither sufficient, each subserved by a different type of memory system. They therefore contribute two separate neurofunctional subsystems to the verbal communicative system. The use of implicit competence is automatic, that is, without conscious effort, awareness of the process involved, or attention focused on the task. Conversely, the use of metalinguistic knowledge is consciously controlled, with full awareness of the rules that are applied (whether they are actually (normatively) correct or not) at the morphosyntactic and phonological levels. Depending on the level of formality, unilinguals will rely more or less on conscious knowledge, using it mostly to monitor their production by checking the form of their inner speech before implementing it vocally. In the absence of implicit competence, incipient second-language speakers will have to rely entirely on metalinguistic knowledge and to compensate for their deficiencies in both competence and knowledge by relying on pragmatic devices.

Both implicit linguistic competence and explicit metalinguistic knowledge receive input from the cognitive system that prepares the message to be communicated. Pragmatic elements will determine the language to be selected for encoding and, within the language subsystems, which constructions and lexical items are most suitable to convey the intended message. The outputs of both linguistic competence and metalinguistic knowledge are instructions to the articulatory apparatus for verbalization. This process may be stopped prior to the actual vocalization of the utterance (inner speech) and consciously monitored before implementation. It may also remain at the stage of inner speech and not be produced out loud.

Both linguistic competence and metalinguistic knowledge are subject to the effects of an activation threshold. Both are influenced by motivation and affect during appropriation and use. The Subsystems Hypothesis applies only to implicit linguistic competence. Thus, aphasia may (temporarily or permanently) selectively affect one whole subsystem, a module of one subsystem, or a module across subsystems. Metalinguistic knowledge is not affected by aphasia and can thus serve as a compensatory mechanism.

However, although the conscious knowledge of words may be intact, access to lexical items, being implicit, may be affected in one or both languages. The raising of lexical items' activation thresholds is what is assumed to cause word-finding difficulty.

In their recent examination of how naming treatment is transferred in a case of bilingual aphasia, Galvez & Hinckley (2003) highlight the importance, in bilingual language therapy, of implicit and explicit memory and of language system organization. One can see how conscious and unconscious processing as well as the organization of languages into subsystems are underlyingly associated with all neurolinguistic aspects of bilingualism.

The integration of motivation and affect

Motivation has been shown to be an important factor in the ability to appropriate and use a second language. As illustrated in cases of dynamic aphasia, it is a prerequisite to the production of any utterance. No speech event would take place without some motivation. It is the motor that drives the acquisition, learning and use of both first and second language. Motivation may have the same facilitating effect as repeated practice.

The emotional input from the relevant parts of the limbic system into the processing of utterances may be assumed to lower activation thresholds in the same way that frequency of use does. This is compatible with the observation that emotional impact seems to have the same effect as rehearsal in strengthening a memory trace. This would be a direct way in which motivation could affect L2 acquisition. An additional indirect effect is that motivation also encourages practice, which in turn positively affects L2 acquisition.

The integration of the various hypothetical constructs

The Direct Acces Hypothesis is compatible with both the Three-Store Hypothesis and the Subsystems Hypothesis. The direct access hypothesis assumes that the acoustic signal that carries a particular word, regardless of its language identity (i.e., whether it is English or Spanish for an English-Spanish bilingual), automatically activates the corresponding lexical representation in the relevant language subsystem, which in turn activates the matching conceptual features in the (nonlinguistic) conceptual system and gives rise to a particular mental representation.

Two words within the same language are distinguished by their specific phonological properties: *cat* /kæt/ is distinguished from *bat* /bæt/ and *cash* [kæʃ]). Two words from different languages are distinguished from each other in the same way: *hat* [hæt] is distinguished from *chatte* [ʃæt]; the first happens to refer to a piece of clothing, the second to a female domestic animal. Likewise, the first happens to be an English word, the second a French word, i.e., the lexical end-point of [ʃæt] happens to be situated within the French subsystem whereas that of [hæt] lies in the English subsystem. This is no different in kind from [kæt] ending up at the lexical representation of {cat} (and nowhere else) and [dɔg] at the {dog} representation (not {cat} or {*chien*}).

At the conceptual level, however, to the extent that words and their closest translation equivalents have meanings that correspond to the respective native speakers' norms, [ʃæ] will activate some of the same features as [kæt] but not all (e.g., it could not refer to lions or leopards, irrespective of context).

The Subsystems Hypothesis is compatible with the Three-Store Hypothesis. The lexical constraints of each language subsystem determine which set of conceptual features is activated when a word (say, in the English subsystem) or its translation equivalent (say, in the French subsystem) is perceived.

The activation threshold hypothesis is a fundamental principle that applies to all items in all neurofunctional cognitive systems, subsystems and modules, whether subserved by procedural or declarative memory. Within the language system, it applies to syllables, lexical items, syntactic constructions, etc. In the case of extremely frequently used items, such as closed-class grammatical morphemes, the threshold may be so low as to show no fluctuation because of the strong frequency effect. Only pathology may interfere with such items' activation threshold and raise it artificially by inhibiting certain pathways. Affect may lower the threshold by providing a surge of appropriate neurotransmitters.

An integration of the Subsystems Hypothesis and the Activation Threshold hypothesis is able to account for all reported cases of bilingual aphasia as well as normal phenomena such as how the speaker-hearer controls two competing language systems and avoids dynamic grammatical interference while retaining the ability to mix at will and to translate from one language to the other, as discussed earlier.

Basic principles of a neurolinguistic theory of bilingualism

It is the basic nature of a theory to integrate a number of hypotheses about a particular domain into a coherent whole. Each component of the proposed theory is necessary but not sufficient. It needs all the other components which, working together, subserve the very complex function of verbal communication. Each major component is itself a complex system composed of several parts. The hypothetical constructs proposed in this volume have the merit of at least being compatible with all known phenomena and of complementing each other to form a cohesive framework. The theory (and all of its parts) is not only compatible with the observable data of normal behavior, but consistent with a number of pathological conditions; in addition, it makes predictions about others (e.g., aphasia vs. amnesia; Alzheimer's vs. Parkinson's) and fits within a larger framework of cognitive functions in general.

The proposed neurolinguistic theory of bilingualism suggests that, in a brain where virtually everything is connected to everything else, there are still some portions of the network that are dedicated to the processing of specific functions. While the basic physiological functioning principles are essentially the same throughout the brain, each dedicated portion of the network subserves its own set of representations, the internal structure of which is independent of that of other neurofunctional systems, while the neurofunctional subsystems are instantiations of specific parameters of their system's principles.

Languages are represented as neurofunctional subsystems of the language system. The neurofunctional language system is a component of the verbal communication system which, in addition to implicit linguistic competence (the language system), contains metalinguistic knowledge, pragmatic ability and motivation. The verbal communication system is connected to the cognitive system where intentions to communicate particular messages are formulated and where verbal messages received are interpreted in accordance with the lexical and grammatical semantic constraints of each language that selectively activate the corresponding concepts, and with pragmatic inferences based on the various contexts of the utterance. Cognitive functions are neurofunctionally modularized during ontogeny as a result of both genetic capacities and experience, and are for the most part stored as microanatomically separate systems, susceptible to selective impairment and nonpathological inhibition.

There is not a single mechanism in the bilingual brain that is not also available to unilingual speakers. Late second-language speakers compensate for the lacunae in their L2 implicit competence by relying more on metalinguistic knowledge and pragmatic ability, but these resources are also available to unilingual speakers.

Every time an item is used, its activation threshold is lowered, making it easier to activate again; the threshold slowly rises again when the item is not used, eventually leading to attrition. Normal age-related functional changes raise the activation thresholds of items in declarative memory, often leading to the gradual degradation of a late-learned second language. Aphasia affects implicit competence, including lexical access.

Within the proposed theory, everything that is said about bilingualism also applies *mutatis mutandis* to multilingualism. For example, trilingual speakers have three language subsystems instead of two, all differentially connected to a single conceptual system. If two languages have been acquired from the crib, and a third has been learned, the third will behave in all respects like the second language of a late bilingual. If two or more languages have been learned, they both (or all) possess the characteristics of learned languages. There may be quantitative differences (such as possible proportional increases in reaction times in psycholinguistic experiments and in the amount and direction of interference in the representations) but no qualitative differences in *the way* the items are represented and processed. The schematic representation in Figure 7.4 is an attempt to highlight the connections between the sensory perceptions and the conscious cognitive representations that feed into the conceptual system, which is connected to both the linguistic and pragmatic components of each language. Feelings give rise to motivation, which sets the conceptualizer in motion.

Conclusion

At least five neurofunctional mechanisms are directly involved in normal language use: (1) The part of the cognitive system which formulates the message to be verbalized and decodes the message to be understood; (2) the implicit linguistic competence system, which provides the grammar (phonology, morphology, syntax and semantics); (3) the metalinguistic system, which monitors the correctness of the sentences (about to be) produced, and in some circumstances also provides conscious knowledge of surface structures to be implemented or understood; (4) the pragmatic system, which selects the linguistic and paralinguistic elements most appropriate to the message to be conveyed and infers the interlocutor's intention from the various contexts of the utterance; and (5) the motivational system without which no utterance would ever be produced.

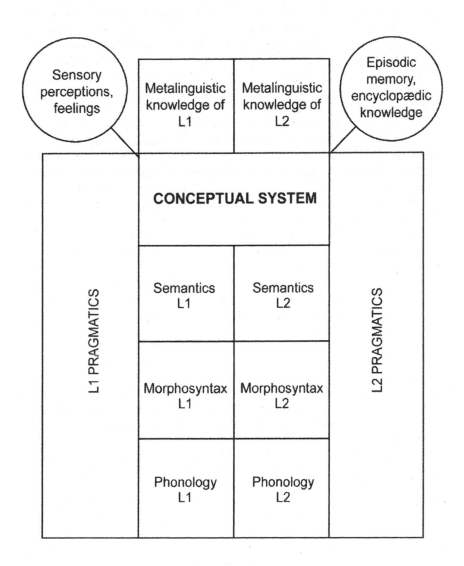

Figure 7.4. *A schematic representation of the components of verbal communication*

Each system constitutes a neurofunctional module that interacts with other modules without modifying (or being modified by) their intrinsic structure. They all work in parallel or in rapid succession, with the output of one possibly serving as input for another. Items may be selected from one module for processing by another but without modifying the internal structure of either module. The performance of a complex task depends on the collaboration of a number of independent neurofunctional modules, each capable of selective impairment. Each language of a bilingual speaker is represented as a complex subsystem comprising several modules.

The intention to communicate provides the impetus to verbalize the message formulated within the cognitive system (corresponding to what psycholinguists have called the conceptualizer—cf. Levelt, 1989; de Bot, 1992). The grammar (implicit linguistic competence) offers possible choices and constrains how a message may be encoded. Pragmatics selects from among the available grammatical choices (languages, registers, direct or indirect speech acts, literal or figurative speech).

Pathology limits the available choices, either in grammar (circumscribed left-hemisphere damage—aphasia), in pragmatics (circumscribed right-hemisphere damage—dyshyponoia), or in metalinguistic knowledge—including vocabulary (diffuse bilateral damage—retrograde amnesia). It may also reduce the desire to communicate verbally (limbic damage—dynamic aphasia), or impair the conceptual system (dementia).

Conceptual mental representations are independent of language. Lexical semantic representations, on the other hand, are a constituent of the language subsystem. The conceptual representation that corresponds to the semantic representation of a lexical item is a specific grouping of conceptual features. The elements included in that grouping and in that of its translation equivalent overlap only partly. The degree of overlap depends on how genetically close two languages are; for each language pair, it varies from word to word.

All speakers (bilinguals of various types and unilinguals alike) make use of all four cerebral mechanisms involved in verbal communication (implicit linguistic competence, metalinguistic knowledge, pragmatics, and affect) to different extents depending on a number of circumstances, such as degree of mastery of the language, degree of formality of the speech event, degree of affective relevance, and to some extent, the cognitive style of the speaker. When pathology reduces access to one of these mechanisms, speakers compensate by relying more heavily on the remaining ones. Thus, aphasic patients may rely on pragmatics and/or metalinguistic knowledge, and the level of emotional arousal will influence their performance as well; conversely, a patient with dyshyponoia will rely on implicit linguistic competence.

Insofar as one word, expression or language is used more often than another, its activation threshold will be lowered. If a language is not used at all for a long time, its activation threshold will be raised, culminating in attrition. To the extent that a word or expression is used more often (or used more recently) than its translation equivalent, it will be selected when the speaker is in a bilingual mode of communication (yielding a nonce borrowing), because its activation threshold is lower, and it will also cause word-finding difficulty in the other language when the speaker is communicating with unilingual speakers of that language.

Bilingual individuals with aphasia recover their languages in one of at least six patterns: parallel, differential, successive, selective, blended, and antagonistic (including alternating antagonism). These patterns show that when a language is not available, it is not physically destroyed but physiologically inhibited, The two languages of a bilingual individual are hypothesized to be represented as subsystems of the larger neurofunctional language system. Each item within each language has an activation threshold that is lowered each time it is used and then slowly rises again until the next use. Just as in a unilingual system some items have a lower activation threshold than some of their synonyms because of frequency and/or recency of use, in bilingual subsystems some items have a lower activation threshold than their translation equivalents. (*Synonym* here refers not only to lexical items with similar meanings, but to any item such as a word, phrase, or syntactic construction that is interchangeable. For example, two syntactic constructions that yield roughly the same meaning (e.g., an active and passive construction) within the same language, or a corresponding morphosyntactic structure in the other language, such as a specific word order or a preposition in one language that has a case-marker as its equivalent in the other, are considered to be synonymous.

There is no mechanism at work in the bilingual speaker's brain that is not also operative, at least to some extent, in the unilingual brain. All speakers rely on the same cerebral substrates, albeit to different extents. There may be qualitative differences at the level of *what* is represented but there are only quantitative differences with regard to *how* it is represented and processed. The contents of each grammar and the semantics of each lexical item (i.e., whether or not they contain only items that legitimately belong to each particular language) are orthogonal to the organization of two (or more) languages in the brain. These factors have no impact on whether the various languages are organized as one (i.e., extended), two (i.e., dual), three (i.e., tripartite) systems or as two or more subsystems. The same is true of the Three-Store Hypothesis. In both cases, grammar and lexical items are treated by the brain in the same way, whether or not they correspond to legitimate items in either language.

In the face of these possibilities, the configuration proposed here on empirical grounds is one in which, irrespective of the degree of static interference in the grammar and lexical representations, the languages of bilingual speakers are represented in the brain as two subsystems, each containing the grammar of their respective language (the subsystems hypothesis) whose individual lexical semantic definitions group together the conceptual features that correspond to the respective language (the three-store hypothesis). Auditory and written words of each language are automatically perceived by the appropriate subsystem, with the same degree of ambiguity as exists in unilingual situations (the direct access hypothesis). There is no special bilingual mechanism needed to identify language identity before an utterance can be processed. To the extent that interlingual quasi-homophones can be distinguished by phonemic or subphonemic features, they will be automatically perceived as different words, provided that the speaker has internalized these properties in both languages.

In the bilingual brain, the form of a representation, and its contents may differ from the L1 norm, but the manner in which these representations are subserved (i.e., the mechanisms and neuropsychological processes involved) is identical for all languages. A phoneme is represented in both languages as a phoneme, though its parameters may be different in each, along one or more featural dimensions (e.g., aspiration, fronting, shorter or longer voice onset time). These differences may be augmented or diminished relative to the norm in one or both bilingual subsystems, but a phoneme modified in this way is treated as an Lx phoneme by the individual's Lx subsystem even when that individual systematically exhibits what is termed interference. This interference applies at the level of representations, not of processing. Independently, dynamic interference may also occur occasionally, in the same way as it does in unilingual speech.

A number of neurofunctional modules have been identified which, in the form of neural systems and subsystems, operate according to a set of parametric variations on basic principles. In comprehension, words are hypothesized to be accessed directly, irrespective of the subsystem in which they are represented. In production, the intended subsystem is selected and the activation threshold of the other subsystem(s) is automatically raised. The proposed theory stresses the need to distinguish between representation and control, between what is represented and how it is represented, between what is represented and how it is accessed, and between what is represented in each language and how these language representations are organized in the brain into systems or subsystems.

But as Henry Hécaen pointed out when neurolinguistics was being established as an independent discipline, it is characteristic of a neurolinguistic theory that it will evolve as new empirical discoveries reshape it, so that it can be used to interpret new data. The discipline itself has broadened its focus since Hécaen stated its objectives and methods some thirty years ago. It has branched into different subfields, with some researchers seeking the confirmation of specific linguistic hypotheses in data from language pathology, while others attempt to account for the observed clinical and experimental phenomena in terms of a neuropsychology of language that leads to further investigations of how language, and by extension verbal communication, are represented and processed in the human brain.

The present work falls into the latter category, focusing on two or more languages in one brain, and proposes what may currently be considered our best working hypotheses. These hypotheses account for the facts now available to us. They should stand until one of them is shown to be in conflict with the new facts arising from our explorations with new, more accurate techniques. If and when that happens, parts of this theory will have to be modified or the theory discarded entirely in favor of another, more explanatory, coherent set of hypotheses.

Glossary

Many words have more than one meaning, depending on the context in which they are used. Some receive a technical definition within a specific domain of discourse. The following definitions correspond to the specific meaning these words have in the context of this book. The intention is not to give a word's general, true, or complete meaning, but to specify the precise acceptation in which it is used in this book. Sometimes these definitions may correspond to the ordinary meaning of the term, as found in dictionaries (and must be taken in this sense rather than a theory-laden sense); sometimes they are idiosyncratically constrained for the purpose of clarity of the argument. The intent is to eliminate ambiguities as much as possible so as to avoid barren controversies and distracting red herrings. It is also estimated that over half the readers of this book, like its author, will not be native speakers of English. If a term is not listed in this glossary, it is to be read with its everyday, ordinary meaning, as found in common dictionaries.

(Language) Acquisition
The incidental appropriation of a language in informal, interactive conversational settings, without formal instruction—as opposed to learning. The outcome of acquisition is *implicit* linguistic *competence*, which linguists generally refer to as an internalized grammar. Under normal circumstances, the native language (L1) is acquired. Languages appropriated later in life are generally learned. See (Language) Learning.

Alexia
Acquired reading disorder. In British English, the term *(acquired) dyslexia* is generally used. Etymologically, *alexia* would mean total inability to read whereas *dyslexia* would mean partial disability. *Dyslexia*, in the United States, generally refers to developmental dyslexia.

Analogy
An analogy is generally defined as a likeness in one or more ways between things that are otherwise unlike. An analogy points to something similar in one or more respects to something else, but not homologous. In the text, all analogies are used heuristically; that is, in order to help the reader grasp a particular concept which actually resembles its analog but with respect to only some of its aspects, the others being irrelevant to the point being made.

Anopia
Blindness in part of the visual field.

(Language) Appropriation
A generic term used when the type of appropriation (i.e., acquisition or learning)
is irrelevant to the issue at hand or when the point made is valid for both. See
(Language) Acquisition and *(Language) Learning.*

Automatic
Self-controlling, i.e., not under conscious control, without awareness of the
computational procedures underlying an observable phenomenon. The production
of speech, for example, is automatic: We are not aware of the programs that
control the scores of muscles involved in articulation and phonation—nor even of
which muscles do what during performance. The generation of sentences prior to
their articulation in the form of utterances is also automatic, that is, without
conscious awareness or control.

Bilingualism
The ability to use two languages. Bilingualism is not a monolithic concept. There
are many types of bilingualism and of bilingual individuals, classified in accordance
with varied criteria. See the section on the definitions of *bilingualism* in the
introduction (p. 2), and Baetens Beardsmore (1982).

Cingulate gyrus
A gyrus (i.e., a convolution) on the medial surface of the cerebrum situated above
the corpus callosum (i.e., the band of fibers that link the two hemispheres). It is
also referred to as the cingulate cortex.

Commissurotomy
Section (cutting) of the band of white fibers that connect the two cerebral
hemispheres, generally performed in order to prevent epileptic seizures that are
unresponsive to medication from crossing from one hemisphere to the other.

Competence
Ability to perform a skill automatically, without conscious control; cerebral
representation of the computational procedures required to perform a skilled act.
Competence is said to be implicit because we are not aware of the form or
structure of the procedures (programs, *modus operandi*) that underlie it. Some
researchers believe that implicit computational procedures are represented in the
brain in the form of algorithms, others that they take the form of parallel
distributed processing networks. Thus, *competence interference* refers to a static
interference in the representation, as opposed to a processing error (a dynamic
type of interference).

Connotative meaning
Secondary meanings commonly associated with a word; qualities, feelings, situations suggested by a word, both conventionally (language/culture-specific (e.g., dog = food, pet, danger, insult—in Korea, England, France, Arab world, respectively), and personally, as influenced by subjective experience (e.g., cat = cuddly, playful, smelly, scratching and hissing, depending on the individual). Connotative meanings are not listed as such in dictionaries and exhibit much individual variability.

Contents (of a representation)
The *contents* of a representation here refers to what is represented, including the form in which it is represented (e.g., whether or not it contains a deviant semantic, morphosyntactic or phonological feature), as opposed to the *organization* of the representations of two languages (e.g., in one common system or two independent systems). It is argued that the way languages are organized in the brain is *orthogonal* (q.v.) to the contents of the representations in the respective languages.

Crossed aphasia
Aphasia subsequent to a right-hemisphere lesion in a right-handed person. It is estimated that, for unknown reasons, about 2% to 3% of right-handers worldwide have their language functions represented in the right hemisphere.

Cytoarchitecture
The arrangement of different types of neurons (brain cells) into layers of varying structure in the cerebral cortex.

Declarative memory
Memory system that underlies the representation of explicit knowledge that is consciously learned and of which we can be aware. It contains both episodic (i.e., experiential) and semantic (i.e., general knowledge) memories, and contrasts with *procedural memory* (q.v.).

Deviant
A statistical term devoid of any valuative judgment. It refers to tokens that deviate from the norm in some respect, i.e., from properties of the vast majority of tokens of this type (e.g., as used by the vast majority of unilingual native speakers); different in some respect from the standard. In a like manner, terms such as *illegitimate* and *inappropriate* mean inappropriate with respect to the L2 norm. Items that are deviant with respect to the norm are nevertheless an integral part of the grammar of individual speakers and their brain treats them as such.

Double dissociation
A double dissociation is obtained between two tasks when, for example, patients can perform task X but not task Y when their right hemisphere is put to sleep, whereas the same patients can perform task Y but not task X when their left hemisphere is put to sleep. It is then said that there is a double dissociation between performance on tasks X and Y, and it is inferred that task X needs the left hemisphere and task Y needs the right hemisphere to be performed.

Dyshyponoia
Impairment of the use of linguistic pragmatics (e.g., the inability to draw correct inferences from the context or from general knowledge, leading to problems in the interpretation of indirect speech acts, metaphors, affective prosody, and in general of the unspoken component of an utterance). From the Greek ὑπονοώ: to imply without actually saying what one means, in the sense of the French *sous-entendre* and Spanish *sobrentender*.

Early bilingual
An individual having acquired both languages by the age of five (or seven, allowing for individual variation in the cerebral maturity rate). An early bilingual is considered to have two native languages (two L1s), contrasted with *late bilinguals* (q.v.).

Evocation, self-activation, retrieval
These terms refer to access to a representation without the help of an external stimulus that would serve as a prompt as it impinges on the senses; retrieval from memory rather than activation of the representation via the perception of its referent. Recognition (comprehension in the case of language) is easier than retrieval (production—independently of the extra difficulty involved in possible motor contributions), because retrieval requires self-activation of the memory trace, without external help.

Figurative meaning
A conventional metaphorically derived meaning (listed as such in dictionaries, sometimes as "secondary" meaning); usually opposed to literal. (Hence may be assumed to be listed in the individual's mental lexicon.)

fMRI
Functional magnetic resonance imagery. A neuroimaging technique that monitors regional cerebral blood flow by recording changes in the magnetic field of red blood cells, taken as an index of cognitive functioning. BOLD fMRI: blood oxygenation-level-dependent functional magnetic resonance imagery.

Gating
Measuring, in milliseconds, from its onset, the portion of a word that must be heard or seen to identify it. For a description of this experimental paradigm, see Grosjean (1980).

Genetic dysphasia
A subset of specific language impairment (SLI). A genetically linked developmental dysphasia characterized by an inability to incidentally internalize those aspects of phonology and morphology that are described by linguists as rule-governed (e.g., marking the regular plural of nouns and regular past tense of verbs in English).

Grammar
The structure of language, comprising phonology, morphology, syntax and semantics, as inferred by linguists from speakers' systematic verbal behavior. Grammar is an attempt to describe, in terms of rules, the observed systematic verbal behavior of speaker-listeners. It is a theoretical construct, at the linguistic level of description. Grammars are abstract representations in the form of systems of rules, the implicit application of which is compatible with the generation of every possible sentence in the language.

Gricean maxims
Maxims describing the characteristics that utterances must have to be understood in context: The maxims of quantity (the speaker provides the right amount of information), quality (the information is assumed to be true), relation (what is said must be relevant to the conversation) and manner (what is said is clear and plain to the understanding); see Grice (1975).

Hebbian cell assembly
The notion, presented by Donald Hebb, that a representation is accessed by the activation of constellations of neurons that are strongly connected because they have frequently been active simultaneously in the various cortical areas that were involved during the appropriation of the representation. A cell assembly is the set of neurons that subserve a representation; see Hebb (1949).

Homographs
Words that are spelled the same way though they have different meanings and possibly different pronunciations (e.g., *wind* (blowing air) and *wind* (to twist and turn)). Cross-linguistic homographs are words that have the same spelling in two languages, though not necessarily the same meaning (e.g., the French word *son* (bran) and the English word *son* (male offspring).

Homophones

Words that have the same sound but different meanings (e.g., *bat* as a piece of baseball equipment and as a flying mammal; *bank* as a financial institution and as rising ground bordering a river).

Idiot-savant

Contrary to ordinary usage, *idiot* is not a derogatory term but a technical label for a specific well-defined condition. *Idiot-savant* is a medical term that refers to a person with a severe mental deficiency (*idiot*, old term for mentally deficient) who has nevertheless developed a unique cognitive capacity to an exceptionally high degree (*savant*). Just as *gender* is not *sex*, an *idiot-savant*, *pace* political correctness and sanctimoniousness, is not just a *savant*, i.e., a scholar. (It is ironic that most recent publications that refer to *savants* in their title list *idiot-savant* among their key words, e.g., Nettelbeck & Young, 1996; Miller, 1998, 1999; Heavey, Pring & Hermelin, 1999; Nettelbeck & Young, 1999; Hermelin et al., 1999; Bolte, Uhlig & Poustka, 2002; Gonzalez-Garrido et al., 2002; Cowan, O'Connor & Samella, 2003.) It would be confusing to refer to *sex* as *gender* in a context where gender also refers to an arbitrary grammatical category, and likewise an idiot-savant is to be distinguished from a savant in the context of neurofunctional modularity. This does not prevent idiot-savants from accomplishing extraordinary intellectual feats in calendrical calculation, for example.

Illocutionary force

The portion of the meaning of the message that pertains to the speaker's intentions; the intended message transmitted by an utterance, e.g., whether it is meant as a question or a request, as a rebuke or a joke, sarcasm or a compliment, irrespective of its actual propositional content (e.g., "Do you know what time it is?" is propositionally a question but its illocutionary force may be a rebuke, such as reproaching the interlocutor with being late, or reminding the children that it is long past bedtime). See *pragmatic meaning*.

Implicit

Inferred from observable phenomena, but not directly observable; covert; opaque to introspection; not available to conscious awareness. Implicit computational procedures are operations by which the brain sustains the production and comprehension of utterances, whatever the nature and form of these procedures may be.

iOIS

Intraoperative optical imaging of intrinsic signals. A technique used during neurosurgery to measure the degree of blood flow optical reflection, taken as an index of cognitive functioning.

Incidental
Not the object of focus. Something is acquired incidentally when the learner focuses on some aspect of the stimulus other than the one which is internalized, i.e., is not consciously aware of what is being acquired.

Interference
Representational (or static) interference: The presence, in a language system, of a feature that actually belongs to another language, and is thus considered deviant with respect to the norm.
Processing (or dynamic) interference: (1) The unintended activation of an element (lexical or grammatical morpheme, word, syntactic feature, pronunciation) of one language while in the process of speaking another, or (2) the co-activation of elements of two systems during processing, resulting in blends. Static interference is systematic; it is a constituent part of the speaker's language representation. Dynamic interference is accidental. It is the result of an inadvertent activation of an inappropriate element.

Jargonaphasia
A form of aphasia characterized by unintelligible speech, in which words are jumbled and neologisms (nonwords) may be present.

Kinesthetic
Related to a motor program, as opposed to kinetic, related to the actual implementation of the motor program.

Knowledge
Information kept in memory that can be recalled to consciousness and stated. Knowledge is said to be explicit since we are aware of what we know (i.e., of the contents of our knowledge).

L1
The native language, that is, the first language acquired in infancy. More than one language may be acquired concurrently from the start. In this case, the speaker is said to possess two or three L1s. The overwhelming majority of children acquire their L1 under similar circumstances (informal communicative interaction with speakers in the environment).

L2
A second language appropriated after the age of five, once a first language has been acquired. Such a language may be informally acquired from the environment or formally learned in school. In contrast with the acquisition of L1, there are many different manners in which, and ages at which, an L2 may be appropriated.

Language
In this volume, in order to avoid confusion as to the possible meanings of the word *language* (given that different authors have used it to refer to different things), this word, when not qualified, refers to the language system (phonology, morphology, syntax and semantics), often referred to as "the grammar" or "implicit linguistic competence" by contemporary linguists within the generative-grammar framework. Language is a necessary but not sufficient component of verbal communication.

Language processing
Language processing refers to the generation of an utterance from the intention to communicate a message to its acoustic realization (production), or from the perception of the acoustic signal to the extraction of a message (comprehension). The message itself is in the conceptual domain, hence not linguistic; it is alternately the output and input of the linguistic system. A message may be conveyed by linguistic means, such as a sentence, but may also be conveyed by other means (e.g., gestures, facial expressions, cries, growls or hums).

Language-specific
Pertaining to a specific language (e.g., German or Italian), rather than to the language faculty as opposed to another cognitive faculty.

Language switching
The passage from one language to another, also referred to as *code-switching*. When the switch occurs within a sentence, it is referred to as *code-mixing*. When only one word or short phrase from one language is incorporated into a sentence in another language, it is called a *nonce borrowing* (q.v.)

Late bilingual
Individual who, after the acquisition of a first language, began the appropriation of one or more languages after the age of five (or seven, allowing for individual variation in the cerebral maturity rate), contrasted with *early bilingual* (q.v.).

(Language) Learning
The controlled, conscious appropriation of a language through formal instruction, as opposed to *acquisition*. Some acquisition may take place in the classroom independently of formal learning, in the course of the actual use of a language in communicative situations. The outcome of learning is *metalinguistic knowledge* (q.v.).

Lexical items
Content words, that have a specific lexical meaning, also referred to as open-class words (e.g., nouns, verbs, adjectives and most adverbs), as opposed to grammatical

words, also referred to as closed-class words (e.g., articles, prepositions, conjunctions).

Lexicon
The set of words represented in the brain, including their default meanings and their implicit phonological, morphological and syntactic properties, such as count/mass for nouns and the number of obligatory arguments for verbs. Implicit aspects of the lexicon are part of the grammar (implicit linguistic competence). *Access* to the lexicon is also implicit. Aspects that are consciously observable or teachable (the pairing of sound and standard referential meaning of words) are referred to as *vocabulary* (q.v.).

Limbic system
Cerebral system placed both phylogenetically and anatomically between the brain stem (the primitive sensory-motor system) and the neocortex (the later evolved outer layer of neural structure in the brain that subserves higher cognitive functions). The limbic system contains structures that are responsible for affect, drives and motivation. See Lamendella (1977b) and Patterson and Schmidt (2003).

Literal meaning
The meaning of a sentence derived solely from the meanings of its words and its grammatical structure.

Meaning
See *Connotative, Figurative, Literal, Metaphorical, Pragmatic meaning.*

MEG (or MSI)
Magnetoencephalography or Magnetic source imaging. A neuroimaging technique that monitors changes in the magnetic fields produced by electrochemical signals among neurons, taken as an index of cognitive functioning. Unlike PET and fMRI that rely on changes in hemodynamics, MEG relies on changes in magnetic flux distributions that arise directly from brain activity (Billingsley et al., 2003).

Metalinguistic
Pertaining to knowledge of the form and structure of a language, either as observed, or as described in grammar books. Metalinguistic awareness is awareness of elements of language, whether they have been formally learned or simply consciously noticed (e.g., the linguistic awareness of speech sounds and words (as opposed to nonwords) by children).

Metaphor
Metaphors draw a parallel between some aspect of the referent and the item to which it is compared. It is unproductive to criticize a metaphor because it does not

reflect those aspects of the referent that are not meant to be taken into account. As a response to "the customs officer was a brick wall", only a right-hemisphere-damaged patient could be expected to object to the fact that the customs officer's complexion was not brick-colored, or that he was not made of baked clay. Likewise, it would be unproductive to reject a hypothetical construct because it did not possess some characteristic of its metaphorical referent. Neurofunctional modularity is such a metaphor: A way of apprehending the anatomico-physiological reality that subserves a particular cognitive function.

Metaphorical meaning
Meaning derived from the particular contexts in which an utterance is produced, without a conventional figurative meaning, and hence not listed as such in the lexicon. It must be inferred from the circumstances of use of the word or phrase. Some metaphors become conventional through frequent use and may eventually become idiomatic expressions.

Microgenesis
The unfolding process of the production of a sentence from the intention to communicate a message to its acoustic realization.

Mind
Emergent property of systems of neurons which allows one to perceive, think, will, reason, and in general perform all cognitive operations (mental processes). For a discussion of the emergence of mind, see Bunge (1980) and Voneida (1998).

Modularity
The neurofunctional modularity of language refers to the fact that comprehension and production of utterances are implemented through the activity of interrelated components, each of which has its own internal structure and *modus operandi* which are unaffected by those of the other components. Each such component (a neurofunctional module) can be selectively inhibited or impaired, and selectively operative. Deficits in the verbal communicative process arise from damage to its component neurofunctional modules or their interconnections. Neurofunctional modules involved in the processing of a complex task may work in parallel or in succession and the output of one may serve as input to another. Neurofunctional modules are not necessarily located in a single circumscribed area, but may be represented in various *dedicated* portions of an interconnected network, such as a cell assembly (i.e., cells that fire together or in rapid sequence as part of a pattern correlated with a specific task). The criterion for neurofunctional modularity is the demonstration of *double dissociation* (q.v.) between two cognitive skills or between two components of a cognitive skill (e.g., A is impaired but not B; B is impaired but not A, in different patients or at different times in the same individual). There is no need to postulate a module on the basis of *simple*

dissociation (e.g., A is impaired but not B; if B is impaired, so is A). If the dissociation is always in the same direction, then a hierarchy of difficulty (or vulnerability, or level of activation) may be assumed.

Nonce borrowing
The incorporation, on the spur of the moment, of a word or phrase from one language into an utterance in another language, when the borrowed word or phrase is not part of the lexicon of native speakers of that language (as opposed to regular borrowings which have become part of the language over the past decades or centuries).

Normal
A statistical term devoid of any valuative judgment. It simply refers to properties of the vast majority of cases of a given type (see *deviant*). When referring to persons, it is used in comparison with brain-damaged.

Orthogonal
Completely independent; having no correlation.

Paradigmatic
In accordance with a set of substitutable elements of the same type. See *Syntagmatic*.

Parameter (of a principle)
Specific instantiation of a principle among a set of possible instantiations.

Paraphasia
A speech error characterized by the substitution of phonemes (in English). Also, the substitution of one word for another that is similar either in sound or in meaning.

Paresis
Partial paralysis

PET
Positron emission tomography. A neuroimaging technique monitoring regional cerebral blood flow by recording the levels of regional metabolism, taken as an index of cognitive functioning.

Pragmatic meaning
The pragmatic meaning of an utterance is its intended meaning (including its illocutionary force), which requires, in addition to the semantic meaning,

inferences from various contexts (paralinguistic, situational, general knowledge). See *semantic meaning* and *illocutionary force*.

Pragmatics
Pragmatics has been used with different meanings in different areas of research, particularly in philosophy, psychology and linguistics. For the purpose of our discussion, it will refer to what relates to the meaning of the unsaid portion of an utterance, specifically what is inferred, based on the context of use and general knowledge, concerning the speaker's purpose in producing the utterance—what the speaker intends to communicate. It also relates to discourse structure, inasmuch as it relies on inferences and implications.

Paragrammatism
A form of language defect characterized by the inability to arrange words grammatically (generally, in English, by the substitution of grammatical morphemes).

Priming
A change in the ability to identify or produce an item (e.g., shorter reaction times, improved identification of degraded stimuli) as a result of a prior encounter with that item. The term comes from the verb *to prime*, i.e., to prepare by supplying a prime, as in pouring water into a pump to get it to work after it has been idle for some time. Items may prime related items of a similar kind (e.g., words in the same semantic field).

Procedural memory
Memory system that underlies the representation of skilled competence. Implicit competence: An inferred set of underlying computational procedures that generate automatic behavior; contrasted with *declarative memory* (q.v.).

Proprioception
The brain's awareness of muscle movement, position, and changes in tonus (contraction, decontraction).

Semantic
This term has at least three different meanings depending on the context of its use:
(1) Semantic memory, a phrase used by psychologists to refer to the memory for general knowledge, as opposed to the recollection of actual events in which the individual participated (episodic memory).
(2) Lexical semantics refers to the study of the intrinsic meanings of words in isolation.

(3) In linguistics, *semantic* refers to the meaning of sentences (i.e., the meaning derived from the meanings of the words plus the grammatical structure of the sentence).

Semantic meaning
The semantic (or propositional) meaning of a sentence is the meaning retrievable solely on the basis of linguistic means: the default meanings of words and the grammatical structure of the sentence (i.e., not taking pragmatic features into consideration), contrasted with *pragmatic meaning* (q.v.) of an utterance, in which its context is taken into account.

Sentence
A theoretical linguistic construct that represents a self-contained, complete syntactic and semantic unit. Implicit linguistic competence, as studied by linguists and subserved by left-hemisphere cortical and subcortical areas, generates sentences.

Somesthetic
Pertaining to bodily sensations.

Speech act
The act performed when producing an utterance, e.g., giving a warning or making a request, a promise, or a claim.

Stroop experiment
In a Stroop test, the participant is asked to name the color in which a word is written. When the word is a color word written in a noncongruent color (e.g., GREEN written in red ink), participants take longer to name the color of the ink (red) than when naming the color of shapes or squiggles. The additional reaction time is the *Stroop effect*. Participants may occasionally give the name of the written word (green) instead of the requested ink color (red), showing how difficult it is to suppress perception of the written word.

Switching
See Language switching.

Syntagmatic
In accordance with the combinatory possibilities between elements; items that frequently occur together. See *Paradigmatic*.

Theory of Mind
Also known as *theory of other minds*: The ability to figure out what other people's beliefs and intentions must be, given a set of circumstances from which these beliefs and intentions can be inferred.

Time-sharing paradigm
Experimental procedure based on the assumption that functions that are subserved by different hemispheres are less likely to interfere with each other than two functions subserved by the same hemisphere (e.g., tapping a certain rhythm with the right hand, as compared to the left hand. while speaking).

Type/token ratio
The number of *different* lexical words (types) in a corpus divided by the total number of lexical words (all tokens of the different types) yields a type/token ratio that is indicative of the richness of the vocabulary (the diversity of words used). A corpus in which every word is of a different type (i.e., in which no two words would be the same) would yield a ratio of 1. The closer to 1 the ratio is, the richer the vocabulary.

UG (Universal Grammar)
A set of general abstract principles implemented in the grammar of any natural language, assumed to be innate by generative grammarians. The actual principles of UG depend on the linguistic theory current at the time of their formulation, i.e., the set of principles taken to be innate within the Government-binding paradigm differs from that within the Minimalist program.

Unilingual
Speaking one language. In the same way that most people would not use the terms *uniglot*, *polylingual*, and *multiglot*, the term unilingual is preferred here to *monolingual*, because the latter is ill-formed with a Greek prefix on a Latin root.

Utterance
A functional unit in verbal communication. An utterance may consist of either a sentence or a string of words shorter than a sentence (possibly even a single word). Its interpretation depends on the context in which it is used, as well as on general knowledge assumed to be shared between the speaker and the listener. Utterances are meaningful verbal units produced and understood in a context (semantic propositional meaning + pragmatic inferences).

Verbal fluency test
A test designed to assess lexical accessibility. The subject is asked to produce, in one minute, as many words as possible that either (1) start with a certain letter (or

phoneme) or (2) are members of a certain semantic category (e.g., animals, tools, etc.).

Vocabulary

The set of explicit word sound-meaning (and grapheme-meaning) pairings. The conscious knowledge of the (default, dictionary) sound-meaning pairing of a word is demonstrated by the speaker's ability to point to a dog when asked to point to [dɔg] and to say [dɔg] when asked to name the animal; see *Lexicon*. The terms *vocabulary* and *lexicon* have not been selected totally arbitrarily. The word *lexicon* has been chosen to include implicit properties because it is the one generally used by linguists. The term *vocabulary* is traditionally used in second language learning/teaching contexts. While the proposed contrast between these terms is not systematic in the literature, the choice of words is nevertheless not unrelated to usage. In the context of this book, *lexicon* and *vocabulary* refer to two different sets of properties of words.

Wada test

Intracarotid injection of sodium amytal (a sedative) alternately into the right and left carotid arteries, allowing one to ascertain which functions are subserved by each hemisphere. Tasks relying on functions subserved by areas in the injected hemisphere cannot be performed during the period of sedation. When such a task can be performed by the left hemisphere when the right hemisphere is selectively sedated, but cannot be performed when the left hemisphere is sedated, it is said to be subserved unilaterally in the left hemisphere. This procedure is performed prior to brain surgery in order to ascertain which hemisphere subserves language (and help the surgeon avoid making incisions where there is a risk of causing language impairments).

References

Abel, B. 2003. English idioms in the first language and second language lexicon: A dual representation approach. *Second Language Research*, 19: 329-358.

Abutalebi, J., Cappa, S.F., & Perani, D. 2001. The bilingual brain as revealed by functional neuroimaging. *Bilingualism: Language and Cognition*, 4: 169-178.

Abutalebi J., Miozzo A., & Cappa, S.F. 2000. Do subcortical structures control 'language selection' in polyglots? Evidence from pathological language mixing. *Neurocase*, 6: 51-56.

Aglioti, S., & Fabbro, F. 1993. Paradoxical selective recovery in a bilingual aphasic following subcortical lesions. *Neuroreport*, 4: 1359-1362.

Alajouanine, T., & Lhermitte, F. 1964. Non-verbal communication in aphasia. In A.V.S. de Reuck & M. O'Connor (eds.), *Disorders of language* (pp. 168-182). London: Churchill.

Alajouanine, T., Pichot, P., & Durand, M. 1949. Dissociation des altérations phonétiques avec conservation relative de la langue la plus ancienne dans un cas d'anarthrie pure chez un sujet français bilingue. *L'Encéphale*, 28: 245-265.

Albanèse, J.F. 1985. Language lateralization in English-French bilinguals. *Brain and Language*, 24: 284-296.

Albert, M.L., & Obler, L.K. 1975. Mixed polyglot aphasia. Paper presented at the Academy of Aphasia, Victoria, B.C.

Albert, M.L., & Obler, L.K. 1978. *The bilingual brain*. New York: Academic Press.

Albyn Davis, G., O'Neil-Pirozzi, T., & Coon, M. 1997. Referential cohesion and logical coherence of narration after right hemisphere stroke. *Brain and Language*, 56: 183-210.

Alexander, M.P., Benson, D.F., & Stuss, D.T. 1989. Frontal lobes and language. *Brain and Language*, 37: 656-691.

Alexiadou, A., & Stavrakaki, S. 2003. Adverb placement as evidence for clause structure and parameterization of verb movement in a bilingual Greek-English speaking patient with Broca's aphasia. *Brain and Language*, 87: 19-20.

Altenberg, M.L., & Cairns, H.S. 1983. The effects of phonotactic constraints on lexical processing in bilingual and monolingual subjects. *Journal of Verbal Learning and Verbal Behavior*, 22: 174-188.

Andersen, R.W. 1982. Determining the linguistic attributes of language attrition. In: R. Lambert & B. Freed (eds.), *The loss of language skills* (pp. 83-118). Rowley, MA: Newbury House.

April, R.S. 1979. Concepts actuels sur l'organisation cérébrale à partir de quelques cas d'aphasie croisée chez les orientaux bilingues. *Revue Neurologique*, 135: 395-378.

April, R.S., & Han, M. 1980. Crossed aphasia in a right-handed bilingual Chinese man—A second case. *Archives of Neurology*, 37: 342-346.

Aram, D.M., & Whitaker, H.A. 1988. Cognitive sequellae of unilateral lesions acquired in early childhood. In D.L. Molfese & S.J. Segalowitz (eds.), *Brain Lateralization in children* (pp. 417-436). New York: The Guilford Press.

Ardal, S., Donald, M.W., Meuter, R., Muldrew, S., & Luce, M. 1990. Brain responses to semantic incongruity in bilinguals. *Brain and Language*, 39: 187-205.

Ashby, F.G., & Ell, S.W. 2002. Single versus multiple systems of category learning: Reply to Nosofsky and Kruschke (2002). *Psychonomic Bulletin and Review*, 9: 175-180.

Ashby, F.G., Ell, S.W., Casale, M.B., Valentin, V.V., & Waterhouse, E. 2002. Biologically plausible models of rule-based and implicit categorization. *Journal of Cognitive Neuroscience*: D77 Suppl. S.

Ashby, F.G., & Waldron, E.M. 1999. On the nature of implicit categorization. *Psychonomic Bulletin and Review*, 6: 363-378.

Ashby, F.G., & Waldron, E.M. 2000. The neuropsychological bases of category learning. *Current Directions in Psychological Science*, 9: 10-14.

Aten, J.L. 1986. Functional communication treatment. In R. Chapey (ed.), *Language intervention strategies in adult aphasia* (pp. 266-276). Baltimore: Williams & Wilkins.

Baddeley, A.D. 1986. *Working memory*. Oxford: Psychology Press.

Baetens Beardsmore, H. 1982. *Bilingualism: Basic principles*. Clevedon: Multilingual Matters.

Bain, B. 1974. Bilingualism and cognition: Toward a general theory. In S.T. Carey (ed.), *Bilingualism, biculturalism and education* (pp. 119-128). Edmonton,AB: University of Alberta.

Bain, B., & Yu, A. 1978. Towards an integration of Piaget and Vygotsky: A cross-cultural replication (France, Germany, Canada) concerning cognitive consequences of bilingualism. In M. Paradis (ed.), *Aspects of bilingualism* (pp. 113-126). Columbia, SC: Hornbeam Press.

Bakker, D.J., van der Vlugt, H., & Claushuis, M. 1978. The reliability of dichotic ear asymmetry in normal children. *Neuropsychologia*, 1: 753-757.

Balkan, L. 1970. Les effets du bilinguisme français-anglais sur les aptitudes intellectuelles. Brussels: AIMAV.

Barrios, M., & Guardia, J. 2001. Relation of the cerebellum with cognitive function: Neuroanatomical, clinical and neuroimaging evidence. *Revista de Neurologia*, 33: 582-591.

Barton, M., Goodglass, H., & Shai, A. 1965. Differential recognition of tachistoscopically presented English and Hebrew words in right and left visual fields. *Perceptual and Motor Skills*, 21: 431-437.

Basso, K.H. 1979. *Portraits of "the whiteman": Linguistic play and cultural symbols among the Western Apache*. New York: Cambridge University Press.

Bastian, C. 1880. *The brain as an organ of mind*. London: Kegan Paul.

Bavelier, D., Corina, D., Jezzard, P., Clark, V., Karni, A., Lalwani, A., Rauschecker, J., Braun, A., Turner, R., & Neville, H. 1998. Hemispheric specialization for English and ASL: Left invariance—right variability. *NeuroReport*, 9: 1537-1542.

Bay, E. 1964. General discussion. In A.V.S. De Reuck & M. O'Connor (eds.), *Disorders of language* (pp. 115-121). Boston: Little Brown.

Beaumont, J.G., Kenealy, P.M., & Rogers, M.J.C. 1996. *The Blackwell dictionary of neuropsychology*. Oxford: Blackwell.

Behrens, S.J. 1989. Characterizing sentence intonation in a right hemisphere damaged population. *Brain and Language*, 37: 181-200.

Ben Amar, M., & Gaillard, F. 1984. Langage et dominance cérébrale chez les monolingues et les bilingues au seuil de l'école. *Les Sciences de l'éducation pour l'ère nouvelle*, 1-2: 93-111.

Bergh, G. 1986. *The neuropsychological status of Swedish-English subsidiary bilinguals*. Göteborg: Acta Universitatis Gothoburgensis.

Berquier, A., & Ashton, R. 1992. Language lateralization in bilinguals: More not less is needed: A reply to Paradis (1990). *Brain and Language*, 43: 528-533.

Berthier, M., Starkstein, S., Lylyk, P., & Leiguarda, R. 1990. Differential recovery of languages in a bilingual patient.: A case study using selective amytal test. *Brain and Language*, 38: 449-453.

Best, C.Y. 1988. The emergence of cerebral asymmetries in early human development: A literature review and a neuroembryological model. In D.L. Molfese & S.J. Segalowitz (eds.), *Brain Lateralization in children* (pp. 5-34). New York: The Guilford Press.

Bialystok, E. 1981. Some evidence for the integrity and interaction of two knowledge sources. In R.W. Andersen (ed.), *New dimensions in second language acquisition research* (pp. 62-74). Rowley, MA: Newbury House.

Bialystok, E. 1994. Representation and ways of knowing: Three issues in second language acquisition. In N. Ellis (ed.), *Implicit and explicit learning of second languages* (pp. 549-569). London: Academic Press.

Bialystok, E. 2004. Consequences of bilingualism for cognitive development. In J.F. Kroll & A.M. de Groot (eds.), *Handbook of bilingualism*. Oxford: Oxford University Press. (in press)

Bihrle, A.M., Brownell, H.H., & Gardner, H. 1988. Humor and the right hemisphere: A narrative perspective. In H.A. Whitaker (ed.), *Contemporary Reviews in Neuropsychology* (p. 109-126). New York: Springer Verlag.

Bihrle, A.M., Brownell, H.H., Powelson, J.A., & Gardner, H. 1986. Comprehension of humorous and non-humorous materials by left and right brain-damaged patients. *Brain and Cognition*, 5: 399-411.

Billingley, R.L., Simos, P.G., Castillo, E.M., Maestú, F., Sarkari, S., Breier, J.I., & Papanicolaou, A.C. 2003. Functional brain imaging of language: criteria for scientific merit and supporting data from magnetic source imaging. Journal of Neurolinguistics, 16: 255-275.

Binder, J.R. 1995. Functional magnetic resonance imaging of the language cortex. *International Journal of Imaging Systems and Technology*, 6: 280-288.

Binder, J., & Price, C.J. 2001. Functional neuroimaging of language. In R. Cabeza and A. Kingstone (eds.), *Handbook of functional neuroimaging of cognition* (pp. 187-251). Cambridge, MA: MIT Press.

Blonder, L.X., Bowers, D., & Heilman, K.M. 1991. The role of the right hemisphere in emotional communication. *Brain*, 114: 1115-1127.

Bloom, L. 1974. Talking, understanding, and thinking. In R.L. Schiefelbusch & L.L. Lloyd (eds.), *Language perspectives—acquisition, retardation and intervention* (pp. 285-311). Baltimore: University Park Press.

Blum-Kulka, S., House, J., & Kasper, G. (eds.) 1989. *Cross-cultural pragmatics: Requests and apologies*. Norwood, NJ: Ablex.

Blumstein, S., Goodglass, H., & Tatter, V. 1975. The reliability of ear advantage in dichotic listening. *Brain and Language*, 2: 226-236.

Bolte, S., Uhlig, N., & Poustka, F. 2002. The savant syndrome: A review. *Zeitschrift für Psychologie und Psychotherapie*, 31: 291-297.

Bond, S.L. 1984. Bilingualism and aphasia, Word retrieval skills in a bilingual anomic aphasic. Unpublished M.A. thesis. North Texas State University.

Bonvillian, J.D., & Patterson, F.G.P. 1993. Early language acquisition in children and gorillas: Vocabulary content and sign iconicity. *First Language*, 13: 315-338.

Bordag, D. 2003. Grammatical gender in first and second language production. *Ceskoslovenska Psychologie*, 47: 105-121.

Borod, J.C., Cicero, B.A., Obler, L.K., Welkowitz, C., Grunwald, I., & Agosti, R.M. 1998. Right hemisphere emotional perception: Evidence across multiple channels. *Neuropsychology*, 12: 446-458.

Bottini, G., Corcoran, R., Sterzi, R., Paulesu, E., Schenone, P., Scarpa, P., Frackowiak, R.S.J., & Frith, C.D. 1994. The role of the right hemisphere in the interpretation of figurative aspects of language. A positron emission tomography activation study. *Brain*, 117: 1241-1253.

Bowers, D., Coslett, H.B., Bauer, R.M., Speedie, L.J., & Heilman, K.M. 1987. Comprehension of emotional prosody following unilateral hemispheric lesions: Processing defect versus distraction effect. *Neuropsychologia*, 25: 317-328.

Bradshaw, J.L., Burden, V., & Nettleton, C. 1986. Dichotic and dichhaptic techniques. *Neuropsychologia*, 24: 79-90.

Brass, M., Zysset, S., & von Cramon, D.Y. 2001. The inhibition of imitative response tendencies. *NeuroImage*, 14: 1416-1423.

Brauer, M. 1998. Stroop interference in bilinguals: The role of similarity between the two languages. In A.F. Healy & L.E. Bourne, Jr. (eds.), *Foreign language learning: Psycholinguistic studies on training and retention* (pp. 317-337). Mahwah, NJ: Lawrence Erlbaum Associates.

Brookshire, R.H., & Nicholas, L.E. 1984. Comprehension of directly and indirectly stated main ideas and details in discourse by brain-damaged and non-brain-damaged listeners. *Brain and Language*, 21: 21-36.

Brown, C.M., & Hagoort, O. 2000. The cognitive neuroscience of language: Challenges and future directions. In C.M. Brown & P. Hagoort (eds.), *The neurocognition of language* (pp. 3-14). Oxford: Oxford University Press.

Brownell, H.H. 1988. Appreciation of metaphoric and connotative word meaning by brain-damaged patients. In C. Chiarello (ed.), *Right hemisphere contributions to lexical semantics* (pp. 19-32). New York: Springer-Verlag.

Brownell, H.H., & Martino, G. 1998. Deficits in inference and social cognition: The effects of right hemisphere damage on discourse. In M. Beeman, & C. Chiarello (eds.),. *Right hemisphere language comprehension: Perspectives from cognitive neuroscience* (pp309-328). Mahwah, NJ: Lawrence Erlbaum Associates.

Brownell, H.H., Michel, D., Powelson, J., & Gardner, H. 1983. Surprise but not coherence: Sensitivity to verbal humor in right-hemisphere patients. *Brain and Language*, 18: 20-27.

Brownell, H.H., Potter, H.H., Bihrle, A.M.,, & Gardner, H. 1986. Inference deficits in right brain-damaged patients. *Brain and Language*, 27: 310-321.

Brownell, H.H., Potter, H.H., Michelow, D., & Gardner, H. 1984. Sensitivity to lexical denotation and connotation in brain-damaged patients: A double dissociation? *Brain and Language*, 22: 253-265.

Brownell, H.H., Simpson, T.L., Bihrle, A.M., Potter, H.H., & Gardner, H. 1990. Appreciation of metaphoric alternative word meanings by left and right brain-damaged patients. *Neuropsychologia*, 28: 375-383.

Brownell H.H., & Stringfellow, A. 1999. Making requests: Illustrations of how right-hemisphere brain damage can affect discourse production. *Brain and Language*, 68: 442-465.

Bruce, L.C. 1895. Notes of a case of dual brain action. *Brain*, 18: 54-65.

Bryan, K.L. 1988. Assessment of language disorders after right hemisphere damage. *British Journal of Disorders of Communication*, 23: 111-125.

Bryan, K.L. 1989. Language prosody and the right hemisphere. *Aphasiology*, 3: 285-299.

Bub, D. 2000. Methodological issues confronting PET and fMRI studies of cognitive function. *Cognitive Neuropsychology*, 17: 467-484.

Bullinaria, J.A., & Chater, N. 1996. Double dissociation, modularity, and distributed organization. *Behavioral and Brain Sciences*, 19: 632.

Bunge, M. 1980. *The mind-body problem: A psychobiological approach*. Oxford: Pergamon Press.

Bychowski, Z. 1919. Über die Restitution der nach einem Schädelschuss verlorenen Umgangssprache bei einem Polyglotten. *Monatsschrift für Psychiatrie und Neurologie*, 45: 183-201. Translated in Paradis (1983), 130-144.

Byng, S., Coltheart, M., Masterson, J., Prior M., & Riddoch, J. 1984. Bilingual biscriptal deep dyslexia. *Quarterly Journal of Experimental Psychology*, 36A: 417-433.

Calabrese, P., Neufeld, H., Falk, A., et al. 2001. Word generation in bilinguals—fMRI study with implications for language and memory processes. *Fortschritte der Neurologie und Psychiatrie*, 69: 42-49.

Canavan, A.G.M., Hömberg, V., & Stelmach, G.E. 1992. Separating declarative memory and procedural learning in alcoholic amnesics. Paper presented at the 22nd Annual Meeting of the Society for Neuroscience, Anaheim, California, 28 October.

Cancelliere, A.E., & Kertesz, A. 1990. Lesion localization in acquired deficits of emotional expression and comprehension. *Brain and Cognition*, 13: 133-147.

Caplan, D. 1987. *Neurolinguistics and linguistic aphasiology*. Cambridge: Cambridge University Press.

Carr, Y.H. 1998. Mechanisms of control in activating and deploying lexical knowledge. *Bilingualism: Language and Cognition*, 1: 83-85.

Carroll, F. 1980. Neurolinguistic processing in bilingualism and second language. In R. Scarcella, & S. Krashen (eds.), *Research in second language acquisition* (pp. 81-86). Rowley, MA: Newbury House.

Carter, C.S., Braver, T.S., Barch, D.M., Botvinick, M.M., Noll, D.C., & Cohen, J.D. 1998. Anterior cingulate cortex, error detection, and the on-line monitoring of performance. *Science*, 280: 747-749.

Carter, C.S., MacDonald, A.W., Ross, L.L., & Spenger, V.A. 2001. Anterior cingulate cortex activity and impaired self-monitoring of performance in patients with schizophrenia: An event-related fMRI study. *American Journal of Psychiatry*, 158: 1423-1428.

Casey, B.J, Trainor, R., Giedd, J., Vauss, Y., Vaituzis, C.K., Hamburger, S., Kozuch, P., Rapoport, J.L. 1997. The role of the anterior cingulate in automatic and controlled processes: A developmental neuroanatomical study. *Developmental Psychobiology*, 30: 61-69.

Cermak, L.S. 1993. Automatic versus controlled processing and the implicit task performance of amnesic patients. In P. Graf & M.E.G. Masson (eds.), *Implicit memory: New directions in cognition, development, and neuropsychology* (pp. 287-301). Hillsdale, NJ: Lawrence Erlbaum Associates.

Chapman, R.M., McCrary, J.W., Chapman, J.A., & Martin, J.K. 1980. Behavioral and neural analyses of connotative meaning: Word classes and rating scales. *Brain and Language*, 11: 319-339.

Chapman, S.B. 1996. Facilitating communicative intent in patients with progressive disorders: Alzheimer's dementia and progressive aphasia. Paper presented at the Bruton Conference, University of Texas, Dallas, 28 September.

Chary, P. 1986. Aphasia in a multilingual society: A preliminary study. In J. Vaid (ed.), *Language processing in bilinguals: Psycholinguistic and neuropsychological perspectives* (pp. 183-197). Hillsdale, NJ: Erlbaum.

Chee, M.W, Caplan, D., Soon, C.S., Sriram, N., Tan, E.W.L., Thiel, T., & Weekes, B. 1999a. Processing of visually presented sentences in Mandarin and English studied with fMRI. *Neuron*, 23: 127-137.

Chee, M.W, Hon, N., Lee, H.L., & Soon, C.S. 2001. Relative language proficiency modulates BOLD signal change when bilinguals perform semantic judgments. *NeuroImage*, 13: 1155-1163.

Chee, M.W.L., & Soon, C.S. 2003. Seeing how we think about words using BOLD contrast MR imaging. *Annals Academy of Medicine Singapore*, 32: 490-494.

Chee, M.W., Tan, E.W., & Thiel, T. 1999b. Mandarin and English single word processing studied with functional magnetic resonance imaging. *The Journal of Neuroscience*, 19: 3050-3056.

Chee, M.W, Weekes, B., Lee, K.M., Soon, C.S., Schreiber, A., Hoon, J.J., & Chee, M. 2000. Overlap and dissociation of semantic processing of Chinese characters, English words, and pictures: Evidence from fMRI. *NeuroImage*, 12: 392-403.

Chertkow, H., & Murtha, S. 1997. PET activation and language. *Clinical Neuroscience*, 4: 78-86.

Chiarello, C., Dronkers, N., & Hardyck, C. 1984. Choosing sides: On the variability of language lateralization in normal subjects. *Neuropsychologia*, 22: 363-373.

Chlenov, L.G. 1948. Ob afazii u poliglotov. *Izvestiia Akademii Pedagogicheskikh NAUK RSFSR*, 15: 783-790.

Chomsky, N. 1965. *Aspects of the theory of syntax.* Cambridge, MA: MIT Press.

Chomsky, N. 1981. *Lectures on government and binding.* Dordrecht: Foris

Chomsky, N. 1995. *The minimalist program.* Cambridge, MA.: MIT Press.

Christoffels, I.K., & de Groot, A.M.B. 2004. Simultaneous interpreting: A cognitive perspective. In J.F. Kroll, & A.M.B. de Groot (eds.), *Handbook of bilingualism: Psycholinguistic approaches.* Oxford: Oxford University Press (in press).

Clark, C.R., Egan, G.F., McFarlane, A.C., Morris, P., Weber, D., Sonkkilla, C., Marcina, J., & Tochon-Danguy, H.J. 2000. Updating working memory for words: A PET activation study. *Human Brain Mapping*, 9: 42-54.

Clark, II.II., & Clark, E.V. 1977. *Psychology and language.* New York: Harcourt Brace Jovanovitch.

Clyne, M.G. 1980. Triggering and language processing. *Canadian Journal of Psychology*, 34: 400-406.

Coggins, P.E., Kennedy, T.J., & Armstrong, T.A. 2004. Bilingual corpus callosum variability. *Brain and Language*, 89: 69-75.

Cohen, M., Prather, A., Town, P., & Hynd, G. 1990. Neurodevelopmental differences in emotional prosody in normal children and children with left and right temporal lobe epilepsy. *Brain and Language*, 38: 122-134.

Cohen, N. 1984. Preserved learning capacity in amnesia: Evidence for multiple memory systems. In L.R. Squire & N. Butters (eds.), *The neuropsychology of human memory* (pp. 83-103). New York: Guilford Press.

Cohen, N. 1991. Memory, amnesia and the hippocampal system. Paper presented at the Cognitive and Neuroscience Colloquium, McGill University, 6 November.

Cohen, N., & Eichenbaum, H. 1993. *Memory, amnesia, and the hippocampal system.* Cambridge, MA: MIT Press.

Cohen, N., & Squire, L. 1980. Preserved learning and retention of pattern-analyzing skill in amnesia: Dissociation of "knowing how" and "knowing that." *Science*, 210: 207-209.

Colbourn, C. 1978. Can laterality be measured? *Neuropsychologia*, 16: 283-289.

Collette, F. Salmon, E., Van der Linden, M., Chicherio, C., Belleville, S., Degueldre, C., Delfiore, G., & Franck, G. 1999. Regional brain activity during tasks devoted to the central executive of working memory. *Cognitive Brain Research*, 7: 411-417.

Corina, D.P, Jose-Robertson, L.S., Guillemin, A., High, J., & Braun, A.R. 2003. Language lateralization in a bimanual language. *Journal of Cognitive Neuroscience*, 15: 718-730.

Corina, D., Poizner, H., Bellugi, U., Feinberg, T., Dowd, D., & O'Grady-Batch, L. 1992. Dissociation between linguistic and nonlinguistic gestural systems: A case for compositionality. *Brain and Language*, 43: 414-447.

Cork, R.C., Kihlstrom, J.F., & Hameroff, S.R. 1992. Explicit and implicit memory dissociated by anesthetic technique. Paper presented at the 22nd Annual Meeting of the Society for Neuroscience, Anaheim, California, 26 October.

Cork, R.C., Kihlstrom, J.F., & Schacter, D.L. 1992. Absence of explicit or implicit memory in patients anesthetized with sufentamil/nitrous oxide. *Anesthesiology*, 76: 892-898.

Corkin, S. 1992. Implicit memory. Paper given at the Seminar in Cognitive Neuroscience, Montreal Neurological Institute and Hospital, 9 April.

Costa, A., Colomé, A., & Caramazza, A. 2000. Lexical access in speech production: The bilingual case. *Psicológica*, 21: 403-437.

Coulmas, F. 1978. Routineformen und pragmatische Interferenzen. In W. Kühlwein & A. Raasch (eds.), *Kongressberichte der 8. Jahrestagung der Gesellschaft für Angewandte Linguistic* (Vol. 11, pp. 3-40). Stuttgart: Hochschulverlag.

Cowan, R., O'Connor, N., & Samella, K. 2003. The skills and methods of calendrical savants. *Intelligence*, 31: 51-65.

Crowder, R.G. 1989. Modularity and dissociations in memory systems. In H.L. Roediger, III & F.L.M. Craik (eds.), *Varieties of memory and consciousness* (pp. 271-294). Hillsdale, NJ: Lawrence Erlbaum Associates.

Cubelli, R., Foresti, A., & Consolini, T. 1988. Reeducation strategies in conduction aphasia. *Journal of Speech and Hearing Disorders*, 21: 239-249.

Cummins, J. 1978. Bilingualism and the development of metalinguistic awareness. *Journal of Cross-Cultural Psychology*, 9: 139-149.

Cummins, J., & Gulutsan, M. 1974. Some effects of bilingualism on cognitive functioning. In S. Carey (ed.) *Bilingualism, Biculturalism and Education*. Edmonton: University of Alberta.

Curtis, S. 1977. *Genie*. New York: Academic Press.

Dagge, M., & Hartje, W. 1985. Influence of contextual complexity on the processing of cartoons by patients with unilateral lesions. *Cortex*, 21: 607-616.

Damasio, A. 1989. Concepts in the brain. *Mind and Language*, 4: 24-28.

Damasio, A. 1994. *Descartes's error: Emotion, reason, and the human brain.* New York: G. P. Putnam's Sons.

Damasio, A. 1999. *The feeling of what happens.* New York: Harcourt Brace and Company.

Damasio, A., Bellugi, U., Damasio, H., Pozner, H., & van Gilcer, J. 1986. Sign language aphasia during left-hemisphere amytal injection. *Nature*, 322, 363-365.

Davis, G.A., & Wilcox, M.J. 1985. *Adult aphasia rehabilitation: Applied pragmatics.* San Diego, CA: College-Hill Press.

de Bot, K. 1992. A bilingual production model: Levelt's "speaking" model adapted. *Applied Linguistics*, 13: 1-24.

de Bot, K. 2002. Cognitive processing in bilinguals: Language choice and code-switching. In R.B. Kaplan (ed.), *The Oxford handbook of applied linguistics* (pp. 287-300). Oxford: Oxford University Press.

de Bot, K., & Clyne, M. 1989. Language reversion revisited. *Studies in Second Language Acquisition*, 11: 167-177.

de Bot, K., & Schreuder, R. 1993. Word production and the bilingual lexicon. In R. Schreuder & B. Weltens (eds.), *The bilingual lexicon* (pp. 191-214). Amsterdam: John Benjamins.

Dehaene, S. 1999. Fitting two languages into one brain. *Brain*, 122: 2207-2208.

Dehaene, S., Dupoux, E., Mehler, J., Cohen, L., Paulesu, E., Perani, D., van Moortele, P.-F., Lehéricy, S., & Le Bihan, D. 1997. Anatomical variability in the cortical representation of first and second language. *NeuroReport*, 8: 3809-3815.

Delacato, C.H. 1966. *Neurological organization and reading.* Springfield, IL: Thomas.

Delis, D.C., Wapner, W., Moses, J.A., & Gardner, H. 1983. The contribution of the right hemisphere to the organization of paragraphs. *Cortex*, 19: 43-50.

Demb, J.B., Desmond, J.E., Wagner, A.D., Vaidya, A.D., Glover, C.J., & Gabrieli, J.D. 1995. Semantic encoding and retrieval in the left prefrontal cortex: A fMRI study of task difficulty and process specificity. *The Journal of Neuroscience*, 15: 5870-5878.

Démonet, J.F., & Thierry, G. 2001. Language and brain: What is up? What is coming up? *Journal of Clinical and Experimental Neuropsychology*, 23: 49-73.

Denès, P.-A. 1914. *Contribution à l'étude de quelques phénomènes aphasiques.* Thèse de Doctorat, Paris: Ollier-Henry.

Dennis, I. 1984. Predicting brain organization from dichotic listening performance: A note on Sidtis. *Brain and Language*, 21: 351-353.

Dennis, M., & Whitaker, H.A. 1976. Language acquisition following hemidecortication: Linguistic superiority of the left over the right hemisphere. *Brain and Language*, 3: 404-433.

de Saussure, F. 1915. *Cours de linguistique générale.* Paris: Payot.

Devinsky, O., Morrell, M.J., & Vogt, B.A. 1995. Contributions of anterior cingulate cortex to behaviour. *Brain*, 118: 279-306.

De Zulueta, F.I.S., Gene-Cos, N., & Grachev, S. 2001. Differential psychotic symptomatology in polyglot patients: Case reports and their implications. *British Journal of Medical Psychology*, 74: 277-292.

Dick, F., Bates, E., Wulfeck, B., Utman, J.A., Dronkers, N., & Gernstacher, M.A. 2001. Language deficits, localization, and grammar: Evidence from a distributive model of language breakdown in aphasic patients and neurologically intact individuals. *Psychological Review*, 108: 759-788.

Dijkstra, A., & Van Heuven, 1998. The BIA model and bilingual word recognition. In J. Grainger & A.M. Jacobs (eds.), *Localist connectionist approaches to human cognition* (pp. 189-225). Mahwah, NJ: Lawrence Erlbaum Associates.

Ding, G., Perry, C., Peng, D., Ma, L., Li, D., Xu, S., Luo, Q., Xu, D., & Yang, J. 2003. Neural mechanisms underlying semantic and orthographic processing in Chinese-English bilinguals. *NeuroReport*, 14: 1557-1562.

Donald, M. 1993. Précis of origins of the modern mind: The stages in the evolution of culture and cognition. *The Behavioral and Brain Sciences*, 16: 737-791.

Dove, A., Pollmann, S., Schubert, T., Wiggins, C.J., & von Cramon, D.Y. 2000. Prefrontal cortex activation in task switching: An event-related fMRI study. *Cognitive Brain Research*, 9: 103-109.

Dravins, C., & Bradvik, B. 1996. Figures of speech and context awareness following right hemisphere infarcts. *Logopedics & Phoniatrics Vocology*, 21: 149-155.

Dronkers, N., Yamasaki, Y., Ross, G.W., & White, L. 1995. Assessment of binguality in aphasia: Issues and examples from multicultural Hawaii. In M. Paradis (ed.), *Aspects of bilingual aphasia* (pp. 57-65). Oxford: Pergamon Press.

Durieu, C. 1969. *La rééducation des aphasiques*. Brussels: Dessart.

Dwyer, J., & Rinn, W. 1981. The role of the right hemisphere in contextual inference. *Neuropsychologia*, 19: 479-482.

Eling, P. 1983. Comparing different measures of laterality: Do they relate to a single mechanism? *Journal of Clinical Neuropsychology*, 5: 135-147.

Ellis, N. 1994. Implicit and explicit language learning—An overview. In N. Ellis (ed.), *Implicit and explicit learning of Second Languages* (pp. 1-32). London: Academic Press.

Ellis, N. 2002. Frequency effects in language processing. *Studies in Second language Acquisition*, 34: 143-188.

Ellis, R. 1994. A theory of instructed second language acquisition. In N. Ellis (ed.), *Implicit and explicit learning of second languages* (pp. 79-114). London: Academic Press.

Erriondo Korostola, L. 1995. *Afasiko Elebidunen Hizkuntz Trebetasunen Azterketa*. Donostia: Argitarapen Zerbitzua Euscal Herriko Unibertsitatea.

Evans, J., Workman, L., Mayer, P., & Crowley, P. 2002. Differential bilingual laterality: Mythical monster found in Wales. *Brain and Language*, 83: 291-299.

Fabbro, F. 1999. *The neurolinguistics of bilingualism: An introduction*. Hove, UK: Psychology Press.

Fabbro, F. 2000. Introduction to language and cerebellum. *Journal of Neurolinguistics*, 13: 83-94.

Fabbro, F., DeLuca, G., & Vorano, L. 1996. Assessment of language rehabilitation with the BAT in four multilingual aphasics. *Journal of the Israeli Speech Hearing and Language Association,* 19: 46-53.

Fabbro, F., Moretti, R., & Bava, A. 2000. Language impairments in patients with cerebellar lesions. *Journal of Neurolinguistics*, 13: 173-188.

Fabbro, F., & Paradis, M. 1995. Acquired aphasia in a bilingual child. In M. Paradis (ed.), *Aspects of bilingual aphasia* (pp. 67-83). Oxford: Pergamon Press.

Fabbro, F., Skrap, M., & Aglioti, S. 2000. Pathological switching between languages after frontal lesions in a bilingual patient. *Journal of Neurology, Neurosurgery and Psychiatry*, 68: 650-652.

Falk, K. 1973. Die aphasischen Störungen aus der Sicht des Logopäden. *Die Sonderschule.* 18 (2). Volkseigener Verlag.

Farah, M. O'Reilley, R.C., & Vecera, S.P. 1993. Dissociated overt and covert recognition as an emergent property of a lesioned neural network. *Psychological Review*, 100: 571-588.

Favreau, M., & Segalowitz, N. 1983. Automatic and controlled processes in reading a second language. *Memory and Cognition*, 11: 565-574.

Fillmore, C.J. 1968. The case for case. In E. Bach and T. Harms (eds.), Universals in linguistic theory (pp. 1-88). Holt, Rinehart & Winston.

Fillmore, C.J. 1988. The mechanisms of construction grammar. *Berkeley Linguistics Society: Proceedings of the 14th annual meeting* (pp. 35-55). Berkeley, CA: BLS.

Flege, J.E., Schirru, C., & MacKay I.R.A. 2003. Interaction between the native and second language phonetic subsystems. *Speech Communication*, 4: 467-491.

Fodor, J. 1983. *The modularity of mind.* Cambridge, MA: MIT Press.

Fodor, J. 1985. Précis of The modularity of mind.*The Behavioral and Brain Sciences*, 8: 1-42.

Fodor, J.D. 2002. Prosodic disambiguation in silent reading. In M. Hirotani (ed.), *Proceedings of NELS*, 32: 113-132.

Foldi, N.S. 1987. Appreciation of pragmatic interpretations of indirect commands: Comparison of right and left hemisphere brain-damaged patients. *Brain and Language*, 31: 88-108.

Foldi, N.S., Cicone, M., & Gardner, H. 1983. Pragmatic aspects of communication in brain-damaged patients. In S.J. Segalowitz (Ed.), *Language functions and brain organization* (pp. 51-86). New York: Academic Press.

Francis, W.S. 1999. Analogical transfer of problem solutions within and between languages in Spanish-English bilinguals. *Journal of Memory and Language,* 40: 301-329.

Frederiksen, C.H., & Stemmer, B. 1993. Conceptual processing of discourse by a right hemisphere brain-damaged patient. In H.H. Brownell & Y. Joanette (eds.),

Narrative discourse in neurologically impaired and normal aging adults (pp. 239-278). San Diego: Singular.

Fredman, M. 1975. The effect of therapy given in Hebrew on the home language of the bilingual or polyglot adult in Israel. *British Journal of Disorders of Communication*, 10: 61-69.

French, R.M. 1998. A simple recurrent network model of bilingual memory. *Proceedings of the Twentieth Annual Cognitive Science Society Conference* (pp. 368-373). Mahwah, NJ: Lawrence Erlbaum Associates.

Gabrieli, J.D.E., Reminger, S.L., Grosse, D.A., & Wilson, R.S. 1992. Implicit memory for representational and novel visual materials in patients with Alzheimer's Disease. Paper presented at the 22nd Annual Meeting of the Society for Neuroscience, Anaheim, California, 27 October.

Gagnon, L., Goulet, P., Giroux, F., & Joanette, Y. 2003. Processing of metaphoric and non-metaphoric alternative meanings of words after right- and left-hemispheric lesion. *Brain and Language*, 87: 217-226.

Galloway, L., & Krashen, S.D. 1980. Cerebral organizatin in bilingualism and second language. In R.C. Scarcella and S.D. Krashen (ed.) *Research in Second Language Acquisition* (pp. 74-80). Rowley, MA: Newbury House.

Galloway, L., & Scarcella, R. 1982. Cerebral organization in adult second language acquisition: Is the right hemisphere more involved? *Brain and Language*, 16: 56-60.

Galvez, A., & Hinckley, J.J. 2003. Transfer patterns of naming treatment in a case of bilingual aphasia. *Brain and Language*, 87: 173-174.

Gandour, J., Larsen, J., Dechongkit, S., Ponglorpisit, S., & Khunadorn, F. 1995. Speech prosody in affective contexts in Thai patients with right hemisphere lesions. *Brain and Language*, 51: 422-443.

Ganis, G., & Chater, N. 1991. Can double dissociation uncover the modularity of cognitive processes? *Proceedings of the 13th annual meeting of the Cognitive Science Society* (pp. 714-718). Chicago.

Garavan, H., Ross, T., Li, S., & Stein, E. 2000. A parametric manipulation of central executive functioning. *Cerebral Cortex*, 10: 585-592.

Gardner, H. 1985. The centrality of modules. *The Behavioral and Brain Sciences*, 8: 12-14.

Gardner, H., Brownell, H., Wapner, W., & Michelow, D. 1983. Missing the point: The role of the right hemisphere in the processing of complex linguistic materials. In E. Perecman (ed.) *Cognitive processing in the right hemisphere*. (pp. 169-191). Orlando: Academic Press.

Gardner, H., Ling, K., Flamm, L., & Silverman, J. 1975. Comprehension and appreciation of humor in brain-damaged patients. *Brain*, 93: 399-412.

Gardner, R.C., & Lambert, W.E. 1972. *Attitudes and motivation in second-language learning*. Rowley, MA: Newbury House.

Gardner, R.C., & Smythe, P.C. 1974a. Second-language acquisition: Motivational considerations. In S.T. Carey (ed.), *Bilingualism, biculturalism and education* (pp. 11-30). Edmonton, AB: University of Alberta.

Gardner, R.C., & Smythe, P.C. 1974b. The integrative motive in second-language acquisition. In S.T. Carey (ed.), *Bilingualism, biculturalism and education* (pp. 31-45). Edmonton, AB: University of Alberta.

Garfield, J.L., Peterson, C.C., & Perry, T. 2001. Social cognition, language acquisition and the development of the theory of mind. *Mind and Language*, 16: 494-541.

Gazzaniga, M.S. 1967. The split brain in man. *Scientific American*, 217: 24-29.

Gazzaniga, M.S. 2000. Right-hemisphere language following brain bisection: A 20-year perspective. In M. Gazzaniga (ed.), *Cognitive neuroscience: A reader* (pp. 411-430). Oxford: Blackwell Publishers.

Geary, D.C., & Huffman, K.J. 2002. Brain and cognitive evolution: Forms of modularity and functions of mind. *Psychological Bulletin*, 128: 667-698.

Geffen, G., Bradshaw, J.L., & Wallace, G. 1971. Interhemispheric effects on reaction time to verbal and non-verbal stimuli. *Journal of Experimental Psychology*, 87: 415-4222.

Geffen, G., & Caudrey, D. 1981. Reliability and validity of the dichotic monitoring test for language laterality. *Neuropsychologia*, 19: 413-423.

Gelb, A. 1937. Zur medizinischen Psychologie und philosophischen Anthropologie. *Acta Psychologica*, 3: 193-211. Translated in Paradis (1983), 383-384.

Gerrans, P. 2002. Modularity reconsidered. *Language and Communication*, 22: 259-268.

Gloning, I., & Gloning, K. 1965. Aphasien bei Polyglotten. Beitrag zur Dynamik des Sprachabbaus sowie zur Lokalisationsfrage dieser Störungen. *Wiener Zeitschrift für Nervenheilkunde*, 22: 362-397.

Gold, B., & Buckner, R. 2002. Anterior left inferior prefrontal cortex is specific to controlled but not semantic processing. *Journal of Cognitive Neuroscience*, 14 (April Suppl.): A59

Goldstein, K. 1948. Disturbances of language in polyglot individuals with aphasia. *In Language and language disturbances* (pp. 138-146). New York: Grune and Stratton.

Gomez-Tortosa, E., Martin, E.M., Gaviria, M., Charbel, F. & Ausman, J.I. 1995. Selective deficit in one language in a bilingual patient following surgery in the left perisylvian area. *Brain and Language*, 48: 320-325.

Gomez-Tortosa, E., Martin, E., Gaviria, M., Charbel, F., & Ausman, J. 1996. Selective defiicit in one language in a bilingual patient: Reply to Paradis and Hines. *Brain and Language*, 54: 174-175.

Gonzáles-Álvarez, J., Parcet-Ibars, M.A., Avila, C., & Geffner-Scalarsky, D. 2003. Una rara alteración del habla de origen neurológico: El síndrome del accento extranjero. *Revista de Neurologia*, 36: 227-234.

Gonzalez-Garrido, A.A., Ruiz-Sandoval, J.L., Gomez-Velazquez, F.R., de Alba, J.L.O., & Villasenor-Cabrera, T. 2002. Hypercalculia in savant syndrome: Central executive failure? *Archives of Medical Research,* 33: 586-589.

Goodglass, H. 1978. Acquisition and dissolution of language. In A. Caramazza & E. Zurif (eds.), *Language acquisition and language breakdown* (pp. 101-108). Baltimore: The Johns Hopkins Press.

Goral, M. 2001. Aphasia in Hebrew speakers. *Journal of Neurolinguistics,* 15: 297-312.

Goral, M., Levy, S., & Obler, L.K. 2002. Neurolinguistic aspects of bilingualism. *The International Journal of Bilingualism,* 6: 411-440.

Gordon, H.W. 1980. Cerebral organization in bilinguals. I. Lateralization. *Brain and Language,* 9: 255-268.

Gordon, H.W., & Weide, R. 1983. La contribution de certaines fonctions cognitives au traitement du langage, à son acquisition et à l'apprentissage d'une langue seconde. *Langages,* 73: 45-56.

Gordon, N. 1996. Speech, language, and the cerebellum. *European Journal of Disorders of Communication,* 31: 359-367.

Graf, P., & Masson, M.E.G. (eds.) 1993. *Implicit memory: New directions in cognition, development, and neuropsychology.* Hillsdale, NJ: Lawrence Erlbaum Associates.

Graf, P., & Schacter, D. 1987. Selective effects of interference on implicit and explicit memory for new associations. *Journal of Experimental Psychology: Learning, Memory, and Cognition,* 13: 45-53.

Grainger, J. 1993. Visual word recognition in bilinguals. In R. Schreuder & B. Weltens (eds.), *The bilingual lexicon* (pp. 11-25). Amsterdam: John Benjamins.

Green, D.W. 1986. Control, activation, and resource: A framework and a model for the control of speech in bilinguals. *Brain and Language,* 27: 210-223.

Green, D.W. 1998. Mental control of the bilingual lexico-semantic system. *Bilingualism: Language and Cognition,* 1: 67-82.

Green, D.W. 2002. Representation and control: Exploring recovery patterns in bilingual aphasics. In F. Fabbro (ed.), *Advances in the neurolinguistics of bilingualism* (pp. 239-260). Udine: Forum-Udine University Press.

Green, D.W., & Newman, S. 1985. Bilingualism and dysphasia: process and resource. In S. Newman and R. Epstein (eds.), *Current perspectives in dyslexia* (pp. 155-177). London: Churchill Livingstone.

Green, D.W., & Price, C.J. 2001. Functional imaging in the study of recovery patterns in bilingual aphasia. *Bilingualism: Language and Cognition,* 4: 191-201.

Grice, H.P. 1975. Logic and conversation. In P. Cole & J.L. Morgan (eds.), *Syntax and semantics* (vol. 3, pp. 41-58). New York: Academic Press.

Grodzinsky, Y. 1984. The syntactic characterization of agrammatism. *Cognition,* 16: 99-120.

Grodzinsky, Y. 1986. Language deficits and the theory of syntax. *Brain and Language,* 27: 135-159.

Grodzinsky, Y. 1990. *Theoretical perspectives on language deficits.* Cambridge, MA: MIT Press.

Grodzinsky, Y. 1995. Trace deletion, theta roles and cognitive strategies. *Brain and Language,* 51: 469-497.

Grosjean, F. 1980. Spoken word recognition processes and the gating paradigm. *Perception and Psychophysics,* 38: 299-310.

Grosjean, F. 1982. *Life in two languages: An introduction to bilingualism.* Cambridge, MA: Harvard University Press.

Grosjean, F. 1985. Polyglot aphasics and language-mixing: A comment on Perecman (1984). *Brain and Language,* 26: 349-355.

Grosjean, F. 1988. Exploring the recognition of guest words in bilingual speech. *Language and Cognitive Processes,* 3: 233-274.

Grosjean, F. 1989. Neurolinguists, beware! The bilingual is not two monolinguals in one person. *Brain and Language,* 36: 1-15.

Grosjean, F. 1995. A psycholinguistic approach to code-switching: The recognition of guest words by bilinguals. In L. Milry & P. Muysken (eds.), *One speaker, two languages* (pp.259-275). Cambridge: Cambridge University Press.

Grosjean, F. 1997. Processing mixed language: Issues, findings, and models. In A. de Groot & J. Kroll (eds.), *Tutorials in bilingualism: Psycholinguistic Perspectives* (pp. 225-254), Mahwah, NJ: Lawrence Erlbaum Associates.

Grosjean, F. 1998. Studying bilinguals: Methodological and conceptual issues. *Bilingualism: Language and Cognition,* 1: 131-149.

Grosjean, F. 2001. The bilingual's language modes. In J. Nicol (ed.), *One mind, two languages: Bilingual language processing* (pp. 1-22). Oxford: Blackwell.

Grosjean, F., & Miller, J. 1994. Going in and out of languages: An example of bilingual flexibility. *Psychological Science,* 5: 201-206.

Grosjean, F., & Soares, C. 1986. Processing mixed language: Some preliminary findings. In J. Vaid (ed.), *Language processing in bilinguals: Psycholinguistic and neuropsychological perspectives* (pp. 145-179). Hillsdale, N.J.: Erlbaum.

Gumperz, J.J. 1982. *Discourse strategies.* Cambridge: Cambridge University Press.

Gurd, J.M., & Marshall, J.C. 1993. Aphasia and intelligence. In G. Blanken, J. Dittmann, H. Grimm, J.C. Marshall, & K. Wallesch (eds.), *Linguistic disorders and pathologies* (pp. 310-317). Berlin: Walter de Gruyter.

Haarmann, H.J., & Kolk, H.H. 1991. A computer model of the temporal course of agrammatic sentence understanding: The effects of variation in severity and sentence complexity. *Cognitive Science,* 15: 49-87.

Hakuta, K., & Diaz, R. 1980. In K.E. Nelson (ed.), *Children's language* (vol. 5, pp. 319-344). Hillsdale, NJ: Lawrence Erlbaum Associates.

Halsband, U., Krause, B.J., Sipilä, H., Teräs, M., & Laihinen, A. 2002. PET studies on the memory processing of word pairs in bilingual Finnish-English subjects. *Behavioural Brain Research,* 132: 47-57.

Harris, L.J. 1988. Right-brain training: Some reflections on the application of research on cerebral hemispheric speialization to education. In D.L. Molfese & S.J.

Segalowitz (eds.), *Brain Lateralization in children* (pp. 207-235). New York: The Guilford Press.

Hasegawa, M., Carpenter, P.A., & Just, M.A. 2002. An fMRI study of bilingual sentence comprehension and workload. *Neuroimage*, 15: 647-660.

Heavey, L., Pring, I., & Hermelin, B. 1999. A date to remember: The nature of memory in savant calendrical calculators. *Psychological Medicine*, 29: 145-160.

Hebb, D.O. 1949. *The organization of behavior*. New York: John Wiley.

Hebb, D.O. 1972. *Textbook of psychology*. Philadelphia, PA: W.B. Saunders Co.

Hécaen, H. 1968. L'aphasie. In A. Martinet (ed.), *Le langage* (pp. 390-414). Paris: Gallimard.

Hécaen, H. 1972. Neurolinguistique et neuropsychologie. *Langages*, 25: 3-5.

Hécaen, H., & Dubois, J. 1971. La neurolinguistique. In G.E. Perren & J.L. Trim (eds.), *Applications of linguistics* (pp. 85-89). Cambridge: Cambridge University Press.

Hegler, C. 1931. Zur Aphasie bei Polyglotten. *Deutsche Zeitschrift für Nervenheilkunde*, 117: 236-239. Translated in Paradis (1983), 317-319.

Heilman, K.M., Bowers, D., Speedie, L., & Coslett, H.B. 1984. Comprehension of affective and nonaffective prosody. *Neurology*, 34: 917-921.

Helm-Estabrooks, N., Fitzpatrick, P.M., & Barresi, B. 1982. Visual action therapy for global aphasia. *Journal of Speech and Hearing Disorders*, 47: 385-389.

Hemphill, R.E. 1976. Polyglot aphasia and polyglot hallucinations. In S. Krauss (ed.), *Encyclopedic handbook of medical psychology* (pp.398-400). London: Butterworth.

Hermans, D., Bongaerts, T., de Bot, K., & Schreuder, R. 1998. Producing words in a foreign language: Can speakers prevent interference from their first language? *Bilingualism: Language and Cognition*, 1: 213-229.

Hermelin, B., Pring, I., Buhler, M., Wolff, S., & Heaton, P. 1999. A visually impaired savant artist: Interacting perceptual and memory representations. *Journal of Child Psychology and Psychiatry and Applied Disciplines*, 40: 1129-1139.

Hernandez, A.E, Dapretto, M., Mazziotta, J., & Bookheimer, S. 2001a. Picture naming in early and late bilinguals: An fMRI study. *NeuroImage*, 13 (Part 2): S540.

Hernandez, A.E, Dapretto, M., Mazziotta, J., & Bookheimer, S. 2001b. Language switching and language representation in Spanish-English bilinguals: An fMRI study. *Neuroimage*, 14: 510-520.

Hernandez A.E., Martinez, A., & Kohnert, K. 2000. In search of the language switch: An fMRI study of picture naming in Spanish-English bilinguals. *Brain and Language*, 73: 421-431.

Hess, E.H. 1965. Attitude and pupil size. *Scientific American*, 212 (April): 46-54.

Hickok, G., & Avrutin, S. 1995. Representation, referentiality, and processing in agrammatic comprehension. *Brain and Language*, 50: 10-26.

Hilton, L.M. 1980. Language rehabilitation strategies for bilingual and foreign-speaking aphasics. *Aphasia, Apraxia, Agnosia*, 3 (2): 7-12.

Hinckley, J.J. 2003. Picture naming treatment in aphasia yields greater improvement in L1. *Brain and Language*, 87: 171-172.

Hirschman, M. 2000. Language repair via metalinguistic means. *International Journal of Language and Communication Disorders*, 35: 251-268.

Hirst, W., LeDoux, J., & Stein, S. 1984. Constraints on the processing of indirect speech acts: Evidence from aphasiaology. *Brain and Language*, 23: 26-33.

Hodges, J.R., Patterson, K., & Tyler, L.K. 1994. Loss of semantic memory: Implications for the modularity of mind. *Cognitive Neuropsychology*, 11: 504-542.

Hoffman, E.J., & Phelps, M.E. 1992. *Positron emission tomography: Principles and quantitations*. New York: Academic Press.

Holland, A. 1991. Pragmatic aspects of intervention in aphasia. *Journal of Neurolinguistics*, 6: 197-211.

Holland, A., & Penn, C. 1995. Inventing therapy for aphasia. In L. Menn, M. O'Connor, L.K. Obler, & A. Holland (eds.), *Non-fluent aphasia in a multilingual world* (pp. 144-155). Amsterdam: John Benjamins.

Hoosain, R., & Shiu, L.-P. 1989. Cerebral lateralization of Chinese-English bilingual functions. *Neuropsychologia*, 27: 705-712.

Hough, M.S. 1990. Narrative comprehension in adults with right and left hemisphere brain-damage: Theme organization. *Brain and Language*, 38: 253-277.

Hough, M.S., & Pierce, R.S. 1993. Contextual and thematic influences on narrative comprehension of left and right hemisphere brain-damaged adults. In H.H. Brownell & Y. Joanette (eds.), *Narrative discourse in neurologically impaired and normal aging adults* (pp. 213-238). San Diego: Singular.

Huitbregtse, I., & de Bot, K. 2002. Measuring patterns of recovery, impairment or residual language proficiency in bilingual aphasia. In F. Fabbro (ed.), *Advances in the neurolinguistics of bilingualism* (pp. 219-238). Udine: Forum-Udine University Press.

Hyltenstam, K. 1995. The code-switching behaviour of adults with language-disorders—With special reference to aphasia and dementia. In L. Milroy & P. Muysken (eds.), *One speaker, two languages* (pp. 302-343). Cambridge: Cambridge University Press.

Hyltenstam, K., & Stroud, C. 1993. Second language regression in Alzheimer's dementia. In K. Hyltenstam & Å. Viberg (eds.), *Progression and regression in language* (pp. 222-242). Cambridge: Cambridge University Press.

Hynd, G., Teeter, A., & Stewart, J. 1980. Acculturation and lateralization of speech in the bilingual native American. *International Journal of Neuroscience*, 11: 1-7.

Illes, J., Francis, W., Desmond, J., Gabrieli, J., Glover, G., et al. 1999. Convergent cortical representation of semantic processing in bilinguals. *Brain and Language*, 70: 347-363.

Jackendoff, R. 1987. *Consciousness and the computational mind*. Cambridge, MA: MIT Press.

Jackendoff, R. 1992. *Languages of the mind: Essays on mental representation.* Cambridge, MA: MIT Press.

Jacobs, J.F., & Pierce, M.L. 1966. Bilingualism and creativity. *Elementary English,* 43: 499-503.

Jacoby, L.L. 1991. A process dissociation framework: Separating automatic from intentional uses of memory. *Journal of Memory and Language,* 30: 513-541.

Jakobovits, L.A. 1970. *Foreign language learning.* Rowley, MA: Newbury House.

Jamkarian, T. 2001. Language amnesia heading, in the link "répond à vos questions," <http://www.amnesique.com>.

Jäncke, L., Steinmetz, H., & Volkmann, J. 1992. Dichotic listening: What does it measure? *Neuropsychologia,* 30: 941-950.

Joanette, Y., Goulet, P., & Hannequin, D. 1990. *Right hemisphere and verbal communication.* New York: Springer-Verlag.

Joanette, Y., Goulet, P., Ska, B., & Nespoulous, J.-L. 1986. Informative content of narrative discourse in right-brain-damaged right-handers. *Brain and Language,* 29: 81-105.

Joanette, Y., Lecours, A.R., Lepage, Y., & Lamoureux, M. 1983. Language in right-handers with right-hemisphere lesions: A preliminary study including anatomical, genetic, and social factors. *Brain and Language,* 20: 217-249.

Johns, D.F., & Lapointe, L.L. 1976. Neurogenic disorders of output processing: Apraxia of speech. In H. Whitaker and H.A. Whitaker (eds.), *Studies in Neurolinguistics,* Vol.1. New York: Academic Press.

Joubert, S. 1999. Etude des soubassements cognitifs et neurologiques de la lecture sublexicale en langue française. Unpublished doctoral dissertation, Université de Montréal.

Juncos-Rabadán, O. 1994. The assessment of bilingualism in normal aging with the Bilingual Aphasia Test. *Journal of Neurolingiuistics,* 8: 67-73.

Juszyk, P.W., & Cohen, A. 1985. What constitutes a module? *The Behavioral and Brain Sciences,* 8: 20-21.

Kandel, E.R., Schwartz, J.H., & Jessell, T.M. 1991. *Principles of neural science* (Third Edition). New York: Elsevier.

Kandel, E.R., Schwartz, J.H., & Jessell, T.M. 2000. *Principles of neural science* (Fourth Edition). New York: McGraw-Hill.

Kaplan, J.A., Brownell, H.H., Jacobs, J.R., & Gardner, H. 1990. The effects of right hemisphere damage on the pragmatic interpretation of conversational remarks. *Brain and Language,* 38: 315-333.

Karanth, P., & Rangamani, G.N. 1988. Crossed aphasia in multilinguals. *Brain and Language,* 34: 169-180.

Karmiloff-Smith, A. 1986. Stage/structure versus phase/process in modelling linguistic and cognitive development. In I. Levin (ed.), *Stage and structure: Reopening the debate.* Norwood, NJ: Ablex.

Kasher, A. 1991. Pragmatics and the modularity of mind. In S. Davis (ed.), *Pragmatics. A reader* (pp. 567-582). Oxford: Oxford University Press.

Keane, M.M., Clarke, H., & Corkin, S. 1992. Impaired perceptual priming and intact conceptual priming in a patient with bilateral posterior cerebral lesions. Paper presented at the 22nd Annual Meeting of the Society for Neuroscience, Anaheim, California, 26 October.

Kent, R. 1998. Neuroimaging studies of brain activation for language, with an emphasis on functional magnetic resonance imaging: A review. *Folia Phoniatrica et Logopaedica*, 50: 291-304.

Kershner, J., & Jeng, A. 1972. Dual functional hemispheric asymmetry in visual perception: Effects of ocular dominance and post-exposural processes, *Neuropsychologia*, 10: 437-445.

Kertesz, A. 1994. Localization and function. In A. Kertesz (ed.), *Localization and neuroimaging in neuropsychology* (pp. 1-33). New York: Academic Press

Kihlstrom, JF., Schacter, D.L., Cork R.C., Hurt, C.A., & Behr, S.E. 1990. Implicit and explicit memory following surgical anesthesia. *Psychological Sciences*, 1: 303-306.

Kim, H., & Cohen Levine S. 1991. Inferring patterns of hemispheric specialization for individual subjects from laterality data: A two-task criterion. *Neuropsychologia*, 29: 93-105.

Kim, K.H., Relkin, N.R., Lee, K.-M., & Hirsch, J. 1997. Distinct cortical areas associated with native and second languages. *Nature*, 388: 171-174.

Kinsbourne, M. 1981. Neuropsychological processes in language acquisition: General discussion. In H. Winitz (ed.), *Native language and foreign language acquisition* (Annals of the New York Academy of Sciences, Vol. 379, pp. 87-91). New York: New York Academy of Sciences.

Kircher, T.T.J., Brammer, M., Andreu, N.T., Williams, S.C.R., & McGuire, P.K. 2001. Engagement of right temporal cortex during processing of linguistic context. *Neuropsychologia*, 39: 798-809.

Kiroy, V.N., & Kotik, B. 1985. Electrographic correlates of speech activity in morther tongue and foreign language. *Phisiologia Cheloveka*, 11: 223-227.

Klein, D. 2003. A positron emission tomography study of presurgical language mapping in a bilingual patient with a left posterior temporal cavernous angioma. *Journal of Neurolinguistics*, 16: 417-427.

Klein, D., Milner, B., Zatorre, R., Visca, R., & Olivier, A. 2002. Cerebral organization in a right-handed trilingual patient with right-hemisphere speech: A positron emission tomography study. *Neurocase*, 8: 369-375.

Klein, D., Milner, B., Zatorre, R., Zhao, V., & Nikelski, J. 1999. Cerebral organization in bilinguals: A PET study of Chinese-English verb generation. *NeuroReport*, 10: 2841-2846.

Klein, D., Zatorre, R.J., Milner, B., Meyer, E., & Evans, A.C. 1994. Left putaminal activation when speaking a second language: Evidence from PET. *NeuroReport*, 5: 2295-2297.

Klein, D., Watkins, K., Milner, B., & Zatorre, R. 2001. Functional imaging study of word and nonword repetition in bilingual subjects. *NeuroImage*, 13 (6, Part 2): S552.

Klein, D., Zatorre, R.J., Milner, B., Meyer, E., & Evans, A.C. 1995a. The neural substrates of bilingual language processing: Evidence from positron emission tomography. In M. Paradis (ed.), *Aspects of bilingual aphasia* (pp. 23-36). Oxford: Pergamon Press.

Klein, D., Zatorre, R.J., Milner, B., Meyer, E., & Evans, A.C. 1995b. The neural substrates underlying word generation: A bilingual functional-imaging study. *Proceedings of the National Academy of Science USA*, 92: 2899-2903.

Klein, D., Zatorre, R.J., Milner, B., & Zhao, V. 2001. A cross-linguistic PET study of tone perception in Mandarin Chinese and English speakers. *NeuroImage*, 13: 646-653.

Klosty Beaujour, E. 1989. *Alien tongues*. Ithaca, NY: Cornell University Press.

Kolers, P.A. 1966. Reading and talking bilingually. *The American Journal of Psychology*, 3: 357-375.

Kolers, P.A. 1968. Bilingualism and information processing. *Scientific American*, 218 (March): 78-86.

Konishi, S., Jimura, K., Asari, T., & Miyashita, Y. 2003. Transient activation of superior prefrontal cortex during inhibition of cognitive set. *Journal of Neuroscience*, 23: 7776-7782.

Köpke, B. 2002. Activation threshold and non-pathological first language attrition. In F. Fabbro (ed.), *Advances in the neurolinguistics of bilingualism* (pp. 119-142). Udine: Forum-Udine University Press.

Kotik, B. 1975. Lateralization in multilinguals. Thesis, Moscow State University, USSR.

Kotik-Friedgut, B. 2001. A systemic-dynamic Lurian approach to aphasia in bilingual speakers. *Communication Disorders Quarterly*, 22: 100-109.

Kotik-Friedgut, B.S. 2002. A.R. Luria's systemic dynamic conception and neuropsychology today. *Voprosy Psikhologii*, 4: 68-76.

Krapf, E.E. 1961. Aphasia in polyglots. *Proceedings of the VIIth International Congress of Neurology* (vol. 1, pp. 741-742) Rome.

Krashen, S. (1973). Lateralization, language learning and the critical period: Some new evidence, *Language Learning*, 23: 63-74.

Krashen, S. 1977. The Monitor Model for adult second language performance. In M. Burt, H. Dulay, & M. Finocchiaro (eds.), *Viewpoints on English as a second language*. New York: Regents.

Krashen, S. 1981. *Second language acquisition and second language learning*. Oxford: Pergamon Press.

Krashen, S. 1982. *Principles and practice in second language acquisition*. Oxford: Pergamon.

Kremin H., Chomel-Guillaume, S., Ferrand, I., & Backnine, S. 2000. Dissociation of reading strategies: Letter-by-letter reading in the native language and normal reading in the learned language. A case study. *Brain and Cognition*, 43: 282-286.

Kroll, J.F., & de Groot, A.M.B. 1997. Lexical and conceptual memory in the bilingual: Mapping form to meaning in two languages. In A. de Groot & J. Kroll (eds.), *Tutorials in bilingualism: Psycholinguistic perspectives* (pp. 169-199). Mahwah, NJ: Lawrence Erlbaum Associates.

Kroll, N.E.A., & Madden, D.J. 1978. Verbal and pictorial processing by hemisphere as a function of the subjects' Verbal Scholastic Aptitude Test score. In J. Requin (ed.), *Attention and Performance VII* (pp. 375-390). Hillsdale, NJ: Lawrence Erlbaum Associates.

LaBerge, D. 2001. Attentional control: brief and prolonged. *Psychological Research*, 66: 220-233.

Laganaro, M., & Overton Venet, M. 2001. Acquired alexia in multilingual aphasia and computer-assisted treatment in both languages: Issues of generalisation and transfer. *Folia Phoniatrica et Logopaedica*, 53: 135-144.

Lai, C.S.L., Fisher, S.E., Hurst, J.A., Vargha-Khadem, F., & Monaco, A.P. 2001. A forkhead-domain gene is mutated in a severe speech and language disorder. *Nature*, 413: 519-523.

Lamb, S. 1966. *Outline of stratificational grammar*. Washington, DC: Georgetown University Press.

Lamb, S. 1994. Relational network linguistics meets neural science. *LACUS Forum*, 20: 109-120.

Lambert, W.E. 1968. Psychological asoects of motivation in language learning. A paper presented at the 4th Southern Conference on Language Teaching in New Orleans, Feb. 22nd. Reprinted from the May 1969 issue of *the Bulletin of the Illinois Foreign Language Teachers Association* in A. S. Dil (ed.), *Language, psychology, and culture* (pp. 290-299). Stanford: Stanford University Press, 1972.

Lambert W.E., & Fillenbaum, S. 1959. A pilot study of aphasia among bilinguals. *Canadian Journal of Psychology*, 13: 28-34.

Lambert, W.E., & Tucker, G.R. 1972. *The bilingual education of children*. Rowley MA: Newbury House.

Lamendella, J. 1977a. General principles of neurofunctional organization and their manifestation in primary and secondary language acquisition. *Language Learning*, 27: 155-196.

Lamendella, J. 1977b. The limbic system in human communication. In H. Whitaker & H.A. Whitaker (eds.), *Studies in neurolinguistics* (vol. 3, pp.154-222). New York: Academic Press.

Landry, R.G. 1974. A comparison of second language learners and monolinguals on divergent thinking tasks at the elementary school level. *Modern Language Journal*, 58: 10-15.

Langacker, R. 1991. *Foundations of cognitive grammar*. Stanford: Stanford University Press.

Langdon, R., Coltheart, M., Ward, P.B., & Catts, S.V. 2002. Disturbed communication in schizophrenia: The role of poor pragmatics and poor mind-reading. *Psychological Medicine*, 32: 1273-1284.

Larsen, S.F., Schrauf, R.W., Fromholt, P., & Rubin, D.C. 2002. Inner speech and bilingual autobiographical memory: A Polish-Danish cross-cultural study. *Memory*, 10: 45-54.

Lassen, N.A., Ingvar, D.H., & Skinhøj, E. 1978. Brain function and blood flow. *Scientific American*, 239 (October): 52-71.

Lauter, J.L. 1998. Neuroimaging and the trimodal brain: Applications for developmental communication neuroscience. *Folia Phoniatrica et Logopaedica*, 50: 118-145.

Lebrun, Y. 1978. Evaluation of language-impaired children. In F. Peng & W. von Raffler-Engel (eds.), *Language acquisition and developmental kinesics* (pp. 182-193*)*. Hiroshima: Bunka Hyokon.

Lebrun, Y. 1981. Bilingualism and the Brain: A brief appraisal of Penfield's views, in H. Baetens-Beardsmore (ed.), *Elements of Bilingual Theory* (pp. 66-76). Brussels: Vrije Universiteit Brussel.

Lebrun, Y. 1988. Multilinguisme et aphasie. *Revue de Laryngologie*. 109, 299-306.

Lebrun, Y. 2002. Implicit competence and explicit knowledge. In F. Fabbro (ed.), *Advances in the neurolinguistics of bilingualism* (pp.299-313). Udine: Forum-Udine University Press.

Lecours, A.R., Branchereau, L., & Joanette, Y. 1984. La zone du langage et l'aphasie: Enseignement standard et cas particuliers. *META*, 29: 10-26.

Lecours, A.R., & Joanette, Y. 1980. Linguistic and other psychological aspects of paroxysmal aphasia. *Brain and Language*, 10: 1-23.

Lee, W.L., Hong, W.T., Chua, C.L., Nowinski, W.L., Chai, S.P., Chua, G.E., & Sitoh, Y.Y. 2002. fMRI comparison of orthographic, phonological and semantic components of word recognition in English and Chinese. NeuroImage Human Brain Mapping Meeting, Poster No. 10012. (Cited by Pillai et al., 2003.)

Leiner, H.C., Leiner, A.L., & Dow, R.S. 1991. The human cerebro-cerebellar system: Its computing, cognitive and language skills. *Behavioural Brain Research*, 11: 113-128.

Leischner, A. 1943. Die "Aphasie die Taubstummen." Beitrag zur Lehre von der Asymbolie. *Archiv für Psychiatrie*, 115: 469-548.

Lenneberg, E. 1967. *Biological foundations of language*. New York: John Wiley & Sons.

Lepsien, J., & Pollmann, S. 2002. Covert reorienting and inhibition of return: An event-related fMRI study. *Journal of Cognitive Neuroscience*, 14: 127-144.

Levelt, W.J.M. 1989. *Speaking: From intention to articulation*. Cambridge, MA: MIT Press.

Lewandowsky, S., Dunn, J.C., & Kirsner, K. (eds.) 1989. *Implicit memory: Theoretical issues*. Hillsdale, NJ: Lawrence Erlbaum Associates.

Lieberman, P. 1996. Neuroanatomical structures and segregated circuits. *Behavioral and Brain Sciences*, 19: 641.

Liepman, D., & Saegert, J. 1974. Language tagging in bilingual free recall. *Journal of Experimental Psychology*, 103: 1137-1141.

Linebarger, M.C., Schwartz, M.F., & Saffran, E., 1983. Sensitivity to grammatical structure in so-called agrammatic aphasics. *Cognition*, 13: 361-392.

Linke, D. 1979. Zur Therapie polyglotter Aphasiker. In G. Peuser (ed.), *Studien zur Sprachtherapie*. Munich: Wilhelm Fink Verlag.

Lockhart, R.S. 1984. What do infants remember? In M. Moscovitch (ed.), *Infant memory*. New York: Plenum.

Lockhart, R.S., & Parkin, A.J. 1989. The role of theory in understanding implicit memory. In S. Lewandowsky, J. C. Dunn, & K. Kirsner (eds.), *Implicit memory: Theoretical issues* (pp.3-13). Hillsdale, NJ: Lawrence Erlbaum Associates.

Loew, R.C., Kegl, J.A., & Poizner, H. 1997. Fractionation of the components of role play in a right-hemisphere lesioned signer. *Aphasiology*, 11: 263-281.

Logan, G.D., & Cowan, W.B. 1984. On the ability to inhibit thought and action: A theory of an act of control. *Psychological Review*, 91: 295-327.

Long, M. 1983 Does second language instruction make a difference? A review of the research. *TESOL Quarterly*, 17: 359-382.

Luke, K.K., Liu, H.L., Wai, Y.Y., Wan, Y.L., & Tan, L.H. 2002. Functional anatomy of syntactic and semantic processing in language comprehension. *Human Brain Mapping*, 16: 133-145.

Luria, A.R. 1973. *The working brain: An introduction to neuropsychology*. New York: Penguin Education.

Luria, A.R. 1974. Basic problems of neurolinguistics. In T.A. Sebeok (ed.), *Current trends in linguistics* (vol. 12, pp. 2561-2593). The Hague: Mouton.

Luria, A.R., & Hutton, T. 1977. A modern assessment of the basic forms of aphasia. *Brain and Language*, 4: 129-151.

Mack, M.A. 1984. Early bilinguals: How monolingual-like are they? in M. Paradis & Y. Lebrun (eds.), *Early Bilingualism and Child Development*, (pp. 161-173). Lisse: Swets & Zeitlinger.

Mack, M.A. 1986. A study of semantic and syntactic processing in monolinguals and fluent early bilinguals. *Journal of Psycholinguistic Research*, 15: 463-488.

MacNab, G.L. 1979. Cognition and bilingualism: A reanalysis of studies. *Linguistics*, 17: 231-255.

Macnamara, J. 1969. How can one measure the extent of a person's bilingual proficiency? In L.G. Kelly (ed.), *Description and measurement of bilingualism* (pp. 80-119). Toronto: University of Toronto Press.

Macnamara, J. 1970. Bilingualism and thought. *Georgetown University Monograph Series in Linguistics*, 23: 25-40.

Macnamara, J., & Kushnir, S.L. 1971. Linguistic independence of bilinguals: The input switch. *Journal of Verbal Learning and Verbal Behavior,* 10: 480-487.

MacWhinney, B. 1997. Second language acquisition and the competition model. In A. de Groot & J. Kroll (eds.), *Tutorials in bilingualism: Psycholinguistic perspectives* (pp. 113-142). Hillsdale, NJ: Lawrence Erlbaum Associates.

Maddox, W.T., Ashby, F.G., & Bohil, C.J. 2003. Delayed feedback effects on rule-based and information-integration category learning. *Journal of Experimental Psychology: Learning, Memory, and Cognition,* 29: 650-662.

Maddox, W.T., Ashby, F.G., & Waldron, E.M. 2002. Multiple attention systems in perceptual categorization. *Memory and Cognition,* 30: 325-339.

Mägiste, E. 1992. Leaning to the right: Hemispheric involvement in bilinguals. In R.J. Harris (ed.), *Cognitive processing in bilinguals.* Amsterdam: Elsevier.

Malmkjær, K., & Anderson, J.M. 1991. *The linguistics encyclopedia.* London and New York: Routledge.

Mandler, G. 1975. *Mind and emotion.* New York: Wiley.

Marian, V., & Spivey, M. 2003. Bilingual and monolingual processing of competing lexical items. *Applied Psycholinguistics,* 24: 173-193.

Marian, V., Spivey, M., & Hirsch, J. 2001. A levels-of-processing approach to bilingual language processing. Abstract presented at the Neurological Basis of Language Conference, University of Groningen, Groningen, The Netherlands. (Cited by Pillai et al., 2003.)

Marian, V., Spivey, M., & Hirsch, J. 2003. Shared and separate systems in bilingual language processing: Converging evidence from eyetracking and brain imaging. *Brain and Language,* 86: 70-82.

Marien, P., Engelbroghs, S., Fabbro, F., & De Dijn, P.P. 2001. The lateralized linguistic cerebellum: A review and a new hypothesis. *Brain and Language,* 79: 580-600.

Marrero, M.Z., Golden, C.J., & Espe-Pfeifer, P. 2002. Bilingualism, brain injury, and recovery: Implications for understanding the bilingual and for therapy. *Clinical Psychology Review,* 22: 463-478.

Marshall, J.C. 1984. Multiple perspectives on modularity. *Cognition,* 17: 209-242.

Martin, I., & McDonald, S. 2003. Weak coherence, no theory of mind, or executive dysfunction? Solving the puzzle of pragmatic language disorders. *Brain and Language,* 85: 451-466.

Martinet, A. 1960. *Eléments de linguistique générale.* Paris: Armand Colin.

Martinet, A. 1975. *Studies in functional syntax.* Munich: Fink.

Mayberry, M., Taylor, M., & Obrien-Malone, A. 1995. Implicit learning—Sensitive to age but not IQ. *Australian Journal of Psychology,* 47: 8-17.

Mazoyer, B.M., Tzourio, N., Frak, V., Syrota, A., Murayama, N., Levrier, O., Salamon, G., Dehaene, S., Cohen, L., & Mehler, J. 1993. The cortical representation of speech. *Journal of Cognitive neuroscience,* 5: 467-479.

McCormack, P.D. 1977. Bilingual linguistic memory: The independence-interdependence issue revisited. In P.A. Hornby (ed.), *Bilingualism* (pp. 57-66). New York: Academic Press.

McKeever, W.F., & Hunt, L. 1984. Failure to replicate the Scott et al. findings of reversed ear dominance in the Native American Navajo. *Neurologia*, 22: 539-541.

McKiernan, K.A., Kaufman, J.N., Kucera-Thompson, J., Binder, J.R. 2003. A parametric manipulation of factors affecting task-induced deactivation in functional neuroimaging. *Journal of Cognitive Neuroscience*, 15: 394-408.

Meguro, K., Senaha, M., Caramelli, P., Ishizaki, J., Chubacci, R., Meguro, M., Ambo, H., Nitrini, R., & Yamadori, A. 2003. Language deterioration in four Japanese-Portuguese bilingual patients with Alzheimer's disease: A transcultural study of Japanese elderly immigrants in Brazil. *Psychogeriatrics*, 3: 63-68.

Mendelsohn, S. 1988. Language lateralization in bilinguals: Facts and fantasy. *Journal of Neurolinguistics*, 3: 261-292.

Mendez, M.F., Perryman, K. M., Pontón, M.O., & Cummings, J.L. 1999. Bilingualism and dementia. *Journal of Neuropsychiatry and Clinical Neuroscience*, 11: 411-412.

Menon, V., Adleman, N.E., White, C.D., Glover, G.H., & Reiss, A.L. 2001. Errr-related brain activation during a Go/NoGo response inhibition task. *Human Brain Mapping*, 12: 131-143.

Miller, L.K. 1998. Defining the savant syndrome. *Journal of Developmental and Physical Disabilities*, 10: 73-85.

Miller, L.K. 1999. The savant syndrome: Intellectual impairment and exceptional skill. *Psychological Bulletin*, 125: 31-46.

Milner, B. 1966. Amnesia following operation on the temporal lobes. In C.W.M Whitty & O.L. Zangwill (eds.), *Amnesia*. London: Butterworth.

Milner, B., Corkin, S., & Teuber, H.-L. 1968. Further analysis of the hippocampal amnesic syndrome: 14-year follow up study of H.M. *Neuropsychologia*, 6: 215-234.

Milner, B., Taylor, L., & Sperry, R.W. 1968. Lateralized suppression of dichotically presented digits after commissural section in man. *Science*, 161: 184-186.

Mimouni, Z., Béland, R., Danault, S., & Idrissi, A. 1995. Similar language disorders in Arabic and French in an early bilingual aphasic patient. *Brain and Language*, 51: 132-134.

Mimouni, Z. , & Jarema, G. 1997. Agrammatc aphasia in Arabic. *Aphasiology*, 11: 125-144.

Minkowski, M. 1928. Sur un cas d'aphasie chez un polyglotte. *Revue Neurologique*, 49: 361-366.

Minkowski, M. 1949. Sur un cas particulier d'aphasie avec des réactions polyglottes, de fabulation et d'autres troubles après un traumatisme cranio-cérébral. *Contes rendus du congrès des médecins aliénistes et neurologistes de langue française* (pp. 315-328). *Clermont-Ferrand.*

Minkowski, M. 1963. On aphasia in polyglots. In L. Halpern (ed.), *Problems of dynamic neurology* (pp. 119-161). Jerusalem: Hebrew University.

Minkowski, M. 1965. Considérations sur l'aphasie des polyglottes. *Revue Neurologique*, 112: 486-495.

Mogford-Bevan K. 2000. Developmental language impairments with complex origins: Learning from twins and multiple birth children. *Folia Phoniatrica et Logopaedica*, 52: 74-82.

Molloy, R., Brownwell, H.H., & Gardner, H. 1990. Discourse comprehension by right hemisphere stroke patients: Deficits of prediction and revision. In Y. Joanette and H. Brownell (Eds.), *Discourse Ability and Brain Damage: Theoretical and Empirical Perspectives*. (Pp. 113-130). New York: Springer Verlag.

Morais, J. 1981. Le test d'écoute dichotique en tant que prédicteur de la dominance cérébrale chez les normaux. *Acta Neurologica Belgica*, 81: 144-152.

Moretti, R., Bava, A., Torre, P., Antonello, R.M., & Cazzato, G. 2002a. Reading errors in patients with cerebellar vermis lesions. *Journal of Neurology*, 249: 461-468.

Moretti, R., Bava, A., Torre, P., Antonello, R.M., Ukmar, M., Longo, R., Cazzato, G., & Bava, A. 2002b. Complex distal movement in cortical-basal ganglionic degeneration. A functional evaluation. *Functional Neurology*, 17: 71-76.

Moretti, R., Torre, P., Antonello, R.M. Capus, L., Gioulis, M., Marsala, S., Cazzato, G., & Bava, A. 2001a. Effects on cognitive abilities following subthalamic nucleus stimulation in Parkinson's disease. *European Journal of Neurology*, 8: 726-727.

Moretti, R., Torre, P., Antonello, R.M., Capus, L., Gioulis, M., Marsala, S.Z., Cazzato, G., & Bava, A. 2002e. Cognitive changes following subthalamic nucleus stimulation in two patients with Parkinson disease. *Perceptual and Motor Skills*, 95: 477-486.

Moretti, R., Torre, P., Antonello, R.M., Capus, L., Marsala, S.Z., Cattaruzza, T., Cazzato, G., & Bava, A. 2003. Neuropsychological changes after subthalamic nucleus stimulation: A 12 month follow-up in nine patients with Parkinson's disease. *Parkinsonism and Related Disorders*, 10: 73-79.

Moretti, R., Torre, P., Antonello, R.M., Carraro, N., Cazzato, G., & Bava, A. 2002d. Complex cognitive disruption in motor neuron disease. *Dementia and Geriatric Cognitive Disorders*, 14: 141-150.

Moretti, R., Torre, P., Antonello, R.M., Carraro, N., Zambito-Marsala, S., Ukmar, M., Capus, L., Gioulis, M., Cazzato, G., & Bava, A. 2002c. Peculiar aspects of reading and writing performance in patients with olivopontocerebellar atrophy. *Perceptual and Motor Skills*, 94: 667-694.

Moretti, R., Torre, P., Antonello, R.M., De Masi, R., & Cazzato, G. 2001b. Complex cognitive disruption in frontal dementia related to motor neuron disease. *Perceptual and Motor Skills*, 92: 1213-1229.

Moss, E.M., Davidson, R.J. & Saron, C. 1985. Cross-cultural differences in hemisphericity: EEG asymmetry discriminates between Japanese and Westerners. *Neuropsychologia,* 23: 131-135.

Mountcastle, V.B. 1978. An organizing principle for cerebral function: The unit module and the distribution system. In G.M. Edelman & V.B. Mountcastle (eds.), *The mindful brain* (pp. 7-50). Cambridge: MIT Press.

Müller, R.A. 1996. Innateness, autonomy, universality? Neurobiological approaches to language. *Behavioral and Brain Sciences,* 19: 611-675.

Müller, R.-A., Rothermel, R.D., Behen, M.E., Muzik, O., Mangner, T.J. & Chugani, H.T. 1997. Receptive and expressive activation for sentences: A PET study. *NeuroReport,* 8: 3767-3770.

Muñoz, M.L., & Marquardt, T.P. 2003. Picture naming and identification in bilingual speakers of Spanish and English with and without aphasia. *Aphasiology,* 17: 115-1132.

Muñoz, M.L., Marquardt, T.P., & Copeland, G. 1999. A comparison of the codeswitching patterns of aphasic and neurologically normal bilingual speakers of English and Spanish (Appendix). *Brain and Language,* 66: 249-274.

Myers, P.S., & Linebaugh, C. 1981. Comprehension of idiomatic expressions by right hemisphere damaged adults. *Clinical Aphasiology—Proceedings of the Conference* (pp. 254-261). Minneapolis, MN: BRK Publishing.

Naeser, M.A. 1975. A structural approach teaching aphasics basic sentence types. *British Journal of Disorders of Communication,* 10: 70-76.

Nakada, T. 2002. Time to jettison extreme localizationism: Reply to the comment of Tomioka and Paradis. *Neuroscience Research,* 43: 91-92.

Nakada, T., Fujii, Y., & Kwee, I.L. 2001. Brain strategies for reading in the second language are determined by the first language. *Neuroscience Research,* 40: 351-358.

Nakai, T., Matsuo, K., Kato, C., Matsuzawa, M., Okada, T., Glover, H., Moriya, T., & Inui, T. 1999. A functional magnetic resonance imaging study of listening comprehension of languages in human at 3 tesla-comprehension level and activation of the language areas. *Neuroscience Letters,* 263: 33-36.

Nass, R., & Gutman, R. 1997. Boys with Asperger disorder, exceptional verbal intelligence, tics, and clumsiness. *Developmental Medicine and Child Neurology,* 39: 691-695.

Nazzi, T., Bertoncini, J., & Mehler, J., 1998. Language discrimination by newborns: Towards an understanding of the rolr of rhythm. *Journal of Experimental Psychology: Human Perception and Performance,* 24: 1-11.

Nelson, K. 1988. The ontogeny of memory for real events. In U. Neisser & E. Winograd (eds.), *Remembering reconsidered: Ecological and traditional approaches to the study of memory.* (pp. 244-276) Cambridge, MA: Cambridge University Press.

Nettelbeck, T., & Young, R. 1996. Intelligence and savant syndrome: Is the whole greater than the sum of the fragments? *Intelligence,* 22: 49-67.

Nettelbeck, T., & Young, R. 1999. Savant syndrome. *International Review of Research in Mental Retardation*, 22: 137-173.

Neville, H.J., Mills, D.L., & Lawson, D.S. 1992. Fractionating language: Different natural subsystems with different sensitive periods. *Cerebral Cortex*, 2: 244-258.

Nichelli, P., Grafman, J., Pietrini, P., Clark, K., Lee, K.Y., & Miletich, R. 1995. Where the brain appreciates the moral of a story. *NeuroReport*, 6: 2309-2313.

Nicholas, L., & Brookshire, R. 1995. Comprehension of spoken and narrative discourse by adults with aphasia, right hemisphere brain damage, or traumatic brain injury. *American Journal of Speech Language Pathology*, 4: 69-81.

Nilipour, R. 1988. Bilingual aphasia in Iran: A preliminary report. *Journal of Neurolinguistics*, 3: 185-232.

Nilipour, R., & Ashayeri, H. 1989. Alternating antagonism between two languages with successive recovery of a third in a trilingual aphasic patient. *Brain and Language*, 36: 23-48.

Nilipour, R., & Paradis, M. 1995. Breakdown of functional categories in three Farsi-English bilingual aphasic patients. In M. Paradis (ed.), *Aspects of bilingual aphasia* (pp. 123-138). Oxford: Pergamon Press.

Nilsson, L.G. & Bäckman, L. 1989. Implicit memory and the enactment of verbal instructions. In S. Lewandowsky, J.C. Dunn, & K. Kirsner (eds.), *Implicit memory: Theoretical issues* (pp. 173-183). Hillsdale, NJ: Lawrence Erlbaum Associates.

Norman, D.A., & Shallice, T. 1986. Attention to willed action: Willed and automatic control of behavior. In R.J. Davidson, G.E. Schwartz, & R.L. Shapiro (eds.), *Conscious and self-regulation: Advances in research*. Vol. 4 (pp. 1-18). New York: Plenum.

Norris, J.M., & Ortega, L. 2000. Effectiveness of L2 instruction: A research synthesis and quantitative meta-analysis. *Language Learning*, 50: 417-528.

Norris, J.M., & Ortega, L. 2001. Does type of instruction make a difference? Substantive findings from a meta-analytic review. *Language Learning*, 51: 157-213, Supplement 1.

Obler, L.K. 1999. Language in dementia: Implications for neurolinguistic theory. In J.A. Argenter (ed.), *Language, brain and verbal behaviour. Neurobiological aspects of linguistic capacities and language processing* (pp. 63-76). Barcelona: Institut d'Estudis Catalans.

Obler, L.K., & Albert, M.L. 1977. Influence of aging on recovery from aphasia in polyglots. *Brain and Language*, 4: 460-463.

Obler, L.K., & Albert, M. 1978. A monitor system for bilingual language processing. In M. Paradis (ed.) *Aspects of bilingualism* (pp. 156-164). Columbia, NC: Hornbeam Press.

Obler, L.K. & Mahecha, N.R. 1991. First language loss in bilingual and polyglot aphasics. In H.W. Seliger & R.M. Vago (eds.), *First language attrition* (pp. 53-65). Cambridge: Cambridge University Press.

Obler, L.K., Zatorre, R.J., Galloway, L., & Vaid, J. 1982. Cerebral lateralization in bilinguals: Methodological issues. *Brain and Language* , 15: 40-54.

Obrzut, J.E., Conrad, P.F., Bryden, M.P, & Boliek, C.A. 1988. Cued dichotic listening with right-handed, left-handed, bilingual and learning disabled children. *Neuropsychologia*, 26: 119-131.

Ojemann, G.A., & Whitaker, H.A. 1978. The bilingual brain. *Archives of Neurology*, 35: 409-412.

Okoh, N. 1980. Bilingualism and divergent thinking among Nigerian and Welsh school children. *The Journal of Social Psychology*, 110: 163-170.

Orbach, J. 1967. Differential recognition of Hebrew and English words in right and left visual fields as a function of cerebral dominance and reading habits. *Neuropsychologia*, 5: 127-134.

Owen, W.J., Borowsky, R., & Sarty, G.E. 2004. FMRI of two measures of phonological processing in visual word recognition: Ecological validity matters. *Brain and Language*, in press (available online at www.sciencedirect.com).

Ozonoff, S., & Miller, J.N. 1996. An exploration of right-hemisphere contributions to the pragmatic impairments of autism. *Brain and Language*, 52: 411-434.

Paivio, A., & Desrochers, A. 1980. A dual-coding approach to bilingual memory. *Canadian Journal of Psychology*, 34: 388-399.

Pallier, C., Colomé, A., & Sebastián-Gallés, N. 2001. The influence of native-language phonology on lexical access: Exemplar-based versus abstract lexical entries. *Psychological Science*, 12: 445-449.

Paller, K.A., Hutson, C.A., Miller, B.B., & Boehm, S.G. 2003. Neural manifestations of memory with and without awareness. *Neuron*, 38: 507-516.

Papagno, C. 2001. Comprehension of metaphors and idioms in patients with Alzheimer's disease—a longitudinal study. *Brain*, 124: 1450-1460.

Papanicolaou, A.C., & Billingsley, R.L. 2003. Functional neuroimaging contributions to neurolinguistics. *Journal of Neurolinguistics*, 16: 251-254.

Paradis, M. 1977. Bilingualism and aphasia. In H. Whitaker & H.A. Whitaker (eds.), *Studies in neurolinguistics*, (vol.3, pp. 65-121). New York: Academic Press.

Paradis, M. 1978. Bilingual linguistic memory: Neurolinguistic considerations. Paper presented at the Annual Meeting of the Linguistic Society of America, Boston, 28 December.

Paradis, M. 1979. Baby talk in French and Québécois. *LACUS Forum*, 5: 355-365.

Paradis, M. 1980a. The language switch in bilinguals: Psycholinguistic and neurolinguistic perspectives. *Zeitschrift für Dialektologie und Linguistik Beihefte*, 32: 501-506.

Paradis, M. 1980b. language and thought in bilinguals. *LACUS Forum*, 6: 420-431.

Paradis, M. 1981. Neurolinguistic organization of a bilingual's two languages. *LACUS Forum*, 7: 486-494.

Paradis, M. (ed.) 1983. *Readings on aphasia in bilinguals and polyglots*. Montreal: Marcel Didier.

Paradis, M. 1984. Aphasie et traduction. *META: Translator's Journal*, 29: 57-67.

Paradis, M. 1985. On the representation of two languages in one brain. *Language Sciences*, 7: 1-39.

Paradis, M. 1987a. Le bilinguisme. In J. Rondal & J.-P. Thibaut (eds.), *Problèmes de psycholinguistique* (pp. 421-489). Brussels: Mardaga.

Paradis, M. 1987b. Neurolinguistic perspectives on bilingualism. In M. Paradis & G. Libben, *The assessment of bilingual aphasia* (pp.1-17). Hillsdale, NJ: Lawrence Erlbaum.

Paradis, M. 1987c. The neurofunctional modularity of cognitive skills: Evidence from Japanese alexia and polyglot aphasia. In E. Keller & M. Gopnik (eds.), *Motor and sensory processes of language* (pp. 277-289). Hillsdale, NJ: Lawrence Erlbaum Associates.

Paradis, M. 1989a. Bilingual and polyglot aphasia. In F. Boller & J. Grafman (eds.), *Handbook of neuropsychology* (vol. 2, pp.117-140). Amsterdam: Elsevier.

Paradis, M. 1989b. Linguistic parameters in the diagnosis of dyslexia in Japanese and Chinese. In P.G. Aaron and R. M. Joshi (eds.), *Reading and writing disorders in different orthographic systems* (pp. 231-266). (NATO ASI Series D, vol. 52.) Dordrecht: Kluwer.

Paradis, M. 1990a. Language lateralization in bilinguals: Enough already! *Brain and Language*, 39: 576-586. Reprinted in L. Wei (ed.) *The bilingualism reader* (pp.394-401). London: Routledge, 2000.

Paradis, M. 1990b. A psycholinguistic model of bilingual performance. Paper presented at the International Interdisciplinary Symposium on the Linguistic Brain: Models of Language Performance, University of Toronto, 23 February.

Paradis, M. 1992a. The Loch Ness Monster approach to bilingual language lateralization: A response to Berquier and Ashton. *Brain and Language*, 43: 534-537.

Paradis, M. 1992b. Neurosciences et apprentissage des langues. in D. Girard (ed.), *Enseignement des langues dans le monde d'aujourd'hui* (pp. 21-31). Paris: Hachette.

Paradis, M. 1993a. Linguistic, psycholinguistic, and neurolinguistic aspects of "interference" in bilingual speakers: The Activation Threshold Hypothesis. *International Journal of Psycholinguistics*, 9: 133-145.

Paradis M. 1993b. Multilingualism and aphasia. In G. Blanken, J. Dittmann, H. Grimm, J.C. Marshall, and C.-W Wallesch (eds.), *Handbooks of linguistics and communication sciences* (vol. 9, pp. 278-288). New York: Walter de Gruyter.

Paradis, M. (ed.) 1993c. *Foundations of aphasia rehabilitation*. Oxford: Pergamon Press.

Paradis, M. 1993d. Bilingual aphasia rehabilitation. In M. Paradis (ed.), *Foundations of aphasia rehabilitation* (pp. 413-426). Oxford: Pergamon Press.

Paradis, M. 1994. Neurolinguistic aspects of implicit and explicit memory: Implications for bilingualism. In N. Ellis (ed.), *Implicit and explicit learning of second languages* (pp. 393-419). London: Academic Press.

Paradis, M. 1995a. Another sighting of differential language laterality in multilinguals, this time in Loch Tok Pisin: Comments on Wuillemin, Richardson & Lynch (1994). *Brain and Language*, 49: 173-186.

Paradis, M. 1995b. The need for distinctions. In M. Paradis (ed.), *Aspects of bilingual aphasia* (pp. 1-9). Oxford: Pergamon Press.

Paradis, M. 1996. Selective deficit in one language is not a demonstration of different anatomical representation. Comments on Gomez-Tortosa et al. (1995). *Brain and Language*, 54: 170-173.

Paradis, M. 1997a. The cognitive neuropsychology of bilingualism. In A. de Groot & J. Kroll (eds.), *Tutorials in bilingualism: Psycholinguistic perspectives* (pp. 331-354). Hillsdale, NJ: Lawrence Erlbaum Associates.

Paradis, M. 1997b. Représentation lexicale et conceptuelle chez les bilingues: Deux langues, trois systèmes. In J. Auger & Y. Rose (eds.), *Explorations du lexique* (pp. 15-27). Quebec City: CIRAL.

Paradis, M. (ed.) 1998a. *Pragmatics in neurogenic communication disorders*. Oxford: Pergamon press.

Paradis, M. 1998b. Neurolinguistic aspects of the native speaker. In R. Singh (ed.), *The native speaker: Multilingual perspectives* (pp. 205-219). London: Sage Publications.

Paradis, M. 1998c. The other side of language. *Journal of Neurolinguistics*, 11: 1-10.

Paradis, M. 2000a. An integrated neurolinguistic theory of bilingualism (1976-2000). Presidential address at the 27th LACUS Forum, Rice University, Texas, 29 July. Published in *LACUS Forum*, 27: 5-15, 2001.

Paradis, M. 2000b. Cerebral representation of bilingual concepts. *Bilingualism: Language and Cognition*, 3: 22-24.

Paradis, M. 2000c. Generalizable outcomes of bilingual aphasia research. *Folia Phoniatrica et Logopaedica*, 52: 54-64.

Paradis, M. 2001a. Bilingual and polyglot aphasia. In R.S. Berndt (ed.), *Handbook of neuropsychology* (Second Edition, vol. 3, pp. 69-91). Oxford: Elsevier Science.

Paradis, M. (ed.) 2001b. *Manifestations of aphasia symptoms in different languages*. Oxford: Pergamon Press.

Paradis, M. 2001c. The need for awareness of aphasia symptoms in different languages. *Journal of Neurolinguistics*, 14: 85-91.

Paradis, M. 2003. The bilingual Loch Ness Monster raises its non-asymmetric head again—Or, why bother with such cumbersome notions as validity and reliability? Comments on Evans et al. (2002). *Brain and Language*, 87: 441-448.

Paradis, M., & Goldblum, M.-C. 1989. Selective crossed aphasia in one of a trilingual's languages followed by antagonistic recovery. *Brain and Language*, 36: 62-75.

Paradis, M., Goldblum, M.-C., & Abidi, R. 1982. Alternate antagonism with paradoxical translation behavior in two bilingual aphasic patients. *Brain and Language*, 15: 55-69.

Paradis, M., & Gopnik, M. 1997. Compensatory strategies in familial language impairment. *Journal of Neurolinguistics*, 10: 173-185.

Paradis, M. Hagiwara, H., & Hildebrandt, H. 1985. *Neurolinguistic aspects of the Japanese writing system*. New York: Academic Press.

Paradis, M., & Lecours, A.R. 1979. L'aphasie chez les bilingues et les polyglottes. In A.R. Lecours, F. Lhermitte et al., *L'Aphasie* (pp. 605-616). Paris: Flammarion.

Paradis, M., & Libben, G. 1987. *The assessment of bilingual aphasia*. Hillsdale, NJ: Lawrence Erlbaum Associates.

Paradis, M., & Libben, G. 1993. *Evaluación de la afasia en los bilingües*. Barcelona: Masson.

Paradis, M., & Libben, G. 1999. *Valutazione dell'afasia bilingue*. Bologna: EMS.

Paradis, M., & Libben, G. 2003. *Shuangyu shiyuzheng de pinggu*. Guangzhou: Jinan daxue chubanshe.

Parker, T.W. 1992. Verbal implicit recall of subject performed tasks but not verbal tasks in alcoholic Korsakoff's amnesics. Paper presented at the 22nd Annual Meeting of the Society for Neuroscience, Anaheim, California, 28 October.

Parkin, A.J. 1989. The development and nature of implicit memory. In S. Lewandowsky, J.C. Dunn, & K. Kirsner (eds.), *Implicit memory: Theoretical issues* (pp. 231-240). Hillsdale, NJ: Lawrence Erlbaum Associates.

Parkin, A.J., & Russo, R. 1990. Implicit and explicit memory and the automatic/effortful distinction. *European Journal of Cognitive Psychology*, 2: 71-80.

Parkin, A.J., & Streete, S. 1988. Implicit and explicit memory in young children and adults. *British Journal of Psychology*, 79: 361-369.

Patterson, D.W., & Schmidt, L.A. 2003. Neuroanatomy of the human affective system. *Brain and Cognition*, 52: 24-26.

Pavlenko, A. 1999. New approaches to concepts in bilingual memory. *Bilingualism: Language and Cognition*, 2: 209-230.

Pavlenko, A. 2002. Conceptual change in bilingual memory: A NeoWhorfian approach. In F. Fabbro (ed.), *Advances in the neurolinguistics of bilingualism* (pp. 69-94). Udine: Forum-Udine University Press.

Peal, E. & Lambert, W.E. 1962. The Relation of Bilingualism to Intelligence. *Psychological Monographs, General and Applied*, 76: 1 - 23.

Penfield, W. 1965. Conditioning the uncommitted cortex for language learning. *Brain*, 88: 787-798.

Penfield, W., & Roberts, L. 1959. *Speech and brain-mechanisms*. Princeton, NJ: Princeton University Press.

Perani, D., Abutalebi, J., Paulesu, E., Brambati, S., Scifo, P., Cappa, S.F., & Fazio, F. 2003. The role of age of acquisition and language usage in early, high-proficient bilinguals: An fMRI study during verbal fluency. *Human Brain Mapping*, 19: 170-182.

Perani, D., Dehaene, S., Grassi, F., Cohen, L., Cappa, S., Paulesu, E., Dupoux, E., Fazio, F., & Mehler, J. 1996. Brain processing of native and foreign languages. *NeuroReport*, 7: 2439-2444.

Perani, D., Paulesu, E., Sebastian-Gallés, N., Dupoux, E., Dehaene, D., Bettinardi, V., Cappa, S., Fazio, F., & Mehler, J. 1998. The bilingual brain: Proficiency and age of acquisition of the second language. *Brain*, 121: 1841-1852.

Perecman, E. 1984. Spontaneous translation and language mixing in a polyglot aphasic. *Brain and Language*, 23: 43-53.

Perkins, L., & Lesser, R. 1993. Pragmatics applied to aphasia rehabilitation. In M. Paradis (ed.), *Foundations of aphasia rehabilitation* (pp. 211-246). Oxford: Pergamon Press.

Persinger, M.A., Chellew-Belanger, G., & Tiller, S.G. 2002. Bilingual men but not women display less left ear but not right ear accuracy during dichotic listening compared to monolinguals. *International Journal of Neuroscience*, 112: 55-63.

Peuser, G. 1978. Vergleichende Aphasieforschung und Aphasie bei Polyglotten. *Folia Phoniatrica*, 12: 123-128.

Piazza Gordon, D., & Zatorre, R.J. 1981. A right-ear advantage for dichotic listening in bilingual children. *Brain and Language*, 13: 389-396.

Pihko, E., Ilmoniemi, R.J., Mäkälä, A.M., & Mäkinen, V. 2001a. Processing of native versus later-acquired languages. *NeuroImage*, 13 (6 Part 2): 585.

Pihko, E., Mäkinen, V., Nikouline, V.V., Mäkälä, A.M., Ilmoniemi, R.J. 2001b. Visual attention to words of native versus later acquired languages: A magnetoencephalographic study in humans. *Neuroscience Letters*, 310: 33-36.

Pihko, E., Nikulin, V.V., & Ilmoniemi, R.J. 2002. Visual attention to words in different languages in bilinguals: A magnetoencephalographic study. *NeuroImage*, 17: 1830-1836.

Pike, K. 1971. Crucial questions in the development of tagmemics: The sixties and seventies. In Richard J. O'Brien (ed.), Report of the 22nd Annual Round Table Meeting of Linguistics and Language Studies (pp. 79-98). *Monograph Series on Languages and Linguistics*, 24. Washington, DC: Georgetown University Press.

Pillai, J.J., Araque, J., Allison, J.D., & Lavin, T. 2001. Functional MRI study of semantic and phonological language processing in bilingual subjects. *Radiology*, 221 (3, suppl.): 487.

Pillai, J.J., Araque, J.M., Allison, J.D., Sethuraman, S., Loring, D.W., Thiruvaiyaru, D., Ison, C.B., Balan, A., & Lavin, T. 2003. Functional MRI study of semantic and phonological language processing in bilingual subjects: Preliminary findings. *NeuroImage*, 19: 565-576.

Pilotti, M., Meade, M.L., & Gallo, D.A. 2003. Implicit and explicit measures of memory for perceptual information in young adults, healthy older adults, and patients with Alzheimer's disease. *Experimental Aging Research*, 29: 15-32.

Pitres, A. 1895. Etude sur l'aphasie chez les polyglottes. *Revue de Médecine*, 15: 873-899.

Pizzamiglio, L., De Pascalis, C. & Vignati, A. 1974. Stability of dichotic listening test. *Cortex*, 10: 203-205.

Poeppel, D. 1996. A critical review of PET studies of phonological processing. *Brain and Language*, 55: 317-351.

Poulisse, N. 1999. *Slips of the tongue: Speech errors in first and second language production*. Amsterdam: John Benjamins

Poulisse, N., & Bongaerts, T. 1994. First language use in second language production. *Applied Linguistics*, 15: 36-57.

Pouratian, N., Bookheimer, S., O'Farrell, A., Sicotte, N., Cannestra, A., Becker, D., & Toga, A. 2000. Optical imaging of bilingual cortical representations. *Journal of Neurosurgery*, 93: 676-681.

Price, C.J., & Friston, K.J. 1999. Scanning patients with tasks they can perform. *Human Brain Mapping*, 8: 102-108.

Price, C., Green, D., & von Studnitz, R. 1999. A functional imaging study of translation and language switching. *Brain*, 122: 2221-2235.

Price, C.J., Wise, R.J., Warburton, E.A., Morre, C.S., Howard, D., Patterson, K., Frackowiak, R.S., & Friston, K.J. 1996. Hearing and saying—The functional neuro-anatomy of auditory word processing. *Brain*, 119: 919-931.

Pricewilliams, D., & Ramirez, M. 1977. Divergent thinking, cultural difference, and bilingualism. *The Journal of Social Psychology*, 103: 3-11.

Proverbio, A.M., Cok, B., & Zani, A. 2002. Electrophysiological measures of language processing in bilinguals. Journal of Cognitive Neuroscience, 14: 994-1017.

Pu, Y.L., Liu, H.L., Spinks, J.A., Mahankali, S., Xiong, J.H., Feng, C.M., Tan, L.H., Fox, P.T., & Gao, J.H. 2001. Cerebral hemodynamic response in Chinese (first) and English (second) language processing revealed by event-related functional MRI. *Magnetic Resonance Imaging*, 19: 643-647.

Pugh, K.R., Shaywitz, B.A., Shaywitz, S.E., Constable, R.T., Shudlarski, P., Fulbright, R.K., Bronen, R.A., Shankweiler, D.P., Katz, L., Fletcher, J.M., & Gore, J.C. 1996. Cerebral organization of component processes in reading. *Brain*, 119: 122-11238.

Pulvermüller, F. 1992. Constituents of a neurological theory of language. *Concepts in Neuroscience*, 3: 157-200.

Rafal, R., & Henik, A. 1994. The neurology of inhibition: Integrating controlled and automatic processes. In D. Dagenbach & T.H. Carr (eds.), *Inhibitory processes in attention, memory, and language* (pp. 1-51). San Diego: Academic Press.

Raichle, M.E., Fiez, J.A., Videen, T.O., MacLeod, A.-M.K., Pardo, J.V., Fox, P.T., & Petersen, S.E. 1994. Practice-related changes in human brain functional anatomy during nonmotor learning. *Cerebral Cortex*, 4: 8-26.

Ramsey, N.F., Sommer, I.E.C., Rutten, G.J., & Kahn, R.S. 2001. Combined analysis of language tasks in fMRI improves assessment of hemispheric dominance for language functions in individual subjects. *NeuroImage*, 13: 719-733.

Ramsey, N.F., Tallent, K., van Gelderen, P., Frank, J.A., Moonen, C.T.W., Weinberger, D.R. 1996. Reproducibility of human 3D fMRI brain maps acquired during a motor task. *Human Brain Mapping*, 4: 113-121.

Rangamani, G.N. 1989. Aphasia and multilingualism: Clinical evidence towards the cerebral organization of language. Unpublished Ph.D. dissertation, The University of Mysore.

Ranganath, C., Johnson, M.K., & D'Esposito, M. 2003. Prefrontal activity associated with working memory and episodic long-term memory. *Neuropsychologia*, 41: 378-389.

Rapport, R.L., Tan, C.T., & Whitaker, H.A. 1983. Language function and dysfunction among Chinese- and English-speaking polyglots: Cortical stimulation, Wada testing, and clinical studies. *Brain and Language*, 18: 342-366.

Rasmus, F., Nespor, M., & Mehler, J. 1999. Correlates of the linguistic rhythm in the speech signal. *Cognition*, 73: 265-292.

Reber, A.S. 1976. Implicit learning of synthetic languages: The role of instructional set. *Journal of Experimental Psychology: Human Learning and Memory*, 2: 88-94.

Reber, A.S., Kassin, S., Lewis, S., & Cantor, G. 1980. On the relationship between implicit and explicit modes in the learning of a complex rule structure. *Journal of Experimental Psychology: Human Learning and Memory*, 6:. 492-502.

Rehak, A., Kaplan, J.A., & Gardner, H. 1992. Sensitivity to conversational deviance in right-hemisphere-damaged patients. *Brain and Language*, 42: 203-217.

Rehak, A., Kaplan, J.A., Weylman, S.T., Kelly, B., Brownell, H.H., & Gardner, H. 1992. Story processing in right-hemisphere brain-damaged patients. *Brain and Language*, 42: 320-336.

Ribot, T. 1881. *Les maladies de la mémoire*. Paris: G. Baillère.

Ricciardelli, L.A. 1992. Bilingualism and cognitive development in relation to threshold theory. *Journal of Psycholinguistic Research*, 21: 301-316.

Richardson, B., & Wuillemin, D. 1995. Reply. *Brain and Language*, 49: 187.

Robinson, P. 1995. Attention, memory, and the "noticing" hypothesis. *Language Learning*, 45: 283-331.

Rodriguez-Fornells, A., Rotte, M., Heinze, H.J., Nösselt, T., & Münte, T.F. 2002. Brain potential and functional MRI evidence for how to handle two languages with one brain. *Nature*, 415: 1026-1029.

Roelofs, A. 2003a. Shared phonological encoding processes and representations of languages in bilingual speakers. *Language and Cognitive Processes*, 18: 175-204.

Roelofs, A. 2003b. Goal-referenced selection of verbal action: Modeling attentional control in the Stroop task. *Psychological Review*, 110: 88-125

Rohde, A. 2001. The early bird catches the worm: Bilingual preschool education in Germany —A psycholinguistic perspective. *Drustvena Istrazivanja*, 10: 991-1023.

Rolls, E.T. 1999. *The brain and emotion*. Oxford: Oxford University Press.

Roman, M., Brownell, H.H., Potter, H.H., Seibold, M.S., & Gardner, H. 1987. Script knowledge in right hemisphere damaged and in normal elderly adults. *Brain and Language*, 31: 151-170.

Ross, E.D., Edmondson, J.A., Seibert, G.B., & Homan, R.W. 1988. Acoustic analysis of affective prosody during right-sided Wada test: A within-subjects verification of the right hemisphere's role in language. *Brain and Language*, 33: 128-145.

Rouleau, I., & Labrecque, R. 1991. Selective and permanent retrograde amnesia following a unilateral lesion: A case study. *Journal of Clinical and Experimental Neuropsychology*, 13: 22.

Roux, F.E., & Tremoulet, M. 2002. Organization of language areas in bilingual patients: a cortical stimulation study. *Journal of Neurosurgery*, 97: 857-864.

Rumsey, J.M., & Hanahan, A.P. 1990. National-Institute-of-Mental-Health getting it right—Performance of high-functioning autistic adults on a right hemisphere battery. *Journal of Clinical and Experimental Neuropsychology*, 12: 81.

Saint-Cyr, J.A., Taylor, A.E. & Lang, A.E., 1987. Procedural learning impairment in basal ganglia disease. *Journal of Clinical and Experimental Neuropsychology*, 9: 280.

Samuels, R. 1998. Evolutionary psychology and the massive modularity hypothesis. *British Journal for the Philosophy of Science*, 49: 575-602.

Samuels, R. 2000. Massively modular minds: Evolutionary psychology and cognitive architecture. In P. Carruthers & A. Chamberlain (eds.), *Evolution and the mind: Modularity, language and meta-cognition* (pp. 13-46). Cambridge: Cambridge University Press.

Sasanuma, S., & Park, H.S. 1995. Patterns of language deficits in two Korean-Japanese bilingual aphasic patients—A clinical report. In M. Paradis (ed.), *Aspects of bilingual aphasia* (pp. 111-122). Oxford: Pergamon Press.

Satz, P. 1977. Laterality tests: An inferential problem. *Cortex*, 13: 208-212.

Savignon, S.J. 1976. On the other side of the desk: Teacher attitudes and motivation in second language learning. *Canadian Modern Language Review*, 32: 295-305.

Scarborough, D., Gerard, L., & Cortese, C. 1984. Independence of lexical access in bilingual word recognition. *Journal of Verbal Learning and Verbal Behavior*, 23: 84-99.

Schacter, D.L., & Moscovitch, M. 1984. Infants, amnesics, and dissociable memory systems. In M. Moscovitch (ed.), *Infant memory* (pp.173-216). New York: Plenum.

Schall, J.D., Stuphorn, V., & Brown, J.W. 2002. Monitoring and control of action by the frontal lobes. *Neuron*, 36: 309-3222.

Scheibel, A.B. 1991. Some structural and developmental correlates of human speech. In K.R. Gibson & A.C. Peterson (eds.), *Brain maturation and cognitive development* (pp. 345-353). New York: Aldine De Gruyter.

Schlanger, B.B., Schlanger, P., & Gerstman, L.J. 1986. The perception of emotionally toned sentences by right hemisphere-damaged and aphasic subjects. *Brain and Language*, 3: 396-403.

Schlosser, M.J., Aojagi, N., Fulbright, R.K., Gore, J.C., & McCarthy, G. 1998. Functional MRI studies of auditory comprehension. *Human Brain Mapping*, 6: 1-13.

Schmidt, R. 1990. The role of consciousness in second language learning. *Applied Linguistics*, 11: 129-158.

Schmidt, R. 1994. Implicit learning and the cognitive unconscious: Of artificial grammars and SLA. In N. Ellis (ed.), *Implicit and explicit learning of second languages* (pp. 165-209). London: Academic Press.

Schneiderman, E.I., & Desmarais, C. 1988. A neuropsychological substrate for talent in second-language acquisition. In L.K. Obler & D. Fein (eds.), *The exceptional brain* (pp. 103-126). New York: Guilford Press.

Schneiderman, E.I., Murasugi, K.F., & Saddy, J.D. 1992. Story arrangement ability in right brain-damaged patients. *Brain and Language*, 43: 107-120.

Schönle, P., & Breuninger, H. 1977. Untersuchungen mit dichotischen Hörtesten bei Zweisprachigkeit. *Archiv für Ohren - Nasen - und Kehlkopfheilkunde*, 26: 574.

Schulpen, B., Dijkstra, T., Schriefers, H.J, & Hasper, M. 2003. Recognition of interlingual homophones in bilingual auditory word recognition. *Journal of Experimental Psychology—Human Perception and Performance*, 29: 1155-1178.

Schulze, H.A.F. 1968. Unterschiedliche Rückbildung einer sensorischer und einer ideokinetischen motorischen Aphasie bei einem Polyglotten. *Psychiatrie, Neurologie und medizinische Psychologie*, 20: 441-445.

Schumann, J.H. 1990. The role of the amygdala as a mediator of affect and cognition in second language acquisition. In J.E. Alatis (ed.), *Georgetown University Round Table on Languages and Linguistics* (pp. 169-176). Washington, DC: Georgetown University Press.

Schumann, J.H 1998. The neurobiology of affect in language. *Language Learning*, 48: Supplement 1.

Schwalbe, J. 1920. Über die Aphasie bei Polyglotten. *Neurologisches Zentralblatt*, 39: 265. Translated in Paradis (1983), 155.

Schwartz, M.F., Saffran, E.M., & Marin, O.S. 1980. The word order problem in agrammatism. *Brain and Language*, 10: 249-262.

Schwartz, S., & Kirsner, K. 1982. Laterality effects in visual information processing: Hemispheric specialization or the orienting of attention? *Quarterly Journal of Experimental Psychology*, 34A: 61-67.

Schwartz, S., & Kirsner, K. 1984. Can group differences in hemispheric asymmetry be inferred from behavioral laterality indices? *Brain and Cognition*, 3: 57-70.

Scoresby-Jackson R.E: 1867. Case of aphasia with right hemiplegia. *Edinborough Medical Journal*: 12: 696-706.

Scovel, T. 1982. Questions concerning the application of neurolinguistic research to second language learning/teaching. *TESOL Quarterly*, 6: 323-331.

Scoville, W.B., & Milner, B. 1957. Loss of recent memory after bilateral hippocampal lesions. *Journal of Neurological and Neurosurgical Psychiatry*, 20: 11-12.

Sebastian-Gallés, N., & Bosch, L. 2001. On becoming and being bilingual. In E. Dupoux (ed.), *Language, brain and cognitive development* (pp. 379-393). Cambridge, MA: MIT Press.

Segalowitz, N, 1986. Skilled reading in the second language. In Jyotsna Vaid (ed.), *Language Processing in Bilinguals: Psycholinguistic and Neuropsychological perspectives* (pp. 3-19). Hillsdale, NJ: Erlbaum.

Segalowitz, N. 2000. Automaticity and attentional skill in fluent performance. In H. Riggenbach (ed.), *Perspectives on fluency* (pp. 200-219). Ann Arbor, MI: University of Michigan Press.

Segalowitz, N., Poulsen, C., & Segalowitz, S. 1999. RT coefficient of variation is differentially sensitive to executive control involvement in an attention switching task. *Brain and Cognition*, 40: 255-258.

Segalowitz, N., & Segalowitz, S. 1993. Skilled performance, practice, and the differentiation of speed-up from automatization effects: Evidence from second language word recognition. *Applied Psycholinguistics*, 14: 369-385.

Segalowitz, S.J. 1983. *Two sides of the brain*. Englewood Cliffs, NJ: Prentice-Hall.

Segalowitz, S.J. 1986. Validity and reliability of noninvasive measures of brain lateralization. In J. Obrzut & D. Hines (eds.), *Child neuropsychology*, (vol.1, pp. 191-208). Orlando: Academic Press.

Segalowitz, S., Segalowitz, N., & Wood, A. 1998. Assessing the development of automaticity in second language word recognition. *Applied Psycholinguistics*, 19: 53-67.

Seliger, H.W. 1982. On the possible role of the right-hemisphere in 2nd language-acquisition. *TESOL Quarterly*, 16: 307-314.

Semenza, C., Spacal, M., Girelli, L., & Kobal., J. 1999. Derivation and prefixation in Slovenian: A study in aphasia. *Brain and Language*, 69: 276-278.

Sergent, J., Zuck, E., Levesque, M., & MacDonald, B. 1992. Positron emission tomography study of letter and object processing: Empirical findings and methodological considerations. *Cerebral Cortex*. 2: 68-80.

Service, R.F. 1993. Making modular memories. *Science*, 260: 1876.

Shallice, T. 1982. Specific impairments of planning. *Philosophical Transactions of the Royal Society London* B, 298: 199-209.

Shallice, T. 1988. *From neuropsychology to mental structure*. Cambridge: Cambridge University Press.

Shallice, T. 2001. Fractionating the supervisory system. *Brain and Cognition*, 47: 30.

Shammi, P., & Stuss, D. 1999. Humor appreciation: A role of the right frontal lobe. *Brain*, 122: 657-666.

Shannahoff-Khalsa, D. 1984. Rhythms and reality: The dynamics of the mind. *Psychology Today*, Sept.: 72-73.

Shanon, B. 1982. Lateralization effects in the perception of Hebrew and English words. *Brain and Language*, 17: 107-123.

Shapiro, B.E., & Danly, M. 1985. The role of the right hemisphere in the control of speech prosody in propositional and affective contexts. *Brain and Language*, 25: 19-36.

Sherry, D.F., & Schacter, D.L., 1987. The evolution of multiple memory systems. *Psychological Review*, 94: 439-454.

Sidtis, J. 1982. Predicting brain organization from dichotic listening performance: Cortical and subcortical functional asymmetries contribute to perceptual asymmetries. *Brain and Language*, 17: 287-300.

Siegal, M., Carrington, J., & Radel, M. 1996. Theory of mind and pragmatic understanding following right hemisphere damage. *Brain and Language*, 53: 40-50.

Silverberg, R., & Gordon, H.W. 1979. Differential aphasia in two bilinguals. *Neurology*, 29: 51-55.

Silveri, M.C., & Misciagna, S. 2000. Language, memory, and the cerebellum. *Journal of Neurolinguistics*, 13: 129-143.

Simos, O., Castillo, E., Francis, J. et al. 2001. Mapping receptive language cortex in bilingual volunteers by using magnetic source imaging. *Journal of Neurosurgery*, 95: 76-81.

Simpson, G.B., & Burgess, C. 1985. Activation and selection processes in the regognition of ambiguous words. *Journal of Experimental Psychology: Human Perception and Performance*, 11: 28-39.

Skutnabb-Kangas, T. 1980. Semilingualism and the education of migrant children as a means of reproducing the caste of assembly-line workers. *Tijdschrift van de Vrije Universiteit Brussel*, 21: 100-136.

Soares, C. 1982. Converging evidence for left hemisphere language lateralization in bilinguals. *Neuropsychologia*, 20: 653-660.

Soares, C. 1984. Left-hemisphere language lateralization in bilinguals: Use of the concurrent activities paradigm. *Brain and Language*, 23: 86-96.

Soares, C., & Grosjean, F. 1981. Left hemisphere language lateralization in bilinguals and monolinguals. *Perception and Psychophysics*, 29: 599-604.

Soares, C. & Grosjean, F. 1984. Bilinguals in a monolingual and a bilingual speech mode: The effect of lexical access. *Memory and Cognition*, 12: 380-386.

Solin, D. 1989. The systematic misrepresentation of bilingual crossed aphasia data and its consequences. *Brain and Language*, 36: 92-116.

Smith N., & Tsimpli, I.M. 1995. *The Mind of a Savant. Language Learning and Modularity*. Oxford: Blackwell.

Sperber, D. & Wilson, D. 2002. Pragmatics, modularity and mind-reading. *Mind and Language*, 17: 3-23.

Sperry, R.W. 1974. Lateral specialization in surgically separated hemispheres. In F.O. Schmitt and F.G. Worden (eds.), *The neurosciences, third study program* (pp. 5-19). Cambridge, MA: MIT Press.

Sperry, R.W., Gazzaniga, M.S., & Bogen, J.E., 1969. Interhemispheric relationships: The neocortical commisures; syndromes of hemisphere disconnection. In P.J.

Vinken and G.W. Bruyn (eds.), *Handbook of clinical neurology* (vol. 4, pp. 273-290). Amsterdam: North Holland.

Spivey, M.S. & Marian, V. 1999. Cross talk between native and second languages: Partial activation of an irrelevant lexicon. *Psychological Science*, 10: 201-284.

Sridhar, S.N. & Sridhar, K.K. 1980. The syntax and psycholinguistics of bilingual code mixing. *Canadian Journal of Psychology*, 34: 407-416.

Starck, R., Genesee, F., Lambert, W., & Seitz, M. 1977. Multiple language experience and the development of cerebral dominance. In S. Segalowitz & F. Gruber (eds.)., *Language development and neurological theory* (pp. 48-55). New York: Academic Press.

Stemmer, B., & Whitaker, H.A. 1997. *Handbook of neurolinguistics*. San Diego: Academic Press.

Stephan, K.E., Marshall, J.C., Friston, K.J., Rowe, J.B., Ritzl, A., Zilles, K., & Fink, G.R. (2003). Lateralized cognitive processes and lateralized task control in the human brain. *Science*, 301: 384-386.

Straüssler, E. 1912. Ein Fall von passagerer systematischer Sprachstörung bei einem Polyglotten, verbunden mit rechtsseitigen transitorischen Gehörshalluzinationen. *Zeitschrift für die gesamte Neurologie und Psychiatrie*, 9: 503-511. Translated in Paradis (1983), 94-101.

Sussman, H. 1989. A reassessment of the time-sharing paradigm with ANCOVA. *Brain and Language*, 37: 514-520.

Sussman, H., Franklin, P., & Simon, T. 1982. Bilingual speech: Bilateral control? *Brain and Language*, 15: 125-142.

Talairach, J., & Tournoux, P. 1988. *Co-planar stereotaxic atlas of the human brain*. Stuttgart: Thieme.

Tan, L.H., Feng, C.M., Liu, H.L., Shen, G., & Gao, J.H. 2001a. Semantic representations in the bilingual brain. *NeuroImage, 13* (6 Part 2): S611.

Tan, L.H., Spinks, J.A., Feng, C.M., Siok, W.T., Perfetti, C.A., Xiong, J.H., Fox, P.T., & Gao, J.H. 2003. Neural systems of second language reading are shaped by native language. *Human Brain Mapping*, 18: 158-166.

Tan, L., Spinks, J., Perfetti, C., Fox, P. & Gao, J-H. 2001b. Neural systems of second language learning are shaped by native language. *NeuroImage, 13* (6 Part 2): S612.

Taylor Sarno, M. (ed.) 1998. *Acquired aphasia* (3rd edition). San Diego: Academic Press.

Teng, E.L. 1981. Dichotic ear difference is a poor index for the functional asymmetry between the cerebral hemispheres. *Neuropsychologia*, 19: 235-240.

Tenyi, T., Herold, R., Szili, I.M., & Trixler, M. 2002. Schizophrenics show a failure in the decoding of violations of conversational implicatures. *Psychopathology*, 35: 25-27.

Terrace, H.S. 1979. *Nim*. New York: Alfred A. Knopf.

Thiery, C. 1976. Le bilinguisme vrai. *Etudes de linguistique appliquée*, 24: 52-63.

Thompson, C.K., & Shapiro, L.P. 1995. Training sentence production in agrammatism: Implications for normal and disordered language. *Brain and Language*, 50: 201-224.

Tomioka, N. 2002a. How to distinguish procedural and declarative memory use in L2 processing with a behavioral test. Paper presented at the International Linguistics Association 47th Annual Conference. York University, Toronto, 6 April.

Tomioka, N. 2002b. A bilingual language production model. Paper presented at the International Symposium on the Multimodality of Human Communication, University of Toronto, 5 May.

Tomioka, N., & Paradis, M. 2002. Cerebral processes involved in reading as a function of the structure of various writing systems. Comments on Nakada et al. (2001). *Neuroscience Research*, 43: 87-89.

Tompkins, C.A. 1990. Knowledge and strategies for processing lexical metaphor after right- or left-hemisphere brain damage. *Journal of Speech and Hearing Research*, 33: 307-316.

Tompkins, C.A., Baumgaertner, A., Lehman, M.L., & Fossett, T.R. 1995. Suppression and discourse comprehension in right-brain-damaged adults. *Brain and Language*, 51: 181-183.

Tompkins, C.A., Baumgaertner, A., Lehman, M.L., & Fossett, T.R. 1997. Suppression and discourse comprehension in right-brain-damaged adults: A preliminary report. *Aphasiology*, 11: 505-519.

Tompkins, C.A., Boada, R., & McGarry, K. 1992. The access and processing of familiar idioms by brain-damaged and normally aging adults. *Journal of Speech and Hearing Research*, 35: 626-637.

Tompkins, C.A., & Flowers, C.R. 1985. Perception of emotional intonation by brain-damaged adults: The influence of task processing levels. *Journal of Speech and Hearing Research*, 28: 527-538.

Tompkins, C.A., & Mateer, C.A. 1985. Right hemisphere appreciation of prosodic and linguistic indication of implicit attitude. *Brain and Language*, 24: 185-203.

Torrance, A.P., Gowan, J.C., Wu, J.M., & Alliotti, N.C. 1970. Creative functioning of monolingual and bilingual children in Singapore. *Journal of Educational Psychology*, 61: 72-75.

Trudeau, N., Colozzo, P., Sylvestre, V., & Ska, B. 2003. Language following functional left hemispherectomy in a bilingual teenager. *Brain and Cognition*, 53: 384-388.

Tulving, E. 1983. *Elements of episodic memory*. Oxford: Oxford University Press.

Turkewitz, G. 1988. A prenatal source for the development of hemispheric specialization. In D.L. Molfese & S.J. Segalowitz (eds.), *Brain Lateralization in children* (pp. 73-81). New York: The Guilford Press.

Turner, C.W., & Fischler, I.S. 1993. Speeded tests of implicit knowleedge. *Journal of Experimental Psychology—Learning Memory and Cognition*, 19: 1165-1177.

Ullman, M.T., Corkin, S., Coppola, M., Hickok, G., Growdon, J.H., Koroshetz, W.J., & Pinker, S. 1997. A neural dissociation within language: Evidence that the mental dictionary is part of declarative memory, and that grammatical rules are processed by the procedural system. *Journal of Cognitive Neuroscience*, 9: 266-276.

Urbanik, A., Binder, M., Sobiecka, B., & Kozub, J. 2001. fMRI study of sentence generation by early bilinguals differing in proficiency level. *Rivista di Neuroradiologia*, 14: 11-16.

Vaid, J. 1983. Bilingualism and brain lateralization. In S. Segalowitz (ed.) *Language functions and brain organization* (pp. 315-339). New York: Academic Press.

Vaid, J. 2002. Bilingualism. In V.S. Ramachandran (ed.), *Encyclopedia of the Human Brain* (Vol. 1, pp. 417-434). San Diego, CA : Academic Press.

Vaid, J., & Chengappa, S. 1988. Assigning linguistic roles: Sentence interpretation in normal and aphasic Kannada-English bilinguals. *Journal of Neurolinguistics*, 3: 161-184.

Vaid, J., & Genesee, F. 1980. Neuropsychological approaches to bilingualism: A critical review. *Canadian Journal of Psychology*, 34: 417-445.

Vaid, J., & Hall, D.G. 1991. Neuropsychological perspectives on bilingualism: Right, left, and center. In A. Reynolds (ed.), *Bilingualism, multiculturalism and second language learning* (pp. 81-112). Hillsdale, NJ: Lawrence Erlbaum Associates.

Vaid, J., & Hull, R. 2002. Re-envisioning the bilingual brain using functional neuroimaging: Methodological and interpretive issues. In F. Fabbro (ed.), *Advances in the neurolinguistics of bilingualism* (pp. 315-356). Udine: Forum-Undine University Press.

Vaid, J., & Lambert, W.E. 1979. Differential cerebral involvement in the cognitive functioning of bilinguals. *Brain and Language*, 8: 92-110.

Valin, R. 1994. *L'envers des mots: Analyse psychomécanique du langage.* Sainte-Foy, QC: Presses de l'Université Laval.

Van Hell, J.G., & de Groot, A.M.B. 1998. Conceptual representation in bilingual memory: Effects of concreteness and cognate status in word association. *Bilingualism: Language and Cognition*, 1: 193-211.

Van Orden, G.C., Pennington, B.F., & Stone, G.O. 2001. What do double dissociations prove? *Cognitive Science*, 25: 111-172.

Varley, R., & Siegal, M. 2000. Evidence for cognition without grammar from causal reasoning and "theory of mind" in an agrammatic aphasic patient. *Current Biology*, 10: 723-726.

Verdolini, K. 2002. Memoria procedurale e sue implicazioni. Paper presented at the congress on *L'Adulto che non parla*, Centro Congressi, Tabiano, Italy, 22 March.

Vilariño, I., Prieto, J.M., Robles, A., Lema, M., & Noya, M. 1997. Estudio de pacientes afásicos bilingües gallego-castellano. *Revista de Neurología*, 25: 1165-1167.

Vingerhoets, G., Van Borsel, J., Tesink, C., van den Noort, M., Deblaere, K., Seurinck, R., Vandemaele, P., & Achten, E. 2003. Multilingualism: An fFMI study. *NeuroImage*, 20: 2181-2196.

Voinescu, I., Vish, E., Sirian, S., & Maretsis, M. 1977. Aphasia in a polyglot. *Brain and Language*, 4: 165-176.

Voneida, T.J. 1998. Sperry's concept of mind as a emergent property of brain function and its implications for the future of humankind. *Neuropsychologia*, 36: 1077-1082.

von Raffler-Engel, W. 1961. Investigation of Italo-American bilinguals. *Zeitschrift für Phonetik, Sprachwissenschaft und Kommunikationsforschung*, 14: 127-130.

Voyer, D. 1998. On the reliability and validity of noninvasive laterality measures. *Brain and Cognition*, 36: 209-236.

Voyer, D. 2003. Reliability and magnitude of perceptual asymmetries in a dichotic word recognition task. *Neuropsychology*, 17: 393-401.

Wald, I. 1958. Zagadnienie afazji poliglotów. *Postepy Neurologii Neurochirurgii i Psychiatrii*, 4: 183-211.

Wald, I. 1961. Problema afazii poliglotov. Moscow: *Voprosy Kliniki i Patofiziologii Afazii*, 140-176.

Waldron, E.M., & Ashby, F.G. 2001. The effects of concurrent task interference on category learning: Evidence for multiple category learning systems. *Psychonomic Bulletin and Review*, 8: 168-176.

Walters, J., & Zatorre, R.J. 1978. Laterality differences for word identification in bilinguals. *Brain and Language*, 6: 158-167.

Wang, 1973. Phonological theory. Course given at the LSA Institute, University of Michigan, East Lansing, August 1973.

Warburton, E., Wise, R.J., Price, C.J., Weiller, C., Hadar, U., Ramsay, S., & Frackowiak, R.S. 1996. Noun and verb retrieval by normal subjects. Studies with PET. *Brain*, 119: 159-180.

Wartenburger, I., Heekeren, H.R., Burchert, F., De Bleser, R., & Villringer, A. 2003. Grammaticality judgments on sentences with and without movement of phrasal constituents—an event-related fMRI study. *Journal of neurolinguistics*, 16: 301-314.

Watamori T., & Sasanuma, S. 1976. The recovery process of a bilingual aphasic. *Journal of Communication Disorders*, 9: 157-166.

Watamori T., & Sasanuma, S. 1978. The recovery process of two English-Japanese bilingual aphasics. *Brain and Language*, 6: 127-140.

Wattendorf, E., Westerman, B., Zappatore, D., Franceschini, R., Ludi, G., Radu, E.-W., & Nitsch, C. 2001. Different languages activate different subfields in Broca's area. *NeuroImage*, 13 (6 Part 2): S624.

Watzlawick, P. 1976. *How real is real?* New York: Vintage Books.

Weber-Fox, C. & Neville, H. 1996. Maturational constraints on functional specializations for language processing: ERP and behavioral evidence in bilingual speakers. *Journal of Cognitive Neuroscience*, 8: 231-256.

Wegner, M.L., Brookshire, R.H., & Nicholas, L.E. 1984. Comprehension of main ideas and details in coherent and noncoherent discourse by aphasic and nonaphaisc listeners. *Brain and Language*, 21: 37-51.

Weinreich, U. 1953. *Languages in contact*. New York: Publications of the Linguistic Circle of New York.

Weintraub, S., Mesulam, M., & Kramer, L. 1981. Disturbance in prosody: A right hemisphere contribution to language. *Archives of Neurology*, 38: 742-744.

Weisenburg, T.H., & McBride, K.E. 1935. *Aphasia, a clinical and psychological study*. New York: Commonwealth Fund.

Weissenborn, J., & Klein, W. (eds.) 1982. *Here and there: Cross-linguistic studies on deixis and demonstration*. Amsterdam: John Benjamins.

Werntz, D., Bickford, R., Bloom, F., & Shannahoff-Khalsa, D. 1983. Alternating cerebral hemispheric activity and the lateralization of autonomic nervous function. *Human Neuropsychology*, 2: 39-43.

Wexler, B., Halwes, T., & Heninger, G. 1981. Use of a statistical significance criterion in drawing inferences about hemispheric dominance for language function from dichotic listening data. *Brain and Language*, 13: 13-18.

Weylman, S.T., Brownell, H.H., Roman, M., & Gardner, H. 1989. Appreciation of indirect requests by left and right brain-damaged patients: The effects of verbal context and conventionality of wording. *Brain and Language*, 36: 580-591.

Whitaker, H.A. 1971. *On the representation of language in the human brain*. Champaign, IL: Linguistic Research.

Wierzbicka, A. 1985. Different cultures, different languages, different speech acts. *Journal of Pragmatics*, 9: 145-178.

Wilcox, J., Albyn Davis, G., & Leonard, L.B. 1978. Aphasics' comprehension of contextually conveyed meaning. *Brain and Language*, 6: 362-377.

Wilson, F.A.W., Scalaidhe, S.P.Ó, & Goldman-Radic, P.S. 1993. Dissociation of object and spatial processing domains in primate prefrontal cortex. *Science*, 260: 1955-1958.

Winner, S.T., Brownell, H.H., Happé, F., Blum, A., & Pincus, D. 1998. Distinguishing lies from jokes: Theory of mind deficits and discourse interpretation in right hemisphere brain-damaged patients. *Brain and Language*, 62: 89-106.

Winocur, G., Moscovitch, M., & Stuss, D. 1996. Explicit and implicit memory in the elderly: Evidence for double dissociation involving medial temporal- and frontal-lobe functions. *Neurology*, 10: 57-65.

Wolfson, N. 1981. Compliments in cross-cultural perspective. *TESOL Quarterly*, 15: 117-124.

Workman, L., Brookman, F., Mayer, P., Rees, V., & Bellin, W. 2000. Language laterality in English/Welsh bilinguals: Language-acquisitional and language-specific factors in the development of lateralisation. *Laterality*, 5: 289-313.

Wulfeck, B., Juarez, L., Bates, E., & Kilborn, K. 1986. Sentence interpretation strategies in healthy and aphasic bilingual adults. In J. Vaid (ed.), *Language processing in bilinguals* (pp. 199-219). Hillsdale, NJ: Lawrence Erlbaum Associates.

Xiang, H.D., Lin, C.Y., Ma, X.H., Zhang, Z.Q., Bower, J.M., Weng, X.C., & Gao, J.H. 2003. Involvement of the cerebellum in semantic discrimination: An fMRI study. *Human Brain Mapping*, 18: 208-214.

Yetkin, O., Yetkin, Z., Haughton, V., & Cox, R.W. 1996. Use of functional MR to map language in multilingual volunteers. *American Journal of Neuroradiology*, 17: 473-477.

Zanini, S., Melatini, A., Capus, L., Gioulis, M., Vassallo, A., & Bava, A. 2003. Language recovery following subthalamic nucleus stimulation in Parkinson's disease. *NeuroReport*, 14: 511-516.

Zatorre, R.J. 1983. La représentation des langues multiples dans le cerveau: Vieux problèmes et nouvelles orientations, *Langages*, 72: 15-31.

Zatorre, R.J. 1989. On the representation of multiple languages in the brain: Old problems and new directions. *Brain and Language*, 36: 127-147.

Zeithamová, D. 2003. Theories of categorization and category learning: Why a single approach cannot be sufficient to account for the phenomenon. *Studia Psychologia*, 45: 169-185.

Zivadinov, R., Sepcic, J., Nasuelli, D., De Masi, R., Gragadin, L., Tommasi, M. et al. 2001. A longitudinal study of brain atrophy and cognitive disturbances in the early phase of relapsing-remitting multiple sclerosis. *Journal of Neurology Neurosurgery and Psychiatry*, 70: 773-780.

Zizzo, D.J. 2003. Verbal and behavioral learning in a probability compounding task. *Theory and Decision*, 54: 287-314.

Subject index

In the series *Studies in Bilingualism* (SiBil) the following titles have been published thus far or are scheduled for publication:

32 KONDO-BROWN, Kimi (ed.): Heritage Language Development. Focus on East Asian Immigrants. 2006. ix, 281 pp.

31 BAPTISTA, Barbara O. and Michael Alan WATKINS (eds.): English with a Latin Beat. Studies in Portuguese/ Spanish – English Interphonology. 2006. vi, 214 pp.

30 PIENEMANN, Manfred (ed.): Cross-Linguistic Aspects of Processability Theory. 2005. xiv, 303 pp.

29 AYOUN, Dalila and M. Rafael SALABERRY (eds.): Tense and Aspect in Romance Languages. Theoretical and applied perspectives. 2005. x, 318 pp.

28 SCHMID, Monika S., Barbara KÖPKE, Merel KEIJZER and Lina WEILEMAR (eds.): First Language Attrition. Interdisciplinary perspectives on methodological issues. 2004. x, 378 pp.

27 CALLAHAN, Laura: Spanish/English Codeswitching in a Written Corpus. 2004. viii, 183 pp.

26 DIMROTH, Christine and Marianne STARREN (eds.): Information Structure and the Dynamics of Language Acquisition. 2003. vi, 361 pp.

25 PILLER, Ingrid: Bilingual Couples Talk. The discursive construction of hybridity. 2002. xii, 315 pp.

24 SCHMID, Monika S.: First Language Attrition, Use and Maintenance. The case of German Jews in anglophone countries. 2002. xiv, 259 pp. (incl. CD-rom).

23 VERHOEVEN, Ludo and Sven STRÖMQVIST (eds.): Narrative Development in a Multilingual Context. 2001. viii, 431 pp.

22 SALABERRY, M. Rafael: The Development of Past Tense Morphology in L2 Spanish. 2001. xii, 211 pp.

21 DÖPKE, Susanne (ed.): Cross-Linguistic Structures in Simultaneous Bilingualism. 2001. x, 258 pp.

20 POULISSE, Nanda: Slips of the Tongue. Speech errors in first and second language production. 1999. xvi, 257 pp.

19 AMARA, Muhammad Hasan: Politics and Sociolinguistic Reflexes. Palestinian border villages. 1999. xx, 261 pp.

18 PARADIS, Michel: A Neurolinguistic Theory of Bilingualism. 2004. viii, 299 pp.

17 ELLIS, Rod: Learning a Second Language through Interaction. 1999. x, 285 pp.

16 HUEBNER, Thom and Kathryn A. DAVIS (eds.): Sociopolitical Perspectives on Language Policy and Planning in the USA. With the assistance of Joseph Lo Bianco. 1999. xvi, 365 pp.

15 PIENEMANN, Manfred: Language Processing and Second Language Development. Processability theory. 1998. xviii, 367 pp.

14 YOUNG, Richard and Agnes Weiyun HE (eds.): Talking and Testing. Discourse approaches to the assessment of oral proficiency. 1998. x, 395 pp.

13 HOLLOWAY, Charles E.: Dialect Death. The case of Brule Spanish. 1997. x, 220 pp.

12 HALMARI, Helena: Government and Codeswitching. Explaining American Finnish. 1997. xvi, 276 pp.

11 BECKER, Angelika and Mary CARROLL: The Acquisition of Spatial Relations in a Second Language. In cooperation with Jorge Giacobbe, Clive Perdue and Rémi Porquiez. 1997. xii, 212 pp.

10 BAYLEY, Robert and Dennis R. PRESTON (eds.): Second Language Acquisition and Linguistic Variation. 1996. xix, 317 pp.

9   FREED, Barbara F. (ed.): Second Language Acquisition in a Study Abroad Context. 1995. xiv, 345 pp.

8   DAVIS, Kathryn A.: Language Planning in Multilingual Contexts. Policies, communities, and schools in Luxembourg. 1994. xix, 220 pp.

7   DIETRICH, Rainer, Wolfgang KLEIN and Colette NOYAU: The Acquisition of Temporality in a Second Language. In cooperation with Josée Coenen, Beatriz Dorriots, Korrie van Helvert, Henriette Hendriks, Et-Tayeb Houdaïfa, Clive Perdue, Sören Sjöström, Marie-Thérèse Vasseur and Kaarlo Voionmaa. 1995. xii, 288 pp.

6   SCHREUDER, Robert and Bert WELTENS (eds.): The Bilingual Lexicon. 1993. viii, 307 pp.

5   KLEIN, Wolfgang and Clive PERDUE: Utterance Structure. Developing grammars again. In cooperation with Mary Carroll, Josée Coenen, José Deulofeu, Thom Huebner and Anne Trévise. 1992. xvi, 354 pp.

4   PAULSTON, Christina Bratt: Linguistic Minorities in Multilingual Settings. Implications for language policies. 1994. xi, 136 pp.

3   DÖPKE, Susanne: One Parent – One Language. An interactional approach. 1992. xviii, 213 pp.

2   BOT, Kees de, Ralph B. GINSBERG and Claire KRAMSCH (eds.): Foreign Language Research in Cross-Cultural Perspective. 1991. xii, 275 pp.

1   FASE, Willem, Koen JASPAERT and Sjaak KROON (eds.): Maintenance and Loss of Minority Languages. 1992. xii, 403 pp.